México
ESTADOS UNIDOS
Golfo de México
OCÉANO PACÍFICO
Golfo de California
BAJA CALIFORNIA
SIERRA MADRE OCCIDENTAL
SIERRA MADRE ORIENTAL
Bahía de Campeche
Canal de Yucatán
Golfo de Tehuantepec
ISTMO DE TEHUANTEPEC
YUCATÁN
Trópico de Cáncer
Río Colorado
Río Gila
Río Grande
Río Bravo
Río Conchos
Río Misisipí
Río Balsas
Tijuana
Mexicali
Nogales
Nogales
El Paso
Ciudad Juárez
Hermosillo
Chihuahua
Houston
San Antonio
Laredo
Nuevo Laredo
Brownsville
Reynosa
Matamoros
Monterrey
Saltillo
Torreón
Ciudad Victoria
La Paz
Cabo San Lucas
Mazatlán
Tula
Zacatecas
Tampico
San Luis Potosí
Aguascalientes
León
Guanajuato
Puerto Vallarta
Guadalajara
Teotihuacán
México, D.F.
Morelia
Toluca
Cuernavaca
Uruapan
Taxco
Jalapa
Puebla
Orizaba
Veracruz
Tlapa
Oaxaca
Acapulco
Villahermosa
Campeche
Uxmal
Mérida
Tizmín
Cancún
Chichén Itzá
Cozumel
Islas Revillagigedo
Lago Petén Itzá
Lago Isabel
Belmopan
BELICE
GUATEMALA
Guatemala
Copán
San Pedro Sula
HONDURAS
Tegucigalpa
San Salvador
EL SALVADOR
0 100 200 300 400 Km.
0 100 200 300 400 Mi.

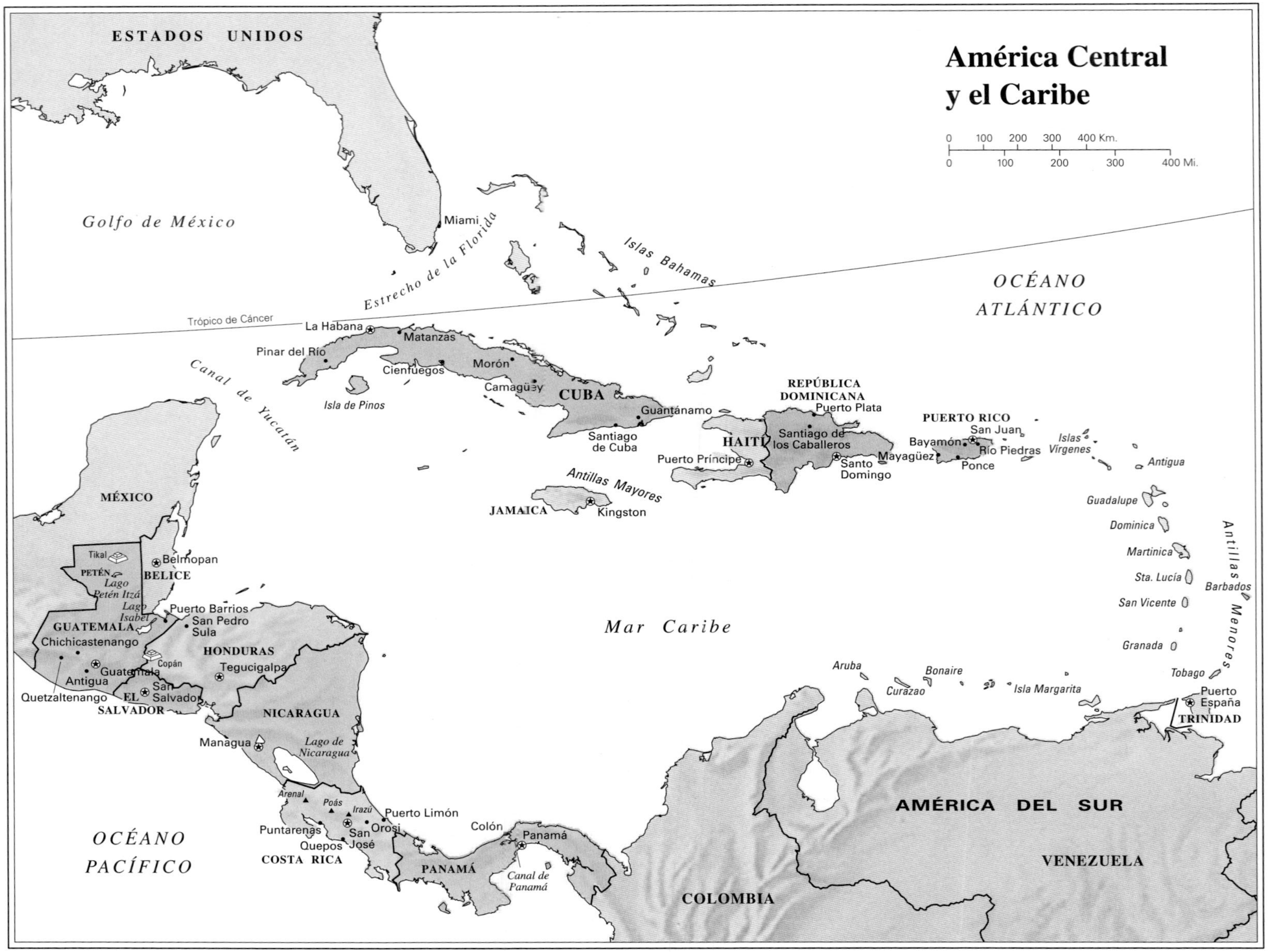
América Central
y el Caribe
0 100 200 300 400 Km.
0 100 200 300 400 Mi.
ESTADOS UNIDOS
Golfo de México
Miami
Estrecho de la Florida
Islas Bahamas
Trópico de Cáncer
OCÉANO
ATLÁNTICO
La Habana
Matanzas
Pinar del Río
Cienfuegos
Morón
Camagüey
CUBA
Isla de Pinos
Canal de Yucatán
Guantánamo
Santiago
de Cuba
REPÚBLICA
DOMINICANA
Puerto Plata
Santiago de
los Caballeros
HAITÍ
Puerto Príncipe
Santo
Domingo
PUERTO RICO
San Juan
Bayamón
Río Piedras
Mayagüez
Ponce
Islas
Vírgenes
Antigua
Antillas Mayores
JAMAICA
Kingston
Guadalupe
Dominica
Martinica
Sta. Lucía
Barbados
San Vicente
Granada
Antillas Menores
Tobago
Puerto
España
TRINIDAD
MÉXICO
Tikal
PETÉN
Lago
Petén Itzá
Belmopan
BELICE
Lago
Isabel
Puerto Barrios
San Pedro
Sula
GUATEMALA
Chichicastenango
Copán
HONDURAS
Tegucigalpa
Guatemala
Antigua
Quetzaltenango
EL
SALVADOR
San
Salvador
NICARAGUA
Mar Caribe
Managua
Lago de
Nicaragua
Arenal
Poás
Irazú
Puerto Limón
Puntarenas
San
José
Orosi
Quepos
COSTA RICA
Colón
Panamá
PANAMÁ
Canal de
Panamá
OCÉANO
PACÍFICO
COLOMBIA
AMÉRICA DEL SUR
VENEZUELA
Aruba
Curazao
Bonaire
Isla Margarita

THE BASIC SPANISH SERIES

BASIC SPANISH FOR BUSINESS AND FINANCE

ENHANCED SECOND EDITION

Ana C. Jarvis
Chandler-Gilbert Community College

Luis Lebredo

HEINLE
CENGAGE Learning

Australia • Brazil • Japan • Korea • Mexico • Singapore • Spain • United Kingdom • United States

HEINLE
CENGAGE Learning

Basic Spanish for Business and Finance, Enhanced Second Edition
Ana C. Jarvis and Luis Lebredo

Publisher: Beth Kramer

Acquisitions Editor: Lara Semones

Assistant Editor: Joanna Alizio

Associate Media Editor: Patrick Brand

Marketing Program Manager: Courtney Wolstoncroft

Executive Brand Manager: Ben Rivera

Manufacturing Planner: Betsy Donaghey

Rights Acquisitions Specialist: Jessica Elias

Art and Design Direction, Production Management, and Composition: PreMediaGlobal

Cover Image: istock

Library of Congress Control Number: 2009939977

ISBN-13: 978-1-285-05223-6

ISBN-10: 1-285-05223-4

Heinle
20 Channel Center Street
Boston, MA 02210
USA

Cengage Learning is a leading provider of customized learning solutions with office locations around the globe, including Singapore, the United Kingdom, Australia, Mexico, Brazil, and Japan. Locate your local office at: **international.cengage.com/region**

Cengage Learning products are represented in Canada by Nelson Education, Ltd.

For your course and learning solutions, visit **www.cengage.com**

Purchase any of our products at your local college store or at our preferred online store **www.cengagebrain.com**

Printed in the United States of America
1 2 3 4 5 6 7 16 15 14 13 12

CONTENTS

PREFACE

The Basic Spanish Series Enhanced Second Edition offers a more dynamic teaching and learning experience than ever before with advanced online tools designed to address the needs of today's students and professionals requiring a working knowledge of Spanish. This flexible, concise introduction to Spanish grammar and communication offers an extensive technology program, which now features outstanding video footage from the incomparable National Geographic collection, additional interactive grammar practice, as well as note-sharing and highlighting capabilities. This state-of-the-art technology combined with a focus on applied Spanish for every-day use gives students the advantage they need to be successful in the workplace and beyond.

Basic Spanish for Business and Finance

As a key component of *The Basic Spanish Series, Basic Spanish for Business and Finance* is a communication manual designed to serve those in the world of business who seek basic conversational skills in Spanish. Written for use in two-semester or three-quarter courses, it presents typical everyday situations that business and accounting students, pre-professionals, and professionals may encounter at their workplace, on business travel, or while communicating with business partners abroad.

Basic Spanish for Business and Finance introduces essential business vocabulary and *Notas culturales* written from a cross-cultural perspective. It provides students with opportunities to apply, in a wide variety of practical contexts, the grammatical structures presented in the corresponding lessons of the *Basic Spanish* core text.

Organization of the Text

Basic Spanish for Business and Finance contains a preliminary lesson (*Lección preliminar*), twenty regular lessons, four review sections (*Repasos*), and three supplementary sections (*Suplementos*) with Spanish business forms and documents such as a customs form, credit card application, job applications, and business letters.

Each lesson contains the following sections:

- A **lesson opener** consists of the lesson objectives divided into two categories: Structures practiced from *Basic Spanish* and Business Communication.
- A **Spanish dialogue** introduces and employs key vocabulary and grammatical structures in the context of the lesson theme. Divided into manageable segments, they feature business-specific contexts. Audio recordings of the dialogues can be found on The Basic Spanish Resource Center in downloadable MP3 format. Translations of the dialogues can be found on the Instructor's side of the Basic Spanish Resource Center.
- The ***¡Escuchemos!*** activity, together with recordings on the In-Text Audio MP3s, encourages students to listen to the dialogue and check their comprehension with true/false questions.
- The ***Vocabulario*** section summarizes new, active words and expressions presented in the dialogue and categorizes them according to their parts of speech. The vocabulary highlights the most important communication tools needed in a variety of professional situations. A special subsection of cognates heads up the vocabulary list so students can readily identify these terms. The *Vocabulario adicional* subsection supplies supplementary vocabulary related to the lesson theme.

- ***Notas culturales*** give students up-to-date information that highlights Hispanic business customs and practices. The Enhanced edition features video footage from National Geographic™ to better reflect the rich cultures of each country featured in the chapter. Clips may be viewed in the iLrn™: Heinle Learning Center.
- ***Dígame...*** questions check students' comprehension of the dialogue.
- The ***Hablemos*** section provides personalized questions based on the lesson theme, where students are encouraged to work in pairs, asking and answering each of the questions presented.
- ***Vamos a practicar*** activities review grammar topics that students need to know before proceeding in the lesson.
- The ***Sirva usted de intérprete*** activities develop students' listening and speaking skills through tasks that provide contextualized practice of vocabulary and grammatical structures in form of role-plays.
- The ***Sirva usted de traductor*** section provides practice in written Spanish-to-English translation through realistic business document formats that employ the *Vocabulario adicional* of each lesson.
- The ***En estas situaciones*** section develops students' communication skills through role-playing in pairs or small groups and encourages more interactive speaking practice.
- Open-ended ***Casos*** activities offer additional opportunities for improving oral proficiency as students interact in situations they might encounter in their work as business and finance professionals. These role-plays require spontaneous use of Spanish and are intended to underscore the usefulness of language study.
- ***Un paso más*** features activities that practice the supplementary words and expressions in the *Vocabulario adicional* section, some through realia.
- ***Lecturas*** sections present short readings that address cultural notions within the business world. They are followed by questions to aid students' comprehension and promote discussion.
- All lessons conclude with ***Un dicho,*** a saying frequently used in the Spanish-speaking business world.

- Pair and group icons indicate pair and group activities.
- Audio icons show what is available as downloadable In-Text Audio MP3s.
- iLrn icons indicate that there are additional resources and practice available at the *Basic Spanish for Business and Finance* iLrn Learning Center.
- Search Web-search icons indicate activities related to the *Notas culturales.*
- Audio Web-audio icons indicate vocabulary available in audio flashcards on The Basic Spanish Series Resource Center.
- Grammar Web-grammar icons indicate grammar help is available through Grammar Tutorials and Grammar videos iLrn™: Heinle Learning Center.
- **Five maps** of the Spanish-speaking world are included in the front and back of the text.

- For easy reference and to aid in lesson planning, the table of contents lists the **grammar structures** presented in the corresponding *Basic Spanish* text and practiced in *Basic Spanish for Business and Finance,* plus the communication objective for each lesson.
- The text's grammatical sequence parallels the core text of the series, *Basic Spanish.*
- A supplementary section, ***Suplemento,*** appears after every five lessons, providing explanations and numerous models of business documents such as letters, memos, job applications, and receipts. Accompanying activities guide students through the documents and provide practice in formulating appropriate responses.

Organization of the *Repasos*

After every five lessons, a review section contains the following materials:

- ***Práctica de vocabulario*** exercises check students' cumulative knowledge and use of active vocabulary in a variety of formats: selecting the appropriate word to complete a sentence, identifying related words, matching, true/false, and puzzles.
- ***Situaciones del mundo de las empresas*** reviews cultural knowledge and competency of the business customs, practices, and conventions presented in the *notas culturales* of the preceding five lessons.

Appendixes

The appendixes of this book include the following:

- **Appendix A, Introduction to Spanish Sounds and the Alphabet,** presents the alphabet and briefly explains vowel sounds, consonant sounds, linking, rhythm, intonation, syllable formation, and accentuation.
- **Appendix B, Verbs,** presents charts of the three regular conjugations and of the **-ar, -er,** and **-ir** stem-changing verbs, as well as lists of orthographic-changing verbs and some common irregular verbs.
- **Appendix C, Más Sobre Del Tema,** consists of a list of the most common expressions and directions that are related to the theme of each chapter.
- **Appendix D, Weights and Measures,** features conversion formulas for temperature and metric weights and measures, as well as Spanish terms for U.S. weights and measures.

End Vocabularies

Comprehensive Spanish-English and English-Spanish vocabularies contain all words and expressions from the *Vocabulario* sections. Each term is followed by the lesson number where the active vocabulary is introduced. All passive vocabulary items found in the *Vocabulario adicional* sections, in marginal glosses to readings, and in glosses of direction lines or exercises are also included.

New to the Enhanced Second Edition

The newly enhanced Second Edition of the Basic Spanish Series fully integrates the most advanced version of iLrn™: Heinle Learning Center yet. The upgraded eBook features note-sharing capabilities, highlighting, and direct video links.

- New Más práctica grammar activities provide extra practice outside of class, freeing up precious class time for more high-level discussion.

- Diagnostics tools enable students to test their own knowledge while instructors can track their progress and assign and review practice activities around specific grammar points.
- All-new video content from National Geographic™ along with corresponding activities introduce students to the cultures and landscapes of twenty-one different Spanish-speaking countries.
- Más sobre del tema appendices bring a sharper focus on the most commen terms and expressions for professional contexts.

Assets

Available on the Basic Spanish Series Resource Center

For Students

- The **in-text audio** is available in downloadable MP3 format.
- Brief **grammar videos** feature a professor teaching specific grammar topics presented in the core text; Flash-based **grammar tutorials** help students learn and understand Spanish grammar through succinct, interactive explanations and quizzes.
- **Activities** encourage students to learn more about the target country and coordinate with the culture notes in each chapter of *Basic Spanish for Business and Finance.*
- Short **podcasts,** downloadable to a computer or MP3 device, review Spanish grammar and pronunciation for studying on-the-go.
- **Text glossaries** provide support for learning and practicing vocabulary.
- The downloadable **audio *Basic Spanish for Business and Finance Phrasebook*** provides vocabulary and phrases for real-life situations.
- The **Resource Center** includes additional quizzes, web-search activities, related links, downloadable In-Text Audio MP3s, audio-enabled flashcards, and Spanish pronunciation help.

For Instructors

- Instructors have access to **all Resource Center content,** including resources for students. Instructor-specific content is password-protected and is not available to students.
- For instructors transitioning to *The Basic Spanish Series* from a different text, a **sample syllabus** offers suggestions for dividing the material evenly through the course of a typical semester.
- A series of **PowerPoint presentations** include explanations of Spanish grammar and correlate to each chapter of *Basic Spanish.* An additional set of PowerPoints review Spanish vocabulary from *Basic Spanish for Business and Finance.*
- **Translations** of dialogues in *Basic Spanish for Business and Finance* are available for download.
- **Answer keys** are provided for exercises in *Basic Spanish for Business and Finance,* as well as for the self-directed tests.
- **Situation cards** and the corresponding guide provide ideas for oral assessment and in-class role-play.

Acknowledgments

We wish to thank our colleagues who have used previous editions of *Basic Spanish for Business and Finance* for their many constructive comments and suggestions:

Robert L. Adler, *University of North Alabama*
Sissy Alloway, *Morehead State University*
Asuncion Amedo, *Dickinson College*
Liz Barcena, *Florida National College*
Valeria Barragon, *Coastline Community College*
Pierina Beckman, *University of North Texas*
Lori Bernard, *State University of New York, College at Geneseo*
Sally R. Brecher, *Buena Vista University*
Antonio Carrillo, *Northern Arizona University*
Maria Jesus Centeno, *University of Alabama at Birmingham*
Kirby Chadwick, *Scottsdale Community College*
Olivia Elias, *Guilford College*
Amos Etukudoh, *Johnson C. Smith University*
Bruce Fox, *Wayne State University*
Amalia Garson, *Northern Arizona University—Yuma campus*
Angelo Glaviano, *Middlesex Community College*
Deborah Hubbard, *Brown Mackie College*
Kathleen M Jiménez, *Miami-Dade Community College*
Suzanne Morrison-Williams, *Art Institute of Fort Lauderdale*
Kati Pletsch de García, *Mount Ida College*
Tracey Robinson, *Devry University*
Dianna Rodríguez-Lozano, *Mount Saint Mary's College*
Claudia Sokol, *Northeastern University*
Carmen Sotomayor, *University of North Carolina at Greensboro*
Sara Ulloa, *Utah Valley University*
Bárbara Villalonga, *San José State University*
David Walczak, *Art Institute of Fort Lauderdale*
Nicole Wilson, *Advanced Career Training*
David Young, *Missouri Western State College*

We also extend our sincere appreciation to the World Languages team at Heinle, Cengage Learning: Publisher, Beth Kramer; Executive Editor, Lara Semones; Assistant Editor, Joanna Alizio, Associate Media Editor, Patrick Brand, and Senior Media Editor, Morgen Gallo; Senior Art Director, Linda Jurras; Marketing Program Manager, Courtney Wolstoncroft; and Project Manager, Arul Joseph Raj.

Ana C. Jarvis
Luis Lebredo

LECCIÓN PRELIMINAR

CONVERSACIONES BREVES (*BRIEF CONVERSATIONS*)

OBJECTIVES

Structures

- Gender and number
- The definite and indefinite articles
- Subject pronouns
- The present indicative of **ser**
- Cardinal numbers 0–39

Business Communication

- Greetings, farewells, and introductions in personal and telephone interaction

A. —Buenos días, señor Martínez. ¿Cómo está usted?
—Muy bien, gracias, señorita Vega. ¿Y usted?
—Bien, gracias.

B. —Buenas tardes, señora.
—Buenas tardes, señor. Pase y tome asiento, por favor. ¿En qué podemos servirle?

Nombre ______________________ Sección ____________ Fecha ____________

C. —Buenas noches, señorita, y muchas gracias. Hasta mañana.
—De nada. Para servirle. Adiós.

D. —¿Con quién desea usted hablar?
—Con la jefa de compras.
—Lo siento, pero la línea está ocupada.
—Entonces llamo más tarde.

E. —Agencia de Publicidad Morales, buenos días.
—Buenos días, señorita. Con el[1] señor Romero, por favor. Soy la gerente de la empresa Alfa.
—Un momento, por favor.

F. —¿Nombre y apellido?
—José Luis Torres Fuentes.
—¿Dirección?
—Calle Palma, número diez.
—¿Número de teléfono?
—Ocho-dos-ocho-cero-seis-uno-dos.
—¿Es Ud.[2] casado, soltero...?
—Yo soy divorciado.

---

[1]When referring to someone as a third person, and using a title such as **señor, señora,** or **señorita,** a definite article is used in Spanish: e.g., ***el* señor Paz** (*Mr. Paz*).
[2]**Usted** is abbreviated **Ud.**

Nombre ______________________ Sección ____________ Fecha ____________

VOCABULARIO

Audio

Saludos y despedidas (*Greetings and farewells*)

adiós *good-bye*
Bien. *Fine., Well.*
buenas noches *good evening, good night*
buenas tardes *good afternoon*
buenos días *good morning, good day*
¿Cómo está usted (Ud.)? *How are you?*
Hasta mañana. *See you tomorrow.*
Muy bien, gracias. *Very well, thank you.*

Títulos (*Titles*)

señor (Sr.) *Mr., sir, gentleman*
señora (Sra.) *Mrs., lady, Ma'am, Madam*
señorita (Srta.) *Miss, young lady*

Nombres (*Nouns*)

el apellido *last name, surname*
la calle *street*
la dirección, el domicilio *address*
el (la) gerente (general) *(general) manager, administrator, director*
el (la) jefe(a) de compras *purchasing manager*
el nombre *name*

Adjetivos (*Adjectives*)

casado(a) *married*
divorciado(a) *divorced*
soltero(a) *single*

Verbo (*Verb*)

ser *to be*

Otras palabras y expresiones (*Other words and expressions*)

agencia de publicidad *advertising agency*
con *with*
¿Con quién desea usted hablar? *With whom do you wish to speak?*
las conversaciones breves *brief conversations*
¿Cuál es su giro? *What is your line of work?*
De nada. *You're welcome.*
¿En qué puedo (podemos) servirle? *How may I (we) help you? What can I (we) do for you?*
energías alternativas *alternative energies*
Entonces llamo más tarde. *I'll call later, then.*
La línea está ocupada. *The line is busy.*
Lo siento. *I'm sorry.*
Muchas gracias. *Thank you very much.*
el número de teléfono *telephone number*
para hogares *for homes*
para servirle *at your service*
Pase. *Come in.*
por favor *please*
un momento *one moment*
y *and*

Search

iLrn

Notas Culturales

- Personal interactions in the Spanish-speaking business world are generally more formal than they are in the United States. Expressions of familiarity that often characterize business relations in this country—calling a client by his or her first name right from the start, for example—may be interpreted in the Hispanic world as a lack of respect rather than a sign of friendship. Rituals of business life in the Spanish-speaking world that might seem excessively ceremonious to an American, such as making sure to greet and bid farewell to one's colleagues at the beginning and end of the business day, or taking care to greet a client with **Buenos días** rather than the more informal **Hola,** are simply part of the Hispanic concept of proper etiquette.

Nombre ______________________ **Sección** __________ **Fecha** __________

- The title **señorita** (*Miss*) is only used to address or refer to women who have never been married. To address or refer to a woman who is married, divorced, or a widow, the title **señora** (*Mrs.*) is used.
- In Spanish-speaking countries people use different expressions when answering the telephone. The following are the most commonly used.

  In Mexico: **Bueno.**

  In Spain: **¿Sí?, Diga, Dígame.**

  In Cuba and other Caribbean countries: **Oigo.**

  In Argentina: **¿Sí?, Hable, Hola.**

In many countries throughout Latin America (Argentina, Perú, Puerto Rico), the expression **¿Aló?** is also used.

Actividades

Dígame... (*Tell me . . .*) Write appropriate responses to the following statements.

1. Buenos días.

   ____

2. Buenas tardes. ¿Cómo está usted?

   ____

3. Muchas gracias.

   ____

4. Buenas noches.

   ____

5. Pase y tome asiento, por favor.

   ____

6. Lo siento, pero la línea está ocupada.

   ____

7. Hasta mañana.

   ____

8. ¿Es usted casado(a), soltero(a), divorciado(a)...?

   ____

Nombre ______________________ **Sección** ______________ **Fecha** ______________

Quiz

VAMOS A PRACTICAR (*LET'S PRACTICE*)

A Write in Spanish the name of the place and the telephone number you would call in each of the following situations. Since many of the words are cognates, guess at their meaning.

MODELO You need to make a dinner reservation.
Restaurante Acapulco 256-7819
Restaurante Acapulco: dos, cinco, seis, siete, ocho, uno, nueve

Aerolíneas Argentinas	257-8493
Agencia de Personal Temporal "Dicho y Hecho"	465-9267
Hotel El Porteño	741-4228
Agencia de Publicidad Otero	931-0476
Banco Industrial	338-0164
Alquiler de computadoras	637-0053

1. You need to take out a loan for your company.

____

2. You need to make a plane reservation to travel to Buenos Aires.

____

3. You need to book a hotel room for your business trip.

____

4. You want to rent a computer.

____

5. You want to hire a temporary secretary.

____

6. You want to advertise your business.

____

B You are scheduling appointments with your clients. In order to verify that you have written the following names correctly in the appointment book, spell each one in Spanish.

MODELO Figueroa
efe, i, ge, u, e, ere, o, a

1. Sandoval ______________________________
2. Fuentes ______________________________

3. Varela ______________________

4. Ugarte ______________________

5. Barrios ______________________

6. Zubizarreta ______________________

C Write the definite article before each word and then write the plural form.

MODELO __________ domicilio
el domicilio **los domicilios**

1. __________ apellido __________________

2. __________ dirección __________________

3. __________ señora __________________

4. __________ señor __________________

5. __________ nombre __________________

6. __________ conversación __________________

7. __________ calle __________________

8. __________ número __________________

D Complete the following exchanges, using the present indicative of the verb **ser.**

1. —¿Tú __________ Isabel Martínez?

   —No, yo __________ Maribel Vigo. ¿Y usted? ¿ __________ usted el señor Morales?

   —Sí, yo __________ el señor Morales.

2. —¿ __________ ella la gerente?

   —No, (ella) __________ la jefa de compras.

   —¿ __________ el Sr. Vega el gerente?

   —Sí, él __________ el gerente.

3. —¿Tú __________ casada?

   —No, yo __________ divorciada.

   —Y ellas, ¿ __________ solteras?

   —María __________ soltera y Rosa __________ casada.

   —¿Y el señor Varela?

   —Él __________ divorciado.

En estas situaciones (*In these situations*) With a partner, act out the following situations in Spanish.

1. You greet your boss in the morning and ask how he/she is.
2. You greet a client, Miss Vega, in the evening.
3. Someone knocks on the door of your office.
4. You want to thank someone for a favor.
5. You call to speak to a business associate, but his/her line is busy.
6. You are helping someone to fill out a form. First you identify yourself, and then you ask for the following information.
   a. first name and last name
   b. address
   c. telephone number
   d. marital status

Words and accents Long words are more frequent in Spanish than in English, and each Spanish word, with the exception of some compound ones, has only one stressed syllable. Spanish dictionaries do not mark the stressed syllables of words because it is not necessary to mark them: Spanish has very precise rules to indicate where the stressed syllable occurs in a word. Find these rules in *Basic Spanish.*

Reading and writing in Spanish In business, reading and writing well is a must. Reading and writing in Spanish is easy when we limit the scope of reading and writing to converting letters into sounds and vice versa. Although reading and writing are not complete without comprehension, knowing how to pronounce written Spanish words is very helpful when dealing with cognates and with the equivalent of English words found in an English–Spanish dictionary.

Both English and Spanish use the same written alphabet, except for the Spanish **ñ** which is not used in English (See Appendix A). In the same way, most phonemes in both languages are similar, although only a few are identical. In Spanish, with a few exceptions, each letter represents one and only one phoneme, and each phoneme is represented by one and only one letter. On the other hand, in English, only the vowels in the stressed syllables are distinctly pronounced, but in Spanish all vowels are pronounced distinctly, and Spanish has no equivalent to the English *schwa,* the neutralized sound of many unstressed syllables in English. Listen to your instructor and the audio material to learn to match sounds (phonemes) and signs (letters).

It is much more difficult for the student to avoid the English interference when trying to follow the Spanish patterns of syllabification. Syllable patterns are totally different in both languages.

The following cognates illustrate the way phonemes and letters are put together to form syllables in each language.

Spanish	**English**
abrasivo (a-bra-si-vo)	*abrasive (a-bra-sive)*
americano (a-me-ri-ca-no)	*American (A-mer-i-can)*
calendario (ca-len-da-rio)	*calendar (cal-en-dar)*
civilizado (ci-vi-li-za-do)	*civilized (civ-i-lized)*
descender (des-cen-der)	*descend (de-scend)*
documento (do-cu-men-to)	*document (doc-u-ment)*
frívolo (frí-vo-lo)	*frivolous (friv-o-lous)*
gasolina (ga-so-li-na)	*gasoline (gas-o-line)*
operar (o-pe-rar)	*operate (op-er-ate)*
positivo (po-si-ti-vo)	*positive (pos-i-tive)*
sistemático (sis-te-má-ti-co)	*systematic (sys-tem-at-ic)*
típico (tí-pi-co)	*typical (typ-i-cal)*
vigilancia (vi-gi-lan-cia)	*vigilance (vig-i-lance)*

El español que ya usted conoce (*The Spanish you already know*)

Those words used as examples above are cognates (***cognados***). Cognates are words that are similar in spelling and meaning in two languages. Some Spanish cognates are identical to English words. In other instances, the words differ only in minor or predictable ways. There are many Spanish cognates related to the business world, as illustrated in the following list. Learning to recognize and use cognates will help you to acquire vocabulary more rapidly and to read and speak Spanish more fluently.

With a partner, practice reading and writing the following Spanish cognates. One of you reads and the other writes; then switch roles. You may want to further practice using words from any lesson in the book.

la administración	*administration*	**el beneficiario**	*beneficiary*
el administrador	*administrator*	**la calculadora**	*calculator*
la agencia	*agency*	**el cheque**	*check*
el (la) agente	*agent*	**la cláusula**	*clause*
la asociación	*association*	**comercial**	*commercial*
el banco	*bank*	**la compañía**	*company*

Nombre ______________________ Sección ____________ Fecha ____________

la computadora	*computer*	**la oficina**	*office*
la condición	*condition*	**la opción**	*option*
el contrato	*contract*	**el plan**	*plan*
la copia	*copy*	**el producto**	*product*
el costo, el coste	*cost*	**el programa**	*program*
el crédito	*credit*	**el (la) recepcionista**	*receptionist*
la factoría	*factory*	**la reservación**	*reservation*
la firma	*firm*	**el restaurante**	*restaurant*
la fotocopiadora	*photocopier*	**el sistema**	*system*
el hotel	*hotel*	**las telecomunicaciones**	*telecommunications*
industrial	*industrial*	**el teléfono**	*telephone*
la información	*information*	**el transporte**	*transport*
el interés	*interest*	**válido(a)**	*valid*
la mercancía	*merchandise*	**la zona**	*zone*

Un dicho (*A saying*)

El tiempo es oro. **Time is money.**

Trivia

Los diez idiomas más hablados del mundo

Posición	Idioma	No. de hablantes (en millones)
1	mandarín	1120
2	inglés	510
3	hindi	490
4	**español**	**425**
5	árabe	255
6	ruso	254
7	portugués	218
8	bengalí	215
9	malayo-indonesio	175
10	francés	130

Sources: Ethnologue: Languages of the World; The KryssTal Web Site

Nombre ______________________ Sección ____________ Fecha ____________

Número de habitantes de los países en que el español es lengua oficial[1]

Posición	País	Población (en millones)
1	México	111,2
2	Colombia	45,6
3	Argentina	40,9
4	España	40,5
5	Perú	29,5
6	Venezuela	26,8
7	Chile	16,6
8	Ecuador	14,5
9	Guatemala	13,2
10	Cuba	11,4
11	Bolivia	9,8
12	República Dominicana	9,6
13	Honduras	7,8
14	El Salvador	7,2
15	Paraguay	7,0
16	Nicaragua	5,9
17	Costa Rica	4,3
18	Puerto Rico	4,0
19	Uruguay	3,5
20	Panamá	3,4
21	Guinea Ecuatorial	0,5

[1]Spanish is the official language of 21 countries, but the following countries have more than one official language: Spain (Spanish–Castilian, Catalan, Basque, and Galician); Puerto Rico (Spanish, English); Peru and Bolivia (Spanish, Quechua, and Aymara); Paraguay (Spanish, Guaraní); and Equatorial Guinea (Spanish, French).

According to the 2007 American Community Survey conducted by the United States Census Bureau, Spanish is the primary language spoken at home by 34.5 million people aged five or older.

Source: World Fact Book (Estimates for 2009)

LECCIÓN 1 EL VIAJE DE NEGOCIOS

OBJECTIVES

Structures

- The present indicative of regular **-ar** verbs
- Interrogative and negative sentences
- Forms and position of adjectives
- Telling time
- Cardinal numbers 300–1,000
- Uses of **hay**

Business Communication

- Traveling by plane
- Making plane reservations
- Arriving in a foreign country

La señora López, compradora de la firma Kids Fashion de Nueva York, viaja a Aguascalientes, México.

Por teléfono:

Empleada —Aeroméxico, buenos días. ¿En qué puedo servirle?
Sra. López —Buenos días. Necesito viajar a Aguascalientes, México. Deseo reservar un asiento.
Empleada —¿Desde dónde?
Sra. López —Desde Nueva York.
Empleada —¿Para cuándo?
Sra. López —Para mañana por la mañana, en primera clase.
Empleada —Hay un vuelo a las ocho y quince, con escala en México, D.F.[1]
Sra. López —¡Perfecto!
Empleada —¿Pasaje de ida y vuelta o de ida solamente?
Sra. López —De ida y vuelta.
Empleada —¿Cuándo desea regresar?
Sra. López —El jueves, en el último vuelo de la tarde.
Empleada —Muy bien. ¿Desea un asiento de ventanilla o de pasillo?
Sra. López —De ventanilla, por favor.
Empleada —Bien, fila ocho, asiento F.

[1]**D.F.** stands for **Distrito Federal.**

Nombre ______________________ **Sección** ____________ **Fecha** ____________

En el mostrador de Aeroméxico:

Sra. López	—¿A qué hora anuncian el vuelo a México?
Empleado	—Veinte minutos antes de la salida, por la puerta número veinticuatro.

En el avión:

Sra. López	—Señorita, por favor, necesito una almohada y una cobija.
Auxiliar de vuelo	—En seguida. ¿Desea un periódico o una revista?
Sra. López	—Un periódico mexicano, por favor.
Auxiliar de vuelo	—Cómo no.
Sra. López	—Y, por favor, ¿qué hora es?
Auxiliar de vuelo	—Son las nueve y cinco. Llegamos a México a las doce y treinta.

Por el altavoz:

—¡Atención a todos los pasajeros! Favor de llenar ahora la declaración de aduana para evitar demoras en el aeropuerto.

La Sra. López llena la declaración de aduana y luego conversa con una pasajera.

¡Escuchemos!

While listening to the dialogue, circle **V (verdadero)** if the statement is true or **F (falso)** if it is false.

1.	La Sra. López viaja a Nueva York.	V	F
2.	Ella desea viajar en primera clase.	V	F
3.	Hay un vuelo con escala en México.	V	F
4.	La Sra. López desea comprar un asiento.	V	F
5.	Hay un vuelo a las ocho y quince de la mañana.	V	F
6.	Ella desea regresar en el último vuelo de la mañana.	V	F
7.	La Sra. López desea un asiento de pasillo.	V	F
8.	Anuncian el vuelo por el altavoz.	V	F
9.	La Sra. López llena la declaración de aduana en el avión.	V	F
10.	Ella llega a Aguascalientes a las doce y media.	V	F

Nombre ______________________ Sección ____________ Fecha ____________

VOCABULARIO

Audio

Cognados

el aeropuerto
atención
mexicano(a)
México
el minuto
la sección

Nombres

la aduana *customs*
la almohada *pillow*
el altavoz, el altoparlante *loudspeaker*
el asiento *seat*
el asiento de pasillo *aisle seat*
el asiento de ventanilla *window seat*
el (la) auxiliar de vuelo *flight attendant*
la cobija (*Méx.*), **la frazada, la manta** *blanket*
el (la) comprador(a) *buyer*
la declaración de aduana *customs form*
la demora *delay*
el (la) empleado(a) *employee, clerk*
la escala *stopover*
la fila *row*
la firma, la casa *firm, business, company*
el jueves *Thursday*
el mostrador *counter*
el negocio, los negocios *business*
el número *number*
el pasaje, el billete, el boleto *ticket*
el pasaje (billete, boleto) de ida *one-way ticket*
el pasaje (billete, boleto) de ida y vuelta *round-trip ticket*
el (la) pasajero(a) *passenger*
el periódico *newspaper*
la puerta *door, gate*
la revista *magazine*
la salida *departure, exit*
la tarde *afternoon*
el viaje de negocios *business trip*
el vuelo *flight*

Verbos

anunciar *to announce*
conversar *to talk, to converse*
desear *to wish, to want*
evitar *to avoid*
llegar (a) *to arrive (in)*
llenar, rellenar, completar *to fill out (a form)*
necesitar *to need*
regresar *to return, to come (go) back*
reservar *to reserve*
viajar *to travel*

Adjetivos

todos(as) *all*
último(a) *last (in a series)*

Otras palabras y expresiones

a *to, at*
a las (+ time)[1] *at (+time)*
¿A qué hora? *At what time?*
ahora, ahorita[2] *now*
antes (de) *before*
cómo no *certainly, of course*
¿cuándo? *when?*
de *of, from*
desde *from*
¿dónde? *where?*
en *in, on, at*
en primera clase *in first class*
en seguida, enseguida *right away*

---

[1]**A la una** is used to express *At one o'clock.*
[2]In some Spanish-speaking countries, **ahorita** means *in a while.*

favor de (+ inf.) *please (do something)*
luego *then, later*

Otras palabras y expresiones

o *or*
para *to, for, in order to*
por *by, on, through*
por la mañana *in the morning*
¿qué? *what?, which?*
¿Qué hora es? *What time is it?*
sí *yes*
solamente, sólo *only*
Son las (+ *time*).[1] *It's (+ time).*

Audio VOCABULARIO ADICIONAL

arma de fuego *firearm*
cantidad *amount*
carretilla *cart*
clase económica *economy (turist) class*
control de seguridad *security check*
equipaje documentado (facturado) *checked baggage*
mayores a (de) *greater than*
mostrador de facturación *check-in desk*
permitido *permitted, allowed*
puerta *gate(at an airport)*
recogida de equipajes *baggage claim*
recomendación *recommendation*
sangre *blood*
terminal de llegadas *arrivals*
terminal de salidas *departures*
tienda libre de impuestos *duty-free store*
tijeras *scissors*
veneno *poison*

Para viajar en avión (*To travel by plane*)

a la llegada, al llegar *upon arrival*
abrocharse el cinturón de seguridad *to fasten one's seat belt*
la aerolínea *airline*
el aterrizaje *landing*
el baño, el servicio, el escusado (*Méx.*) *bathroom, toilet*
el caballero *gentleman*
la clase turista *tourist class*
confirmar *to confirm*
la dama *lady*
debajo (de) *underneath*
el despegue *take-off*
durante *during*
la emergencia *emergency*
los equipos electrónicos *electronic devices*
facturar (despachar) el equipaje *to check the luggage*
el pase de abordar, la tarjeta de embarque *boarding pass*
pagar exceso de equipaje *to pay excess luggage*
prohibido(a) *forbidden*
¿quién(es)? *who?*
reclinar *to recline*
la reservación, la reserva *reservation*
el salvavidas *life preserver*
usar *to use*

[1]**Es la una** is used to express *It's one o'clock.*

Nombre ______________________ Sección ____________ Fecha ____________

Search

iLrn

Notas Culturales

- The saying, "you buy in your own language, but you sell in the customer's language" is being taken to heart by U.S. firms hoping to do business in Latin America, in Spain, and with Latinos in this country, and they are increasingly hiring employees fluent in Spanish.

  As new markets emerge in the Spanish-speaking world—as a result of America's free-trade agreements with Mexico, Chile, Peru, Central America, and the Dominican Republic—mastering Spanish has become an important asset for people who do business in Latin America. Many Latino executives speak English, but communicating with them in their own language makes them more comfortable.

- To avoid confusion when planning business travel, it is important to be familiar with the ways in which dates and times are expressed in Spanish-speaking countries. The numeral indicating the day is written before the month: for example, 3/12/10 (or 3-x-10) refers to **el 3 de diciembre de 2010,** not to March 12, 2010.

- For many countries, schedules for planes, trains, buses, and public events often use a twenty-four hour clock system, so that the departure time for a 3:30 P.M. flight would be listed as 15:30 or 15.30.

Actividades

Dígame... Answer the following questions, basing your answers on the dialogue.

1. ¿Quién es la señora López? ¿Es de México o de Nueva York?

   ____

2. ¿Para cuándo desea reservar un asiento la señora López? ¿En qué aerolínea? ¿En qué clase?

   ____

3. ¿Desea un pasaje de ida o de ida y vuelta?

   ____

4. ¿La señora López desea un asiento de pasillo o de ventanilla?

   ____

5. ¿A qué hora anuncian el vuelo? ¿Por qué puerta?

   ____

6. ¿Qué necesita la señora López?

   ____

7. ¿La señora López desea un periódico de Los Ángeles?

   ____

8. ¿A qué hora llega el avión a México?

______

9. ¿Qué llenan todos los pasajeros?

______

Hablemos (*Let's talk*)

Interview a classmate, using the following questions. When you have finished, switch roles.

1. ¿Viaja Ud. en primera clase?
2. ¿Desea un asiento de pasillo?
3. ¿Desea viajar a Aguascalientes?
4. ¿Viaja Ud. con boletos de ida y vuelta?
5. ¿Necesita una almohada ahora? ¿Necesita una frazada?
6. ¿Desea un periódico ahora? ¿Desea una revista mexicana?

Quiz

Vamos a practicar

A Write affirmative sentences using the subjects and verbs given. Then rewrite them in the negative.

MODELO nosotros / completar
Nosotros completamos la declaración de aduana.
Nosotros no completamos la declaración de aduana.

1. ella / anunciar

______

______

2. yo / viajar

______

______

3. tú / desear

______

______

4. usted / evitar

______

______

5. la señora López / llegar

____

____

6. nosotros(as) / necesitar

____

____

7. ustedes / llenar

____

____

8. él y yo / reservar

____

____

9. los auxiliares de vuelo / regresar

____

____

B Write questions to elicit the following answers.

MODELO **—¿Es usted de Lima?**
—Sí, soy de Lima.

1. ____

—Deseo reservar dos asientos para el último vuelo de mañana.

2. ____

—De pasillo, por favor.

3. ____

—Quince minutos antes de la salida.

4. ____

—Por la puerta número dos.

5. ____

—A las cinco de la tarde.

Nombre ______________________ Sección ____________ Fecha ____________

6. ____

—Una revista en español, por favor.

7. ____

—No, no somos de Bogotá; somos de Caracas.

C Write in Spanish the numbers of the following flights and their departure times.

1. Vuelo 807, 9:15 A.M.

____

2. Vuelo 943, 10:00 A.M

____

3. Vuelo 612, 11:45 A.M.

____

4. Vuelo 594, 1:30 P.M.

____

5. Vuelo 414, 12:40 P.M.

____

6. Vuelo 1042, 2:50 P.M.

____

D Change each adjective to agree with the new nouns given.

MODELO el periódico colombiano
las revistas **colombianas**

1. buenos días

____________ tardes

2. último vuelo

____________ salida

3. todas las puertas

____________ los asientos

4. los pasaportes argentinos

las aduanas ____________

5. las mujeres norteamericanas

los hombres ____________

6. las conversaciones breves

la conversación ____________

Nombre ______________________ Sección ____________ Fecha ____________

Sirva usted de intérprete (*Be an interpreter*)

With two classmates, play the roles of a Spanish-speaking business traveler, an English-speaking airline employee, and the interpreter who helps them communicate. Switch roles until each of you has played the interpreter's role.

Pasajero(a) —Deseo un asiento para el vuelo de las siete de la noche para Bogotá, Colombia.

Intérprete —______________________

Empleado(a) —*A one-way ticket?*

Intérprete —______________________

Pasajero(a) —No, de ida y vuelta.

Intérprete —______________________

Empleado(a) —*When do you want to return?*

Intérprete —______________________

Pasajero(a) —El miércoles. ¿Necesito confirmar la hora de salida?

Intérprete —______________________

Empleado(a) —*Yes, sir. You need to confirm your reservation in Bogotá, upon arrival.*

Intérprete —______________________

Sirva usted de traductor(a) (*Be a translator*)

You are flying to a Spanish-speaking country. What do the following signs say?

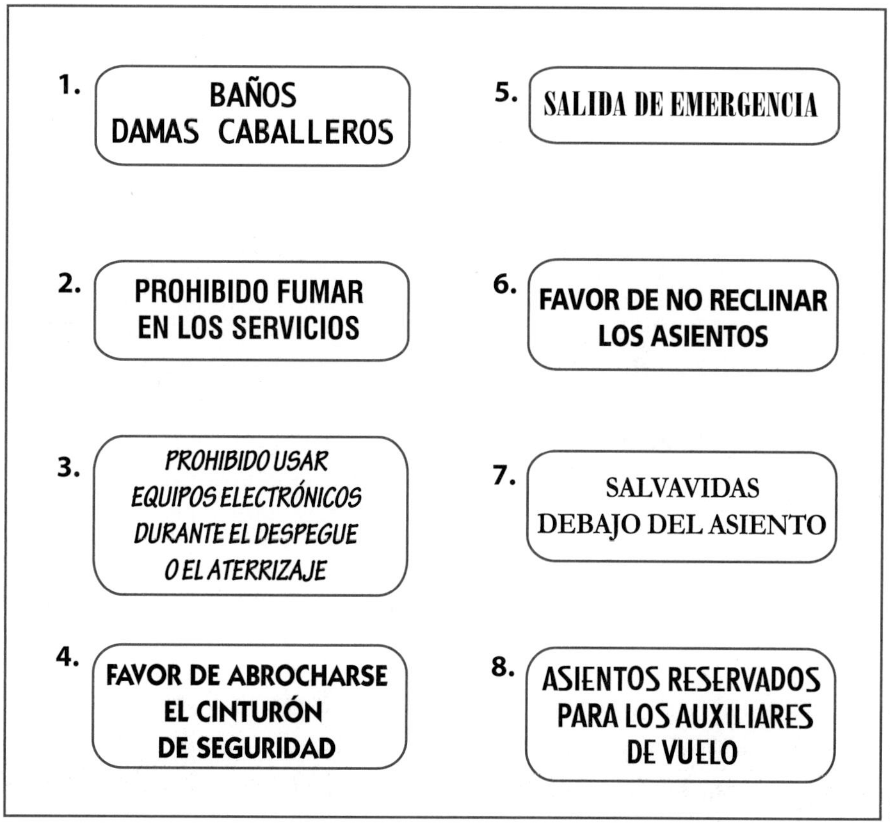

© Cengage Learning

Nombre ______________________ Sección ____________ Fecha ____________

En estas situaciones

With a partner, act out the following situations in Spanish.

1. You are a passenger at an airline counter in Manzanillo, Mexico. Tell the clerk that you want to reserve a seat. Give him/her the time of the flight, and answer his/her questions about the seat you want. Ask the clerk what time the flight arrives in Los Angeles.
2. You are a flight attendant waiting on a Spanish-speaking passenger on an international flight to the United States. You want to find out if he/she wants or needs a blanket, a pillow, a newspaper, or a magazine.
3. You are a passenger on a flight to Chile. When the flight attendant asks the passengers to fill out the customs form, you tell him/her you need a form.

Casos (*Cases*)

With you and a partner playing the roles, work through the following scenarios.

1. At a travel agency in Medellín, Colombia, a travel agent helps a Spanish-speaking customer make plans for air travel.
2. On a flight to Venezuela, a passenger needs some help from a flight attendant.

Un paso más (*One step further*)

A You and a classmate are in training to become flight attendants for an airline that serves Latin America. Review the **Vocabulario adicional** in this lesson and use it and other vocabulary you have learned to create a list of questions, instructions, or statements that you will need to give to passengers.

B Use the information on the boarding pass to identify the passenger's travel plans.

aeromexico

PASE DE ABORDAR	NOMBRE: FLORES LUIS		FECHA: 20/05/10
	VUELO: AM0166	CLASE: Y	ASIENTO: 8D
*VER DORSO		DESTINO: GUADALAJARA	CONTROL: 024
	PASE UD. A LA SALA	C-3 A LAS	1700 HORAS

Nombre ______________________ **Sección** ____________ **Fecha** ____________

1. Passenger: ______________________
2. Flight: ______________________
3. Date: ______________________
4. Class: ______________________
5. Row: ______________ Seat: ______________
6. Time of departure: ______________________

Lectura

After reading this **lectura,** get together with a partner and take turns answering the following questions.

Si va a° México debe saber:°
El signo de pesos es igual al signo de dólares ($).

No todos° los negocios aceptan tarjetas de crédito, cheques de viajero o dólares.

Debe° cambiar su dinero en los bancos. Generalmente las casas de cambio y los hoteles le dan menos° pesos por sus dólares.

Regatear° es una práctica generalizada, pero no en los grandes almacenes° ni en los hoteles de lujo.

Por ley° los precios de los artículos deben incluir° el I.V.A. (impuesto al valor agregado),° pero los hoteles y restaurantes cobran° el I.V.A. sobre el precio anunciado.°

Si... *If you go . . .* / **debe...** *you must know*
No... *not all*
You must
le... *give you less*
bargaining
grandes... *department stores*
Por... *by law* / **deben...** *must include*
impuesto... *value added tax charge (V.A.T.)*
sobre... *above the advertised price*

1. ¿Cómo (*How*) es el signo de pesos?
2. En México, ¿aceptan tarjetas de crédito en todos los negocios?
3. ¿Le dan menos pesos por sus dólares en un hotel o en un banco?
4. ¿Qué es el I.V.A.?

Y usted...

1. ¿Regatea en los grandes almacenes?
2. ¿Paga [(*Do you*) *pay*] impuestos en los restaurantes?

Un dicho

Al país que fueres, haz lo que vieres. *While in Rome, do as Romans do.*

Nombre ______________ Sección ______________ Fecha ______________

Trivia

El español en el mundo: datos significativos

EL ESPAÑOL	DATOS Y FECHAS
Nacimiento:	Hace unos 10 siglos.
Clasificación:	Lengua romance. Proviene principalmente del latín vulgar.
Otras influencias:	Raíces griegas, notables aportaciones del árabe, provenzal, francés, lenguas amerindias y, últimamente, del inglés.
Primera gramática:	Gramática de Antonio Nebrija, 1492. Primera gramática escrita en una lengua romance.
Preceptor:	Real Academia Española (RAE), desde 1713. Periódicamente actualiza y publica sus *Gramática* y *Diccionario.*
Vocabulario:	83.500 palabras sin prefijos ni derivados
Países de habla hispana:	21 países en cinco continentes
Letra emblemática:	Ñ, ñ[1]

[1]Indeed, in Wolof, one of the two main languages of Ethiopia, the 'ñ' is used as a letter and sounds as it does in Spanish.

Sources: Real Academia Española, Banco de datos; La Página del Español www.sergiozamora.com

Spanish is One of the Official Languages of the U.N.

In 1973, Spanish was added to the list of official languages of the United Nations. Now there are six official languages of the United Nations. They are Chinese, English, Spanish, Russian, French, and Arabic. All formal meetings are interpreted in at least these six official languages, and all official documents are translated into all the six languages. In order to become an interpreter or translator for the U.N., the applicant must have a university degree, relevant experience, and a thorough knowledge of at least three of the official languages of the United Nations.

Source: U.N. webpage

Lección 2

En dos aeropuertos mexicanos

Objectives

Structures

- Agreement of articles, nouns, and adjectives
- The present indicative of regular **-er** and **-ir** verbs
- Possession with **de**
- Possessive adjectives
- The personal **a**

Business Communication

- Dealing with immigration officers and custom inspectors
- Exchanging dollars for foreign currencies

A la llegada a México, D.F., la Sra. López habla con un empleado de la aerolínea.

Sra. López —Perdón, señor, ¿debo pasar inmigración y aduana aquí?
Empleado —Sí, señora. ¿Es Ud. ciudadana mexicana?
Sra. López —No, soy extranjera. Soy de los Estados Unidos.
Empleado —Fila de la izquierda, por favor.

Al inspector de inmigración:

Sra. López —Perdón, señor, ¿dónde queda la aduana?
Empleado —En la planta baja, a la derecha. Debe bajar por la escalera.

En el mostrador de la aduana:

Sra. López —¿Abro mi equipaje?
Inspector —Sí, por favor. ¿Algo que declarar?
Sra. López —Sí, una computadora portátil, una cámara de video y una cámara fotográfica.
Inspector —¿Son para su uso personal?
Sra. López —Sí, señor.
Inspector —¿Bebidas alcohólicas, cigarrillos, medicinas?

Sra. López —No, señor. Solamente aspirinas.
Inspector —Entonces no necesita pagar derechos.

A la salida de la aduana, después de mirar el monitor, la Sra. López camina hacia la puerta de salida número siete. Dos horas después toma el avión para Aguascalientes.

En el aeropuerto de Aguascalientes, la Sra. López llama a un maletero que pasa.

Sra. López —Por favor, señor. Primero, a la casa de cambio, y después, a la parada de taxis.
Maletero —Sí, señora.

En la casa de cambio:

Sra. López —¿A cómo está el cambio?
Empleada —A 11,50 pesos[1] por dólar.
Sra. López —Ahora el dólar sube o baja casi todos los días, ¿verdad?
Empleada —Sí, señora, la tasa de cambios no es estable, pero la diferencia de un día a otro es insignificante.
Sra. López —Bien, deseo cambiar doscientos dólares. ¿Aceptan cheques de viajero?
Empleada —Sí, señora. Debe firmar los cheques aquí, y escribir la fecha de hoy.
Sra. López —¿Necesita ver mi pasaporte?
Empleada —Sí, por favor.

A la salida del aeropuerto:

Empleado —Los comprobantes, por favor. (*Mira los comprobantes.*) ¿Dos bultos?
Sra. López —Sí, la maleta grande y el bolso pequeño.
Empleado —Muy bien. Bienvenida a nuestro país.

El maletero lleva el equipaje de la Sra. López a la parada de taxis. La Sra. López toma un taxi.

Search

iLrn

Notas Culturales

In Spanish, commas are used to separate decimals, and periods to indicate thousands ($2.456,87), but Mexico, the Dominican Republic, Puerto Rico, Cuba, El Salvador, Guatemala, and Panama have adopted the Anglo American system ($2,456.87). In Spain, South America, and the rest of Central America, they use the Spanish system.

[1]Mexican currency. This amount of money would be expressed as **trece cincuenta.**

Nombre ______________________ **Sección** __________ **Fecha** __________

¡Escuchemos!

While listening to the dialogue, circle **V (verdadero)** if the statement is true or **F (falso)** if it is false.

1.	La Sra. López no es ciudadana mexicana.	V	F
2.	Ella debe pasar inmigración y aduana a la llegada.	V	F
3.	Debe tomar la fila de la derecha.	V	F
4.	La aduana queda en la planta baja.	V	F
5.	La Sra. López declara cigarrillos y bebidas alcohólicas.	V	F
6.	Ella necesita pagar derechos de aduana.	V	F
7.	Después de mirar el monitor, la Sra. López llama un taxi que pasa.	V	F
8.	Ahora el dólar sube o baja todos los días.	V	F
9.	El empleado de la casa de cambio necesita ver el pasaporte de la Sra. López.	V	F
10.	La tasa de cambio no es estable y la diferencia de un día a otro es grande.	V	F

Audio VOCABULARIO

Cognados

alcohólico(a)
la cámara de video
la diferencia
el dólar
estable
la inmigración
insignificante
el (la) inspector(a)
la medicina, el medicamento
el monitor
el pasaporte
perdón
portátil
el taxi

Nombres

el avión *airplane*
la bebida *drink*
el (la) bolso(a), el maletín de mano, el veliz (*Méx.*) *handbag, carry-on bag*
el bulto *package, bundle*
la cámara fotográfica (*photographic*) *camera*
la casa de cambio *currency exchange office*
el cheque de viajero *traveler's check*
el cigarrillo *cigarette*
el (la) ciudadano(a) *citizen*
el comprobante *claim check,* (*written*) *proof of verification*
el (la) computador(a), el ordenador (*España*) *computer*

Nombre ______________________ Sección ____________ Fecha ____________

el (la) computador(a) portátil, el ordenador portátil *laptop computer*
los derechos, los aranceles, el impuesto *(customs) duty*
el día *day*
el equipaje *baggage*
la escalera *stairs*
el (la) extranjero(a) *foreigner*
la fecha *date*
la fila *line*
la maleta, la valija *suitcase*
el maletero *porter, skycap*
la parada de taxis *taxi stop*
la planta baja *ground floor, downstairs*
la tasa (el tipo) de cambio *exchange rate*

Verbos

abrir *to open*
aceptar *to accept*
bajar *to go down*
cambiar *to change, to exchange*
caminar *to walk*
deber *must, should*
declarar *to declare*
escribir *to write*
firmar *to sign*
llamar *to call*
llevar *to take (someone or something someplace)*
mirar *to look at*
pagar *to pay*
pasar *to pass, to go through*
quedar *to be located*
subir *to go up*
tomar *to take; to drink*
ver[1] *to see*

Adjetivos

bienvenido(a) *welcome*
grande *big, large*
mi *my*
nuestro(a) *our*
pequeño(a) *small*
su *your, his, her, their*

Otras palabras y expresiones

¿A cómo está el cambio? *What's the rate of exchange?*
a la derecha (izquierda) *to the right (left)*
a la llegada *upon arrival*
¿Algo que declarar? *Anything to declare?*
aquí *here*
casi *almost*
después *later*
después (de) *after*
fila de la izquierda (derecha) *left (right) row*
hacia *to, toward*
hoy *today*
para su uso personal *for your personal use*
pasar aduana *to go through customs*
pero *but*
primero *first*
que pasa *passing by*
todos los días *every day*
¿verdad? *right?*

[1]Irregular first person: **yo veo**

Nombre ______________________ Sección ______________ Fecha ______________

VOCABULARIO ADICIONAL

Audio

a quién(es) *whom*
alimentos para bebé *baby food*
la calculadora de bolsillo *pocket calculator*
el centavo *cent*
el dinero en efectivo *cash*
elegir *to choose*
la escalera mecánica *escalator*
el estado *state*
el estado civil *marital status*
emitir *to emit*
es menor a (de) *is lower than*
ingresar *to enter, to come in*
ingreso *entering*
jeringa, la jeringuilla *syringe*
la fecha de nacimiento *date of birth*
la grabadora de video, la videograbadora, la casetera *VCR*
libre de derechos (impuestos) *duty-free*
las mercancías, los géneros *goods*
la moneda *currency*
marcapasos *pacemaker*
mujeres embarazadas *pregnant women*
ocurrir *to happen*
paciente *patient*
el país *country*
la parada de autobuses [camiones (*Méx.*)] *bus stop*
la planta alta *upstairs*
poder *to be able to (can)*
por tal razón *therefore*
portar *to travel with*
el (la)[1] radio de batería (de pilas) *battery-operated radio*
receta (medicine) *prescription*
silla de ruedas *wheelchair*
sin embargo *however*
la tabla de cotizaciones *currency exchange table*
la tarjeta de crédito *credit card*
la tarjeta de residente[2] *resident card*
(teléfono) celular/móvil *cellular telephone*
el televisor portátil *portable television set*

Search

iLrn

Notas Culturales

- Due to the vast distances between major cities, the excessive cost of highway and railroad construction through mountain ranges and other geographical barriers, and the resultant scarcity of good land transportation systems, some Latin American countries have excellent air transportation systems. The well-regarded Colombian airline Avianca, for example, is the oldest airline in the Americas and the second oldest airline in the world. Safety and efficiency standards vary widely among both private and state-owned airlines, however, so air travel should be planned with care. Domestic flights in Latin America are usually booked to capacity, and confirmation of reservations is essential.
- Credit cards and debit cards are widely used, especially in urban areas, and usually offer the most favorable exchange rates available.
- Traveler's checks generally are not accepted as cash at restaurants and shops in some Spanish-speaking countries, as they are in the United States, except at some resort areas. They must be cashed at banks (where exchange rates are generally higher, and transaction fees lower), currency exchanges, or hotels.
- In Ecuador, El Salvador, and Panama, the American dollar (**dólar**) is officially accepted as legal tender.

[1]The feminine form **la radio** (meaning *radio receiver*) is used in some countries, while the masculine form is used in other countries.
[2]In the U.S., **la tarjeta verde** (*green card*).

Nombre ______________________ Sección ____________ Fecha ____________

Los países de habla hispana y sus monedas

País	Moneda	País	Moneda
Argentina	el peso	Honduras	el lempira
Bolivia	el boliviano	México	el peso
Chile	el peso	Nicaragua	el córdoba
Colombia	el peso	Panamá	el balboa, dólar
Costa Rica	el colón	Paraguay	el guaraní
Cuba	el peso CUC (Cuban convertible peso)	Perú	el nuevo sol
		Puerto Rico[1]	el dólar
Ecuador	el sucre, dólar	República Dominicana	el peso
El Salvador	el colón, dólar	Uruguay	el peso
España	el euro	Venezuela	el bolívar fuerte
Guatemala	el quetzal		

Actividades

Dígame... Answer the following questions, basing your answers on the dialogues.

1. ¿Dónde debe pasar inmigración y aduana la Sra. López?

____

2. ¿La Sra. López es mexicana?

____

3. ¿Dónde queda la aduana?

____

4. ¿Quién abre las maletas, el inspector o la Sra. López?

____

5. ¿Qué declara la Sra. López?

____

6. ¿Necesita pagar derechos? ¿Por qué o por qué no?

____

7. A la llegada al aeropuerto de Aguascalientes, ¿a quién llama la Sra. López?

____

[1]U.S. Commonwealth

8. ¿Qué ocurre con el dólar casi todos los días?

____

9. ¿Cuántos dólares desea cambiar la Sra. López?

____

10. ¿Aceptan cheques de viajero?

____

11. A la salida del aeropuerto, ¿qué necesita ver la empleada?

____

12. ¿Qué toma la Sra. López?

____

Hablemos

Interview a classmate, using the following questions. When you have finished, switch roles.

1. ¿Es Ud. ciudadano(a) mexicano(a)?
2. ¿Ud. toma bebidas alcohólicas?
3. ¿Usa Ud. una computadora portátil?
4. ¿Deben o no deben subir el precio de la gasolina?
5. ¿Qué moneda usamos en los Estados Unidos?
6. ¿Cree Ud. que el cambio del dólar por euros es estable?
7. ¿Dónde queda Aguascalientes?
8. ¿Necesita Ud. pasaporte?

Quiz

Vamos a practicar

A Complete the following sentences, using the Spanish equivalent of the possessive adjectives in parentheses. Make sure they agree with the nouns they modify.

Modelo No necesitas abrir __________ equipaje, Lolita. (*your*)
No necesitas abrir **tu** equipaje, Lolita.

1. El maletero sube __________ maletas. (*my*)
2. La inspectora no abre __________ maletas. (*our*)
3. Ella necesita __________ equipaje. (*her*)
4. ¿Las medicinas son para __________ uso personal, Sr. Rojas? (*your*)
5. Ellas deben cambiar __________ cheques de viajero. (*their*)

Nombre ______________________ Sección ______________ Fecha ______________

B Rewrite the following sentences, using the new subjects.

Modelo Ellos necesitan pagar derechos de aduana. (Nosotros)
Nosotros necesitamos pagar derechos de aduana.

1. El inspector abre las maletas de la Sra. López.
   Yo ______________________________.
2. Ella cree que debe cambiar los dólares hoy.
   Nosotros ______________________________.
3. Ud. debe llenar la declaración de aduana.
   Tú ______________________________.
4. Nosotros firmamos los cheques de viajero.
   Ella y tú ______________________________.
5. El dólar sube todos los días.
   La gasolina ______________________________.

C Give the Spanish equivalent of the following.

1. *Elena does not see Carlos.*
   ____
2. *Elena does not see her big suitcase.*
   ____
3. *Estela needs María.*
   ____
4. *Esteban needs his passport.*
   ____
5. *They do not accept traveler's checks.*
   ____

Nombre ______________________ **Sección** ____________ **Fecha** ____________

Sirva usted de intérprete

With two classmates, play the roles of an English-speaking business traveler, a Spanish-speaking currency exchange employee, and the interpreter who helps them communicate. Switch roles until each of you has played the interpreter's role.

Pasajero(a) —*What is the exchange rate?*

Intérprete —______________________________

Empleado(a) —A 13,50 pesos por dólar.

Intérprete —______________________________

Pasajero(a) —*Do you accept personal checks?*

Intérprete —______________________________

Empleado(a) —No, señor(ita), pero aceptamos cheques de viajero.

Intérprete —______________________________

Pasajero(a) —*Well, I want to exchange $50.00.*

Intérprete —______________________________

Empleado(a) —Debe firmar aquí, y necesito ver su pasaporte.

Intérprete —______________________________

Sirva usted de traductor(a)

You encounter the following sign in the international terminal of an airport. Review the **Vocabulario adicional** in this lesson, and then translate the information from the sign on a separate sheet of paper.

© Cengage Learning

Nombre ______________________ Sección ______________ Fecha ______________

En estas situaciones

With a partner, act out the following situations in Spanish.

1. You are a passenger going through customs in a Spanish-speaking country. Declare three items and tell the inspector that they are for personal use. Find out whether you must declare medicine.
2. You are a customs inspector in Miami, assisting a Spanish-speaking traveler. Tell the traveler that he/she must open his/her suitcases, and ask if he/she has anything to declare. Confirm that the traveler must declare a laptop computer.
3. You are at a currency exchange office in a Mexican airport. Ask the clerk what the rate of exchange is, and whether they accept traveler's checks. He/She should tell you where to sign the traveler's checks.

Casos

With you and a partner playing the roles, work through the following scenarios.

1. A passenger goes through customs at a Latin American airport.
2. A traveler changes money at a currency exchange office.

Un paso más

A You and a partner are customs officers. Review the **Vocabulario adicional** in this lesson and use it and other vocabulary you have learned to create a list of questions, instructions, or statements that you will need to be able to give to Spanish-speaking travelers regarding the following issues:

- documentation that must be presented (passport or green card)
- what items travelers must pay duty on and what items are duty free
- travelers should take the escalator upstairs
- there is no currency exchange office in the customs area

B The following document, **Mercancías Libres de Impuestos**, lists what residents and non-residents can bring into Mexico free of charge. Indicate if you can take the following ten items with you to Mexico without paying duty on them, according to the document.

1.	¿Maletas?	Sí	No
2.	¿Una cámara fotográfica?	Sí	No
3.	¿Libros?	Sí	No
4.	¿Animales?	Sí	No
5.	¿Un binocular?	Sí	No
6.	¿Cuatro raquetas de tenis?	Sí	No
7.	¿Treinta cajetillas (*packs*) de cigarrillos?	Sí	No
8.	¿Un instrumento musical?	Sí	No
9.	¿Una bicicleta?	Sí	No
10.	¿Una computadora?	Sí	No

Nombre ______________________ Sección ____________ Fecha ____________

Mercancías Libres de Impuestos

Usted tiene derecho de importar, sin el pago de impuestos, las mercancías que a continuación se detallan:

A) Para residentes en el país:

1) Las de uso personal como ropa, calzado y artículos de aseo o tocador, en cantidad razonable y acorde a la duración de su viaje.

2) Una cámara fotográfica o una cinematográfica o una para videograbación, incluyendo su fuente de poder, excepto equipo profesional; hasta doce rollos de película virgen o DVD, así como el material fotográfico impreso o filmado.

3) Libros y revistas.

4) Un artículo deportivo o un equipo individual de deporte, siempre que pueda ser transportado comúnmente por una persona.

5) Hasta veinte cajetillas de cigarrillos o cincuenta puros o doscientos cincuenta gramos de tabaco, si el pasajero es mayor de edad.

6) Hasta tres litros de vino o licor, si se trata de mayores de edad.

7) Medicamentos de uso personal, con receta médica cuando se trate de sustancias psicotrópicas.

8) Los velices, petacas, báules, maletas en los que se contengan las mercancías.

B) Para residentes en el extranjero:

Además de las señaladas en el apartado A) podrán introducirse las siguientes mercancías:

1) Un binocular y una cámara fotográfica adicional a lo autorizado en el inciso 2 de dicho apartado.

2) Un aparato de televisión portátil.

3) Un aparato de radio portátil para el grabado o reproducción del sonido o uno mixto.

4) Hasta veinte discos compactos propios para la reproducción del sonido.

5) Una máquina de escribir portátil.

6) Un instrumento musical, siempre que pueda ser transportado normal y comúnmente por una persona.

7) Una tienda de campaña y un equipo para acampar.

8) Hasta cinco juguetes usados, cuando el pasajero sea menor de edad.

9) Un juego de avíos para pesca, un par de esquíes y dos raquetas de tenis.

10) Un bote sin motor, de menos de cinco y medio metros de largo (eslora), o un deslizador acuático con o sin vela.

11) Una videocasetera.

12) Una bicicleta con o sin motor.

13) Ropa de casa (habitación).

14) Utensilios y muebles de cocina, estancia y/o alcoba.

Nombre ______________________ **Sección** ____________ **Fecha** ____________

Lectura

After reading this **lectura,** get together with a partner and take turns answering the following questions.

En los Estados Unidos° son frecuentes las historias° de sobornos° a los inspectores de aduana de México y de otros países, pero recuerde° que° el soborno es un delito.° Tratar de° sobornar a un inspector de aduana, a un policía° o a cualquier° otra persona puede llevarlo a la cárcel.° En realidad° la persona que soborna es tan deshonesta° como la que° acepta el soborno.	**Estados...** *United States* *tales / bribe* *remember / that / crime* **Tratar...** *Trying to* *police officer / any* **puede...** *may put you in jail* / **En...** *Indeed* **tan...** as *dishonest* **como...** *as the one who*
En México, llaman al soborno "la mordida".°	*bite*

1. Según (*According* to) las historias, ¿a quiénes sobornan en México?
2. Tratar de sobornar a un inspector puede llevarlo a la cárcel. ¿Por qué (*Why*)?
3. Según la lectura, ¿quiénes (*who*) son deshonestos?
4. ¿Cómo llaman al soborno en México?

Y en los Estados Unidos...

1. ¿El soborno es un delito?
2. ¿Es frecuente sobornar a los policías?

Un dicho

El que compra, manda. *Buyers have the upper hand.*

Trivia

Tips for Travelers

- As of summer 2003, U.S. citizens are allowed to take home up to $800 of merchandise per person without paying taxes—so long as they have been out of the country for at least 48 hours and have not used the exemption in the past 30 days. Nevertheless, antiques over 100 years old and works of art are exempt from the $800 limit.
- One cannot bring plants, fruits, vegetables, meat, and, indeed, most food items out of the foreign country.
- The exchange rate may fluctuate daily, so do not exchange too much of your currency at once.

LECCIÓN

3

EN EL HOTEL

OBJECTIVES

Structures

- The irregular verbs **ir, dar,** and **estar**
- **Ir a** + infinitive
- Uses of the verbs **ser** and **estar**
- Contractions

Business Communication

- Making hotel reservations
- Providing personal and credit card information
- Complaining about hotel accommodations

La Sra. López llama por teléfono al Hotel Fiesta Americana, un hotel para hombres y mujeres de negocios.

Empleado —Hotel Fiesta Americana, buenos días.
Sra. López —Buenos días. Deseo reservar una habitación por cuatro días, a partir de mañana.
Empleado —¿Para cuántas personas?
Sra. López —Para una persona. ¿Cuánto es?
Empleado —Ochocientos cuarenta y cinco pesos por día, más impuestos. ¿A qué hora va a llegar al hotel?
Sra. López —A las nueve y media de la noche, más o menos.
Empleado —Bien, para asegurar su reservación, necesito los datos de su tarjeta de crédito.
Sra. López —Me llamo Sonia López y mi tarjeta es una VISA, número 4723-5561-1096-8289.
Empleado —¿Válida hasta cuándo?
Sra. López —La fecha de vencimiento es junio de 2012.
Empleado —¿Cuál es su dirección, señora?
Sra. López —Calle 124, número 789, apartamento 11, Nueva York.[1]
Empleado —Muy bien, eso es todo.
Sra. López —Por favor, ¿a qué distancia del aeropuerto está el hotel?
Empleado —A unos 25 kilómetros.[2]

---

[1]In a Spanish-speaking country, the name of the street precedes the number of the house, i.e., **Avenida Magnolia (número) 520.**

[2]1 mile = 1.6 kilometers. For an extensive list of weights and measures, their Spanish equivalents, and their equivalents in the metric system, see Appendix D.

A la llegada, en la recepción:

Sra. López —Buenas noches, soy la Sra. López, de los Estados Unidos.
Empleado —¡Bienvenida a Aguascalientes, Sra. López! Su habitación está lista. Ahora debe llenar la tarjeta de huésped, por favor.
Sra. López —¿En qué piso está mi habitación?
Empleado —En el tercer piso.
Sra. López —No da a la calle, ¿verdad? Aquí hay mucho ruido.
Empleado —Sí, estamos situados en el centro de la ciudad, pero su habitación es interior. (*Llama a Antonio, el botones.*) Antonio, a la recámara 334.

El botones toma las maletas de la Sra. López y la llave de la habitación.

Botones —Por aquí, señora. (*Ambos van hacia el ascensor.*)

En la habitación:

Botones —¿Necesita algo más, señora?
Sra. López —Nada más, gracias.

Al poco rato la Sra. López llama por teléfono a la recepción.

Empleado —Recepción.
Sra. López —Soy la Sra. López.
Empleado —¿Quién?
Sra. López —Soy la Sra. López y estoy en la habitación 334. El aire acondicionado no funciona bien.
Empleado —En seguida va para allá el botones para trasladar su equipaje a otra recámara. Lamentamos mucho el inconveniente.

¡Escuchemos!

While listening to the dialogue, circle **V (verdadero)** if the statement is true or **F (falso)** if it is false.

1. La Sra. López desea reservar una habitación para una persona. V F
2. Ella va a llegar al hotel por la mañana. V F
3. La Sra. López pregunta cuánto es el impuesto. V F
4. Su tarjeta de crédito es válida hasta junio de 2012. V F
5. A la llegada al hotel su habitación no está lista. V F
6. El hotel está situado en el centro de la ciudad. V F
7. La habitación de la Sra. López da a la calle. V F
8. Antonio es el botones del hotel. V F
9. Ambos van hacia la escalera. V F
10. El ascensor del hotel funciona bien. V F

Nombre ______________________ Sección ______________ Fecha ______________

VOCABULARIO

Audio

Cognados

el apartamento
el crédito
el hotel
el inconveniente
interior
el kilómetro
la persona
el (la) recepcionista
situado(a)
válido(a)

Nombres

el aire acondicionado *air conditioning*
el ascensor, el elevador *elevator*
el botones *bellhop*
el centro de la ciudad *downtown, center of the city*
los datos *information, data*
la fecha de vencimiento *expiration date*
la habitación, el cuarto, la recámara (*Méx.*) *room*
el hombre (la mujer) de negocios *businessman (woman)*
el (la) huésped *guest*
el impuesto *tax*
la llave *key*
el piso *floor*
la recepción *reception desk, front desk*
el ruido *noise*
la tarjeta *card*
la tarjeta de registro, la tarjeta de huésped *registration card*

Verbos

asegurar *to ensure*
dar *to give*
estar *to be*
funcionar *to work*
ir *to go*
lamentar *to be sorry for, to regret*
trasladar *to move, to relocate*

Adjetivos

ambos(as) *both*
listo(a) *ready*
mucho(a) *much*
tercero(a)[1] *third*

Otras palabras y expresiones

a partir de *starting, as of*
¿a qué distancia? *how far?*
al poco rato *a while later*
¿Algo más? *Anything else?*
allá *there, over there*
¿Cuál? *which?, what?*
¿cuánto(a)? *how much?*
¿cuántos(as)? *how many?*
da a la calle *overlooks the street*
en seguida va para allá *he's/she's on his/her way there*
eso es todo *that's all*
hasta *until, up to*
hay *there is, there are*
ir a (+ ***inf.***) *going to (do something)*
más *plus*
más o menos *more or less, around*
Me llamo... *My name is . . .*
nada *nothing*
nada más *nothing else*
por aquí *this way*
por día *per day*
unos, unas (+ ***number***) *about (+ number)*

---

[1]**Primero** and **tercero** drop the final **o** before a masculine noun.

Nombre ______________________ Sección ____________ Fecha ____________

VOCABULARIO ADICIONAL

Audio

a partir del día (+ ***date***) *as of the* (+ *date*)
el agua[1] **caliente (fría)** *hot* (*cold*) *water*
la bañadera, bañera *bathtub*
el bolígrafo *ballpoint pen*
la calefacción *heating*
el champú *shampoo*
las cortinas *curtains*
cuenta con *has*
desde... hasta, de... a *from . . . to . . .*
discapacitado(a), minusválido(a) *disabled*
desocupar la habitación *to check out, to vacate a room*
la ducha, la regadera (*Méx.*) *shower*
horario limitado *limited hour*
el inodoro *toilet*
el jabón *soap*
el lavabo *bathroom sink*
limpio(a) *clean*
el papel de cartas *stationery*
el papel higiénico *toilet paper*
prender (apagar) la luz *to turn on* (*turn off*) *the light*
la sábana *sheet*
el servicio de habitación *room service*
servicio de habitación(habitaciones) *room service*
sucio(a) *dirty*
la tarjeta postal *postcard*
la televisión *television*
el televisor *TV set*
transporte *shuttle*
la toalla *towel*

Search

iLrn

Notas Culturales

- Hotels in a range of categories, including many owned by North American, European, and Japanese chains, exist in all Latin American cities and can usually be reserved through a travel agent or through the Internet. Information about independent hotels can be obtained through hotel representation firms such as *LARC (Latin American Reservation Center)*. In choosing a hotel, remember that room prices quoted usually don't include taxes, which are very high in some countries.
- Mexicans are very proud of their independence from the United States and are very sensitive about U.S.-Mexican political relationships. Many of them resent U.S. citizens referring to themselves as **"americanos"**, since this term includes North, Central, and South America. Nevertheless, they refer to U.S. citizens as **"norteamericanos",** although this term also includes Canadians and Mexicans.

Actividades

Dígame... Answer the following questions, basing your answers on the dialogue.

1. ¿Para qué llama por teléfono la Sra. López?

____

[1]**Agua** is a feminine noun, but the definite article **el** or the indefinite article **un** is used instead of **la** or **una** with feminine singular nouns beginning with stressed **a** or **ha.**

2. ¿Por cuántos días necesita una habitación?

____

3. ¿A partir de qué día?

____

4. ¿A qué hora va a llegar la Sra. López al hotel?

____

5. ¿Qué necesita la recepcionista para asegurar la reservación?

____

6. ¿Hasta cuándo es válida la tarjeta de crédito de la Sra. López?

____

7. ¿Cuál es el número de la habitación de la Sra. López?

____

8. ¿Da a la calle la habitación de la Sra. López?

____

9. ¿Qué toma el botones?

____

10. ¿Adónde van la Sra. López y el botones?

____

11. ¿Qué problema hay en la habitación de la Sra. López?

____

12. ¿A qué distancia del aeropuerto está el hotel?

____

Hablemos Interview a classmate, using the following questions. When you have finished, switch roles.

1. ¿Cuál es su dirección?
2. ¿En qué piso está su habitación?
3. ¿Su cuarto da a la calle?
4. ¿Hay mucho ruido en su cuarto?
5. ¿Funciona bien el aire acondicionado de su cuarto?

6. ¿Cuál es su número de teléfono?
7. ¿Cuál es su hotel favorito?
8. ¿Paga Ud. el hotel con una tarjeta de crédito?
9. ¿Cuál es la fecha de vencimiento de su tarjeta de crédito?
10. ¿Paga Ud. impuestos? ¿Cuándo?
11. ¿Paga Ud. sus impuestos con la tarjeta de crédito?

Quiz

Vamos a practicar

A Give the Spanish equivalent of the following.

1. *the noise of the elevator*

____

2. *Sir, to Calinda Roma Hotel, please.*

____

3. *the hotel elevator*

____

4. *She is arriving at the airport at 10 A.M.*

____

5. *He calls the bellhop.*

____

6. *Mr. Sosa's room*

____

B Create sentences using the elements given and adding any necessary elements to say what is going to happen.

Modelo Carlos / hablar / gerente
Carlos va a hablar con el gerente.

1. yo / dar / dirección

____

2. ¿tú / estar / en / hotel / favorito?

____

Nombre ______________________ Sección ____________ Fecha ____________

3. ella / no / dar / fecha de vencimiento / tarjeta de crédito

____

4. nosotros / ir / hacia / allá

____

5. ellos / trasladar / el equipaje

____

6. el empleado / llamar / maletero

____

C Choose the correct form of **ser** or **estar.**

1. Yo (soy / estoy) el botones del hotel.
2. La maleta (es / está) a la izquierda de la puerta.
3. Las tarjetas de huésped (son / están) en la recepción.
4. ¿Tú (eres / estás) de Guadalajara?
5. ¿Él (es / está) en Guadalajara?
6. El Sr. Pérez (es / está) aquí.
7. ¿Cuál (es / está) la fecha de vencimiento de su tarjeta?
8. Nosotros (somos / estamos) empleados de la aerolínea.
9. Sus habitaciones no (son / están) listas.

Sirva usted de intérprete

With a partner, play the roles of a Spanish-speaking business traveler, a front desk recepcionist at an American hotel, and the interpreter who helps them communicate. Switch roles until each of you has played the interpreter's role.

Huésped —Buenos días, necesito una habitación para hoy.

Intérprete —______________________________

Recepcionista —*For how many people?*

Intérprete —______________________________

Huésped —Para una sola. ¿Cuánto es?

Intérprete —______________________________

Recepcionista —*Sixty-five dollars a night, plus tax. How many days are you going to stay?*

Intérprete —______________________________

Huésped —Tres o cuatro días. Por favor, deseo una habitación interior. Aquí hay mucho ruido.

Intérprete —______________________________

Nombre ______________________ Sección ______________ Fecha ______________

Sirva usted de traductor You work at an inexpensive hotel. Your boss has just asked you to translate the following note left this morning by a Spanish-speaking guest who seemed upset. Review the **Vocabulario adicional** in this lesson, and then translate the note on a separate sheet of paper. Then, respond to the note of this upset guest and suggest a solution.

Señores:
—¡Su hotel es un desastre!
—La habitación está sucia.
—No hay agua caliente en la ducha[1].
—Necesito una toalla y una sábana limpias.
—El inodoro no funciona bien.
—No hay jabón en el lavabo.
—El servicio de habitación es horrible.
Por eso no dejo propina.

L. Álvarez

En estas situaciones With a partner, act out the following situations in Spanish.

1. You are traveling to Monterrey, Mexico. When you telephone to reserve a room at a hotel, tell the receptionist the purpose of your call and the length of your upcoming stay, and ask for the price of the room.
2. You are the receptionist at a New Jersey motel. Check in a customer who speaks only Spanish. Tell him/her to fill out the guest card, inform him/her where his/her room is located, and tell him/her what kind of room it is.
3. You are a guest in a hotel in Costa Rica. You call the front desk to complain because the room is not ready and it is too noisy. In addition, the air conditioning is not working properly.

Casos With you and a partner playing the roles, work through the following scenarios.

1. A customer calls a hotel to make a reservation.
2. At the registration desk of a hotel, a guest checks in for two nights.
3. A bellhop shows a guest to his/her room.

---

[1]**regadera** in Mexico

Nombre ______________________ **Sección** __________ **Fecha** __________

Un paso más

A Review the **Vocabulario adicional** in this lesson and act out the following dialogues in Spanish with a partner.

1. "At what time do we need to check out today?"
"At eleven o'clock. Are you ready?"
"Yes, I'm ready."

2. "Is there a television set in the room?"
"Yes, but it doesn't work."
"The sheets and the sink are dirty, too."
"And there's no hot water. We need another hotel!"

B Read the registration card filled out by Antonio Zamora Pino during a recent hotel stay and supply the following information. Then draw a similar form and fill in your own data.

1. Guest's first name: ______________
2. Guest's last name: ______________
3. Hotel name: ______________
4. Hotel address: ______________
5. Date of arrival: ______________
6. Number of people occupying room: ______
7. Guest's address: ______________
8. Room number: ______ Floor: ______
9. Credit card number: ______________
10. Credit card expiration date: ______________

TARJETA DE REGISTRO

A. Zamora P.
FIRMA

FECHA DE LLEGADA		FECHA DE SALIDA		DÍAS
DÍA	MES	DÍA	MES	PERMANENCIA
1 | 4	0 | 4			

NOMBRE: Antonio Zamora Pino
DIRECCIÓN: Avenida Madero, 415
CIUDAD: Guadalajara, Jalisco AUTO-PLACAS: 73-425
No. DE PERSONAS: 2 HABITACIÓN: 108 PISO: 2º
HORA DE RECEPCIÓN: 11:15 RESERVADO POR: —

EFECTIVO $ ______ (______)

DEPÓSITO:

TARJETAS DE CRÉDITO: ______ No.: 742-5617 VÁLIDA HASTA: Mayo 2012

TARIFA: $785.00 MÁS I.V.A.

BIENVENIDOS

HOTEL-SOCAVÓN
36060 Guanajuato, 46A Airondiga Tel•2•48•85

Nombre ______________________ Sección ____________ Fecha ____________

Lectura After reading this **lectura,** get together with a partner and take turns answering the following questions.

En la mayoría° de los países	*majority*
latinoamericanos hay dos	
tipos de hoteles: hoteles de lujo,°	**hoteles...** *luxury hotels*
visitados por turistas, hombres y mujeres	
de negocios y las clases altas° del país,	**clases...** *high class*
y hoteles económicos que usa,°	**hoteles...** *economic hotels used by*
principalmente, la clase media.°	*middle class*
El resto de la población,°	*people*
es decir,° la gente pobre,°	**es...** *that is* / **la gente...** *the poor*
va a las casas de huéspedes o pensiones.°	**casas...** *boarding houses*
También,° como° muchas universidades	*Also / as*
no tienen° residencias universitarias,	*don't have*
los estudiantes viven° en pensiones.	*live*

1. ¿Cuántos tipos de hoteles hay en la mayoría de los países latinoamericanos?
2. ¿Quiénes van a los hoteles de lujo?
3. ¿Qué hoteles usa la clase media?
4. ¿Adónde van los pobres?

Y en los Estados Unidos...

1. ¿Hay muchas casas de huéspedes en los Estados Unidos?
2. ¿Piensa Ud. (*Do you think*) que hay muchas o pocas (*a few*) diferencias de clases?

Un dicho

El ahorro es la base del capital. *Saving is the base of capital.*

Trivia

- Generally, in Mexico, the infrastructure for tourism offers very good hotels and restaurants at reasonable prices. The quality of services has improved a lot in recent years and, in this respect, they have reached international standards.
- The "machismo" attitude towards women in Mexican professional circles is history. Today, women doing business in Mexico are not only accepted and respected, but treated both professionally and courteously.

Lección 4

Las comidas

Objectives

Structures

- The irregular verbs **tener** and **venir**
- Expressions with **tener**
- Comparative forms
- Irregular comparative forms

Business Communication

- Dining at a restaurant
- Finding information about typical local food
- Asking about the ingredients and preparation of dishes

Al día siguiente, por la mañana, la Sra. López va a la cafetería del hotel para tomar el desayuno.[1]

Mesera —Buenos días, señora. ¿Cuántos son?
Sra. López —Yo sola.
Mesera —Por aquí, por favor.
Sra. López —¿Cuál es el desayuno típico mexicano?
Mesera —Huevos, frijoles, tortillas... Aquí tiene el menú. ¿Café?
Sra. López —¿El café mexicano es fuerte?
Mesera —Es más fuerte que el café americano,[2] pero no tan fuerte como el café expreso italiano.
Sra. López —¿Tienen café descafeinado?
Mesera —Sí, pero es café instantáneo.
Sra. López —Entonces voy a tomar café con leche.
Mesera —Muy bien, ¿y para comer?
Sra. López —(*Lee el menú.*) ¿Cómo son los huevos rancheros?
Mesera —Vienen con una salsa de tomate y chile.
Sra. López —¿No hay pan tostado u[3] otro tipo de pan? ¡Tengo mucha hambre!
Mesera —Sí, señora, pero aquí las tortillas son más populares que el pan.

---

[1]**Tomar** means *to have, to eat* when referring to breakfast only; **comer** is used with other meals.
[2]Used to describe weaker, American-style coffee.
[3]**U** is used for **o** when preceding a word starting with **o** or **ho.**

Nombre ______________________ **Sección** ____________ **Fecha** ____________

A la hora del almuerzo, la Sra. López va al restaurante La Catrina.[1]

Mesero —¿Desea Ud. tomar algo antes del almuerzo?
Sra. López —No, ahora no. ¿Cuál es la especialidad de la casa?
Mesero —Los mariscos y el pescado.
Sra. López —(*Después de leer el menú*) El lenguado, ¿es fresco o congelado?
Mesero —Solamente servimos pescados frescos: lenguado, huachinango,[2] mero, corbina, bagre...
Sra. López —¿Cuál es el mejor?
Mesero —Todos son buenos, señora. Tan buenos como el lenguado o mejores.
Sra. López —¿Qué es el huachinango?
Mesero —Es el pargo rojo de otros países, y el *red snapper* de los Estados Unidos.
Sra. López —¿Con qué viene?
Mesero —Con arroz y ensalada mixta o vegetales.
Sra. López —Entonces, huachinango asado con vegetales y arroz.
Mesero —¿Algo para tomar?
Sra. López —Una copa de vino blanco Marqués de Riscal.

Cuando la Sra. López termina de comer, llama al mesero.

Mesero —¿Café, postre?
Sra. López —No, gracias. La cuenta, por favor. Tengo prisa. Tengo que estar en la zona industrial a las tres.
Mesero —Tiene tiempo, señora. De aquí a la zona industrial tarda menos de veinte minutos.

La Sra. López paga la cuenta y deja la propina en la mesa.

¡Escuchemos!

While listening to the dialogue, circle **V (verdadero)** if the statement is true or **F (falso)** if it is false.

1. La Sra. López va sola a la cafetería. V F
2. Los mexicanos comen frijoles en el desayuno. V F
3. El café americano es tan fuerte como el café expreso italiano. V F
4. El café descafeinado de la cafetería es café instantáneo. V F
5. En México el pan es tan popular como las tortillas. V F
6. Los mariscos y el pescado son la especialidad del restaurante. V F
7. El restaurante solamente sirve pescados frescos. V F
8. La Sra. López pide una ensalada de tomate. V F
9. Ella desea comer el postre típico. V F
10. La Sra. López tarda una hora para ir del restaurante a la zona industrial. V F

[1]**Catrín(ina)** is said of a person who is dressed up.
[2]Commonly pronounced **guachinango**

Nombre ______________________ Sección ____________ Fecha ____________

VOCABULARIO

Audio

Cognados

la cafetería
el chile (*Méx.*), **el ají**
la especialidad
el menú
popular
el restaurante, el restorán
el tomate
la tortilla[1] (*Méx.*)
los vegetales

Nombres

el almuerzo, la comida (*Esp.*) *lunch*
el arroz *rice*
el bagre *fresh water fish*
el café *coffee*
el café con leche *coffee and milk, café au lait*
el café expreso, el café solo *espresso, strong black coffee*
la casa *house*
la ciudad *city*
la copa *glass*
la corbina *sea bass*
la cuenta *bill*
el desayuno *breakfast*
la ensalada *salad*
el frijol *bean*
el huevo, el blanquillo (*Méx.*) *egg*
la leche *milk*
el lenguado *sole*
el marisco *seafood, shellfish*
el mero *halibut*
la mesa *table*
el (la) mesero(a) (*Méx.*), **mozo, camarero(a), mesonero** (*Ven.*) *waiter, waitress*
el pan *bread*
el pargo, el huachinango (*Méx.*) *red snapper*
el pescado *fish*
el postre *dessert*
la salsa *sauce*
el tipo *type*
la tostada, el pan tostado *toast*
el vino *wine*
la zona (el distrito) industrial *industrial zone*

Verbos

comer *to eat*
dejar *to leave (behind)*
leer *to read*
tardar *to take, to last (a length of time)*
tener *to have*
terminar *to finish*
venir *to come*

Adjetivos

asado(a) *grilled, broiled, roasted*
bueno(a) *good*
congelado(a) *frozen*
descafeinado(a) *decaffeinated*
fresco(a) *fresh*
fuerte *strong*
instantáneo(a) *instant*
mejor *better*
mixto(a) *mixed*
muchos(as) *many*
todos(as) *all of them*

Otras palabras y expresiones

a la hora del almuerzo *at lunch time*
al día siguiente *the next day*
aquí tiene... *here's . . .*
¿cómo? *how?*
¿Cómo son... ? *What are (they) like?*
cuando *when*
cuando termina de comer *when he/she finishes eating*

[1] **Tortilla** means *omelet* in Spain and some Latin American countries. An *omelet* in Mexico is **una omelete.**

menos de *less than*
que *than*
tan... como *as (so) . . . as*
tener hambre *to be hungry*
tener prisa *to be in a hurry*
tener que (+ ***inf.***) *to have to (do something)*
tomar algo *to have something to drink*
ya *already*
yo solo(a) *just me*

VOCABULARIO ADICIONAL

Audio

apagado *off*
charla *chat*
cuidan mucho las reglas de etiqueta *take a lot of attention to ettiquete*
la paga *is paid by*
le toca elegir *you must decide(chose)*
llegar tarde *to be late*
no son muy puntuales *aren't very punctual*
reunión de negocios *business meeting*
salvo *except*
tanto en ….. como *both at . . . as in (on, at)*
una de las partes invita a la otra *one party invites the other*
unos pocos *a few*
usted es quien *you are the one who*
vestimenta más formal *more formal dress*

Ensaladas (*Salads*)

la ensalada de aguacate *avocado salad*
la ensalada de berro *watercress salad*
la ensalada de lechuga *lettuce salad*
la ensalada de tomate *tomato salad*

Pescados (*Fish*)

el atún, el bonito *tuna*
el bacalao *cod*
el salmón *salmon*
la trucha *trout*

Carnes (*Meats*)

el bistec[1] *steak*
la carne de res *beef*
el cordero *lamb*
el puerco, el cerdo *pork*
la ternera *veal*

Vegetales (*Vegetables*)

el apio *celery*
el bróculi, el brécol *broccoli*
los guisantes, los chícharos *peas*
el maíz *corn*
la mazorca de maíz tierno, el elote (*Méx.*) *fresh ear of corn*
la papa, la patata *potato*
la zanahoria *carrot*

Mariscos (*Shellfish*)

las almejas *clams*
los calamares *squid*
los camarones, las gambas (*Esp.*) *shrimp*
el cangrejo *crab*
la langosta *lobster*

Aves (*Poultry, fowl*)

el pato *duck*
el pavo, el guajolote (*Méx.*), **el guanajo** (*Cuba*) *turkey*
el pollo *chicken*

Modos de preparar la comida (*Ways of preparing food*)

al gusto *any style,* to *order, to taste*
al horno (horneado)(a) *baked*

---

[1]Also called **biftec, carne asada** (Mexico), **bife** (Argentina, Uruguay, Paraguay).

Nombre ______________________ **Sección** ____________ **Fecha** ____________

al vapor *steamed*
asado(a) *grilled*
bien cocido(a), bien cocinado(a) *well done*
crudo(a), más bien crudo *rare*
estofado(a), guisado(a) *stewed*
frito(a) *fried*
hervido(a) *boiled*
relleno(a) *stuffed*
término medio *medium*

Search

iLrn

Notas Culturales

- Eating habits in Spanish-speaking countries are different from those in the United States. Not only does the food change from country to country and region to region, but meals are often served at different times.
  Breakfast (**el desayuno**) frequently consists of **café con leche** or **chocolate** and bread with butter or marmalade or a sweet roll. Lunch, the midday meal, (**el almuerzo / la comida**) is a more substantial meal than the typical U.S. lunch. For example, there might be a first course of soup followed by a green salad, a main course of meat or fish with vegetables and potatoes, rice, or beans, and finally dessert (often fruit or cheese). Coffee is served after the meal. Dinner or supper (**la cena**) is usually a lighter meal than lunch unless it is eaten at a restaurant, where it may consist of more than one course.
- Hotel restaurants often cater to the tastes of foreign travelers by serving more substantial, American-style breakfasts and a wide range of international foods, albeit at much higher prices than those in local restaurants. American fast-food restaurants are also a familiar presence in most Hispanic cities. The cuisine of the Spanish-speaking world may not be what one would expect based on the offerings of ethnic restaurants in the United States; Americans accustomed to the taco- and enchilada-based menus of Mexican restaurants in this country, for example, are likely to be pleasantly surprised by the sophisticated seafood dishes and other specialties of fine restaurants in Mexico.
- To avoid health problems when traveling, it is a good idea to stay away from food prepared by street vendors, to avoid raw fruits and vegetables unless you can be sure that they have been properly washed, and to stick to bottled beverages.

Actividades

Dígame... Answer the following questions, basing your answers on the dialogues.

1. ¿Cuándo va a la cafetería la Sra. López?

____

2. ¿Para qué va la Sra. López a la cafetería?

____

3. ¿Qué café es más fuerte, el café mexicano o el café americano?

____

4. ¿Qué comen los mexicanos en el desayuno?

____

5. ¿Cómo son los huevos rancheros?

____

Nombre ______________________ Sección ______________ Fecha ______________

6. ¿Qué es más popular en México, el pan o las tortillas?

____

7. ¿Cuál es la especialidad del restaurante?

____

8. ¿Qué pescados frescos tienen?

____

9. ¿Cuál es el mejor?

____

10. ¿Qué va a comer la Sra. López? ¿Qué va a tomar?

____

11. ¿Cuánto se tarda en ir del restaurante a la zona industrial?

____

12. ¿Tiene prisa la Sra. López? ¿A qué hora tiene que estar allí?

____

13. ¿Qué deja la Sra. López en la mesa?

____

Hablemos Interview a classmate, using the following questions. When you have finished, switch roles.

1. ¿A qué hora toma Ud. el desayuno?
2. ¿Desayuna Ud. todos los días en una cafetería?
3. ¿Qué come Ud. en el desayuno?
4. ¿Toma Ud. café expreso o café americano?
5. ¿Toma Ud. café con leche?
6. ¿Qué bebe Ud. en el almuerzo?
7. ¿Cuál es su pescado favorito?
8. En su opinión, ¿el postre es tan importante como la ensalada?
9. En un restaurante, ¿a quién llamamos cuando terminamos de comer?
10. ¿Siempre deja propina?
11. ¿Cuál es su restaurante favorito? ¿Dónde está?

Nombre ______________________ Sección ____________ Fecha ____________

Quiz

Vamos a practicar

A Rewrite the following sentences according to the new subjects.

Modelo Ella viene por aquí (Nosotros).
Nosotros **venimos** por aquí.

1. La señora tiene que estar en el hotel a las cinco.
   Ud. ______________________________.
2. El mozo viene con la comida.
   Nosotros ______________________________.
3. Tengo el café, pero no tengo leche.
   Tú ______________________________.
4. Ellos vienen a la hora del almuerzo.
   Tú y yo ______________________________.

B Use complete sentences to write down what the following people have to do.

Modelo Elvira / pagar la cuenta
Elvira **tiene que pagar** la cuenta.

1. yo / venir por la mañana
   ____
2. tú y yo / tomar menos café
   ____
3. Pedro y Jorge / terminar mañana
   ____
4. nosotras / dejar una buena propina
   ____

C Use the cues in parentheses to compare the following foods.

Modelo las tortillas / el pan (*more popular*)
Las tortillas **son más populares que** el pan.

1. el pargo / el lenguado (*fresher than*)
   ____

2. el café típico / el café expreso (*less strong than*)

______

3. los mariscos / el pescado (*as good as*)

______

4. el lenguado / la corbina (*better than*)

______

Sirva usted de intérprete

A With three classmates, play the roles of an English-speaking waiter/waitress, a Spanish-speaking couple, and the interpreter. Switch roles until each of you played the interpreter's role.

Mesero(a) —*How many?*

Intérprete —______

Sr. García —Dos.

Intérprete —______

Mesero(a) —*Smoking section or non-smoking section?*

Intérprete —______

Sra. García —Sección de fumar, por favor.

Intérprete —______

Mesero(a) —*Here's the menu. Do you want to have a drink before lunch?*

Intérprete —______

Sr. García —Agua mineral, por favor.

Intérprete —______

Sra. García —Una copa de vino blanco. ¿Cuál es la especialidad de hoy?

Intérprete —______

Mesero(a) —*Grilled red snapper. It comes with rice or vegetables.*

Intérprete —______

Sr. García —¿El pescado es fresco o congelado?

Intérprete —______

Mesero(a) —*The fish and the seafood are fresh.*

Intérprete —______

Sr. García —Bien, lenguado asado y ensalada.

Intérprete —______

Sra. García — Y yo voy a comer el pargo asado con vegetales y ensalada de tomate.

Intérprete —________________________________

Mesero(a) —*And to drink?*

Intérprete —________________________________

Sra. García —Otra copa de vino blanco, por favor.

Intérprete —________________________________

Más tarde (*later*):

Mesero(a) —*How's the fish?*

Intérprete —________________________________

Sra. García —Muy bueno, gracias.

Intérprete —________________________________

Sr. García —¿Aceptan tarjetas de crédito?

Intérprete —________________________________

Mesero(a) —*Yes, sir.*

Intérprete —________________________________

Sirva usted de traductor(a) An American restaurant chain has hired you to create a bilingual menu for its franchises in Latin America. Review the **Vocabulario adicional** in this lesson, and then add Spanish translations below the items listed on the menu.

menú

Soups and Salads

Tomato soup	Mixed salad
______________	______________
Turkey and rice soup	Lettuce, tomato, and avocado salad
______________	______________
Vegetable soup	Chicken and vegetable salad
______________	______________

Nombre ______________________ **Sección** __________ **Fecha** __________

Meat and Poultry

Steak (Rare, medium, or well done) ______	Boiled turkey ______
Roast beef ______	Fried chicken ______
Baked pork ______	Roasted lamb ______

Fish and Seafood

Grilled tuna ______	Steamed clams ______
Baked salmon ______	Shrimp, any style ______
Fried squid ______	Boiled lobster ______

En estas situaciones

With a partner, act out the following situations in Spanish.

1. You are going to have breakfast at a coffee shop in Mexico. When the waiter/waitress asks if you would like coffee, make sure he/she knows what kind you want. Ask him/her to explain a couple of items on the menu before placing your order (you're very hungry). You want to pay with a credit card, but you're not sure if the coffee shop accepts them.
2. You are eating lunch at a restaurant in Guatemala. Tell the waiter/waitress you want to see the menu. After he/she asks if you'd like to have a drink before lunch and you respond, ask if the fish is fresh, and which is the best fish to order. Find out what side dishes come with the meal and place your food order. The waiter/waitress should remember to ask what you would like to drink with your meal.

Casos

With you and a partner playing the roles, work through the following scenarios.

1. A waiter/waitress at a restaurant waits on a customer who is there for breakfast or lunch.
2. Two friends eating together at a restaurant read the menu and discuss what they are going to order for lunch. You can use the menus included in this lesson.

Nombre ______________________ Sección ____________ Fecha ____________

Un paso más

A You are having breakfast at a hotel restaurant. Read the menu and answer the following questions. Try to guess the meaning of unfamiliar words from context.

COMBINACIONES

Mexicano $45	**Americano $50**
Huevos rancheros o chilaquiles con pollo	Huevos al gusto o pan francés[1]
Tortillas	Café americano
Café	Tostadas
Crema	Jugo de naranja

DESAYUNOS A LA CARTA

Huevos con jamón o tocino	$35
Huevos con chorizo	$30
Huevos rancheros	$30
Chilaquiles con pollo	$40
Tortilla de huevos con queso	$40
Panqueques	$30
Pan francés	$25
Cereales fríos con leche	$25

BEBIDAS

Jugo de frutas	$20
Chocolate caliente	$20
Leche	$15
Café	$12
Expreso	$20

EJECUTIVO $60
Huevos "Benedict"
Huevos rancheros con bistec
Tortilla de huevos con mariscos y queso
Tortilla de huevos con camarones
Tortilla de huevos con langosta
(Incluye un platillo principal, jugo de frutas o una copa de champán)

[1] *French toast* (Méx.); in other countries, **torrejas**

1. ¿Qué bebidas hay en el menú?

____

2. ¿Que bebida típica del desayuno americano no está en las combinaciones?

____

3. ¿Con qué vienen los huevos rancheros de los desayunos ejecutivos?

---

4. ¿Qué platos típicos del desayuno americano hay en el menú?

---

5. ¿Qué alimentos típicos del desayuno mexicano están en el menú?

---

6. ¿Qué tipo de pan hay en el menú? ¿Cómo se llama este plato en inglés?

B Read the following advertisement for ***La Catrina*** restaurant. With a partner, take turns asking and answering the following questions.

(Left to Right): Yellowj © 2009 Shutterstock; © Michael Flippo / Fotolia; fdimeo © 2009 Shutterstock; vesilvio © 2009 Shutterstock

© Cengage Learning

1. ¿Dónde está situado el restaurante La Catrina?

---

2. ¿Qué tipo de comida sirven en este restaurante?

Nombre ______________________ Sección ____________ Fecha ____________

3. ¿Qué tipo de ingredientes usan?

___

4. ¿Qué tipo de música hay allí? ¿Cuándo?

___

5. Deseo hacer (*to make*) una reservación. ¿A qué número de teléfono tengo que llamar?

___

C You are traveling to a Spanish-speaking country. Plan what you are going to order from the menu on your first day there.

Desayuno:

Para tomar: ___

Para comer: ___

Almuerzo o comida:

Ensalada o sopa: ___

Plato principal: ___

Postre: ___

Para tomar: ___

Cena:

Ensalada o sopa: ___

Plato principal: ___

Postre: ___

Para tomar: ___

Lectura After reading this **lectura,** get together with a partner and take turns answering the following questions.

En los Estados Unidos muchas personas llaman "Spanish food" a la comida mexicana. Nada está más lejos de la realidad.° La comida mexicana es, fundamentalmente, autóctona,° aunque° en muchos de sus platillos° se aprecia° la influencia de la comida española y de la francesa. La comida española llegó° con los conquistadores; la francesa, con las tropas° francesas que ocuparon° y gobernaron el país por poco tiempo,° pero que dejaron° una gran influencia en las capas más

reality
native / although
dishes (Méx.) / **se...** *is noticeable*
arrived
troops / occupied
poco... *short time*
left

altas de la sociedad.° A pesar de su proximidad geográfica, los Estados Unidos han influido poco° en la comida mexicana. Hoy la comida mexicana es conocida en todo el mundo.

las... *high society*

han... *have had little influence*

1. ¿Es la comida mexicana similar a la comida española?
2. Fundamentalmente, ¿cómo es la comida mexicana?
3. ¿Cómo llegó a México la comida española? ¿Y la francesa?
4. En la comida mexicana, ¿se aprecia la influencia de la comida americana?

Y a usted...

1. ¿Qué comida le gusta más, la mexicana o la americana?
2. ¿Cuál es el mejor restaurante mexicano de la ciudad?

Un dicho

El dinero no tiene patria. *Money has no country.*

Trivia

Healthcare Tips When Traveling Abroad

- Take a first-aid kit with you. Keep it in your handbag, as suitcases are frequently lost.
- In some countries prescription drugs are sold without prescriptions. Avoid buying them this way because it can be dangerous.

Lección 5

Comprando para importar

Objectives

Structures

- Stem-changing verbs **(e:ie)**
- Some uses of the definite article
- The present progressive

Business Communication

- Importing goods
- Making an appointment to buy goods abroad
- Conducting a subsequent interview
- Inquiring about quality and other features of the goods
- Finding out about prices and paying terms and conditions

Por teléfono:

Recepcionista —Confecciones Gomax, S.A. de C.V.[1] (*ese, a de ce ve*). Buenos días.
Sra. López —Buenos días, señorita. Soy Sonia López, compradora de la firma Kids Fashion, una cadena de tiendas al detalle de los Estados Unidos.
Recepcionista —¿En qué podemos servirle, Sra. López?
Sra. López —Necesito hablar con el jefe de ventas al por mayor.
Recepcionista —Un momento, por favor. Voy a llamar a su oficina. (*Por el intercomunicador*) Julia, la Sra. López, compradora de una firma norteamericana, quiere hablar con el Sr. Navarro. (*Escucha un momento.*) Lo siento, Sra. López, pero el jefe de ventas está ocupado. Ahora está atendiendo a un cliente.
Sra. López —Quiero hacer una cita para hablar con él hoy mismo, si es posible. Prefiero ir por la tarde. ¿A qué hora cierran?
Recepcionista —A las cinco, pero el Sr. Navarro está disponible a las tres y media. ¿Tiene la dirección?
Sra. López —Sí, señorita. Muchas gracias y hasta luego.

A las cuatro menos veinticinco de la tarde, en la oficina del Sr. Navarro:

Sra. López —Estoy interesada en comprar confecciones para niños para mi firma en los Estados Unidos.

---

[1]**S.A. de C.V.** stands for **Sociedad Anónima de Capital Variable.** See **Notas culturales** in **Lección 12** for more information on business corporations.

Sr. Navarro —Entonces, primero debe ver la gran[1] variedad de artículos que fabricamos. Vamos al salón de exhibición y venta en el segundo piso.

En el salón de exhibición y venta:

Sr. Navarro —Bien, aquí tenemos prendas de vestir para chamacos de todas las edades, desde conjuntos de dos o tres piezas para bebés hasta ropa para niñas y niños mayores. Al fondo están los accesorios.

Sra. López —¿No tienen artículos de mejor calidad?

Sr. Navarro —Sí, señora. Si prefiere ver artículos más caros, vamos al otro salón.

Sra. López —(*En el otro salón*) Aquí sí tienen lo que estoy buscando.

Sr. Navarro —Sí, todos estos artículos están fabricados en telas de primera calidad, y están muy bien terminados.

Sra. López —¿Los diseños son originales?

Sr. Navarro —Sí, son creaciones exclusivas de la casa.

Sra. López —¿Los precios marcados son para ventas al detalle?

Sr. Navarro —Sí, señora. En las ventas al por mayor damos descuentos hasta del cincuenta por ciento, de acuerdo con la cantidad y con el costo de fabricación de cada artículo.

Sra. López —Bien, yo voy a seleccionar varios artículos y accesorios. Estoy anotando los modelos que prefiero. Después discutimos precios y condiciones.

Sr. Navarro —Comprendo, señora. Estamos a su disposición.

Sra. López —El primer pedido va a ser pequeño. Queremos ver qué aceptación tienen sus productos en el mercado de los Estados Unidos.

Los dos regresan a la oficina y comienzan a discutir las condiciones de venta.

¡Escuchemos!

While listening to the dialogue, circle **V (verdadero)** if the statement is true or **F (falso)** if it is false.

1.	Kids Fashion es una cadena de ventas al por mayor.	V	F
2.	La recepcionista y Julia hablan por el intercomunicador.	V	F
3.	El Sr. Navarro es el jefe de ventas al detalle.	V	F
4.	La recepcionista está ocupada atendiendo a una clienta.	V	F
5.	La Sra. López hace una cita para mañana por la mañana.	V	F
6.	Ella y el Sr. Navarro van al salón de exhibición y venta.	V	F
7.	En el salón de exhibición y venta hay ropa para niños mayores.	V	F
8.	Las prendas de vestir más caras están al fondo.	V	F
9.	Los precios marcados son para venta al detalle.	V	F
10.	La Sra. López está anotando los modelos que prefiere.	V	F

[1]**Grande** becomes **gran** before a masculine or feminine singular noun.

Nombre ______________________ Sección ____________ Fecha ____________

VOCABULARIO

Audio

Cognados

el accesorio
el artículo
el (la) cliente(a)
la calidad
la cantidad
la condición
la creación
exclusivo(a)
el intercomunicador
el modelo
el momento
el (la) recepcionista
la variedad

Nombres

la cadena *chain*
la cita *appointment*
las confecciones *ready-made clothes*
el conjunto *set*
el descuento *discount*
el diseño *design*
la edad *age*
la fabricación *manufacture*
el (la) jefe(a) *boss*
el (la) jefe(a) de ventas *sales manager*
el mercado *market*
el (la) niño(a), el (la) chamaco(a) (*Méx.*) *child*
el pedido, la orden *order*
la pieza *piece*
el precio *price*
la prenda de vestir *garment, clothing*
la ropa *clothing, clothes*
el salón de exhibición *showroom, exhibition hall*
la sociedad anónima (S.A.) *corporation*
la tela *fabric*
la tienda *store*
la venta *sale*

Verbos

anotar *to write, to note, to jot down*
atender (e:ie) *to assist, to attend, to wait on*
buscar *to look for*
cerrar (e:ie) *to close*
comenzar (e:ie), empezar (e:ie) *to start, to begin*
comprar *to buy*
comprender, entender (e:ie) *to understand*
discutir *to discuss*
escuchar *to listen*
fabricar, producir[1] *to manufacture*
hablar *to speak, to talk*
hacer[2] *to do, to make*
importar *to import*
preferir (e:ie) *to prefer*
querer (e:ie) *to want, to wish*
seleccionar *to select*
vender *to sell*

Adjetivos

cada *each*
caro(a) *expensive*
disponible *available*
este(a) *this*
estos(as) *these*
fabricado(a) *manufactured, made*
interesado(a) *interested*
marcado(a) *marked*
ocupado(a) *busy*
primer, primero(a) *first, top*
segundo(a) *second*
terminado *completed, done*
varios(as) *several*

---

[1]Irregular first person: **yo produzco**
[2]Irregular first person: **yo hago**

Nombre ______________________ Sección ____________ Fecha ____________

Otras palabras y expresiones

al detalle, al por menor, al menudeo *retail*
al fondo *in the back*
al por mayor, al mayoreo *wholesale*
aquí sí tienen *here you do have*
bien terminado(a) *well finished*
de acuerdo (con) *according to, in accordance (with)*
de primera calidad *top quality*
¿Está bien si...? *Is it all right if . . . ?*
Estamos a su disposición. *We're at your disposal.*
hoy mismo *this very day*
lo (la) que *that which, what*
por ciento *percent*
que *that, which*
si es posible *if possible*
tener aceptación *to be well received*
Vamos. *Let's go.*

Audio VOCABULARIO ADICIONAL

algo *something*
el almacén *warehouse, department store*
anfitrión(ona) *host(ess)*
el anticipo *advance payment*
barato(a) *inexpensive, cheap*
el cargo *title, employment*
conejo *rabbit*
la compra *purchase*
la compraventa *purchase and sale agreement*
conceder un crédito *to extend credit*
corbata *necktie*
el cuarto *quarter*
la exportación *export*
en punto *sharp*
halagar to *flatter*
la hora *hour, time*
la importación *import*
importado(a) *imported*
el (la) importador(a) *importer*
mal(o)(a) *bad*
la marca de fábrica *manufacturer's trademark*
la materia prima *raw material*
menudo *traditional Mexican dish*
morcilla *blood sausage*
no sean de su agrado are *not to your liking*
oscuro(a) *dark*
pagar a plazos *to pay in installments*
pagar al contado *to pay in cash*
panza de res *beef tripe*
el precio de compra *purchase price*
el precio de venta *selling price*
puntual *on time*
reclamar *to claim*
la reunión, la junta *meeting*
riñón *kidney*
todo tipo *all types*
traje *suit*
la utilidad bruta *gross profit*
la utilidad neta *net profit*

Nombre ______________________ Sección ____________ Fecha ____________

Search

iLrn

Notas Culturales

- Aguascalientes is called "Mexico's little giant" because it is one of the smallest Mexican states, but it has a well-developed infrastructure, and is one of the five states with the highest standard of living in Mexico. Prior to NAFTA's implementation, 33 **maquiladoras**[1] were operating in Aguascalientes. Since then, more than 100 **maquiladoras** have set up operations there, mainly in the apparel sector.
- Hierarchies in Latin American businesses tend to be well defined. Subordinates generally address senior management by title and surname, and use the formal **Ud.** even if a superior addresses them as **tú.** Some bosses use **Ud.** with their employees as a means of maintaining a respectful distance. Male subordinates are usually referred to by their last name, and women by **señora** or **señorita** and their first name. Colleagues at the same level may use **tú** or **Ud.** depending on age difference and the degree of friendship or familiarity between them. Personal space—the distance at which people feel comfortable talking or otherwise interacting with one another—is generally smaller in the Spanish-speaking world than in the United States, especially when people are engaged in lively conversation. This increased physical proximity is not necessarily a sign of familiarity, as it might be in this country.
- Business meetings generally begin and end with handshakes all around, for both men and women. Encounters among people who are friends as well as business associates may be marked by more familiar forms of greeting and farewell.

Actividades

Dígame... Answer the following questions, basing your answers on the dialogue.

1. ¿Cuál es el cargo (*title*) de la Sra. López?

   ____

2. ¿Con quién desea hablar la Sra. López?

   ____

3. ¿Quién es el jefe de ventas?

   ____

4. El Sr. Navarro no está disponible. ¿Qué está haciendo ahora?

   ____

5. ¿Cuándo prefiere la Sra. López tener la cita?

   ____

6. ¿A qué hora está disponible el Sr. Navarro?

   ____

7. ¿Qué quiere comprar la Sra. López?

   ____

[1]**Maquiladoras** are factories that receive special customs privileges because they assemble parts or manufacture products for export only. Hundreds of thousands of Mexicans work in **maquiladoras.**

8. ¿Para qué va la Sra. López al salón de exhibición y venta?

______

9. ¿Los precios marcados son para ventas al por mayor?

______

10. ¿Qué descuentos dan en los precios marcados?

______

11. ¿La Sra. López va a hacer un pedido grande?

______

Hablemos

Interview a classmate, using the following questions. When you have finished, switch roles.

1. ¿Tiene Ud. niños en su familia? ¿Compra prendas de vestir para ellos?
2. En México las confecciones son más baratas que en los Estados Unidos. ¿Por qué?
3. ¿Está Ud. interesado(a) en comprar artículos de diseños originales?
4. ¿Son caras las prendas de vestir de diseños originales?
5. ¿Compra Ud. artículos de calidad cuando viaja?
6. Cuando Ud. compra algo ¿discute precios y condiciones?
7. ¿Desea Ud. ser jefe(a) de ventas de una firma?
8. ¿Tiene el (la) profesor(a) un intercomunicador en su oficina?
9. ¿Quiere Ud. hacer una cita para hablar con el (la) profesor(a)? (¿Para cuándo?)

Quiz

Vamos a practicar

Write sentences to say what the following people are doing right now using the present progressive construction and the elements given. Supply any necessary elements.

Modelo Ella / anotar / el pedido
Ella **está anotando** el pedido.

1. yo / comprar / artículos de primera calidad / mi firma

______

2. la Srta. Julia / hablar / intercomunicador

______

3. esa fábrica / producir / gran variedad de artículos

______

Nombre ______________________ Sección ____________ Fecha ____________

4. nosotros / dar / descuentos / hasta / cincuenta por ciento

____

5. ¿qué / hacer / tú?

____

6. ellos / no / discutir / el precio

____

Sirva usted de intérprete

With two classmates, play the roles of an import company executive from the United States, the sales manager of a Latin American firm, and the interpreter who helps them communicate. Switch roles until each of you has played the interpreter's role.

Ejecutivo(a) —*Good morning, I'm ____________, director of South of the Border Imports of San Antonio, Texas.*

Intérprete —____

Jefe(a) de ventas —Mucho gusto, ____________. Soy ____________, jefe(a) de ventas de esta firma. ¿En qué podemos servirle?

Intérprete —____

Ejecutivo(a) —*We're interested in buying some of your high quality items.*

Intérprete —____

Jefe(a) de ventas —Entonces creo que debemos ir al salón de exhibición y venta. Ud. debe ver la gran variedad de artículos que tenemos.

Intérprete —____

Ejecutivo(a) —*Where are the high quality items for men?*

Intérprete —____

Jefe(a) de ventas —Están en el mostrador de la izquierda.

Intérprete —____

Ejecutivo(a) —*Are the marked prices for retail sales?*

Intérprete —____

Jefe(a) de ventas —Sí, señor(a). Damos descuentos de hasta un 40 por ciento en las ventas al mayoreo.

Intérprete —____

Ejecutivo(a) —*I prefer to select some items first, and then discuss prices and conditions.*

Intérprete —____

Jefe(a) de ventas —Cómo no. Estamos a sus órdenes.

Intérprete —____

Nombre ______________________ **Sección** ____________ **Fecha** ____________

Sirva usted de traductor

Your employer is dealing with a Spanish-speaking manufacturer south of the border. She received a long letter from her prospective supplier; you highlighted the following sentences as those including vital information. After reviewing the **Vocabulario adicional** in this lesson, translate them for her.

1. Nuestra fábrica está situada en Tecate, Baja California.

   ____

2. Nuestra firma es una sociedad anónima.

   ____

3. La marca de fábrica de nuestros productos es "Lorena".

   ____

4. Necesitamos un anticipo para la compra de la materia prima.

   ____

5. Su utilidad bruta debe ser de un 45 por ciento o más.

   ____

6. El precio de venta de cada artículo es un 40 por ciento más del precio de compra.

   ____

En estas situaciones

With a partner, act out the following situations in Spanish.

1. You are a receptionist answering a telephone call. Identify the firm for which you work, and ask the caller how you may help him/her. He/She wants to see the sales manager; say that the sales manager is not available, and that he/she is talking with another client.
2. You are meeting with a sales manager at a factory. Indicate that you want to buy kids' garments, and that you wish to visit the showroom. Tell him/her that you want original designs. In the showroom, say that some items are inexpensive, but that you prefer to pay more and buy better-quality items. Respond when he/she tells you about the quality and price of the items they have in another hall. Ask about the difference between retail and wholesale prices.

Casos

With you and a partner playing the roles, work through the following scenarios.

1. An executive for an American firm makes an appointment for a business meeting with a company's receptionist.
2. A sales manager meets with a client in his/her office and takes him/her to the factory showroom.

Nombre ______________________ Sección ____________ Fecha ____________

Un paso más

Review the **Vocabulario adicional** in this lesson and act out the following dialogues in Spanish with a partner.

1. "Is the client going to pay in cash?"
   "No, we are going to extend credit for the purchase and they're going to pay in installments."
   "For the entire purchase price?"
   "No, for ninety percent. It's in the purchase and sale agreement."
2. "What is the factory's gross profit this year?"
   "Five hundred thousand dollars, but the net profit is much less."
   "Why?"
   "Because of taxes."

Lectura

After reading this **lectura,** get together with a partner and take turns answering the following questions.

El comercio de importación y exportación entre° México y los Estados Unidos es mucho más fácil° desde la firma° del Tratado de Libre Comercio de América del Norte (TLCAN), conocido° aquí como NAFTA, su sigla° en inglés. El tratado° es muy beneficioso para los tres países: Estados Unidos y Canadá aprovechan° la mano de obra barata° de México para producir partes o ensamblar° componentes que requieren° mano de obra intensiva, y así° sus productos terminados pueden° competir en precio con artículos similares importados de otros países. México gana° trabajo y adiestramiento° para su gente,° y las divisas° necesarias para promover su propio desarrollo.°

between
más... *easier*
desde... *since the signing*
known
abbreviation in initials / agreement
take advantage
mano... *cheap labor*
assemble / require
thus, this way / can
profits
training / people / hard currency
promover... *promote its own development*

1. ¿Desde (Since) cuándo es más fácil el comercio entre los Estados Unidos y México?
2. ¿Cuáles son los tres países del TLCAN?
3. ¿Por qué es beneficioso el Tratado de Libre Comercio para los Estados Unidos y Canadá?
4. ¿Qué gana México con el TLCAN?

Y usted...

1. Algunos obreros (*Some workers*) piensan que el TLCAN no es beneficioso para ellos. ¿Sabe por qué (*Do you know why*)?
2. ¿Piensa que los tratados de libre comercio son beneficiosos o que no son beneficiosos?

Nombre ______________________ **Sección** __________ **Fecha** __________

Un dicho

Lo barato sale caro. *You get what you pay for.*

Trivia

Quality Control

In the area of manufacturing and service enterprises, quality control is used to ensure that products and services maintain a consistent standard of quality that meets or exceeds customer requirements. This is neither easy nor inexpensive.

In more developed countries, when consumers buy products, they take for granted that their purchases will have the same quality standards found in similar items they have purchased before. This is not always true of products sold in the developing world, and this is the first major obstacle that industries in developing countries need to overcome in order to succeed in exporting to countries with more rigid quality standards.

A significant part of the impressive growth of Latin-American exports during the last decade is due to the improvement in quality control that has been attained with the assistance of specialized national and international, public and private organizations like the Inter-American Development Bank (**Banco Interamericano de Desarrollo, MexControl,** and others.)

SUPLEMENTO 1 LLENANDO PLANILLAS[1]

- Declaración de aduanas
- Solicitud de tarjeta de crédito
- Solicitud de empleo
- Registro de clientes de una tienda para compras por Internet[2]
- Solicitud de envío de dinero al extranjero

A Fill out the customs declaration on the next page, using the following information. Ud. y su esposo(a) viajan a México por avión. Llevan 4 maletas, $12,000 dólares en efectivo y 50 cajetillas (*packs*) de cigarrillos, pero no llevan animales vivos ni productos alimenticios frescos. (México permite entrar 20 cajetillas de cigarrillos por persona sin pagar impuestos.)

---

[1]**la planilla, el formulario** *blank form.* Note: **la forma,** frequently used by Spanish speakers in the U.S. with this meaning, has not been accepted by the ***Real Academia Española.***

[2]At last, the word **Internet** was accepted by the ***Real Academia Española.*** It will appear in the 23rd edition of its dictionary. The word will be defined as **ambigua** (either *m.* or *f.*). It will appear with small-cap initial, but capital initial is also admitted.

Nombre ______________________ Sección ____________ Fecha ____________

BIENVENIDO A MÉXICO

DECLARACIÓN DE ADUANAS

Cada pasajero o jefe de familia[1] debe llenar esta sección.

Nombre: ______________________ / ______________________
Apellido paterno[2] *Materno*[3]

____
Nombre(s)

Pasaporte: ______________ / ______________
Número *País que lo expide*[4]

Arribo vía: marítima ______________ /aérea ______________
Nombre de la embarcación *Línea/#vuelo*

Número de familiares[5] que viajan con usted: ______________

Número de maletas, bultos o cajas: ______________

País de residencia: ______________

¿Trae[6] consigo más de 10,000 dls. estadounidenses o su equivalente en otras monedas, en efectivo o cheque?* SI ☐ NO ☐

En caso afirmativo, indique cuánto más: ______________ dls. estadounidenses.

Declare si transporta animales vivos,[7] productos alimenticios frescos[8] de origen vegetal o animal: SI ☐ NO ☐

¿Transporta mercancías por las que deba pagar impuestos? *(Ver reverso)* SI ☐ NO ☐

Para el pago de impuestos, favor de pasar al módulo de orientación aduanera en la terminal de arribo, donde estará a su disposición el formato para el pago de contribuciones al comercio exterior y el material explicativo para su llenado.

Sanción:
Cuando usted no declare mercancías por las que deba pagar impuestos, éstas pasarán a propiedad del Fisco Federal, se impondrá una multa de hasta cuatro veces el valor comercial de dichas mercancías y podrá ser sujeto a sanciones penales.

*Traer dinero no es delito, no declararlo sí lo es.

Declaro bajo protesta de decir verdad que los datos asentados en la presente declaración son ciertos.

______________________ ____/____/____
Firma ***día /mes / año***

[1]*head of household* [2]*father's last name* [3]*mother's last name* [4]*issuer*
[5]*relatives* [6]*Bring* [7]*live animals* [8]*fresh food*

Nombre ______________________ **Sección** ____________ **Fecha** ____________

B Fill out the following application to apply for a department store credit card.

1. INFORMACIÓN PERSONAL (Escriba en letra de molde[1])

NOMBRE	INICIAL	APELLIDO	NÚMERO DEL SEGURO SOCIAL

LICENCIA DE CONDUCIR, NÚMERO DE PASAPORTE O DE IDENTIFICACIÓN DEL ESTADO	EDAD	NÚMERO DE DEPENDIENTES

DIRECCIÓN	APARTAMENTO	CIUDAD	ESTADO	CODIGO POSTAL

TIPO DE RESIDENCIA ☐ PROPIETARIO ☐ INQUILINO ☐ OTRO — TELÉFONO DE LA CASA ( )

DIRECCIÓN ANTERIOR[2] (SI SE MUDO EN MENOS DE UN AÑO)	CIUDAD	ESTADO	CODIGO POSTAL

COMPAÑIA DONDE TRABAJA	DIRECCIÓN	CIUDAD	POSICIÓN/TÍTULO	¿DESDE CUANDO? AÑOS / MESES

SUS INGRESOS EN BRUTO[3] (FUENTES)
No tiene que divulgar una pensión de divorcio o separación, mantenimiento de hijos u otros gastos de mantenimiento, si no desea ser tomado en cuenta para el reembolso de esta obligación. $______ /mensual[4]
TELÉFONO DEL TRABAJO O NEGOCIO ( )

NOMBRE DE SU PARIENTE MÁS CERCANO[5] (QUE NO VIVA CON UD.)	RELACIÓN	TELÉFONO ( )

DIRECCIÓN	CIUDAD	ESTADO	CODIGO POSTAL

REFERENCIAS DE CREDITO: (MARQUE TODO LO QUE SE RELACIONE CON UD.)
☐ CUENTA DE CHEQUES[6] ☐ VISA ☐ MASTERCARD ☐ TIENDAS DE ROPA (MENCIÓNELAS) ____________ ____________
☐ CUENTA DE AHORRO[7] ☐ DISCOVER ☐ AMERICAN EXPRESS ☐ OTRO (MENCIÓNELO) ____________ ____________

2. INFORMACIÓN SOBRE EL SOLICITANTE DE CUENTA CONJUNTA[8] (Firma es necesaria)

NOMBRE	INICIAL	APELLIDO	NÚMERO DEL SEGURO SOCIAL

LICENCIA DE CONDUCIR, NÚMERO DE PASAPORTE O DE IDENTIFICACIÓN DEL ESTADO	EDAD	PARENTESCO[9] CON EL SOLICITANTE: ☐ CONYUGE ☐ OTRO: INDIQUE ______

COMPAÑIA DONDE TRABAJA	DIRECCIÓN	CIUDAD

POSICIÓN/TITULO	¿DESDE CUANDO? (AÑOS)	TELÉFONO DE TRABAJO ( )

NOTIFICACIÓN: CUALQUIER PERSONA QUE FIRME ESTE CONTRATO DE CRÉDITO PARA EL CONSUMIDOR, ESTARA SUJETA A TODOS LOS RECLAMOS Y DEFENSAS EN JUICIO QUE EL DEUDOR PUEDA EFECTUAR EN CONTRA DEL VENDEDOR DE BIENES, O SERVICIOS OBTENIDOS EN VIRTUD DEL MISMO, O CON EL INGRESO OBTENIDO POR EL CONTRATO. EL REEMBOLSO DEL DEUDOR DE ESTE ACUERDO NO DEBERA EXCEDER LAS CANTIDADES PAGADAS POR EL DEUDOR EN VIRTUD DE ESTE ACUERDO.
Yo/Nosotros solicito/solicitamos una Cuenta de Crédito de Mervyn's y certifico/certificamos que, según mi/nuestro entender, la informacíon que aparece arriba es correcta.

3. POR FAVOR FIRME AQUÍ:

Firma Del Solicitante FECHA **Firma del Cosolicitante** FECHA

X ______________________ **X** ______________________

STORE USE ONLY

TEAM MEMBER # ____ ____ ____ ____ STORE 3-LETTER CODE AND NUMBER: RDL075

Written accent marks are frequently omitted in printed material when using capital letters.

[1] *print* [2] *previous address* [3] *gross income* [4] *monthly* [5] **pariente...** *closest relative* [6] *checking account* [7] *savings account* [8] **solicitante...** *co-applicant for joint account* [9] *(family) relationship*

Nombre ______________________ Sección ______________ Fecha ______________

C In order to improve your Spanish you want to spend a year in a Spanish-speaking country. Fill out the following form to apply for a job.

SOLICITUD DE EMPLEO

NOVOTEC, S.A.

CONFIDENCIAL

LLÉNESE A MANO USE LETRA DE MOLDE[1]

DATOS PERSONALES

Apellido Paterno	Apellido Materno	Nombre(s)
Lugar de Nacimiento[2]	Fecha de Nacimiento	Edad[3]
Domicilio		

Fecha	
Estado Civil[4]	
Nacionalidad	
Teléfono	Sexo ◯ Femenino ◯ Masculino

REFERENCIAS PERSONALES (No incluya parientes.[5])

NOMBRE COMPLETO	OCUPACIÓN	DIRECCIÓN	TELÉFONO

EXPERIENCIA DE TRABAJO (Empiece por el actual[6] o último empleo.)

DURACIÓN		NOMBRE DE LA EMPRESA	DIRECCIÓN Y TEL.	SALARIO		PUESTO DESEMPEÑADO[7]	MOTIVO(S) DE SU SEPARACIÓN
DESDE	HASTA			INICIAL	FINAL		

ESCOLARIDAD

NOMBRE DE LA EMPRESA	DOMICILIO	No. DE AÑOS QUE ASISTIO	FECHAS		TERMINO UD.	OBTUVO CERTIFICADO DIPLOMA O TÍTULO
			DE	A		
Primaria						
Secundaria						
Universidad						
Estudios de Post-Graduado						
Otros						

Idiomas que domina

Máquinas de oficina que pueda manejar[8]

DATOS GENERALES

Sírvase indicar si tiene alguna experiencia en: ◯ Administración ◯ Contabilidad ◯ Economía ◯ Inv. de Mercado ◯ Producción ◯ Publicidad ◯ Rel. Industriales ◯ Rel. Públicas ◯ Ventas ◯ Compras ◯ Tiendas

¿Está dispuesto a[9] trabajar cualquier turno?[10]
◯ Sí No ◯ (Razones)

¿Algún pariente suyo trabaja con nosotros?
◯ Sí No ◯ (Quién)

¿Qué tipo de trabajo desea Ud. desempeñar?[11]

¿Qué sueldo mensual[12] desea?

¿En qué fecha podría empezar a trabajar?

¿Está dispuesto a cambiar su lugar de residencia?
◯ Sí No ◯ (Razones)

¿Está Ud. dispuesto a viajar?
◯ Sí No ◯ (Razones)

¿Conoce Ud. alguna persona en nuestra compañía?
◯ Sí No ◯ (Quién)

¿Podemos solicitar informes de Ud.?
◯ Sí No ◯ (Razones)

Las declaraciones anteriores hechas por mi son absolutamente verdaderas.[13]

____
Firma del solicitante

[1] **letra de molde:** *printing* [2] **nacimiento:** *birth* [3] **edad:** *age* [4] **estado civil:** *marital status* [5] **parientes:** *relatives* [6] **actual:** *current* [7] **puesto desempeñado:** *position held* [8] **manejar:** *to operate* [9] **Está dispuesto(a) a...** *Would you be willing to . . .* [10] **cualquier turno:** *any shift* [11] **desempeñar:** *to hold, to carry out* [12] **sueldo mensual:** *monthly salary* [13] **verdaderas:** *true*

Nombre ______________________ **Sección** __________ **Fecha** __________

D Fill out the following form with your own data, but do not use your real credit card number.

Registro de clientes de El Corte Inglés

Para que sus visitas o sus compras le resulten más cómodas, le ofrecemos la posibilidad de registrar sus datos personales y elegir una contraseña (*mark*) que le permitirá acceder a todas aquellas zonas que requieran una identificación previa. Esto evitará que, en lo sucesivo, tenga que volver a cumplimentarlos. Todos sus datos quedarán registrados en un **servidor seguro** y serán tratados con **absoluta confidencialidad.**

Para que el registro funcione adecuadamente, es obligatorio rellenar por lo menos todas las casillas indicadas con (*). La casilla **Provincia** sólo es obligatoria para residentes en España y la casilla **DNI/Pasaporte** es obligatoria para los residentes fuera de España.

(*) Nombre: ______________________

(*) Primer Apellido: ______________ (*) Segundo Apellido: ______________

Fecha de nacimiento: Día ________ Mes ____________ Año ________

DNI / Pasaporte: ______________ (*) Sexo: Hombre Mujer

(*) E-mail: ______________________

¿Tiene Tarjeta El Corte Inglés?: Sí No (*) Número de tarjeta: ______________

(*) Domicilio: ______________________

(*) Población: ______________ (*) Provincia (Estado, Departamento...): ______________

(*) Código Postal: ______________ (*) País: ______________

(*) Teléfono 1: ______________ Teléfono 2: ______________

Ahora deberá usted rellenar las dos casillas siguientes y memorizar los datos que introduzca en ellas, pues son las claves que le facilitarán, en adelante, el acceso a nuestras páginas.

En la casilla **Usuario** deberá usted indicar el nombre o número con el que desee ser identificado (mínimo 8 caracteres y máximo 16 caracteres). En la casilla **Contraseña** deberá usted indicar la clave (nombre o número) que le permitirá el acceso a nuestras páginas (entre 4 y 8 caracteres).

(*) Usuario: ______________________

(*) Contraseña: ______________ (*) Confirmar contraseña: ______________

A continuación puede usted indicar, si lo desea, una o varias palabras que en un futuro le puedan ayudar, **únicamente a usted,** a recordar la contraseña que ha introducido, en caso de que la olvide (por ejemplo, "la matrícula de mi coche", "El nombre de mi perro", ...)

Este dato **nunca será publicado** y nuestro servicio de atención al cliente se lo comunicará personalmente cuando usted necesite recordar la contraseña que ha olvidado.

Recordatorio: ______________________

Si no desea recibir información on-line del Grupo de Empresas El Corte Inglés, por favor, indíquenoslo. ❑

El envío de datos en el Grupo de Empresas El Corte Inglés se realiza a través de una conexión segura. De este modo, la información que Ud. nos haga llegar o la que nosotros le enviemos, viajará por Internet encriptada y protegida.

Aceptar ❑

Si usted reside fuera de España, marque la casilla siguiente: ❑

Nombre ______________________ **Sección** __________ **Fecha** __________

E You want to send money to Mexico. Fill out this form.

Para enviar dinero a México

WESTERN UNION®

www.westernunion.com

POR FAVOR ESCRIBA
Número de Tarjeta Western Union

☐ *DINERO EN MINUTOS*® ☐ *DINERO DIA SIGUIENTE* ☐ *DINERO A DOMICILIO* (☐ Efectivo ☐ Cheque) ☐ *GIRO PAISANO Servicio Ocurre* ☐ *GIRO TELEGRÁFICO Servicio Ocurre* ☐ *GIRO TELEGRÁFICO Con Aviso A Domicilio*

Cantidad en dolares* $ ______ Cantidad de Dinero con letra* ______

Destinatario

Nombre ______ Apellido paterno ______ Apellido materno ______

Ciudad ______ Estado ______ No. de Teléfono ______

Destinatario alterno (Dinero a Domicilio sólamente)

Nombre ______ Apellido paterno ______ Apellido materno ______

Información requerida sólamente para envios de Dinero a Domicilio o Giro Telegráfico con notificación.

Dirección ______ Calle y número

Colonia ______ **Código postal** ______

Remitente

Nombre ______ Apellido paterno ______ Apellido materno ______

Dirección ______ Calle y número

Ciudad ______ Estado ______ Código postal ______ No. de Teléfono ______

ALGUNOS TÉRMINOS Y CONDICIONES QUE RIGEN EL SERVICIO DE TRANSFERENCIA DE DINERO QUE USTED HA ELEGIDO, ESTÁN ESPECIFICADOS EN EL REVERSO DE ESTE FORMULARIO. AL FIRMARLO, USTED ESTÁ DE ACUERDO CON ESOS TÉRMINOS Y CONDICIONES.

***ADEMÁS DE LOS CARGOS POR EL SERVICIO DE TRANSFERENCIA, WESTERN UNION GANA DINERO CUANDO CAMBIA SUS DÓLARES AMERICANOS POR PESOS MEXICANOS. POR FAVOR LEA EL REVERSO DE ESTE FORMULARIO PARA MÁS INFORMACÍON SOBRE EL CAMBIO DE MONEDA.**

Al enviar $1,000 ó más, usted deberá presentar una identificación e información adicional. No exceder $5,000.

Firma del remitente ______

No escriba en el área obscura

Número de operador

Fecha / / **Hora de envío**

Tipo de identificacion **Número**

Fecha de nacimiento / / **Ocupación**

Número de Seguro Social/Otro No.

Número de control de transferencia

Cantidad $

Cargo $

Cargo por el mensaje $

Impuesto $

Cantidad total cobrada $

Tipo de cambio* **Cantidad a pagar***

 DFMSMMGGB (02/03G)

Nombre ______________________ Sección ____________ Fecha ____________

LECCIONES 1-5

REPASO

Práctica de vocabulario

A Circle the word or phrase that does not belong in each group.

1. aeropuerto aduana venta
2. periódico papel higiénico revista
3. tarde almohada frazada
4. pasar llenar completar
5. manta mostrador cobija
6. maleta equipaje cigarrillo
7. comprobante bulto escalera
8. inmigración pasaje billete
9. valija chamaca maleta
10. ordenador extranjero computadora portátil
11. hotel botones monitor
12. datos ascensor elevador
13. tela habitación llave
14. café mesa leche
15. pargo lenguado huésped
16. venir beber tomar
17. accesorio cita prenda de vestir
18. disponible descafeinado instantáneo
19. último ocupado primero
20. hacer comprender entender
21. mi su después
22. importar exportar llamar
23. comenzar caminar empezar
24. cadena comprador cliente
25. unos al del

B Circle the word or phrase that best completes each sentence.

1. Deseo reservar un (asiento / altavoz / negocio) para el vuelo de mañana.
2. ¿Cuándo desea (necesitar / buscar / regresar)?
3. Su asiento está en la (almohada / fila / mercancía) tres.
4. ¿A qué hora (llegamos / evitamos / anunciamos) a Guadalajara?
5. El niño mayor llega en el (negocio / pasaporte / vuelo) de la tarde.
6. Debe (abrir / subir / firmar) los cheques aquí.
7. La tasa de cambios no es (estable / grande / cara).
8. Ellas desean reservar (un impuesto / un maletín / una habitación) en el cuarto piso por cuatro días.
9. ¡Bienvenida, señora! Su habitación ya está (mucha / lista / asada).
10. Para (asegurar / funcionar / lamentar) su reservación, necesito los datos de su tarjeta de crédito.
11. ¿Cuál es la (casa / corbina / fecha) de vencimiento de su tarjeta de crédito?
12. En esta habitación hay mucho (país / ruido / postre) porque da a la calle.
13. El aire acondicionado del hotel no (deja / funciona / demora).

Nombre ______________________ Sección ____________ Fecha ____________

14. Aquí comemos pan, pero las tortillas son más (populares / fuertes / mixtas) que el pan.

15. Desean comer huachinango asado con vegetales y (copas / cuentas / arroz).

16. Prefiero hablar con el jefe de (modelos / ventas / accesorios).

17. El Sr. Vargas está (fresco / situado / interesado) en comprar bagre congelado.

18. Los precios marcados son para ventas al (artículo / diseño / menudeo), ¿verdad?

19. Queremos hacer una (cantidad / firma / cita) con el gerente de la firma.

20. Yo voy a seleccionar varios artículos, y después (discutimos / preferimos / fabricamos) precios y condiciones.

21. Ahora voy a (venir / anotar / ir a) los modelos que prefiero.

22. (Soy / Vamos / Es Ud.) al salón de exhibición y ventas.

C Match the questions in column **A** with the answers in column **B**.

A		B
1. ¿Es Ud. ciudadana mexicana?	______	**a.** No, una revista.
2. ¿Tiene algo que declarar?	______	**b.** Huevos hervidos y café.
3. ¿Desea un pasaje de ida?	______	**c.** Una copa de vino.
4. ¿Quiere un asiento de pasillo?	______	**d.** No, pequeño.
5. ¿Desea un periódico?	______	**e.** Sí, y tarjetas de crédito.
6. ¿Cuándo regresa Ud.?	______	**f.** A 11,50 por dólar.
7. ¿Quiere una almohada?	______	**g.** No, de dos piezas.
8. ¿Cuántas maletas tiene Ud.?	______	**h.** No, soy extranjera.
9. ¿A cómo está el cambio?	______	**i.** No, al por mayor.
10. ¿Aceptan aquí cheques de viajero?	______	**j.** Sí, y una manta.
11. ¿Qué desea para el desayuno?	______	**k.** Sí, son creaciones exclusivas.
12. ¿Desea un conjunto de tres piezas?	______	**l.** No, de ida y vuelta.
13. ¿Qué van a tomar ellos?	______	**m.** No, es la gerente.
14. ¿Cuál es la especialidad de la casa?	______	**n.** Sí, una cámara de video.
15. ¿Va a hablar con el gerente?	______	**o.** El cincuenta por ciento.
16. ¿Todos los diseños son originales?	______	**p.** Mañana a las tres.
17. ¿Qué descuento dan Uds.?	______	**q.** Dos, y un bolso.
18. ¿Ella es la camarera?	______	**r.** No, con el jefe de ventas.
19. ¿El pedido va a ser grande?	______	**s.** No, de ventanilla.
20. ¿Las ventas son al menudeo?	______	**t.** Los mariscos y el pescado.

Nombre ______________________ **Sección** ____________ **Fecha** ____________

Situaciones del mundo de las empresas

Review the **Notas culturales** and **Lecturas** of the past five lessons and then read the following scenarios. Find out what went wrong, and propose possible solutions in Spanish. Then discuss the different cultural interpretations represented in the scenarios.

1. Upon arriving at my office, the representative of an exports company from Uruguay has introduced himself to me as Fernando Concha. To be friendly, I replied: "Mucho gusto en conocerte, Fernando."

2. Since I knew the client was a divorcée, I greeted her by saying: "Buenos días, señorita."

3. I am the new sales manager of the Nicaraguan branch of a textile company. I tell one of the office secretaries: "Lorena, ¿puedes traerme la nueva lista de precios?"

4. This morning, I addressed my supervisor, Mr. Cardenas, as follows: "Cárdenas, necesito hablar con Ud."

5. Because some Spanish salespeople visit their prospective clients without previously arranging for an interview, Ms. Robinson did the same thing.

Nombre ______________________ **Sección** ____________ **Fecha** ____________

Advanced Translation

The following translations include some words not presented yet in your book. You may need to use a dictionary.[1]

Translate into English

1. Llego el martes, a las cuatro y veintitrés.

   ____

2. También tenemos varios vegetales congelados.

   ____

3. Estoy interesada en los vestidos con diseños originales.

   ____

4. El jefe de ventas no está aquí hoy. Está enfermo.

   ____

5. Estamos situados en el centro de la ciudad, frente al parque Juárez.

   ____

6. ¿Dónde podemos comprar ingredientes para una comida típica?

   ____

Translate into Spanish

1. My line of business is marketing.

   ____

2. Mr. Ramos arrives in Mexico City on a stopover to Acapulco.

   ____

3. You cannot take this bottle of wine with you.

   ____

4. I want to visit your warehouse to see all the styles you have.

   ____

5. I am going to talk to the manager to try to get an additional discount.

   ____

6. Yes, you can speak with him. I can't authorize discounts.

   ____

[1]Learning to use the dictionary is of paramount importance in the training of translators.

Lección 6

Vendiendo para exportar

Objectives

Structures

- Stem-changing verbs **(o:ue)**
- Affirmative and negative expressions
- Pronouns as object of a preposition
- Direct object pronouns

Business Communication

- Visiting with a prospective client in a Latin American country
- Negotiating to sell merchandise to be exported from the United States

El Sr. Leonard, viajante de la firma Flagler Auto Parts, de Miami, visita al Sr. Rovira, administrador de Nuevos Servicentros, S.A., una cadena de talleres de reparación de automóviles de Antigua, Guatemala.

Sr. Leonard —Estamos tratando de penetrar el mercado de Guatemala, y tenemos buenas ofertas para Ud.

Sr. Rovira —Uds. venden silenciadores y tubos de escape, ¿verdad?

Sr. Leonard —Sí, señor. Además vendemos repuestos para la reparación de los frenos y de los sistemas de suspensión de los carros.

Sr. Rovira —En realidad, estamos satisfechos con nuestros suministradores locales, pero podemos hacer negocio. Todo depende de la calidad y precio de su mercancía.

Sr. Leonard —Sólo vendemos piezas de marcas acreditadas, y estoy seguro de que, en precios, nadie puede competir con nosotros.

Sr. Rovira —Bien, estoy interesado en las líneas de silenciadores y tubos de escape, y también, en los amortiguadores Monroe.

Sr. Leonard —¿No usan Uds. los amortiguadores Gabriel? ¿Por qué no los usan?

Sr. Rovira —Porque aquí esa marca es poco conocida y casi ningún cliente la ordena. No queremos tener en existencia mercancías que tienen poca salida.

Sr. Leonard —Pues esos amortiguadores son de primera calidad y tienen precios competitivos.

Sr. Rovira —Sí, pero nosotros siempre usamos los repuestos que los clientes indican.

Sr. Leonard —Bien, aquí tiene nuestras listas de precios. Éstos son los precios para el consumidor. Los talleres reciben descuentos según el volumen de la compra y la forma de pago.

Sr. Rovira	—¿Estos precios son L.A.B.[1] o C.S.F.?[2]
Sr. Leonard	—Éstos son los precios de las piezas en nuestros almacenes en Ciudad de Guatemala. Desde luego, el transporte de nuestros almacenes a sus talleres va por su cuenta.
Sr. Rovira	—¿Qué descuento hacen en pedidos de mil unidades o más?
Sr. Leonard	—En pedidos de ese volumen descontamos entre el 15 y el 25 por ciento del precio de lista.
Sr. Rovira	—¿Cuáles son las condiciones de pago?
Sr. Leonard	—Las de costumbre en el mercado: 2/30, n/90.[3] ¿Tienen Uds. crédito bancario?
Sr. Rovira	—Sí, aquí en Antigua y en la capital.
Sr. Leonard	—¿Importan directamente de las fábricas?
Sr. Rovira	—Pocas veces. Nuestros pedidos son pequeños y, aunque las piezas cuestan menos en fábrica, el ahorro no compensa las dificultades para importarlas.
Sr. Leonard	—Bien, ¿va a hacer algún pedido ahora?
Sr. Rovira	—Creo que sus precios son buenos, pero necesito compararlos con los de nuestros proveedores actuales.
Sr. Leonard	—Comprendo. ¿Cuándo vuelvo a visitarlo? ¿El jueves está bien?
Sr. Rovira	—A ver... el jueves no voy a estar aquí, ni el viernes tampoco; puede venir a verme el lunes próximo.

¡Escuchemos!

While listening to the dialogue, circle **V (verdadero)** if the statement is true or **F (falso)** if it is false.

1. Flagler Auto Parts tiene buenas ofertas porque está tratando de penetrar el mercado de Guatemala. — V F
2. Ellos sólo venden silenciadores y tubos de escape. — V F
3. El administrador de Nuevos Servicentros no está satisfecho con sus suministradores actuales. — V F
4. La cadena siempre vende piezas de marcas acreditadas. — V F
5. Los clientes prefieren los amortiguadores Gabriel. — V F
6. Los talleres Nuevos Servicentros usan las piezas más baratas. — V F
7. El costo del transporte de las piezas de los almacenes a los talleres va por cuenta del comprador. — V F
8. Los clientes reciben el 2 por ciento de descuento cuando pagan en 30 días. — V F
9. Nuevos Servicentros casi siempre importa las piezas. — V F
10. El Sr. Rovira va a comparar los precios con los de sus suministradores actuales. — V F

---

[1]**L.A.B. (libre a bordo)** *F.O.B. (free on board)*

[2]**C.S.F. (costo, seguro y flete)** *C.I.F. (cost, insurance, and freight)*

[3]**2/30 (dos treinta)** represents a 2 percent discount if the bill is paid within 30 days of purchase, **n/90 (neto noventa)** indicates that the full amount must be paid if the account is satisfied 31–90 days after the date of purchase.

Nombre ______________________ Sección ____________ Fecha ____________

VOCABULARIO

Audio

Cognados

la capital
competitivo(a)
el (la) consumidor(a)
la dificultad
directamente
innecesario(a)
la lista
local
el volumen

Nombres

el ahorro *savings*
el amortiguador *shock absorber*
el automóvil, el auto, el coche, el carro, la máquina (*Cuba*) *automobile, car*
la compra *purchase, buying*
la fábrica, la factoría *factory*
el filtro de aire (aceite) *air (oil) filter*
el freno *brake*
la línea *line*
el lunes *Monday*
la marca *brand*
la mercancía, la mercadería *merchandise*
la oferta *offer, bid, deal*
la pieza *part*
la reparación *repair*
el repuesto *spare part*
el silenciador *muffler*
el (la) suministrador(a), el (la) proveedor(a) *provider, supplier*
el taller de reparación *repair shop*
el tubo de escape *exhaust pipe*
la unidad *unit*
el (la) viajante, el (la) agente viajero(a) *traveling salesperson*
el viernes *Friday*

Verbos

comparar *to compare*
compensar *to compensate*
competir (e:i)[1] *to compete*
costar (o:ue) *to cost*
creer *to think, to believe*
depender (de) *to depend (on)*
descontar (o:ue) *to give a discount of*
exportar *to export*
indicar *to indicate*
ordenar *to order*
penetrar *to penetrate, to enter (i.e., a market)*
poder (o:ue) *can, to be able*
recibir *to receive*
trabajar *to work*
tratar (de) *to try*
usar, utilizar *to use*
visitar *to visit*
volver (o:ue) *to come back*

Adjetivos

acreditado(a) *well-established*
actual *present*
bancario(a) *bank*
próximo(a) *next*
satisfecho(a) *satisfied*

Otras palabras y expresiones

a veces *sometimes*
a ver *let's see*
además *besides*
las (condiciones) de costumbre en la plaza (el mercado) *the usual terms in the market*
las condiciones de pago *terms of payment*
conmigo *with me*
desde luego *of course*

---

[1]**competir: compito, compites, compite, competimos, compiten**

Nombre ______________________ Sección __________ Fecha __________

en existencia *in stock*
estar seguro(a) *to be certain*
la forma de pago *means of payment*
hacer un pedido *to place an order*
ir por su cuenta *to be paid by you*
los de *those*
los (las) nuestros(as) *ours*
nadie *no one*
ni *neither, nor*
ningún *none*
poco *a little*
pocas veces *not frequently*
¿por qué? *why?*
porque *because*
según *according to, depending on*
siempre *always*
el sistema de suspensión *suspension*
tampoco *neither, not either*
todo *all, everything*

VOCABULARIO ADICIONAL

Audio

Vocabulario automovilístico (I)

el acelerador *accelerator*
el acumulador, la batería *battery*
alguien *someone*
añadir *to add*
arroba, at
barril *barrel* (36 gallons)
la bolsa de aire *air bag*
botella *bottle* (0.725 liter)
la bujía *spark plug*
la caja de bolas *ball bearings*
el cambio de aceite *oil change*
la carrocería *body* (*of automobile*)
el chasis *chassis*
el claxon, la bocina, el pito (*coll.*) *horn, klaxon*
los cojinetes *roller bearings*
la defensa, el parachoques *bumper*
dirigirse to *address*
el engrase, la lubricación *lubrication*
el (la) guantero(a) *glove compartment*
el guardabarros, el guardafangos *fender*
hectárea *2.47 acres*
el limpiaparabrisas *windshield wiper*
el líquido de frenos *brake fluid*
litro *liter*
la luz *light*
la llanta (*Méx.*), **el neumático, la goma** (*coll.*) *tire*
el maletero, la cajuela (*Méx.*), **el baúl** *trunk*
manzana (medida de tierra) *10 000 square "varas",* 6 989 m^2 (land)
manzana (en una ciudad) *space limited by four streets*
mayoría de *most of*
el motor *motor, engine*
el motor de arranque *starter*
nuez *nut*
obsequio *present*
onza *ounce*
el parabrisas *windshield*
pie *foot*
pluma *pen*
pulgada *inch*
quintal *100 pounds*
respetuoso(a) *respectful*
se casa *gets married*
la transmisión *transmission gear*
vara *836 meters*
la vestidura, la tapicería *upholstery*
el volante, el timón (*coll.*) *steering wheel*

Nombre ______________________ Sección ____________ Fecha ____________

Notas Culturales

- Before trying to do business in a foreign country, it is necessary to do some legal research. Many countries prohibit or restrict certain imports, or they charge high customs duties in order to protect their national industries. Some countries also prohibit certain exports. Costa Rica, for example, prohibits the export of certain types of wood in order to protect their rain forests. Peru and Mexico do not allow certain pre-Columbian artifacts to be taken out of the country.
- On the other hand, before extending credit, it is a good idea to find about the legal and practical difficulties one might encounter when trying to collect bad debts.
- While conducting business in the Spanish-speaking business world, remember to be punctual for all meetings and appointments, just as you would elsewhere. Do not be offended, however, if your associates do not practice the same concept of time management and arrive up to thirty minutes late for a meeting. Time is a flexible concept in many countries of the Spanish-speaking world, and efficiency and timeliness often bow to courtesy and diplomacy, leading to tardiness by American standards. Be prepared to wait even for scheduled appointments. An exception to the previous rule is Guatemala. Although in daily living time may be a flexible concept, most of the Guatemalan ruling elite has embraced the Neopentecostal's "prosperity ideology," and for them punctuality is very important.
- Generally, the red tape necessary to start a business in Latin-American countries is more complicated and costly than it is in the United States or Canada. According to the report by the World Bank's International Finance Corporation, "Doing Business in 2009," most Latin-American countries are "the world champions in red tape"! For example, it takes an average of 141 days to open a new business in Venezuela, six in the U.S., and only two in Australia. In Venezuela, 16 procedures are necessary to start a business, while in Argentina, 15 steps are required. In contrast, in the U.S. only six are needed and only one in Canada.

Source: World Bank's International Finance Corporation, "Doing Business in 2009"

Actividades

Dígame... Answer the following questions, basing your answers on the dialogue.

1. ¿Cuál es el trabajo (*job*) del Sr. Leonard?

____

2. ¿Qué es Nuevos Servicentros, S.A.?

____

3. ¿Qué está tratando de hacer la firma Flagler Auto Parts?

____

4. ¿Qué piezas de repuesto vende Flagler Auto Parts?

____

5. ¿Por qué no está interesado el Sr. Rovira en los amortiguadores Gabriel?

____

6. ¿Cree Ud. que el Sr. Leonard y el Sr. Rovira van a hacer negocio? ¿Por qué o por qué no?

____

Nombre ______________________ Sección ____________ Fecha ____________

7. ¿Piensa Ud. que Nuevos Servicentros, S.A. es un negocio serio (*serious*)? ¿Por qué o por qué no?

____

8. ¿Quién debe pagar el transporte de la mercancía del almacén a los talleres?

____

9. ¿Por qué no importa Nuevos Servicentros, S.A. siempre?

____

10. ¿Qué va a hacer el Sr. Rovira antes de decidir (*before deciding*) hacer un pedido?

____

Hablemos

Interview a classmate, using the following questions. When you have finished, switch roles.

1. ¿Dónde trabaja Ud.?
2. ¿Qué hace?
3. ¿Qué fábricas de automóviles extranjeros están tratando de penetrar el mercado de los Estados Unidos?
4. ¿Está Ud. satisfecho(a) con su taller de mecánica? ¿Por qué o por qué no?
5. Los productos de marcas acreditadas, ¿son siempre mejores?
6. ¿Qué productos son más caros: los de marcas acreditadas o los genéricos (*generic*)?
7. ¿Tiene Ud. una línea de crédito bancaria? ¿En qué banco?
8. Importar un carro directamente de Japón, ¿cuesta menos que comprarlo aquí?
9. Antes de comprar algo, ¿compara Ud. los precios de varias tiendas? ¿El ahorro compensa las dificultades?

Quiz

Vamos a practicar

A Complete the following sentences with the appropriate form of the verb in parentheses.

Modelo El amortiguador (costar) $23.
El amortiguador **cuesta** $23.

1. Ellas ____________ (poder) tratar de penetrar el mercado de Colombia.

2. Si el administrador no está hoy yo ____________ (volver) mañana.

Nombre ______________________ Sección ______________ Fecha ______________

3. ¿Cuánto ____________ (descontar) Uds. en los tubos de escape?

4. Yo no ____________ (poder) atender a los clientes.

5. Nosotros ____________ (volver) a las cinco.

B Rewrite the following sentences to express the opposite.

MODELO Ella *siempre* come *algo* antes de salir.
Ella **nunca** come **nada** antes de salir.

1. Importamos *algunas* piezas directamente de los Estados Unidos.

____

2. En este taller hay *siempre algún* mecánico disponible.

____

3. *Nadie* compra *nada nunca*.

____

4. *También* damos descuentos en las piezas de repuesto.

____

C You are a salesperson talking with a prospective client. Tell him/her the following.

MODELO I have a good offer for you.
Tengo una buena oferta para Ud.

1. No one can compete with us in price and quality.

____

2. For us, a satisfied client is good business.

____

3. I am going to order the mufflers today.

____

4. You may talk with the manager or with me.

____

Nombre ______________________________ **Sección** ______________ **Fecha** ______________

D Rewrite each sentence by changing the word order, as required by the alternative placement of the direct object pronoun.

MODELO Nosotros *queremos introducirla* en el mercado.
Nosotros **la queremos introducir** en el mercado.

1. *Los estamos importando* de Guatemala.

   ____

2. *Vamos a visitarla* todos los lunes.

   ____

3. *Lo podemos reparar* en este taller.

   ____

4. *Puedo ordenarlas* ahora.

   ____

5. No *tenemos que importarlas; podemos comprarlas* en el mercado local.

   ____

Sirva usted de intérprete

With two classmates, play the role of Mr. Block, Sr. Bernal, and the interpreter who helps them communicate. Switch roles until each of you has played the interpreter's role.

Mr. Block —*Good morning. I am a traveling salesman for Midas.*

Intérprete —____

Sr. Bernal —Mucho gusto en conocerlo, Sr. Block. ¿En qué puedo servirle?

Intérprete —____

Mr. Block —*My company is trying to enter the Ecuador market and we are offering big discounts on all spare parts.*

Intérprete —____

Sr. Bernal —¿Qué piezas venden Uds.?

Intérprete —____

Mr. Block —*We sell shock absorbers, mufflers, exhaust pipes, and everything you may need to repair brakes.*

Intérprete —____

Sr. Bernal —¿Qué marcas de amortiguadores venden Uds.?

Intérprete —____

Mr. Block —*We sell Monroe and Gabriel shock absorbers.*

Intérprete —____

Nombre ______________________ Sección ____________ Fecha ____________

Sr. Bernal —¿Cuáles son los mejores?

Intérprete —____

Mr. Block —*The Monroe shock absorbers are better known in this market, but the Gabriel ones are also top quality, and I sell them at competitive prices.*

Intérprete —____

Sr. Bernal —¿Es ésta la lista de precios para el consumidor?

Intérprete —____

Mr. Block —*Yes, and this month we are offering a 40 percent discount to wholesale buyers.*

Intérprete —____

Sr. Bernal —Muy bien. ¿Cuáles son las condiciones de pago?

Intérprete —____

Mr. Block —*The usual terms in this market: 2/30, n/90.*

Intérprete —____

Sr. Bernal —¿Tienen Uds. existencias de todos estos productos en Ecuador?

Intérprete —____

Mr. Block —*Yes. sir. We have a warehouse here in Quito.*

Intérprete —____

Sirva usted de traductor(a) After visiting with Mr. Leonard, Mr. Rovira sent the following e-mail to his company's president. What does the e-mail say?

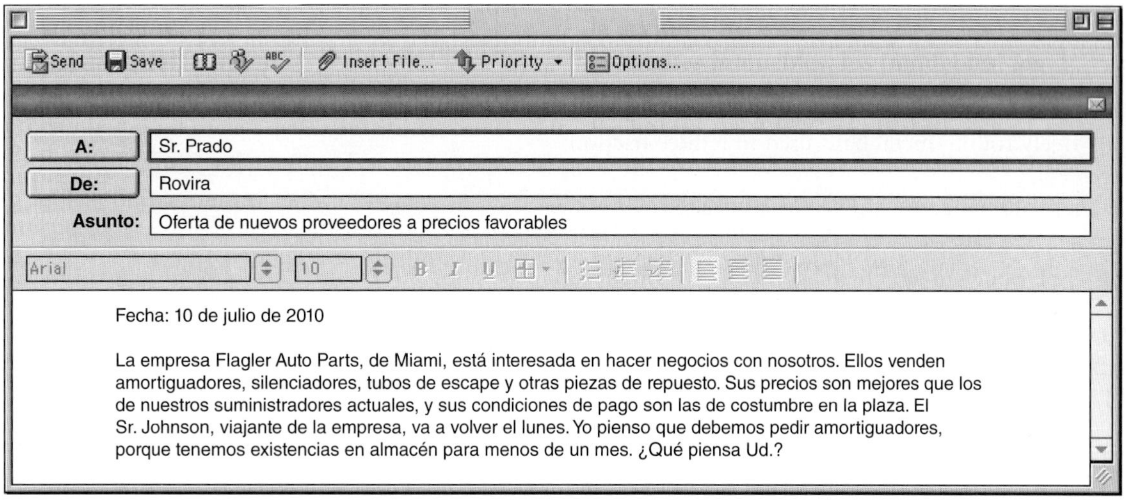

Fecha: 10 de julio de 2010

La empresa Flagler Auto Parts, de Miami, está interesada en hacer negocios con nosotros. Ellos venden amortiguadores, silenciadores, tubos de escape y otras piezas de repuesto. Sus precios son mejores que los de nuestros suministradores actuales, y sus condiciones de pago son las de costumbre en la plaza. El Sr. Johnson, viajante de la empresa, va a volver el lunes. Yo pienso que debemos pedir amortiguadores, porque tenemos existencias en almacén para menos de un mes. ¿Qué piensa Ud.?

Nombre ______________________________ **Sección** ____________ **Fecha** ____________

En estas situaciones

With a partner, act out the following situations in Spanish.

1. You are talking with a sales representative from an automotive parts distributor. You want to know whether a company sells mufflers, exhaust pipes, and shock absorbers. You also wish to find out the price of these products.
2. You are a public relations person and you call a customer to see if he/she is satisfied with the service provided by your company. Ask about the following:
   a. the quality and the prices
   b. the discounts
   c. the terms of payment
   d. other orders

Casos

With you and a partner playing the roles, work through the following scenarios.

1. A salesperson is trying to convince a client to order merchandise from his/her company.
2. A businessperson and a salesperson are discussing discounts and terms of payment.

Un paso más

Review the **Vocabulario adicional** in this lesson and give the Spanish names of the automobile parts described.

1. metal frames over the wheels ____________
2. a connected group of cells storing an electrical charge ____________
3. airbags and seat belts ____________
4. liquid used as fuel ____________
5. covering of the interior of a car ____________
6. a piece fitted into an engine to ignite the fuel ____________
7. freely rolling metal balls used to reduce friction ____________
8. a metal bar across the front or back ____________
9. a device to lessen the force of shocks and jarring ____________
10. a compartment for holding luggage ____________
11. a device for starting the engine ____________
12. glass that protects the riders from wind ____________

Nombre ______________________ Sección ____________ Fecha ____________

Lectura After reading this **lectura**, get together with a partner and take turns answering the questions that follow.

Antigua es el nombre con que hoy se conoce a la antigua° capital de Guatemala. Es una pequeña ciudad de unos 36.000 habitantes, famosa por su bien conservada° arquitectura colonial con gran influencia mudéjar y barroca, y por las espectaculares ruinas de sus iglesias° coloniales.

former
bien... *well preserved*
churches

Antigua fue° la capital de Guatemala por más de 200 años, pero entonces se llamaba° Guatemala. En 1773, cuando un terremoto° destruyó° la mayor parte° de la ciudad, España decidió° construir una nueva ciudad, la actual capital del país. Sin embargo°, no todo el mundo° se fue° de la ciudad, que desde entonces pasó a ser° la Antigua Guatemala, o simplemente, Antigua. Hoy día, esta ciudad es una de las principales atracciones turísticas de América Central.

was
se... *its name was*
earthquake / destroyed / most
decided
Sin... *nevertheless / everybody / left*
pasó... *became*

1. ¿Por qué es famosa Antigua?
2. ¿Cuántos años fue Antigua la capital de Guatemala?
3. ¿Cómo se llamaba entonces?
4. ¿Por qué España decidió construir una nueva ciudad?

Y en los Estados Unidos...

1. ¿Qué ciudad es famosa por su bien conservada arquitectura colonial?
2. ¿Hay terremotos en los Estados Unidos? ¿Dónde son más frecuentes?

Un dicho

Compra en tu idioma; vende en el de tu cliente. *Buy in your language; sell in your client's.*

Nombre ______________________ Sección ____________ Fecha ____________

Trivia

The Export-Oriented Mexican Economy

Today's Mexican economy is amply diversified. Until a few decades ago the country's economy was based primarily on agriculture, but now less than 4% of the GDP (Gross Domestic Product) comes from this sector, while 34% is from industry and more than 62% from the service area. Both agriculture and industry are increasingly export-oriented, and the service sector is dominated by tourism.

In 2008, Mexico exported products for more than $290 billion F.O.B. (free on board). Of this amount, 82.2% went to the U.S., and 2.4% was sent to Canada. These exported products included manufactured goods, oil and oil-related products, silver, beverages, fruits, vegetables, coffee, and cotton. Nevertheless, its commercial balance was unfavorable because in the same year the country imported $305.9 billion F.O.B. in machinery, electrical equipment, car repair parts, and food.

Lección 7

Medios de comunicación

Objectives

Structures

- Stem-changing verbs **(e:i)**
- Irregular first-person forms
- **Saber** contrasted with **conocer**
- Indirect object pronouns

Business Communication

- Inquiring about the availability of communication facilities in a foreign country
- How to procure and use communication facilities

La Sra. Sánchez, compradora de la firma Gaviña and Sons, de California, está en Colombia comprando café. Ahora llama a la telefonista del hotel para pedir información acerca de los medios de comunicación con que cuenta el hotel.

Por teléfono:

Sra. Sánchez —Señorita, necesito llamar a los Estados Unidos. ¿Cómo hago para llamar desde mi habitación?

Telefonista —Primero marca el nueve, después el código de los Estados Unidos y, por último, el código del área y el número de teléfono al que desea llamar.

Sra. Sánchez —¿Cuánto carga el hotel por llamadas de larga distancia?

Telefonista —Mil quinientos pesos, señora.

Sra. Sánchez —¿Y por las llamadas locales?

Telefonista —Nada, señora. El servicio local es gratuito.

Sra. Sánchez —Muy bien. Otra cosa, ¿dónde queda la oficina de correos más cercana? Necesito enviar unas cartas.

Telefonista —A tres cuadras de aquí, pero puede echarlas en el buzón que está en el mostrador de la oficina. El hotel también le ofrece servicios de facsímiles y acceso a la Internet.

Sra. Sánchez —Magnífico. Necesito mandar un fax a mi oficina.

En el correo:

Sra. Sánchez —Por favor, ¿sabe Ud. cuánto tarda un paquete en llegar a su destinatario en Vernon, California?

Empleado —Si lo envía por correo aéreo, le llega en tres días.

Sra. Sánchez —En cuanto al tamaño y al peso de los paquetes, ¿hay alguna regulación?

Empleado —¿Qué contiene el paquete?

Sra. Sánchez —Muestras de café sin valor comercial, varios catálogos y folletos de propaganda.

Empleado —Si envía los impresos en un paquete aparte, ahorra dinero; pues los impresos pagan una tarifa mucho menor.

Sra. Sánchez —¿Cuánto deben medir y pesar los paquetes de impresos?

Empleado —Las medidas no deben exceder de 30 centímetros de largo, 20 de ancho y 10 de alto. Además, el paquete no debe pesar más de 5 kilos, más o menos 11 libras.

Sra. Sánchez —Otra pregunta, ¿puedo enviar por correo bultos de mercancías con valor comercial?

Empleado —Sí, hasta 20 kilos de peso.

Sra. Sánchez —Yo necesito enviar un paquete mucho más grande. ¿Conoce Ud. alguna agencia internacional de envío de paquetes?

Empleado —Nos está prohibido recomendar servicios privados, pero hay una que no está muy lejos de aquí.

Sra. Sánchez —De todos modos, ¿sabe Ud. la dirección?

Empleado —No, no la sé, pero puede buscarla en la guía de teléfonos o pedirle información a la telefonista.

Sra. Sánchez —Gracias, y una pregunta más. ¿Dónde puedo cobrar un cheque, digo, un giro postal internacional?

Empleado —En la tercera ventanilla, a la izquierda.

Sra. Sánchez —Ah, sí, ya la veo. Donde dice "Giros y telegramas", ¿no?

Empleado —Sí, señora.

¡Escuchemos!

While listening to the dialogue, circle **V (verdadero)** if the statement is true or **F (falso)** if it is false.

1. La Sra. Sánchez compra café para exportar a los Estados Unidos. V F
2. El hotel no cobra por las llamadas de larga distancia. V F
3. La oficina de correos más cercana queda a veinte cuadras del hotel. V F
4. La señora puede echar las cartas en el buzón. V F
5. La Sra. Sánchez quiere mandar por correo muestras de café. V F
6. Enviar café cuesta menos que enviar folletos y catálogos. V F
7. Está prohibido enviar por correo mercancías con valor comercial. V F
8. Los empleados de correo pueden recomendar agencias privadas de envío de paquetes. V F
9. La señora puede buscar el nombre de una agencia de envío de paquetes en la guía de teléfonos. V F
10. Para cobrar un giro postal la Sra. Sánchez debe ir a donde dice "Giros y telegramas". V F

Nombre ______________________ Sección ____________ Fecha ____________

VOCABULARIO

Audio

Cognados

el acceso
el área
el centímetro
la comunicación
el facsímil, el facsímile, el fax
internacional
el (la) Internet, la red
el kilo, el kilogramo
el paquete
la regulación, la disposición
el servicio
el telegrama

Nombres

el alto *height, depth (of a container)*
el ancho *width*
el buzón *mailbox*
la carta *letter*
el código, la clave *code*
el correo aéreo *airmail*
el correo electrónico *e-mail*
la cosa *thing*
la cuadra *block*
el (la) destinatario(a) *addressee*
el dinero *money*
el folleto *booklet*
el giro postal *money order*
la guía de teléfonos, el directorio telefónico *telephone book*
el (la) hijo(a) *son, daughter*
el impreso *printed matter*
el informe *report*
el largo *length*
la libra *pound*
la llamada *call*
la (llamada de) larga distancia *long distance (call)*
la medida *measure, measurement, dimension*
los medios de comunicación *means of communication*
la muestra *sample*
la oficina de correos, el correo *post office*
el peso *weight*
la pregunta *question*
la propaganda *advertisement*
el tamaño *size*
la tarifa *tariff, toll, fare*
el (la) telefonista, el (la) operador(a) *telephone operator*
el valor *value, worth*
la ventanilla *(service) window*

Verbos

ahorrar *to save*
cargar, cobrar *to charge*
conocer[1] *to know*
contener[2] *to contain*
decir (e:i)[3] *to say, to tell*
echar *to drop*
enviar,[4] **mandar** *to send*
exceder *to exceed*
marcar *to dial*
medir (e:i) *to measure*
ofrecer[5] *to have available*
pedir (e:i) *to ask for, to request*
pesar *to weigh*
recomendar (e:ie) *to recommend*
saber[6] *to know*

---

[1]Irregular first person singular: **yo conozco**
[2]Conjugated like **tener**
[3]Irregular first person singular: **yo digo**
[4]Present indicative forms: **envío, envías, envía, enviamos, envían**
[5]Irregular first person singular: **yo ofrezco**
[6]Irregular first person singular: **yo sé**

Adjetivos

algún,[1] **alguno, alguna** *any*
cercano(a) *near, close by*
gratuito(a), gratis *free of charge*
menor *less*
privado(a) *private*

Otras palabras y expresiones

a tres cuadras de (aquí) *three blocks from (here)*
acerca de *about*
aparte *separately, in addition to*
con que cuenta *available*
de todos modos *anyway*
digo *I mean*
en cuanto a *in regard to*
lejos (de) *far (from)*
¡Magnífico! *Great!*
nos *to us*
por último *finally, lastly*
pues *because, since*
sin *without*

VOCABULARIO ADICIONAL

Audio

base de retención de datos *retention base*
brecha digital *digital divide*
buscador *search engine*
centro de asistencia técnica *helpdesk*
compatibilidad con sistemas anteriores *backward compatibility*
competidor(a) *the competition*
comprender *to understand*
cuerpo del mensaje *body of text*
datos de inicio de sesión *login information*
desactivar to *unset*
desbloquear to *release*
descarga de canción en MP3 sin protección de derechos de autor *DRM-free MP3 song download*
diseñar una estrategia electrónica to *craft an e-strategy*
dominio público *public domain*
eliminar de la lista de amigo to *unfriend*
empresario(a) *entrepreneur*
estacionamiento de nombre de dominio *domain name parking*
galería de imágenes *photowall*
incluir en favoritos *book page*
informe de actividad reciente *recent activity feed*
introduzca la contraseña *enter password*
juego en red *hosted game*
página de inicio de sesión *login webpage*
página de recuperación de contraseña *password-assistance page*
pista (supercarretera) de la información *information (super) highway*
portal de acceso mundial *global gateway*
proveedores independientes de contenidos *third party content provider*
rastreadores automatizados *automated spiders*

---

[1]Like **bueno, alguno** drops its final **o** when used before masculine singular nouns. When used in this way, it adds a written accent to the **u.**

Nombre ______________________ Sección __________ Fecha __________

redacción de textos publicitarios *copywriting*
rendimiento del sistema de registro de datos *data logging engine performance*
sitio (página) web en construcción *website under construction*
suplantación de correo electrónico *email spoofing*
tablero *dashboard*
tecnología líder en su categoría/clase *best of breed technology*
tendencias del usuario *searchers' behavior*
tienda virtual *webshop*
uso desautorizado *unauthorized use*
velocidad de carga *upload speed*
velocidad de descarga *download speed*
violación de la seguridad *breach of security*
visitado *accessed*

El correo

el apartado postal, la casilla de correo *post office box*
la carta certificada *registered (certified) letter*
el (la) cartero(a) *mail carrier*
con acuso de recibo *return receipt*
la entrega al día siguiente *overnight delivery*
la entrega especial *special delivery*
entregar *to deliver*
la esquina superior derecha *upper right corner*
la esquina superior izquierda *upper left corner*
la estampilla, el sello, el timbre (*Méx.*) *(postage) stamp*
el franqueo *postage*
el matasellos *postmark*
el membrete *letterhead*
porte debido, porte a pagar *postage due*
porte pagado *postage paid*
el (la) remitente *sender*
los servicios de correo y paquetería privados *private couriers*
el sobre *envelope*

Los teléfonos

los audífonos *headset*
la conferencia telefónica *telephone conference*
la llamada a cobrar, la llamada por cobrar *collect call*
la memoria *memory*
el remarcador del último número *last number redial*
la tarjeta telefónica *prepaid phone card*
el teléfono celular *cellular phone*
el teléfono portátil *cordless phone*
el teléfono público *public phone*

Nombre ______________________ Sección ____________ Fecha ____________

Search

iLrn

Notas Culturales

- The quality of telephone service varies widely within the Spanish-speaking world. While most countries have seen vast improvements in their telecommunications systems in recent years, direct dialing and immediate international connections may still not always be available, and connections may be poor, especially in rural areas. Placing a call from one's hotel room is generally the most expensive option, since hefty surcharges are usually applied. Many cities and even smaller towns in Latin American countries have calling centers, run by telephone companies, where long-distance calls can be made and paid for on the spot. Depending on the country, telephones may require coins, special tokens (**fichas**), or phone cards. Operators for U.S. long-distance carriers can also be accessed from most countries to assist in placing international calls.

  The efficiency of mail also should not be taken for granted in most Latin American countries, and General Delivery mail in most of these countries is not a good option.

- First-class hotels throughout Latin America are usually equipped to cater to the needs of business travelers. In addition to providing fax services, many hotels have document centers that provide computers for word processing, as well as for e-mail and Internet access. Also, the telephone lines in the rooms of these hotels are usually upgraded with an additional data jack so that the guest may be able to connect his or her laptop for Internet communication.

Actividades

Dígame... Answer the following questions, basing your answers on the dialogues.

1. ¿Para qué llama la Sra. Sánchez a la telefonista?

   ____

2. ¿Qué tiene que hacer la Sra. Sánchez para llamar a los Estados Unidos desde su habitación?

   ____

3. ¿Cuánto carga el hotel por las llamadas de larga distancia?

   ____

4. ¿Cuánto cobra el hotel por las llamadas locales desde la habitación?

   ____

5. ¿Adónde debe ir la Sra. Sánchez para enviar un fax?

   ____

6. ¿Cuándo va a llegar el paquete de la Sra. Sánchez a su destinatario en Vernon, California?

   ____

7. ¿Qué contiene el paquete de la Sra. Sánchez?

   ____

8. ¿Qué debe hacer la Sra. Sánchez para ahorrar dinero?

____

9. ¿Cuáles son las regulaciones del correo en cuanto al peso de los paquetes?

____

10. ¿Hasta cuánto pueden pesar los paquetes de mercancías con valor comercial?

____

11. ¿Qué tiene que buscar la Sra. Sánchez en la guía de teléfonos?

____

Hablemos Interview a classmate, using the following questions. When you have finished, switch roles.

1. ¿Qué hace Ud. para llamar por teléfono a otro país?
2. ¿Cuánto le cuesta a Ud. llamar por larga distancia a su casa?
3. ¿Necesita utilizar a la operadora para llamar por larga distancia a su casa?
4. ¿Dónde queda el buzón más cercano? ¿Y la oficina de correos más cercana?
5. ¿Envía Ud. sus paquetes por correo o por una agencia privada?
6. ¿Conoce Ud. alguna agencia de envío de paquetes a todo el mundo (*the world over*)?
8. ¿Dónde puedo buscar la dirección de FedEx?
9. ¿Dónde puedo comprar un giro postal?
10. ¿El correo entrega los paquetes a domicilio?

Quiz

Vamos a practicar

A Complete the sentences with the conjugated form of the verb in parentheses.

Modelo Nosotros les (pedir) los catálogos.
Nosotros les **pedimos** los catálogos.

1. Yo no les ___________(pedir) dinero a mis padres.
2. Tú ___________ (medir) el largo y el ancho del paquete.
3. Ella ___________ (decir) que ellos van al correo.
4. El Sr. Fernández ___________ (conseguir—*to get, to obtain*) folletos de propaganda.
5. Ellos ___________ (servir—*to serve*) café de Colombia.

Nombre ______________ Sección ______________ Fecha ______________

B Write sentences using the following elements.

MODELO yo / salir (*leave*) / a las dos
Yo salgo a las dos.

1. yo / saber / dónde hay un buzón

____

2. yo / no conocer / la operadora

____

3. yo / hacer / los bultos

____

4. yo / traer / los catálogos

____

5. yo / ofrecer / mis servicios a la agencia

____

C Mr. Johnson uses UPS services to send packages and letters. The following are the addresses and what he sends to each of them. Form complete sentences using the verb **mandar.** Remember to use the corresponding indirect object pronouns.

MODELO muestras de café / a su jefa
Él le manda muestras de café a su jefa.

1. cartas / a sus hijos

____

2. un giro postal / a nosotros

____

3. a mí / un folleto de propaganda

____

4. a ti / un paquete de impresos

____

5. a Ud. / mercancías

____

6. a ustedes / la dirección del hotel

____

Nombre ______________________ Sección ______________ Fecha ______________

Sirva usted de intérprete

With two classmates, play the roles of a customer **(cliente)**, a post office employee, and the interpreter who helps them communicate. Switch roles until each of you has played the interpreter's role.

Cliente	—Por favor, necesito enviar una carta a España. ¿Cuánto es el franqueo?
Intérprete	—______________________________
Empleado(a)	—*Do you want an airmail stamp?*
Intérprete	—______________________________
Cliente	—Sí, por favor. ¿Cuánto tarda una carta por correo aéreo a Uruguay?
Intérprete	—______________________________
Empleado(a)	—*About four days. Do you want one international stamp?*
Intérprete	—______________________________
Cliente	—Quiero cuatro. ¿Cuánto es?
Intérprete	—______________________________
Empleado(a)	—*Two dollars. Anything else?*
Intérprete	—______________________________
Cliente	—Sí, necesito cambiar un giro postal.
Intérprete	—______________________________
Empleado(a)	—*You need to go to the second window to the left.*
Intérprete	—______________________________
Cliente	—Muchas gracias.
Intérprete	—______________________________
Empleado(a)	—*You're welcome.*
Intérprete	—______________________________

En estas situaciones

With a partner, act out the following situations in Spanish.

1. You are in Mexico and you need to mail a package. Ask the clerk how long it takes for a package to arrive at its address in the United States. Also ask what the limitations are regarding the size and weight of the package. Tell the clerk what the package contains, and ask about a shipping agency, its address, and where you can get a telephone directory.
2. You are a clerk in a post office. Help a customer who doesn't speak English. Say that a postcard takes two weeks to get to Venezuela, but by airmail it takes five days. Also say that packages can weigh up to 40 pounds. Add that a package larger than that must be sent through a shipping agency located five blocks from the post office.

Nombre ______________________ Sección ____________ Fecha ____________

Casos With you and a partner playing the roles, work through the following scenarios.

1. A guest in a Spanish-speaking country tries to find out how to make an international telephone call.
2. A clerk at the post office talks with a customer who speaks only Spanish.
3. A hotel receptionist discusses with a guest the various means of communication offered at the hotel, such as fax, Internet service, photocopying service, etc.

Un paso más

A You are a desk clerk at a hotel in Chile. Review the **Vocabulario adicional** in this lesson and use it and other vocabulary you have learned to create a list of questions, instructions, or statements that you will need to help guests send mail.

1. ______________________________
2. ______________________________
3. ______________________________
4. ______________________________
5. ______________________________

B Use the information on the envelope to answer the questions.

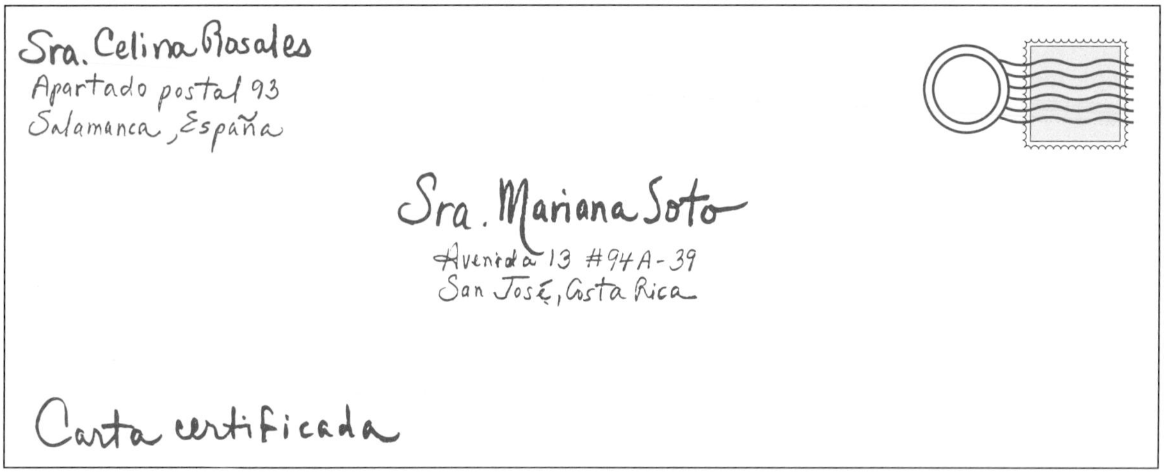

© Cengage Learning

1. ¿Quién es la remitente?
2. ¿Quién es la destinataria?
3. ¿Dónde tiene el sobre un sello?
4. ¿Dónde tiene el matasellos?
5. ¿Es una entrega especial?

Nombre ______________________ **Sección** __________ **Fecha** __________

Lectura After reading this **lectura**, get together with a partner and take turns answering the following questions.

Los colombianos dicen que su café es el mejor del mundo, y son muchos los que están de acuerdo° con ellos, pero la excesiva dependencia del producto limita el desarrollo del país. La Federación Nacional de Cafeteros° (FNC), con más de medio millón de miembros, agrupa° a casi° todos los cosecheros° colombianos, y controla la exportación y la calidad del producto. El logo de Juan Valdés, famoso en todo el mundo,° garantiza que los productos que lo muestran° están hechos° con café 100% colombiano.

Sin embargo,° la Federación no es un monopolio. En Colombia hay unas 40 pequeñas cooperativas independientes de productores y exportadores de café.

están... *agree*
Federación... *National Federation of Coffee Farmers*
includes / almost
growers
en... *the world over*
lo... *exhibit it / made*
Sin... *Nevertheless*

1. ¿Qué limita el desarrollo de Colombia?
2. ¿Quién controla la exportación del café colombiano?
3. ¿Qué garantiza el logo de Juan Valdés?
4. ¿Por qué no es la Federación de Cafeteros de Colombia un monopolio?

Y en los Estados Unidos...

1. ¿Hay muchos monopolios?
2. ¿Algún logo garantiza la calidad de algún producto?

Un dicho

Nunca pongas todos los huevos en una sola canasta. *Don't put all your eggs in one basket.*

Trivia

Communicating with people of a different cultural background involves much more than mastering their language. For example, U.S. and Canadian business people put emphasis on the content of communications (facts and data); consequently, their verbal and written communications are brief, direct, and explicit. On the other hand, Spanish-American business people pay a lot of attention to other factors such as relationship, circumstances, timing and social appropriateness; and their communications reflect it. You must also be aware that nonverbal language is different from one culture to another.

Lección 8

El transporte de pasajeros

Objectives

Structures

- **Pedir** contrasted with **preguntar**
- Special construction with **gustar, doler,** and **hacer falta**
- Demonstrative adjectives and pronouns
- Direct and indirect object pronouns used together

Business Communication

- Using different means of passenger transportation
- Taking a bus or a taxi
- Renting a car
- Requirements for renting and driving a car in a foreign country

La Sra. Soto, propietaria de una tienda de artesanías en Los Ángeles, California, está en Guadalajara en viaje de negocios. Para trasladarse de un lugar a otro de la ciudad, e ir a los pueblos cercanos, utiliza varios medios de transporte. En la acera, frente al hotel, saluda al primer transeúnte que encuentra y le pide información.

Sra. Soto —Por favor, señor, ¿qué autobús debo tomar para ir a Tlaquepaque?
Transeúnte —Aquí, ninguno. Debe caminar dos cuadras hasta la Avenida de la Paz, cruzar la calle y tomar un autobús de la ruta 15, en la parada de la esquina.

Ya en el autobús, le pregunta a otra pasajera.

Sra. Soto —Este autobús va a Tlaquepaque, ¿verdad?
Pasajera —No, señora. Debe hacer transferencia para la ruta 42.
Sra. Soto —¿Dónde hago la transferencia?
Pasajera —En la Plaza de la Bandera. Yo le aviso.
Sra. Soto —¿A quién le pido la transferencia?
Pasajera —Tiene que pedírsela al chofer en el momento de bajarse.
Sra. Soto —Y, ¿dónde tomo el otro autobús?
Pasajera —Tiene que caminar media cuadra por el Boulevard Tlaquepaque y allí debe tomar un camión de la ruta 42.

Cuando la Sra. Soto desea regresar, los autobuses van muy llenos. Cuando ya le duelen los pies de estar parada esperando decide tomar un taxi pero, antes de tomarlo, le pregunta al taxista cuánto le va a costar el viaje.

Sra. Soto —Por favor, ¿cuánto es hasta Guadalajara?
Taxista —¿A qué parte de la ciudad?
Sra. Soto —Al centro, al Hotel Presidente, en la Avenida Juárez 170.
Taxista —Desde aquí el taxímetro va a marcar $90, más o menos.
Sra. Soto —Muy bien, vamos.

Al llegar a la ciudad, la Sra. Soto decide alquilar un carro para manejarlo ella misma.

Sra. Soto —Quiero alquilar un carro compacto por tres días.
Empleada —¿Sabe manejar carros de cambio mecánico?
Sra. Soto —Sí, pero no me gustan. Prefiero uno automático.
Empleada —Lo siento. No tenemos disponible ningún coche pequeño de cambio automático.
Sra. Soto —¿Cuánto me cuesta uno mediano?
Empleada —Ése de cuatro puertas le sale en $350 al día, más el seguro y el I.V.A. (iva), y aquél de dos puertas se lo puedo dejar en $300.
Sra. Soto —¿Qué es el I.V.A.?
Empleada —Es el impuesto al valor agregado.
Sra. Soto —¡Ah! ¿Tengo que comprar seguro? ¿No me cubre el seguro de los Estados Unidos?
Empleada —No, señora. Tiene que comprar un seguro local.
Sra. Soto —Pero puedo conducir con mi licencia de California. No me hace falta también una licencia local, ¿verdad?
Empleada —Sí, si está aquí como turista o en viaje de negocios, puede manejar con su licencia extranjera.
Sra. Soto —¿Necesita verla?
Empleada —Sí, por favor, ¿puede mostrármela? Además, necesito su tarjeta de crédito.

¡Escuchemos!

While listening to the dialogue, circle **V (verdadero)** if the statement is true or **F (falso)** if it is false.

1. En la acera del hotel, la Sra. Soto le pide información a un transeúnte. V F
2. Para ir a Tlaquepaque debe tomar un autobús de la ruta 42. V F
3. No necesita cruzar la calle para tomar el autobús. V F
4. En el autobús, la Sra. Soto le pide información a otra pasajera. V F
5. La otra pasajera no sabe dónde debe hacer transferencia la Sra. Soto. V F
6. Para regresar, el viaje en taxi le cuesta 90 pesos, más o menos. V F
7. A la Sra. Soto le gustan los carros de cambio mecánico. V F
8. El I.V.A. es el impuesto al valor agregado. V F

Nombre ______________________ **Sección** __________ **Fecha** __________

9. Los seguros de los Estados Unidos cubren a los turistas para manejar en México. V F

10. Los hombres y mujeres de negocio no pueden conducir en México con su licencia extranjera. V F

Audio VOCABULARIO

Cognados

automático(a)
el boulevard,[1] **el bulevar**
el (la) chofer
compacto(a)
la licencia
la parte
la ruta
el taxímetro
la transferencia
el (la) turista

Nombres

la acera, la banqueta (*Méx.*) *sidewalk*
la artesanía *artcraft, handicraft*
el autobús, el ómnibus, el camión (*Méx.*), **la guagua** (*I. Canarias, Antillas*) *bus*
la avenida *avenue*
el cambio mecánico, el cambio manual *standard-shift*
la esquina *corner*
la parada (*bus*) *stop*
el pueblo *town*
el (la) taxista *taxi driver*
el (la) transeúnte *passerby*

Verbos

alquilar, rentar[2] *to rent*
avisar *to inform, to give notice*
bajarse *to get off*
cruzar *to cross*
cubrir *to cover*
decidir *to decide*
doler (o:ue) *to hurt, to feel pain*
encontrar (o:ue) *to meet*
gustar *to be pleased, to like*
manejar, conducir,[3] **guiar**[4] *to drive*
marcar *to mark, to indicate*
mostrar (o:ue), enseñar *to show*
saludar *to greet, to say hello*
tomar, coger, agarrar *to take*

Adjetivos

lleno(a) *full*
mediano(a) *medium*

Otras palabras y expresiones

al día, diario(a) (*adj.*) *daily*
de un lugar a otro *from one place to another*
ella misma *herself*
frente (a) *in front (of)*

[1]French words are frequently used in some Latin American countries.
[2]Colloquial (U.S.A.)
[3]Irregular first person singular: **yo conduzco**
[4]Present indicative forms: **guío, guías, guía, guiamos, guían**

hacer falta *to need*
los medios de transporte *means of transportation*
Se lo puedo dejar en... *I can give it to you for . . .*

VOCABULARIO ADICIONAL

Audio

Vocabulario automovilístico (II)

el aceite *oil*
arrancar *to start (i.e., a car)*
boleto para _____. *One ticket for _____.*
la bomba de agua *water pump*
chequear, revisar, checar (*Méx.*) *to check*
coche dormitorio *sleeping car*
compartimento para 4 o 6 pasajeros *sleeping facility for 4 or 6 passengers*
el estacionamiento *parking, parking lot*
estacionar *to park*
la gasolina sin plomo *unleaded gasoline*
la gasolinera, la estación de servicio *service station*
jefe de estación *station master*
el líquido de la transmisión *transmission fluid*
la luz (las luces), el farol *light(s)*
parar *to stop*
el parquímetro *parking meter*
pinchado(a), ponchado(a) (*Cuba, Puerto Rico*) *flat (tire)*
el radiador *radiator*
recalentarse (e:ie) *to overheat*
el remolcador, la grúa *tow truck*
reparar, arreglar *to repair, to fix*
sala de espera *waiting room*
el tanque *tank*
va a llegar a su hora *is arriving on time*
va a llegar adelantado *is coming early*
va a llegar atrasado, está atrasado *is running late*
vacío(a) *empty*
vagón, el carro (Méx.) *wagon*

Search

iLrn

Notas Culturales

- If you decide to take your own car or to rent a vehicle in a Spanish-speaking country, you should definitely purchase insurance. If you travel to Mexico, you are not covered by any foreign insurance. By law, you must buy Mexican insurance.
- Handicrafts constitute the main industry in many small Mexican towns. Every year Mexico sells millions of dollars in handicrafts in the United States, Europe, and Japan. However, most of this money goes to the middlemen.
- The Mexican arts and crafts industry is, for the most part, a family business in which the techniques pass from generation to generation. Children start early to learn and work in the trade. The most famous Mexican arts and crafts are those from Tlaquepaque, Tonalá, and Oaxaca.
- **Tlaquepaque** was originally called *Tlacapan,* which means "Men who make clay utensils with their hands." Today, the town is one of the main pottery production areas in Mexico, and has a reputation for the quality and diversity of its ware, and for the beautiful expressions of its manual arts, especially in ceramics, but also in glass, metals, papier mâché, and yarns and threads.

Nombre ______________________ Sección ____________ Fecha ____________

Actividades

Dígame... Answer the following questions, basing your answers on the dialogues.

1. ¿Dónde habla la Sra. Soto con el transeúnte?

____

2. ¿Adónde va la Sra. Soto para tomar el autobús que va a Tlaquepaque?

____

3. ¿Qué va a hacer la pasajera al llegar a la Plaza de la Bandera?

____

4. ¿Cuándo tiene que pedir la transferencia la Sra. Soto?

____

5. ¿Por qué no regresa la Sra. Soto por autobús?

____

6. ¿Cuesta mucho el viaje hasta Guadalajara por taxi? ¿Cómo lo sabe Ud.?

____

7. ¿Qué tipo de carro quiere alquilar la Sra. Soto?

____

8. ¿Por qué no puede alquilar el coche que quiere?

____

9. ¿Por qué tiene que comprar seguro local la Sra. Soto?

____

10. ¿Quiénes pueden manejar en México con una licencia extranjera?

____

Hablemos Interview a classmate, using the following questions. When you have finished, switch roles.

1. ¿Sabe cuál autobús debo tomar para ir a la estación de servicio más cercana?
2. ¿Dónde está la parada de autobuses?
3. ¿Toma Ud. un autobús para ir a su casa?
4. Si toma el autobús para ir a su casa, ¿necesita hacer transferencia? ¿Dónde?

5. ¿Van siempre llenos los autobuses en esta ciudad?
6. ¿Cuánto cuesta viajar en autobús en esta ciudad?
7. ¿Cuánto tarda el viaje en autobús de su casa al centro de la ciudad?
8. En esta ciudad, ¿cuánto cuesta un viaje de una milla en taxi?
9. Cuando Ud. viaja, ¿alquila coches para manejarlos Ud. mismo(a)?
10. Más o menos, ¿cuánto cuesta alquilar un carro compacto por una semana?
11. ¿Su coche es de cambio automático o de cambio manual?
12. El Focus de Ford, ¿es un coche compacto o un coche mediano?

Quiz

VAMOS A PRACTICAR

A Rewrite the sentences using the correct form of the demonstrative adjective or pronoun. Make all other necessary changes.

MODELO Ese transeúnte me saluda. (pasajera)
Esa pasajera me saluda.

1. Este pasajero quiere una transferencia. (pasajera)

______

2. Esta taxista maneja hasta Guadalajara. (taxistas)

______

3. Aquellos autobuses van a la Plaza de la Bandera. (taxi)

______

4. Ésa es la empleada que habla español. (empleado)

______

5. Aquél es el coche que quiero alquilar. (cámara de video)

______

6. Ésas son las ciudades adonde voy. (pueblos)

______

B Complete the following dialogues using **pedir** and **preguntar** as appropriate.

1. —¿Qué le vas a ______ al chofer?

—Le voy a ______ si ésta es la parada de la Plaza de la Bandera.

Nombre ______________________________ Sección ____________ Fecha ____________

2. —¿Qué le __________ el empleado a Ud.?

—Me __________ la licencia.

3. —¿Cuánto dinero te __________ el taxista?

—Me __________ $25.

4. —¿Qué nos __________ el transeúnte?

—Nos __________ si los autobuses de la ruta 20 paran aquí.

5. —¿Le __________ Uds. la información a ella?

—No, nosotros no se la __________.

C Answer the following questions, using the cues provided. Use direct and indirect object pronouns to substitute the words in italic.

MODELO —¿Quién me dice *dónde debo tomar el autobús?* (yo)
—Yo se lo digo.

1. ¿Quién le pide *una transferencia al chofer*? (la Sra. Soto)

____

2. ¿Quién me puede decir *dónde está la parada*? (Antonio)

____

3. ¿Quién le pide *la licencia a la Sra. Soto*? (el empleado)

____

4. ¿Quién nos pregunta *dónde para el autobús*? (el transeúnte)

____

5. ¿Quiénes les piden *las transferencias a los choferes*? (los pasajeros)

____

6. ¿Quiénes te envían *esos paquetes*? (mis padres)

____

7. ¿A quiénes les envían *Uds. los giros postales*? (a nuestros hijos)

____

8. ¿A quiénes les deja *Ud. las llaves*? (a los vecinos)

____

Nombre ______________________ **Sección** ____________ **Fecha** ____________

Sirva usted de intérprete

With two classmates, play the roles of a rental car employee, a Spanish-speaking customer, and the interpreter who helps them communicate. Switch roles until each of you has played the interpreter's role.

Cliente —Quiero alquilar un coche grande por una semana más o menos.

Intérprete —______________________

Empleado(a) —*Is that one okay?*

Intérprete —______________________

Cliente —¿No tiene otro disponible?

Intérprete —______________________

Empleado(a) —*Yes. We have the red one over there.*

Intérprete —______________________

Cliente —¿En cuánto sale el rojo?

Intérprete —______________________

Empleado(a) —*Thirty-nine, ninety-five a day, or two hundred and fifty a week.*

Intérprete —______________________

Cliente —¿Es automático? ¿Tiene aire acondicionado?

Intérprete —______________________

Empleado(a) —*Yes, sir. How long do you want it for?*

Intérprete —______________________

Cliente —Por ocho o nueve días. ¿Puedo dejar el coche en otro aeropuerto?

Intérprete —______________________

Empleado(a) —*Yes, but it costs fifty dollars more.*

Intérprete —______________________

Cliente —Bien. Voy a dejarlo en el aeropuerto de Chicago.

Intérprete —______________________

Empleado(a) —*Very well. That is two hundred fifty dollars for the first week and thirty-nine dollars and ninety-five cents for each additional day. How are you going to pay?*

Intérprete —______________________

Cliente —Con la tarjeta de crédito de mi compañía.

Intérprete —______________________

Sirva usted de traductor(a)

Wanting to increase business by tourists from the U.S. and Canada, the owner of a service station in a small Mexican city near the U.S. border asks you to translate the following flyer into English. Review the **Vocabulario adicional** in this lesson, and then translate the flyer.

AUTOMUNDO, S.A.

LA MEJOR ESTACIÓN DE SERVICIOS DE ESTA ÁREA

Libertadores, 76
Tecate

VENDEMOS:

Gasolina sin plomo	$4.75 litro
Gasolina regular	$4.05 litro
Aceite de motor	$11.50 litro
Líquido de frenos	$13.50 medio litro
Líquido de la transmisión	$15.00 litro
Limpiaparabrisas desde	$75.00 el par
Baterías nuevas y de uso desde	$350.00

REPARAMOS:

Llantas pinchadas
Bombas de agua
Radiadores
Frenos (Los chequeamos gratis.)

GRATIS:

Aire para las llantas y agua para el radiador si llena aquí su tanque vacío. Si su coche no arranca o se recalienta, le ofrecemos servicio de remolcadores.

AMPLIO ESTACIONAMIENTO
ESTACIONAMIENTO ECONÓMICO 24 HORAS AL DÍA

En estas situaciones

With a partner, act out the following situations in Spanish.

1. You are at a bus stop in Buenos Aires, Argentina. Ask a passerby what bus you must take to go to Calle Florida. Ask someone else if bus number 16 goes by there, if you need to ask for a transfer, and, if so, where you have to take the other bus.
2. You are in Mexico and want to rent a car. Tell the employee that you want to rent a small, standard-shift car for your stay on your business trip. Ask if you need to purchase insurance and if you can drive with your current license.
3. You are an employee of a U.S. rental car company waiting on a Spanish-speaking customer who doesn't speak English. Ask if he/she knows how to drive standard-shift cars. Say that a small car will cost him/her $36 a day, that the car will cost $24 per day if it is rented for a week, and that insurance and tax are to be added to those prices.

Casos

With you and a partner playing the roles, work through the following scenarios.

1. Two people waiting at a bus stop talk about the quickest route to their destinations.
2. An employee at a car rental agency discusses options and preferences with a customer.

Nombre ____________________ Sección __________ Fecha __________

Un paso más

A You own a service station in Uruguay. A customer whose car is falling apart comes to you for help. Review the **Vocabulario adicional** in this lesson and use it and other vocabulary you have learned to create a list of questions to ask your customer to find out what is wrong with the car.

B You are opening a new service station to which you hope to attract many Spanish-speaking customers. Review the **Vocabulario adicional** in this lesson and use it to prepare signs advertising services offered at your garage.

C You work for a Tijuana-based transport company that is considering opening offices in California. Your boss has asked you to identify companies that would be direct competition. Prepare to give her the following information.

1. el nombre de la compañía: ____________________

2. ciudades en donde la compañía tiene oficinas: ____________________

____

3. el número de teléfono de su oficina en Los Ángeles: ____________________

4. el precio que cobra por un viaje de ida y vuelta de Los Ángeles a Tijuana: ____________________

5. para dónde tiene salidas diarias: ____________________

6. otros servicios que ofrece la compañía: ____________________

____

Nombre ______________________ Sección ____________ Fecha ____________

Lectura After reading this **lectura,** get together with a partner and take turns answering the following questions.

En Latinoamérica, los automóviles no están al alcance° de la mayoría del pueblo. En las ciudades, el movimiento de pasajeros se lleva a cabo,° principalmente, en los autobuses de los servicios de transporte público, aunque° unas pocas ciudades tienen trenes subterráneos (Metro).° El servicio interurbano° también depende, generalmente, de los autobuses, pero algunos países cuentan con extensas redes ferroviarias.° Cuando viaje° a Latinoamérica no espere° encontrar la calidad en el servicio de transporte público a que Ud. está acostumbrado° en los Estados Unidos. En la mayor parte° de las ciudades latinoamericanas, los autobuses son viejos,° incómodos,° y pueden no estar en buenas condiciones de mantenimiento.° No espere tampoco poder alquilar, para conducir Ud. mismo, un coche del último modelo y con pocas millas.°

En cuanto a los taxis, a veces no tienen taxímetros y, en algunas ciudades, no tienen un color especial que los identifique. Tomar ese tipo de taxis, en algunas ciudades, puede ser peligroso.°

al... *within reach*
se... *takes place*
although
trenes... *subway*
intercities
redes... *railroads lines*
Cuando... *when traveling / expect*
está... *take for granted*
the majority
old / uncomfortable
maintenance
con... *with low mileage*
risky

1. En Latinoamérica, ¿por qué se realiza el transporte de pasajeros principalmente en autobuses?
2. ¿Qué es el Metro?
3. ¿Cómo son generalmente los autobuses?
4. ¿Qué taxis pueden ser peligrosos en algunas ciudades de Latinoamérica?

Y en los Estados Unidos...

1. ¿Por qué en tantas ciudades la gente apenas (*barely*) usa el servicio de transporte público?
2. ¿Cómo es el servicio del transporte público en relación con el de Latinoamérica?

Un dicho

Al que madruga Dios lo ayuda. *The early bird catches the worm.*

Trivia

Passenger Transportation in Mexico

Land:

Mexico's network of roadways is more extensive than any paved road system in Latin America. Their undivided or two-lane highways are known as **carreteras,** and multi-lane expressways are **autopistas.** The speed limit on **autopistas** is 70 mph (110 km/h) for automobiles and 60 mph (95 km/h) for buses and trucks. Most **autopistas** are toll roads or **autopistas de cuota.** Something peculiar about these cuotas is that they include traveler's insurance (**seguro de viajero**), but the **cuotas** are among the costliest in the world.

Train:

All the regions of the country are connected by railways, but most of the system is used for transportation of merchandise and freight. Exceptions are small sections assigned to the government of the states which are used for passenger transportation and the Copper Canyon railway which is extensively used for tourism. This railway is locally known as **El Chepe** and connects Chihuahua City in central Mexico with **Los Mochis** in the Pacific Ocean. It runs through the Copper Canyon or **Barranca del Cobre,** a group of six canyons in the **Sierra Madre Occidental** or **Sierra Tarahumara.** The entire canyon system is much larger, and portions of it are deeper, than the Grand Canyon in Arizona. A journey through the **Sierra** is enthralling, and the scenery is remarkable.

Air:

Mexico has more than 1,800 airports, and their infrastructure is the most advanced in Latin America. Mexico City International Airport is the largest in Latin America and one of the largest in the world. It transports more than 25 million passengers a year. There are more than 70 domestic airline companies in Mexico, but only two of them, **Aeroméxico** and **Mexicana de Aviación,** are major airlines. Nevertheless, flying even on the small airlines is considered safe.

Sea:

Millions of tourists arrive every year in Cancun, Costa Maya, Cozumel, Acapulco, Puerto Vallarta, and other Mexican ports. They travel to these destinations on popular cruise ships.

Lección 9

El transporte de mercancías

Objectives

Structures

- Possessive pronouns
- Reflexive constructions
- Command forms: **Ud.** and **Uds.**
- Uses of object pronouns with command forms

Business Communication

- Transporting merchandise by air, train, or truck
- Old problems and new solutions regarding the transportation of merchandise between two countries

El Sr. Paz averigua el coste[1] del flete por los distintos medios de transporte disponibles.

En la estación de ferrocarril:

Sr. Paz —Necesito enviar un cargamento de productos de artesanía a Los Ángeles, California, y quiero saber cuáles son sus tarifas.

Empleado —¿Qué tipo de artesanías desea transportar?

Sr. Paz —Alfarería, artículos de vidrio soplado y de cuero, y tejidos de lana, de algodón y de otras fibras.

Empleado —La alfarería y el vidrio soplado son muy frágiles, por eso su tarifa es muy alta: $32,50 por kilogramo de peso. Los demás pagan $825 por metro cúbico de volumen.

Sr. Paz —¿Uds. transportan la mercancía hasta Los Ángeles?

Empleado —No, señor. Nosotros la llevamos hasta la frontera y allí la mercancía se transborda a ferrocarriles americanos. Las líneas de los ferrocarriles de los dos países no son compatibles.

Sr. Paz —Supongo que este transbordo aumenta el riesgo de roturas y averías y aumenta el precio del seguro.

Empleado —Sí, un poco. Pero menos de lo que Ud. ahorra en el flete. Además, si el embalaje es bueno, apenas ocurren daños.

---

[1]**Coste** is mostly used in Spain; in Latin America, **costo** is more commonly used in business.

Sr. Paz —¿Tengo que tratar con la compañía de ferrocarriles americanos?
Empleado —No, señor, nosotros nos responsabilizamos del transporte de la mercancía desde aquí hasta Los Ángeles, y nos encargamos de los trámites de aduana en la frontera.

El Sr. Paz llama por teléfono a la oficina de Camiones Correas, S.A. de C. V.[1]

Empleado —Camiones Correas. Ayude a México utilizando transportes nacionales. Buenos días.
Sr. Paz —Buenos días. ¿Uds. transportan mercancías a los Estados Unidos?
Empleado —Sí, señor, ¿qué se le ofrece?
Sr. Paz —Necesito transportar un cargamento de artesanías desde una fábrica de aquí a Los Ángeles. ¿Cuáles son sus tarifas?
Empleado —¿Se trata de un volumen grande de mercancías?
Sr. Paz —Sí, pero creo que todo cabe en un camión grande. ¿Los suyos son grandes?
Empleado —Sí. Podemos dejarle un contenedor en la fábrica; ellos lo cargan, y nosotros nos encargamos de entregárselo en su establecimiento comercial en Los Ángeles.
Sr. Paz —¿No tienen que transbordar la mercancía en la frontera?
Empleado —No, cambiamos de tráiler, pero los artículos van en el mismo contenedor de aquí a Los Ángeles.
Sr. Paz —¿Los camiones mexicanos pueden entrar en los Estados Unidos?
Empleado —Sí, de acuerdo con el Tratado de Libre Comercio.
Sr. Paz —¿Uds. descargan la mercancía en nuestro almacén?
Empleado —No, señor. La carga y la descarga corren por cuenta del cliente.
Sr. Paz —¿Qué documentos debo entregarles?
Empleado —Mire, mi jefe no está aquí ahora. Llame más tarde o, mejor, venga aquí y hable con él directamente.
Sr. Paz —Está bien. Llamo o voy más tarde.

En la compañía del expreso aéreo:

Sr. Paz —Necesito enviar a Los Ángeles artículos de vidrio soplado que son muy frágiles.
Empleada —Muy bien, señor. Transportamos paquetes a todo el mundo.
Sr. Paz —¿Cuál es la tarifa para ese tipo de artículo?
Empleada —Bueno, de aquí a Los Ángeles es $57,75 por kilogramo o por decímetro cúbico, de acuerdo con la relación entre peso y volumen.
Sr. Paz —Es casi el doble del transporte por tierra.
Empleada —Sí, pero ahorra tiempo.
Sr. Paz —Me pregunto si el ahorro en tiempo compensa el aumento en el coste.
Empleada —Eso depende de su urgencia en recibir la mercancía.
Sr. Paz —Sí, sí. Bueno, voy a pensarlo. Gracias.

---

[1]**S.A. de C.V.** stands for **Sociedad Anónima de Capital Variable.** See ***Notas culturales*** in ***Lección 12*** for more information on business corporations.

Nombre ______________________ Sección ____________ Fecha ____________

¡Escuchemos! While listening to the dialogue, circle **V (verdadero)** if the statement is true or **F (falso)** if it is false.

1.	El Sr. Paz averigua el costo del flete por ferrocarril.	V	F
2.	El cuero y el algodón son muy frágiles.	V	F
3.	Los trenes mexicanos llegan hasta Los Ángeles.	V	F
4.	Las líneas de los ferrocarriles de los Estados Unidos y de México son compatibles.	V	F
5.	El trasbordo de la mercancía aumenta el costo del seguro.	V	F
6.	Si el embalaje es bueno ocurren pocos daños.	V	F
7.	El Sr. Paz cree que toda su mercancía cabe en un camión.	V	F
8.	El costo de la carga y la descarga lo paga Camiones Correas.	V	F
9.	El transporte aéreo de mercancías es barato.	V	F
10.	Si tiene urgencia en recibir la mercancía debe usar el transporte aéreo.	V	F

Audio VOCABULARIO

Cognados

compatible
cúbico(a)
el decímetro
el doble
la estación
expreso(a)
frágil
el metro
nacional
la relación
el tráiler, la rastra (Cuba), la gandola (Venezuela)
la urgencia

Nombres

la alfarería *pottery (i.e., the craft); pottery shop*
el algodón *cotton*
el aumento *increase, raise*
la avería *damage (sustained by merchandise during transport)*
el camión *truck, bus (Méx.)*
el cargamento, la carga *shipment, load*
el contenedor *container*
el daño *damage*
la descarga *unloading*
el embalaje *packing*
el establecimiento *establishment, shop*
el ferrocarril, el tren *railroad, train*
la fibra *fiber*
el flete *freight*
la frontera *border, frontier*
la lana *wool*
el mundo *world*
el riesgo *risk*

Nombre ______________________ Sección ____________ Fecha ____________

la rotura *breakage*
el tejido *fabric*
el tiempo *time*
la tierra *land*
el trámite *procedure*
el transbordo, el trasbordo *transfer*
el transporte por tierra *land transportation*
el Tratado de Libre Comercio (TLC) (*North American*) *Free Trade Agreement* (*NAFTA*)
el vidrio *glass*

Verbos

aumentar *to increase*
averiguar *to find out*
ayudar *to help*
caber *to fit*
cargar *to load*
descargar *to unload*
encargarse (de) *to take charge* (*of*), *to see after*
entrar *to enter*
llevar *to carry*
ocurrir, suceder *to happen, to occur*
preguntarse *to wonder, to ask oneself*
responsabilizarse *to take responsibility for*
suponer[1] *to suppose*
transbordar, trasbordar *to transfer*
transportar *to transport*
tratar *to deal*

Adjetivos

aéreo(a) *air*
alto(a) *high*
distinto(a) *different*
soplado(a) *blown*

Otras palabras y expresiones

a todo el mundo *the whole world over*
apenas *barely, hardly*
bueno... *well . . .*
correr con *to be in charge* (*of*)
los (las) demás *the rest, the others*
más tarde *later*
(un) poco *a little*
¿Qué se le ofrece? *What can I do for you?*
Se trata de... *It is a question of . . .*

VOCABULARIO ADICIONAL

Audio

afianzada y asegurada *bonded and insured*
altura restringida *low clearance*
cargador a granel *bulk loader*
carril adyacente a la acera *curbside bus lane*
carga líquida *wet bulk*
consignado a la orden consigned to order
contenedor sellado y refrigerado *sealed and refrigerated container*
convenio *convention, agreement*
cuneta *roll curb*
empaque (de calidad) industrial *industrial crating*
encomendar [ ] *to entrust,* 9 (**correction not clear. Raise a query)**
entrega a domicilio sin cargo *free house delivery*
estación de peaje *mainline toll*
estadía *lay time*
falta de entrega *non-delivery*
garantía limitada *cost-ceiling warranty*

[1]Conjugates like **poner.**

merma en transporte (tránsito) *transit loss*
porteador(a) *carrier*
prevalecer *to prevail, to predominate*
realizarse *to take place*
retraso *delay*
señal de paso a nivel *crossbuck*
servicio de mensajería aérea *air courier service provider*
servicio de puerta a puerta *first and last mile*
servicio de punta a punta *end-to-end service*
servicio de transporte nocturno *trucking overnight service*
sobrecupo *overcrowding*
tarifas de fletamento *charter rates*
transporte de contenedores *container shipping*
transportista *transporter*
viaje de retorno (regreso) *backhaul*

Otras palabras y expresiones relacionadas con el transporte de mercancías

el barco, el buque *ship, boat*
la camioneta *van*
la carretera *highway*
cobrar o devolver (C.O.D.) *collect on delivery (C.O.D.)*
el (la) consignatario(a) *consignee*
costo, seguro y flete (C.S.F.) *cost, insurance, and freight (C.I.F.)*
el destino *destination*
el itinerario *itinerary*
la guía *consignment note (trucking)*
libre a bordo (L.A.B.), franco a bordo (F.A.B.) *free on board (F.O.B.)*
el peso bruto *gross weight*
el peso muerto *dead weight*
el peso neto *net weight*
por vía aérea *by air*
por vía férrea *by rail*
por vía marítima *by boat*
la tara *tare*
la tonelada *ton*

Search

iLrn

Notas Culturales

- The transportation of merchandise between the United States and Latin American countries is carried out mostly by sea and air, with the exception of Mexico. Land transport between Mexico and the United States is carried out mostly by truck, since railroad lines in the two countries are not compatible. Trucking has increased tremendously as a result of NAFTA (North American Free Trade Agreement) or TLCAN (**Tratado de Libre Comercio de América del Norte**).
- According to the North American Free Trade Agreement (NAFTA) (1994), Mexican trucks were supposed to be allowed to circulate in the United States and Canada beginning December 18, 1995. Nevertheless, for many years, Mexican trucks were not permitted to enter more than 20 miles into the United States territory. At last, after many complaints from Mexico, the U.S. government agreed to fully comply with the treaty beginning June 1, 2002. Since then, 100 Mexican trucking companies have had unlimited legal access to U.S. roads to haul international cargo as part of a pilot program. In return, 100 U.S. trucking companies will be allowed to operate in Mexico, but at a later date. Nevertheless, because of truckers' opposition in both countries, the treaty has not yet been fully implemented.
- Panama has the most important merchant fleet in Latin America. Indeed, the Panamanian merchant navy is the fourth largest in the world, according to the number of its ships, but in most of these ships the only thing that is Panamanian is the flag. Registering a ship in Panama and flying the Panamanian flag are, in most cases, ways to avoid the regulations and high salaries paid in the owner's country.

Nombre ______________________ Sección ____________ Fecha ____________

Actividades

Dígame... Answer the following questions, basing your answers on the dialogues.

1. ¿Qué está haciendo el Sr. Paz?

2. ¿Adónde va primero el Sr. Paz?

3. ¿Qué quiere transportar el Sr. Paz?

4. La tarifa de la alfarería y del vidrio soplado es muy alta. ¿Por qué?

5. ¿Transporta el ferrocarril mexicano la mercancía hasta Los Ángeles?

6. ¿Qué hacen con la mercancía en la frontera?

7. El transbordo de la mercancía hace el seguro más caro. ¿Por qué?

8. ¿Qué sucede si el embalaje no es bueno?

9. ¿Quiénes se responsabilizan del transporte de los artículos del Sr. Paz? ¿Hasta dónde?

10. ¿Cabe toda la mercancía del Sr. Paz en un camión?

11. ¿Se encarga la compañía transportadora de la carga y descarga de la mercancía?

12. ¿Va a utilizar el Sr. Paz la compañía de expreso aéreo?

Nombre ______________________ Sección ____________ Fecha ____________

Hablemos

Hablemos Interview a classmate, using the following questions. When you have finished, switch roles.

1. Cuando Ud. envía paquetes, ¿los envía por tierra o por expreso aéreo?
2. ¿Qué compañías de transporte de paquetes conoce Ud.?
3. ¿Envía Ud. sus paquetes por correo o por una agencia privada de transporte de paquetes?
4. ¿Se responsabiliza la compañía de las averías que ocurren durante el transporte?
5. Cuando Ud. envía paquetes, ¿quién se encarga del embalaje?
6. ¿Prefiere Ud. tejidos de algodón, de lana o de otras fibras?
7. ¿En qué casos piensa Ud. que el ahorro en tiempo compensa el aumento en el costo del transporte?

Quiz

Vamos a practicar

A Rewrite the following sentences, substituting a possessive pronoun for the words in italics.

Modelo Debe comparar las tarifas de ellos con *las tarifas que tenemos nosotros.*
Debe comparar las tarifas de ellos con **las nuestras.**

1. Esa carga es *mi carga.*

____

2. Mi cargamento viene por expreso aéreo. ¿Cómo viene *tu cargamento*?

____

3. Aquellos contenedores son *tus contenedores.*

____

4. Esos precios son altos pero *los precios que tenemos nosotros* son muy bajos.

____

5. Cargamos la mercancía en nuestro establecimiento y la descargamos en el *establecimiento de Ud.*

____

6. Ésta es mi mercancía. ¿Dónde está *la mercancía de él*?

____

Nombre ______________________ Sección ____________ Fecha ____________

7. ¿Puedo utilizar tu camión? *Mi camión* no arranca.

____

8. Mis tarifas son más altas que *las tarifas de ellos.*

____

B Rewrite the following sentences using the **Ud.** and **Uds.** command forms.

MODELO Tienen que utilizar dos contenedores.
Utilicen dos contenedores.

1. Uds. no lo deben compensar por los daños a la mercancía.

____

2. La tienen que transbordar en la frontera.

____

3. Los tienen que transportar por ferrocarril.

____

4. No se deben responsabilizar de la carga.

____

5. Uds. no los deben descargar ahora.

____

6. Lo tiene que ayudar con los trámites de aduana.

____

7. No se la deben entregar ahora.

____

8. No me la debe dejar hoy.

____

9. Ud. nos lo tiene que preguntar.

____

10. Ud. se la tiene que aumentar.

____

Nombre ______________________ Sección ______________ Fecha ______________

Sirva usted de intérprete

With two classmates, play the roles of a shipping company employee, a potential customer, and the interpreter who helps them communicate. Switch roles until each of you has played the interpreter's role.

Cliente —Uds. transportan mercancías a Monterrey, México, ¿verdad?

Intérprete —______________________________

Empleado(a) —*Well, we take them to El Paso, Texas. From there another company takes them to Monterrey, Mexico.*

Intérprete —______________________________

Cliente —¿Hacen transbordo de las mercancías en El Paso?

Intérprete —______________________________

Empleado(a) —*No, sir/ma'am. The merchandise continues in the same containers, although we change the trucks and the drivers.*

Intérprete —______________________________

Cliente —Eso está bien, porque en los transbordos ocurren muchas averías.

Intérprete —______________________________

Empleado(a) —*Yes, sir/ma'am. What type of merchandise do you have?*

Intérprete —______________________________

Cliente —Tejidos de algodón y artículos de cuero.

Intérprete —______________________________

Empleado(a) —*In that case we charge you the volume rate: $50 per cubic meter.*

Intérprete —______________________________

Cliente —El seguro lo cargan aparte, ¿no?

Intérprete —______________________________

Empleado(a) —*Yes, sir/ma'am.*

Intérprete —______________________________

Cliente —Voy a pensar en la posibilidad de enviar la mercancía por expreso aéreo.

Intérprete —______________________________

Empleado(a) —*Do you think that the savings in time compensates for the increase in cost?*

Intérprete —______________________________

Cliente —Eso me pregunto; necesitamos los tejidos con urgencia.

Intérprete —______________________________

Nombre ______________________ **Sección** ____________ **Fecha** ____________

Empleado(a) —*By highway they take only two days. We load the merchandise at your warehouse and deliver it to the factory in Monterrey.*

Intérprete —____

Sirva usted de traductor(a)

Your company needs to transport items from Manzanillo, Mexico. Review the **Vocabulario adicional** in this lesson, and then translate for your boss the following advertisement that appears in the Yellow Pages of the local telephone book.

Transportes

Calinda

SERVICIOS POR TODAS LAS VÍAS

38-71-71

Nos especializamos en el transporte de artesanías frágiles: alfarería, cerámica, vidrio soplado, etc.

Transportamos toda clase de mercancía...

- por vía aérea, desde el aeropuerto local
- por vía marítima, en buques de más de 2.500 toneladas de peso muerto
- por vía férrea, directamente hasta la frontera
- por tierra, en camiones y camionetas nuevos y con poca tara.

Tenemos contratos con varias alfarerías locales que venden sus productos con costo, seguro y flete incluidos o libre a bordo, pero no aceptamos mercancía para cobrar o devolver.

Nos encargamos del embalaje de su mercancía y la entregamos en el domicilio del consignatario.

En estas situaciones

With a partner, act out the following situations in Spanish.

1. You need to ship merchandise from Guadalajara, Mexico to Dallas, Texas. You are now at the office of a local transport company. Ask the clerk if that transport company ships merchandise by highway to Texas, who takes responsibility for the shipment, and if they apply the weight rate or volume rate. Say that you wish to transport fresh vegetables. Ask if they load the merchandise at the warehouse, if they deliver it to the addressee's loading zone, how much they charge per kilogram, and how much the insurance is.

Nombre ______________________ **Sección** __________ **Fecha** __________

2. You are an employee of a shipping agency. Help a customer who doesn't speak English. Ask if his/her merchandise has to be loaded at the factory, what type of merchandise it is, and if the shipment is large. Say that, if the merchandise is fragile, the possibility of damage is greater, which makes insurance costs higher. Let the customer also know that shipping by air costs double the cost of shipping by land transport.

Casos

With you and a partner playing the roles, work through the following scenarios.

1. A shipping agency employee and a customer discuss options for sending goods to the United States from Mexico.
2. An air express employee and a customer talk about the benefits and drawbacks of air transport.

Un paso más

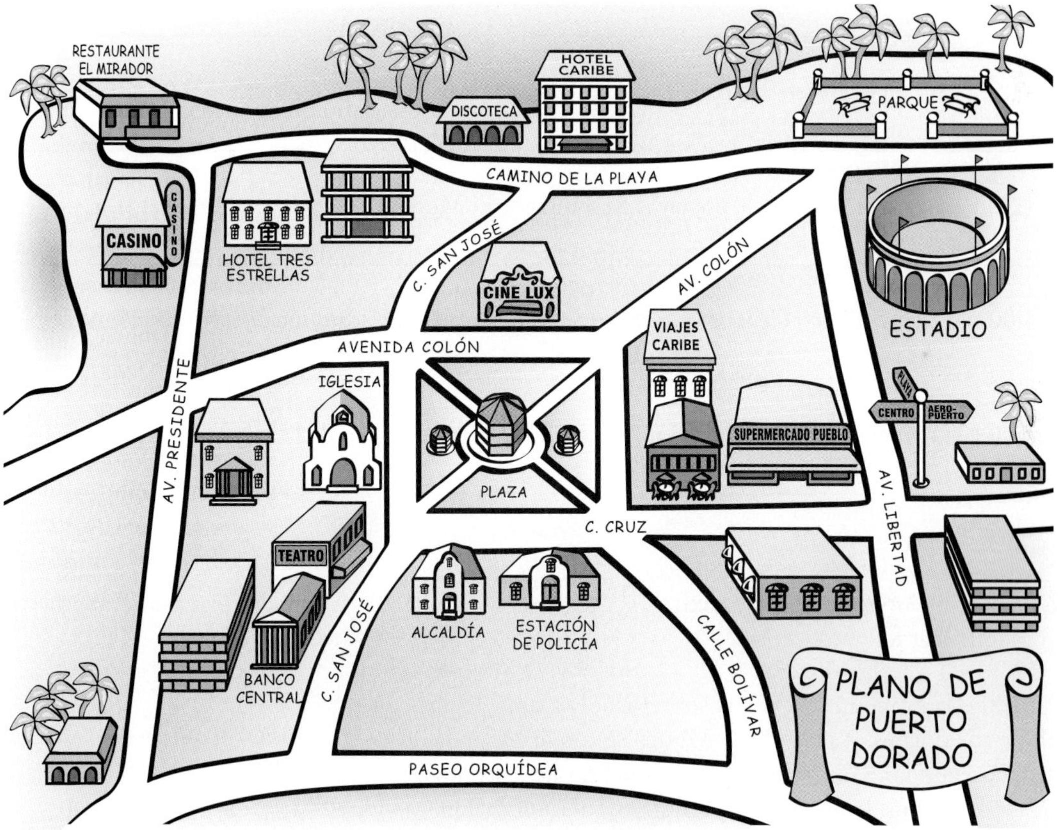

Nombre ______________________ **Sección** __________ **Fecha** __________

You are in Puerto Dorado as a sales representative for a U.S. firm. You are staying at Hotel Caribe on Camino de la Playa. You need to ask for directions to find out the easiest way to get from one sales appointment to another. Work with a partner to ask for directions, and then switch roles. Use the following words and phrases:

a la derecha	*to the right*
a la izquierda	*to the left*
Baje...	*Go down . . .*
Doble (Voltee)...	*Turn . . .*
la esquina de	*the corner of, the intersection of*
hasta..., hasta llegar a...	*up to . . . , until you reach . . .*
Siga derecho.	*Go straight ahead.*
Suba...	*Go up . . .*

1. 9:00 A.M.: en la alcaldía (*City Hall*) en la esquina de las Calles Cruz y San José

   ____

2. 11:00 A.M.: en el Hotel Tres Estrellas, en la esquina de la Avenida Presidente y el Camino de la Playa

   ____

3. 1:30 P.M.: comer con un cliente en el Restaurante El Mirador

   ____

4. 3:00 P.M.: en el Banco Central (*Central Bank*) en la Calle San José

   ____

5. 5:00 P.M.: en el estadio (*stadium*) en Avenida Libertad y Camino de la Playa

   ____

Lectura

After reading this **lectura,** get together with a partner and take turns answering the questions that follow.

En 2004, la economía mexicana sobrepasó° la marca de un billón° de dólares, y en el 2007, México se convirtió° en la decimosegunda° economía más grande del mundo. Como en casi todos los demás países del mundo, su economía ha retrocedido° en los últimos años debido a la crisis financiera mundial.

surpassed
trillion / **se...** *became*
12th
ha... *has grown worse*

Ciertamente, México empezó° a crecer rápidamente desde la firma del Tratado de Libre Comercio de América del Norte, pero desde entonces el país ha

began

firmado° nuevos acuerdos con más de 40 países, entre los que se encuentran° las naciones del Mercado Común Europeo y Japón.

ha... *have signed*
entre... *including*

Actualmente, más del 90% del intercambio comercial mexicano es con los países con que tiene tratados de libre comercio.

1. Entre las economías del mundo, ¿qué lugar ocupó México en 2007?
2. ¿A qué se debe el retroceso de la economía mexicana en los últimos años?
3. ¿Cuándo comenzó a crecer rápidamente la economía mexicana?
4. Actualmente, ¿con qué países comercia México, principalmente?

Y su país...

1. ¿Qué lugar ocupa entre las economías del mundo?
2. ¿Con qué países tiene gran intercambio comercial?

Un dicho

Carro parado no gana flete. *Inactivity kills business.*

Trivia

In the last decade, Latin America's commodity-led export boom revealed the limits of the region's transportation infrastructure, and pushed governments to focus on infrastructure investment in this sector. As political leaders realized that export competitiveness greatly depends on a modern transportation infrastructure, they began to increase public investments, and to attract private-sector investors. Generally, public investment prioritized roads, which carry most of domestic traffic, while private investors were more interested in airports and seaports, which carry most of the hard currency exports.

LECCIÓN 10 CONTRATANDO PERSONAL

OBJECTIVES

Structures

- The preterit of regular verbs
- The preterit of **ser, ir,** and **dar**
- Uses of **por** and **para**

Business Communication

- Conducting an interview to hire personnel

La Sra. Artiles, jefa de personal de la firma Pérez y Hno.,[1] de Puerto Rico, contrata empleados de oficina.

Por teléfono:

Empleada	—Agencia ABC, a sus órdenes.
Sra. Artiles	—¿Es la agencia de empleos?
Empleada	—Sí, señora. ¿En qué puedo servirle?
Sra. Artiles	—Necesito un oficinista con experiencia y buenas referencias.
Empleada	—Tengo dos candidatos: uno que trabajó en la oficina de una fábrica por dos años y otro que trabaja actualmente para un banco.
Sra. Artiles	—Bien, los espero mañana a las nueve. Mi dirección es Calle Hostos 54. Pregunten por la Sra. Artiles.

La primera entrevista:

Recepcionista	—Sra. Artiles, llegó la oficinista que viene de la agencia de empleos.
Sra. Artiles	—Si ya llenó la solicitud de empleo, dígale que pase. (*A la candidata*) Buenos días.
Candidata	—Buenos días, Sra. Artiles. Me llamo María Rodríguez.
Sra. Artiles	—Mucho gusto, Srta. Rodríguez. (*Lee la solicitud.*) ¿Así que Ud. tiene experiencia en todo el trabajo de oficina?

[1]**Hno.: Hermano** (*Brother*)

Candidata	—Sí, señora. Sé trabajar con los sistemas operativos de *Windows* y *Macintosh*. Tengo experiencia con varios programas de composición de textos y de manejo de base de datos para minoristas y para mayoristas. Además, soy bilingüe.
Sra. Artiles	—¿Sabe utilizar los programas para la introducción de datos como *Excel* y *Access*?
Candidata	—Sí, señora. En la fábrica donde trabajé hasta el mes pasado, usé varios, incluidos los que Ud. mencionó.
Sra. Artiles	—¿Por qué no continuó trabajando allí?
Candidata	—Renuncié porque solicité un aumento y no me lo dieron.
Sra. Artiles	—¿Cuándo fue eso?
Candidata	—El día 30 del mes pasado, pero no fui a la agencia de empleos hasta el lunes.
Sra. Artiles	—Bien. Aquí pagamos $450 semanales. El horario de trabajo es de ocho de la mañana a cuatro y media de la tarde. A las doce, tiene treinta minutos para almorzar.
Candidata	—¿Cuáles son los beneficios adicionales?
Sra. Artiles	—Ofrecemos un seguro de salud y un plan de retiro para los empleados.
Candidata	—¿En qué consiste el plan de retiro?
Sra. Artiles	—Es un Keogh en el que nosotros ponemos una cantidad equivalente al 8 por ciento de su sueldo, y Ud. contribuye con una cantidad igual que le descontamos de su sueldo.
Candidata	—¿Quiénes deciden dónde se invierte ese dinero?
Sra. Artiles	—La empresa y Ud., como indica la ley.
Candidata	—El plan de salud, ¿ofrece opciones?
Sra. Artiles	—Sí, puede escoger entre una HMO[1] local y un plan de la Blue Cross, que es mucho más caro.
Candidata	—Está bien. Otra pregunta. ¿Cuánto tiempo dan de vacaciones?
Sra. Artiles	—Dos semanas al año.
Candidata	—Por favor, ¿tiene una descripción del contenido de trabajo del puesto?
Sra. Artiles	—Sí, señorita. La recepcionista le va a dar un paquete con todo el material que debe leer antes de firmar el contrato, si es que decidimos emplearla a Ud.
Candidata	—¿Cuándo voy a tener una respuesta al respecto?
Sra. Artiles	—Mañana por la tarde.
Candidata	—Por favor, si Ud. llama y no estoy en casa, déjeme un mensaje en la máquina contestadora.

¡Escuchemos!

While listening to the dialogue, circle **V (verdadero)** if the statement is true or **F (falso)** if it is false.

1. La Sra. Artiles es la jefa de ventas de la firma Pérez y Hno.	V	F
2. Ella necesita un oficinista con experiencia y buenas referencias.	V	F
3. Uno de los candidatos trabajó en un banco por dos años.	V	F
4. La candidata tiene experiencia en el manejo de programas de base de datos para detallistas.	V	F

[1]**HMO** (*health maintenance organization*) **organización de mantenimiento de la salud**

5. Ella renunció a su trabajo anterior porque no le dieron el aumento que solicitó.	V	F
6. Los empleados de la Sra. Artiles tienen una hora para almorzar.	V	F
7. Solamente los empleados contribuyen al plan de retiro de la empresa.	V	F
8. El plan de salud ofrece solamente dos opciones.	V	F
9. La candidata debe leer el contenido de trabajo del puesto antes de firmar el contrato.	V	F
10. La candidata no tiene máquina contestadora.	V	F

Audio
VOCABULARIO

Cognados

bilingüe
el (la) candidato(a)
equivalente
la experiencia
el material
la opción
el personal
la referencia
el sistema operativo
las vacaciones[1]

Nombres

el año *year*
el beneficio adicional (marginal), las prestaciones adicionales *fringe benefit(s)*
la composición (el procesamiento) de textos *word processing*
el (la) detallista, el (la) minorista *retailer*
el empleo *employment*
la entrevista *interview*
el hermano (hno.) *brother*
el horario *schedule*
la introducción de datos *data entry*
la mañana *morning*
la máquina contestadora *answering machine*
el (la) mayorista *wholesaler*
el mensaje *message*
el mes *month*
el (la) oficinista *office clerk*
el programa de manejo (administración) de base (de datos) *database management program*
el puesto, la posición, el cargo *job, post, position*
la respuesta *answer*
el retiro, la jubilación *retirement*
la salud *health*
la semana *week*
la solicitud *application*
el sueldo, el salario *salary*
el trabajo *work*

Verbos

almorzar (o:ue) *to have lunch*
consistir (en) *to consist (of)*
continuar[2] *to continue*

[1]**Vacaciones** is rarely used in the singular form.
[2]First-person present indicative: **yo continúo**

Nombre ______________________ Sección ____________ Fecha ____________

Adjetivos

igual (que) *equal (to), the same (as)*
incluido(a) *included, including*
pasado(a) *last, past*
semanal, a la semana *weekly*

Otras palabras y expresiones

a sus órdenes *at your service*
actualmente *presently*
al año, anual *yearly*
al respecto *about that, about the matter*
así que *so*
la descripción del contenido de trabajo *job description*
Dígale que pase. *Tell her to come in.*
en casa *at home*
Mucho gusto [en conocerlo(la)]. *Pleased to meet you.*
se invierte *is invested*
contratar, emplear *to hire, to employ*
contribuir *to contribute*
escoger[1] *to choose*
esperar *to expect*
invertir (e:ie) *to invest*
mencionar *to mention*
poner[2] *to put*
preguntar *to ask*
renunciar (a) *to resign (from)*
solicitar[3] *to ask for, to apply for*

VOCABULARIO ADICIONAL

Audio

cada vez más *increasinly*
con sede *based in*
conocimiento de embarque *bill of lading*
en cuanto a *related to, in reference to*
en lugar de *instead of*
enfrentar *to face*
falta de *lack of*
fuente de talento *source of talent*
grado *degree*
manejo management, handling
manifiesto *manifest (A document listing and describing the cargo contents.)*
margen *margin (The difference between the cost of goods sold and the sales price.)*
nación más favorecida *most favored nation*
país de origen *country of origin*
prestan servicios *render services*
retención *keeping back*
sumado(a) *added*

Términos relacionados con un empleo

a medio tiempo, a medio día, a media jornada *part-time*
a tiempo completo, a jornada completa *full-time*
archivar *to file*
el (la) aspirante, el (la) postulante *applicant*
la carta de recomendación *letter of recommendation*

---

[1]First-person present indicative: **yo escojo**
[2]Irregular first-person present indicative: **yo pongo**
[3]**Aplicar** and **calificar,** respectively, do not have such meanings in Spanish.

Nombre ______________________ Sección ____________ Fecha ____________

despedir, cesantear *to fire (i.e. an employee)*
ganar *to earn*
el jornal *daily wage(s)*
mensual *monthly*
la preparación *qualification*
quincenal *biweekly, every two weeks*
el resumen, el resumé, la hoja de vida, el curriculum vitae (*Méx.*) *résumé, vita*
reunir (llenar) los requisitos[4] *to qualify*
el tiempo extra *overtime*

Otros materiales y equipos de oficina

el abrecartas *letter opener*
el archivo, el archivador (*España*) *file, filing cabinet*
la banda elástica, la liga (*Méx., Cuba*), **la goma** (*Puerto Rico*) *rubber band*
la chinche, la tachuela (*Puerto Rico*) *thumbtack*
el destacador *reference marker, highlighter*
el escritorio, el buró *desk*
la grapa, la presilla (*Cuba*) *staple*
la grapadora, la presilladora (*Cuba*), **la corchetera** (*Chile*) *stapler*
el impresor, la impresora *printer*
el lápiz *pencil*
la máquina copiadora, la fotocopiadora *copy machine*
la máquina de escribir *typewriter*
el marcador *marker*
la pizarra, la tablilla de avisos *bulletin board*
el reloj *clock, watch*
la silla *chair*
el sujetapapeles, la presilla (*Cuba*) *paper clip*

Search

iLrn

Notas Culturales

- Big and small enterprises in this country have an increased need for bilingual employees. Some are trying to meet the needs of immigrant customers who do not speak English, some because increasing globalization has made it difficult to do business in one language. In any case, if an enterprise wants to do business with the Hispanic population, here or abroad, it needs to hire and retain Spanish-speaking employees.
- If you plan to start a business abroad, remember that mercantile and labor legislation differ a great deal from country to country. Although Puerto Rico is a U.S. Commonwealth, not all U.S. laws are observed in that country. Besides, while some countries encourage foreign investments, others limit or restrict them.
- In most Spanish-speaking countries, government agencies and some private businesses are required to request bids from suppliers when dealing with major purchases.
- If you are thinking about opening an office or factory in Mexico, it will be important for you to familiarize yourself with Mexican labor laws. According to an article of the Mexican constitution, anybody who is hired and signs a contract to render services is entitled to rights that his/her American counterparts may not have. For example, industrial, agricultural, and mining enterprises must provide housing, schools, medical facilities, and other social services to their employees. Although many Mexican companies do not comply with these regulations, foreign companies may experience serious problems if they do not.
- The Mexican constitution reserves some lines of business for the government or for Mexican nationals. Mining and oil enterprises are two such industries.

---

[4] *requirements*

Nombre ______________________ Sección ____________ Fecha ____________

Actividades

Dígame...

Answer the following questions, basing your answer on the dialogues.

1. ¿Para qué llama la Sra. Artiles a una agencia de empleos?

2. ¿Quiénes son los candidatos que tiene la agencia de empleos?

3. ¿Cuándo debe la agencia enviar a los candidatos a ver a la Sra. Artiles?

4. ¿Qué llenó la candidata cuando llegó a la oficina?

5. ¿Qué sabe hacer la candidata?

6. ¿Con qué programas para computadoras trabajó la señorita en la fábrica?

7. ¿Hasta cuándo trabajó en la fábrica la candidata?

8. ¿Cuándo renunció a su puesto y por qué?

9. ¿Cuánto paga la Sra. Artiles?

10. ¿Cuánto qué por ciento descuenta la compañía del sueldo de los empleados para poner en el plan de retiro?

11. ¿Sabe la candidata si van a emplearla? ¿Cuándo lo va a saber?

12. Si la Sra. Artiles llama a la candidata y ella no está en su casa, ¿qué debe hacer?

Nombre ______________________ Sección ____________ Fecha ____________

13. ¿Reúne la candidata los requisitos para ocupar la posición?

____

Hablemos Interview a classmate, using the following questions. When you have finished, switch roles.

1. ¿Trabajó Ud. alguna vez (*ever*) en un banco?
2. ¿Fue Ud. alguna vez a una agencia de empleos para buscar trabajo?
3. ¿Tiene Ud. experiencia en el trabajo de oficina?
4. ¿Sabe Ud. trabajar con algún programa de composición de textos? ¿Con cuál(es)?
5. ¿Cuál es el horario de trabajo de las oficinas de la universidad?
6. ¿Qué seguro de salud tiene Ud.?
7. ¿Quién paga su seguro de salud?
8. ¿Cuánto tiempo tiene Ud. de vacaciones al año?

Quiz

Vamos a practicar

A Rewrite the following sentences according to the change in the time or date of the event.

Modelo *Today:* La muchacha *llega* a la agencia de empleos a las nueve.
Yesterday: La muchacha **llegó** a la agencia de empleos a las nueve.

1. *Now:* La Sra. Artiles contrata a la candidata.

   An hour ago: ____

2. *Every day:* La oficinista almuerza en la cafetería.

   Last Friday: ____

3. *At present:* La Srta. Rodríguez renuncia a su empleo.

   Two months ago: ____

4. *The present one:* El aumento es pequeño.

   The one we received last year: ____

5. *Right now:* Tú vas a llenar la solicitud de retiro.

   Last June: ____

6. *Today:* Yo le doy el folleto al candidato.

   The day before yesterday: ____

Nombre ______________________ **Sección** ____________ **Fecha** ____________

B Complete the following sentences using **por** or **para,** as needed.

1. La muchacha trabajó en el banco __________ dos años.
2. El candidato va a la oficina __________ el pasillo.
3. El candidato va __________ la oficina.
4. Alguien pregunta __________ la Sra. Artiles.
5. Me dieron 20 minutos __________ comer algo.
6. ¿ __________ qué renunció a su empleo?
7. Las nuevas computadoras llegaron __________ expreso aéreo.
8. Cambiamos el aumento de sueldo __________ mayores prestaciones adicionales.
9. Dígale que necesito los programas __________ mañana.
10. Recibí un aumento __________ mi experiencia en el trabajo con computadoras.

Sirva usted de intérprete

With two classmates, play the roles of the job applicant, the manager, and the interpreter who helps them communicate. Switch roles until each of you has played the interpreter's role.

Candidato(a) —Ésta es la solicitud que llené. Aquí están todos mis datos.

Intérprete —______________________________

Gerente —*Are you working now?*

Intérprete —______________________________

Candidato(a) —No, señor(a), pero trabajé hasta el lunes pasado en un banco.

Intérprete —______________________________

Gerente —*Why did you leave the job?*

Intérprete —______________________________

Candidato(a) —Porque pedí un aumento de cien dólares al mes y me ofrecieron solamente treinta.

Intérprete —______________________________

Gerente —*Do you know how much we pay here?*

Intérprete —______________________________

Candidato(a) —Sí, la recepcionista me lo dijo.

Intérprete —______________________________

Gerente —*Fine, the job is from nine to five.*

Intérprete —______________________________

Nombre ______________________ Sección ____________ Fecha ____________

Candidato(a) —¿Cuánto tiempo dan para almorzar?

Intérprete —______________________

Gerente —*An hour.*

Intérprete —______________________

Candidato(a) —Qué tiempo dan de vacaciones?

Intérprete —______________________

Gerente —*One week a year.*

Intérprete —______________________

Candidato(a) —No es mucho. ¿Tienen plan de retiro?

Intérprete —______________________

Gerente —*Yes, at 65 years of age, our employees can retire at (with) 60% of their salary.*

Intérprete —______________________

Candidato(a) —Eso no es mucho tampoco.

Intérprete —______________________

Sirva usted de traductor

Review the **Vocabulario adicional** in this lesson, and then translate the following memo on a separate sheet of paper so that you can help Miss Martínez with preparations for the arrival of a new employee and the needs of the Sales Department.

MEMO

A: Srta. Paula Martínez, Jefa de Oficina

De: Srta. Mariana Cadena, Jefa de Compras

Asunto: Compra de equipos y material de oficina

Fecha: 3 de mayo de 2006

Tenemos un empleado nuevo. Necesitamos un escritorio con su silla, un archivo de metal y una computadora con su mesa.

Por otra parte, necesitamos una copiadora más y una pizarra de anuncios más grande. Además, necesitamos algunos materiales de oficina: grapadoras y grapas, sujetapapeles, bandas elásticas, lápices y bolígrafos.

Todo lo necesitamos con urgencia. Para evitar las demoras, no haga subasta.

Nombre ______________________ Sección ____________ Fecha ____________

En estas situaciones

With a partner, act out the following situations in Spanish.

1. You work for an employment agency and you are talking with a Spanish-speaking candidate who doesn't speak English. Ask if the applicant can drive a truck, has a driver's license in the United States, and can start to work tomorrow. Also ask him/her to fill out an employment application.
2. You went to Guatemala on vacation and have run out of money! Now you are interviewing for a job. Tell the personnel manager that you have already filled out the employment application, that you know how to operate personal computers, that you have experience with database management programs, and that you learned to work with computers at the university. Ask how much the company pays and if they offer any benefits. Also, find out if they have part-time, as well as full-time, work.
3. You are in Venezuela interviewing job candidates for your company. Ask each candidate about previous jobs, including company names, experience gained, length of employment, and reasons for resignations. Tell the applicants about the daily work schedule, wages, and benefits.

Casos

With you and a partner playing the roles, work through the following scenarios.

1. A personnel manager and an employment agency employee are talking on the telephone.
2. A personnel manager interviews a candidate for an office position.

Un paso más

A You are a new employee at a large company in Buenos Aires. Review the **Vocabulario adicional** in this lesson and use it and other vocabulary you have learned to formulate a list of questions to ask your fellow employees about the company and your job.

B You are in charge of ordering office supplies. Review the **Vocabulario adicional** in this lesson and use it and other vocabulary you have learned to make a list of the items needed.

C You are interested in applying for a job in Latin America, and you have researched job listings via the Internet. Read the ads and answer the questions to see if you are qualified for any of the positions advertised.

TECNOBOLSA

El portal de empleo de las nuevas tecnologías en Internet
(Un servicio gratuito de lanción.com/es)

Nombre ______________________ Sección ____________ Fecha ____________

OFERTA NO. 3

Datos generales de la oferta:
Nombre de la empresa: SKILLSOFT (GRUPO STERIA)
Puesto vacante: ANALISTA PROGRAMADOR ORACLE
Número de vacantes: 5
Descripción de oferta: LABORES DE ANÁLISIS Y DESARROLLO DE APLICACIONES ORACLE
País: Costa Rica
Ciudad: San José

Se ofrece:
Tipo de contrato: Indefinido
Jornada: Jornada completa
Remuneración: A discutir
Remuneración complementaria: Ejemplo: Vales de comida / Transporte

Requisitos personales:
Edad: Indiferente
Sexo: Indiferente
Idiomas: Español e inglés
Permiso de conducir: Sí
Vehículo propio: No
Disponibilidad para viajar: No

Experiencia profesional:
Años de experiencia: 3 o más
Tipo de empresa: Multinacional
Orientación de empresa: Telecomunicaciones y nuevas tecnologías
Puesto: Analista programador
Descripción del puesto/responsabilidades: Labores de análisis y desarrollo de aplicaciones Oracle

Operador Comercial

Información del puesto de trabajo
Jornada Laboral Completa
Sueldo Mensual Líquido: 160.000 pesos
El cargo operador comercial tiene como objetivo la atención integral de clientes en las oficinas comerciales de Chilexpress.
El postulante debe tener experiencia mínima de dos años en servicios de atención al público, iniciativa y ganas de trabajar.
Ubicación: Santiago/Área metropolitana Chile
Llamar al 543-0942 para concertar entrevista personal.

COMESTIBLES LA ROSA

Necesita para su fábrica de Dosquebradas (Pereira)
INGENIERO MECÁNICO para trabajar como **INGENIERO DE PROGRAMACIÓN Y CONTROL DE PROYECTOS,** con:
Experiencia mínima de 2 años en industria
Conocimiento y manejo de sistemas
Buen nivel de inglés técnico
Excelentes relaciones interpersonales, habilidad para manejo de personal y potencial para desarrollo futuro.
Los interesados deben enviar su hoja de vida con fotografía reciente, indicando aspiración salarial, al Apartado Aéreo No. 44 de Pereira.

Nombre ______________________ Sección ____________ Fecha ____________

1. ¿Cuáles son los puestos que se anuncian?

____

2. ¿Qué edad (*age*) deben tener los aspirantes a la oferta No. 3?

____

3. ¿Cuáles deben ser las áreas de especialización del (de la) analista programador(a)?

____

4. ¿Qué idiomas (*languages*) deben hablar el (la) ingeniero(a) (*engineer*) y el (la) analista programador(a)?

____

5. ¿Cuántos años de experiencia deben tener los aspirantes a cada puesto?

____

6. ¿Adónde deben enviar su resumé los/las aspirantes a cada puesto?

____

7. ¿Reúne Ud. los requisitos indicados en los anuncios? ¿Cuáles tiene y cuáles no?

____

Lectura After reading this **lectura,** get together with a partner and take turns answering the following questions.

La presencia en los Estados Unidos de más de treinta millones de hispanos, la mitad de los cuales no habla bien el inglés, obliga° a muchas empresas a contratar empleados bilingües. Esto no siempre es fácil.°

obliga° *compels*
fácil° *easy*

Es tendencia de muchas universidades americanas preparar a sus estudiantes para entenderse con personas de habla hispana, pero no los preparan para hablar con propiedad° y escribir con corrección el español.

con... *correctly*

Nombre ______________________ Sección ____________ Fecha ____________

Al hablar de un(a) empleado(a) no use las palabras "agresivo(a)" y "ambicioso(a)" pensando en las connotaciones que sus equivalentes (*aggressive and ambitious*) tienen en inglés. Agresivo(a) se dice° de una persona que tiende° a la violencia, o a ofender o provocar a los demás.° "Ambicioso(a)" tiene la misma connotación negativa que *ambitious,* pero no tiene la connotación positiva con que se usa frecuentemente en inglés.

se... *is said*
que... *who is prone*
a... *other people*

1. Muchas empresas americanas contratan empleados bilingües. ¿Por qué?
2. ¿Qué hacen algunas universidades de los Estados Unidos?
3. ¿Qué no hacen?
4. ¿Cuál es la diferencia entre **agresivo** y *aggressive*?

Y usted...

1. ¿Piensa que es fácil o difícil contratar empleados bilingües? ¿Por qué?
2. ¿Quiere hablar español para poder comunicarse con personas de habla hispana o para usarlo como una herramienta (*tool*) en su trabajo?

Un dicho

Ser puntual ahorra tiempo. *To be punctual saves time.*

Trivia

Firing Employees in Latin America

According to the World Bank's "Doing Business 2009" report,[1] Latin America is one of the most inflexible labor markets in the world. It is extremely difficult and costly to fire an unnecessary or non-performing employee in most Latin American countries. Indeed, Venezuela and Bolivia don't allow firings at all in the private sector. In Ecuador, Argentina, and Mexico, the cost of firing an employee is the equivalent of his/her salary for 135, 95, and 52 weeks respectively. "In this environment it is no exaggeration to say that almost everyone loses: employers, employees, and the region's competitiveness in general."[2]

[1]Covering the period April 2007 to June 2008
[2]Christopher Sabatini, Labor Reform Boosts Competitiveness, *Latin Business Chronicle*, May 23, 2009 http://www.latinbusinesschronicle.com

Nombre ______________________ **Sección** __________ **Fecha** __________

The World Bank "Doing Business 2009" report

Every year the World Bank ranks the world economies on their ease of doing business. The following is a section of the "Doing Business 2009" report, covering the period April 2007 to June 2008. One hundred and eighty-one countries were ranked.

(This section indicates the position of the economies of Latin American Spanish-speaking countries in the report. The U.S., Canada, and Spain are included for comparison. Cuba was not included in the report.)

PAÍS	POSICIÓN
Estados Unidos	3
Canadá	8
Puerto Rico	35
Chile	40
España	49
Colombia	53
México	56
Perú	62
El Salvador	72
Panamá	81
Rep. Dominicana	97
Nicaragua	107
Uruguay	109
Guatemala	112
Argentina	113
Paraguay	115
Costa Rica	117
Honduras	133
Ecuador	138
Bolivia	150
Venezuela	174

Source: "Doing Business 2009" report http://www.latinbusinesschronicle.com

SUPLEMENTO 2

LA CARTA DE NEGOCIOS

- La correspondencia comercial
- Partes de una carta
- El sobre
- Cartas de negocio típicas

La correspondencia comercial (*Business Correspondence*) Business correspondence includes all written texts referring to business matters. In addition to traditional forms of communication, such as letters, telegrams, and telexes, today's business correspondence includes messages sent by fax or electronic mail.

Spanish business letter writing is characterized by the use of a more formal and formulaic language than that used to write business correspondence in English. But as is the case in English, a well-written business letter in Spanish is clear, concise, complete, and courteous. It contains the following elements:

1. **Membrete** (*Letterhead*)
   The letterhead includes the sender's company name, complete address, telephone number, and other key information, such as a fax number and e-mail address.

ALFA Y OMEGA, S.A.
Importadores de Tejidos
Velarde N. 356, La Paz, Bolivia
Teléfono 453-8090, Fax 453-8097
alfyom@alfyomega.com

2. **Fecha** (*Date*)
   In Spanish, the day is written first, followed by the month and year.

24 de enero de 2010

Sometimes the month is separated from the year by a comma.
24 de enero, 2010

3. **Asunto** (*Reference line*)
   Some letters include a brief reference line under the date line indicating the subject of the letter. Subject lines are often preceded by the word **Asunto** (*Subject*) or the letters **Ref.,** meaning **Con referencia a** (*In regard to*).

Asunto: Solicitud de empleo   **Ref.: Factura No. 83472-01**

4. Destinatario (*Recipient*)

This section of the letter identifies the name and address of the person, business, or other organization to whom the letter is being sent. If the letter is addressed to a specific person, an appropriate title should precede his or her name: **señor (Sr.), señora (Sra.), señorita (Srta.), doctor(a) [Dr(a).], Licenciado(a) [Lic., Ldo(a)., or Ledo(a)**[1]], **Ingeniero(a) (Ing.),** etc. In Spain and in some Latin American countries, the titles **Don (D.)** and **Doña (Dña.)** are also used. Remember that in Spanish, the street name precedes the street number; they may be separated by a comma or not. When there is a postal code, it is placed before or after the city name, depending on the country.

Sr. Gustavo Chavando
San Andrés, 546
Lima 32, Perú

Cía.[2] **Vinatera Torre y Hno.**
Junín 232
1086 Buenos Aires, Argentina

5. Saludo (*Salutation*)

The following are customary salutations for business letters.

Estimado(a) señor(a):
Distinguido(a) señor(a):
Estimado(a) cliente(a):
Estimado(a) Sr(a). ____________:
Muy señor(a) mío(a):

6. Cuerpo de la carta (*Body*)

The body of the letter usually begins with a brief sentence indicating the letter's objective. Introductory sentences for business letters usually begin with one of the following expressions:

La presente tiene por objeto... The purpose of this letter is . . .
En respuesta a su carta de fecha... In response to your letter dated . . .
En relación con su pedido de fecha... With reference to your order dated . . .
Confirmando nuestra conversación (telefónica)... To confirm our (telephone) conversation . . .
Le(s) agradecería(mos) nos informara(n) de... I (We) would appreciate receiving information about . . .
Nos es grato comunicarle(s) que... We are pleased to inform you that . . .
Sentimos tener que comunicarle(s) que... We regret to inform you that . . .
Acusamos recibo de su atenta (carta) de fecha... We acknowledge receipt of your letter dated . . .
Adjunto envío (enviamos) cheque (giro)... Enclosed please find a check (money order) . . .
Estamos interesados en... We are interested in . . .
Le(s) agradezco que me envíe(n)... Please send me . . .

---

[1]The title of **Licenciado(a)** designates that the person has completed one of certain professional degrees such as law, pharmacology, etc. In Mexico it designates any university graduate.
[2]**Cía.** is the abbreviation for **compañía.**

7. **Despedida** (*Closing*)
The expressions most frequently used to close a business letter are the following.

Atentamente,
De usted(es) atentamente,
Sinceramente,

8. **Antefirma** (*Sender's company name*)
The sender's company name follows the closing in uppercase letters.

HIPOTECARIA NORTE, S.A. **LÓPEZ Y CÍA.**

9. **Firma** (*Signature*)
The sender's signature is followed by his or her name and title.

Manuela Ibarra
Jefa de Compras

10. **Posdata** (*Postscript*)
Often a postscript is included after the closing to emphasize a particular fact or idea.

P.D.: Por favor, acuse recibo de la mercancía por correo electrónico.

11. **Anexos o adjuntos** (*Enclosures*)
If additional materials are being sent with the letter, this should be noted at the end of the letter.

Anexo: Factura de fecha 4 de febrero de 2010

12. **Iniciales** (*Initials*)
The letter writer's initials usually appear in uppercase letters at the end of the letter, followed by initials of the typist in lowercase letters.

HB/ha **FG:ml**

Nombre ______________________ Sección ____________ Fecha ____________

Partes de una carta (*Parts of a letter*)

Membrete	**R. Sánchez & Sons** Auto Parts & Accessories 547 W. Orange Avenue Albuquerque, New Mexico 87102 Telephone (505) 921-8074
Fecha	24 de septiembre de 2010
Referencia	Ref. DI-78
Destinatario	Sr. Administrador Sociedad Española de Automóviles Turísticos (SEAT) Recoletos, 765 28000 Madrid, España
Saludo	Estimado señor:
Cuerpo de la carta	Estamos interesados en distribuir en esta área las piezas de repuesto y accesorios para los coches de su acreditada marca. La ciudad de Albuquerque, en donde estamos establecidos, cuenta con más de 330.000 habitantes y, sin embargo, su firma no tiene aquí ningún distribuidor autorizado. Estamos en condiciones de ofrecer las referencias comerciales y las garantías bancarias necesarias.
Despedida	De usted atentamente,
Antefirma	R. SÁNCHEZ & SONS
Firma	*Abel N. González* Abel N. González Jefe de Compras

Nombre ______________________ **Sección** __________ **Fecha** __________

EL SOBRE (*THE ENVELOPE*)

LA CASA SÁNCHEZ Partes y accesorios para autos 547 W. Orange Ave. Albuquerque, NM 87102 U.S.A.	Sello o estampilla de correo
	Sr. Administrador Sociedad Española de Automóviles Turísticos (SEAT) Recoletos, 765 28000 Madrid, España (Spain)
Att. Sr. Alba[1]	

Activity: Answer Mr. Gonzalez's letter, accepting his offer. Use regular stationery and address an envelope appropriately to present your work.

[1]When an envelope is addressed to a business (i.e., Commercial Omega S.A.) the "attention" (**Att.**) line is written two spaces below the address. It is used to require that the matter be taken care of by the person indicated. (i.e., **Att. Sr. Alba**). If the letter is personal or confidential, the word **PERSONAL** or **CONFIDENCIAL** must appear on the lower left-hand corner of the envelope.

Nombre ______________________ **Sección** __________ **Fecha** __________

Cartas de negocio típicas (*Model business letters*)

1. To request samples:

SPORTMART
7689 N. Palm Avenue
San Francisco, CA 94105, U.S.A.
Telephone (415) 345-9402

15 de enero de 2010

Sr. Sergio Fuerte
Jefe de Ventas
Freddy Modas, S.A.
Magnolia No. 9876
Lima 32, Perú

Estimado señor:

En respuesta a su oferta de fecha 4 del presente mes, deseo comunicarle nuestro interés en distribuir en nuestras tiendas[1] la ropa[2] para hombres de su acreditada marca, pero antes de hacer nuestros pedidos,[3] necesitamos ver algunas muestras.[4]

Por favor, si es posible, envíenos las muestras por expreso aéreo.

De usted atentamente,
SPORTMART
Gonzalo Ramos
Administrador

[1]*stores* [2]*clothing* [3]*orders* [4]*samples*

Answer the letter, stating that you are sending samples via express mail as requested. Use regular stationery to present your work.

Nombre ______________________ Sección ____________ Fecha ____________

2. To place an order.

SPORTMART
7689 N. Palm Avenue
San Francisco, CA 94105, U.S.A.
Telephone (415) 345-9402

5 de febrero de 2010

Sr. Sergio Fuerte
Jefe de Ventas
Freddy Modas, S.A.
Magnolia No. 9876
Lima 32, Perú

Ref: Pedido de ropa

Estimado señor Fuerte:

Después de revisar cuidadosamente[1] las muestras recibidas, debo informarle que los precios de la ropa fabricada por ustedes son un poco más elevados que los de otras marcas. No obstante,[2] creemos conveniente hacerles el pequeño pedido que enviamos adjunto, y esperamos recibir algún descuento en caso de pedidos mayores.[3]

Atentamente,
SPORTMART
Gonzalo Ramos
Gonzalo Ramos
Administrador

Adjunto:
1. Nota de pedido.

[1] *carefully* [2] **No...** *Nevertheless* [3] *larger*

Answer the letter, thanking Mr. Ramos for his order. Use regular stationery to present your work.

Nombre ______________________ Sección ____________ Fecha ____________

3. To state an error or a wrong order.

SPORTMART
7689 N. Palm Avenue
San Francisco, CA 94105, U.S.A.
Telephone (415) 345-9402

24 de febrero de 2010

Sr. Sergio Fuerte
Jefe de Ventas
Freddy Modas, S.A.
Magnolia No. 9876
Lima 32, Perú

Estimado señor Fuerte:

Lamentamos tener que informarle que, con esta fecha y a su cargo,[1] estamos devolviéndole[2] 32 pantalones de hombre talla[3] 44, recibidos en el día de ayer, los cuales no fueron pedidos por nosotros. Por otra parte,[4] no recibimos una cantidad igual de pantalones talla 34.

Le agradecemos que trate de hacernos este envío[5] con la mayor rapidez posible.

Atentamente,
SPORTMART
Gonzalo Ramos
Gonzalo Ramos
Administrador

[1] **a...** *at your expense* [2] **estamos...** *we are returning to you* [3] *size* [4] **Por...** *In addition* [5] *shipment*

Answer Mr. Ramos' letter, apologizing for the error. Then write a letter, similar to Mr. Ramos', stating that you are returning merchandise due to an error in the order.

Nombre ______________________ Sección ______________ Fecha ______________

Lecciones 6-10 Repaso

Práctica de vocabulario

A Circle the word or phrase that does not belong in each group.

1. cliente ahorro consumidor
2. amortiguador silenciador suministrador
3. área cadena zona
4. código clave cuadra
5. llamada telefonista impreso
6. marcar enviar mandar
7. medir ahorrar pesar
8. acera banqueta freno
9. caja cuadra esquina
10. manejar conducir decidir
11. carga contenedor carta
12. ferrocarril rotura tren
13. descarga lana algodón
14. encargarse cargar descargar
15. ocurrir pensar suceder
16. año mes respuesta
17. sistema sueldo salario
18. marca coche carro
19. alto ancho auto
20. carta buzón cosa
21. detallista mayorista ordenador
22. pieza repuesto oferta
23. usar indicar utilizar
24. exportar compensar importar
25. a veces al día diario

B Circle the word or phrase that best completes each sentence.

1. No podemos (comparar / competir / descartar) en el precio de los tubos de escape.
2. En realidad, no estamos (conocidos / próximos / satisfechos) con la compra.
3. Nuestros precios son los más (competitivos / acreditados / acompañados).
4. El Sr. Vargas no puede (usar / utilizar / atender) a los visitantes ahora.
5. Me (gusta / duele / penetra) esta mercancía.
6. ¿Cuánto (busca / contiene / carga) el hotel por las llamadas?
7. Necesito enviar unas (cartas / ciudades / avenidas) a los Estados Unidos.
8. La oficina de correos está a tres (dineros / cuadras / camiones) de aquí.
9. ¿Cuánto demora un (destinatario / paquete / administrador) por correo aéreo?
10. Puedo buscar la dirección en la (capital / libra / guía) de teléfonos.
11. Él no sabe (manejar / cruzar / cubrir) coches de cambio mecánico.

12. Deseo alquilar un (carro / turista / transeúnte) automático.
13. Hoy no tenemos ningún coche pequeño (medio / disponible / directamente).
14. El hotel está en el (pueblo / folleto / área) comercial.
15. Ud. debe pedirle la (avería / transferencia / libra) al chofer del autobús.
16. Necesito enviar un (ahorro / daño / cargamento) de artesanías.
17. Los artículos de (lana / algodón / vidrio) soplado son muy frágiles.
18. Si el (embalaje / flete / tejido) es bueno, no ocurren daños en la mercancía.
19. Nosotros llevamos la mercancía hasta la (rotura / medida / frontera).
20. El seguro es caro, pero Ud. ahorra en el (flete / taller / tamaño).
21. Ud. tiene treinta minutos para (poner / almorzar / ofrecer).
22. Hoy tengo una (fábrica / salud / entrevista) de trabajo.
23. Nosotros le (descontamos / renunciamos / trasladamos) el ocho por ciento de su sueldo.
24. Antes de firmar el (puesto / beneficio / contrato) debo saber el horario de trabajo.
25. El año pasado me dieron un (empleado / aumento / almacén) de treinta dólares al mes.

C Match the questions in column **A** with the answers in column **B.**

A		B
1. ¿Cuáles son las condiciones de pago?	______	a. Tres días.
2. ¿Tenemos que pagar el seguro?	______	b. No, a la semana.
3. ¿Va a ver Ud. los productos de metal ahora?	______	c. Tres cuadras.
4. ¿Dónde está el buzón?	______	d. Dos semanas al año.
5. ¿Cuánto tarda en llegar el paquete?	______	e. Alfarería y artículos de cuero.
6. ¿Cuánto deben pesar los paquetes?	______	f. Las condiciones de venta.
7. ¿Cuánto debo caminar para tomar el autobús?	______	g. Sí, y el retiro.
8. ¿Qué necesita saber Ud.?	______	h. No, mediano.
9. ¿El coche es compacto?	______	i. Sí, en los almacenes.
10. ¿A quién le pido la transferencia?	______	j. No, sólo el transporte.
11. ¿Qué tipo de artesanía va a transportar Ud.?	______	k. Treinta minutos.
12. ¿Los tejidos son de lana?	______	l. No, hasta la frontera solamente.
13. ¿Cuánto tiempo tengo para almorzar?	______	m. No, no puedo. Tengo prisa.
14. ¿Los pagos son mensuales?	______	n. No más de cinco kilos.

Nombre ______________________ Sección ____________ Fecha ____________

A		B
15. ¿Descuentan el seguro de salud?	______	**o.** Sí, y pregúntale las condiciones de pago.
16. ¿Uds. transportan la mercancía hasta California?	______	**p.** No me dieron el aumento que solicité.
17. ¿Por qué renunció Ud.?	______	**q.** Al chofer del autobús.
18. ¿Cuánto tiempo dan Uds. de vacaciones?	______	**r.** 3/30, n/60
19. ¿Tienen un gran volumen de mercancías en existencia?	______	**s.** No, de algodón.
20. ¿Le pido la lista de precios al viajante?	______	**t.** En la esquina.

Situaciones del mundo de las empresas Review the **Notas culturales** and **Lecturas** of the past five lessons and then read the following scenarios. Find out what went wrong, and propose possible solutions in Spanish.

1. I am in Bogota, Colombia, doing business. I know that time is a flexible concept in many countries, and therefore I arrived at 11:10 for an 11:00 A.M. appointment.

____

____

____

____

2. I went to Mexico by car. I did not buy insurance in Mexico since I am insured in the U.S., and my insurance therefore guarantees coverage all over the world.

____

____

____

____

3. I opened my company in Puerto Rico, a U.S. commonwealth. Since business there is carried out under U.S. law, I am automatically fulfilling all legal obligations governing my business in that U.S. territory.

____

____

____

____

4. I need to translate a document from English to Spanish. I know that one of my employees' last name is **Carmona,** a Spanish last name, so I'll ask him to do the translation.

5. When I wrote a letter commending an employee's work I said this about him: **El Sr. Fernández es ambicioso y agresivo.**

Advanced Translation

The following translations include some words not presented yet. You may need to use a dictionary.

Translate into Spanish

1. This bus stops near the post office, right?
2. The rules of the postal offices of the Latin American countries and Spain are similar.
3. In some Latin American countries cellular phones are a solution in isolated areas.
4. You must be punctual for all meetings.
5. You may rent a hybrid car. It costs more, but you save a lot on gas.
6. The transportation of merchandise between Canada and Mexico has doubled.
7. Mexican trucks circulate in the United States and Canada.
8. Before opening a factory in Mexico, you must familiarize yourself with Mexican laws.

LECCIÓN 11

LA CONTABILIDAD DE LA EMPRESA (I)

OBJECTIVES

Structures

- Time expressions with **hacer**
- Irregular preterits
- The preterit of stem-changing verbs (**e:i** and **o:u**)
- Command forms: **tú**

Business Communication

- Dealing with accounting and accountants

Tan pronto como el segundo candidato sale de la oficina de la Sra. Artiles, la secretaria la llama por el intercomunicador:

Secretaria —Sra. Artiles, el Sr. Villalba la está esperando.
Sra. Artiles —¿Cuánto hace que espera?
Secretaria —Hace unos pocos minutos que está aquí.
Sra. Artiles —Bien. En cinco minutos, hazlo[1] pasar a mi oficina. Gracias.
Secretaria —Sí, señora. (*Al rato, la secretaria mira la hora y le dice al Sr. Villalba*) La Sra. Artiles lo espera en su oficina.
Sr. Villalba —Buenos días, Sra. Artiles. Mi nombre es Jorge Villalba y represento a la firma Allied Business Consultants.
Sra. Artiles —Buenos días y perdone la demora. No pude terminar antes la entrevista anterior, y después tuve que hacer una llamada.
Sr. Villalba —No importa. Por favor, dígame cuál es su problema.
Sra. Artiles —Quiero modernizar el sistema de contabilidad del negocio.
Sr. Villalba —¿Quién lleva la contabilidad de la firma?
Sra. Artiles —Los empleados de la oficina hacen los asientos de diario y los pases al mayor.
Sr. Villalba —¿Ellos también preparan los estados financieros?
Sra. Artiles —No, ahora tenemos un arreglo con un contador que periódicamente prepara los balances de comprobación, los balances generales y los estados de pérdidas y ganancias.

[1]Irregular command (**tú** form) of **hacer: haz**

Nombre ______________________ Sección ____________ Fecha ____________

Sr. Villalba —Bien, explíqueme las dificultades que tiene con su sistema contable actual.

Sra. Artiles —El problema es que el negocio creció mucho el año pasado y ahora estamos sufriendo demoras y errores costosos en los informes a los clientes.

Sr. Villalba —¿Y qué desea hacer ahora, reorganizar su oficina contable o encargar la contabilidad del negocio a una firma de contadores?

Sra. Artiles —Bueno, como le dije por teléfono a la persona con quien hablé, no quise tomar una decisión final sin antes consultar con Uds.

Sr. Villalba —Hizo bien. Y en ese caso necesito evaluar sus necesidades. ¿Están aquí todos los libros?

Sra. Artiles —Sí, se los pedí al contador y él los trajo ayer. (*A su asistente por el intercomunicador*) Eva, no prepares hoy la nómina. Trae los libros de contabilidad y trabaja con el Sr. Villalba, por favor.

La Sra. Artiles le sirve una taza de café al Sr. Villalba y siguen hablando.

¡Escuchemos!

While listening to the dialogue, circle **V (verdadero)** if the statement is true or **F (falso)** if it is false.

1. El contador tuvo que esperar mucho tiempo en la oficina. V F
2. La secretaria mira la hora antes de hacer pasar al contador a la oficina. V F
3. La Sra. Artiles no recibió antes al contador porque estaba hablando por teléfono. V F
4. Ahora, los empleados de la oficina preparan los balances generales y los estados de pérdidas y ganancias. V F
5. La empresa de la Sra. Artiles tiene que modernizar su contabilidad porque el negocio creció mucho el año pasado. V F
6. Ahora el negocio de la Sra. Artiles está teniendo errores costosos en los informes a los clientes. V F
7. La Sra. Artiles tomó una decisión antes de hablar con el contador. V F
8. El contador quiere saber dónde están los libros de contabilidad. V F
9. Los libros no están en la oficina. V F
10. Eva va a preparar la nómina hoy. V F

Nombre ______________________ Sección ____________ Fecha ____________

VOCABULARIO

Audio

Cognados

el caso
el error
final
la necesidad
periódicamente
el problema
el (la) secretario(a)
el sistema

Nombres

el arreglo, la iguala (*Cuba*) *arrangement*
el asiento de diario *journal entry*
el (la) asistente, el (la) ayudante *assistant*
el balance de comprobación *trial balance*
el balance general *balance sheet*
la contabilidad *accounting*
el (la) contador(a) *accountant*
la empresa *enterprise, company*
el estado de pérdidas y ganancias *profit-and-loss statement*
el estado financiero *financial statement*
la ganancia *profit, earnings*
el libro *book*
el (libro) diario *journal*
el (libro) mayor *general ledger*
la nómina *payroll*
el pase al mayor *general ledger entry*
la pérdida *loss*
la taza *cup*

Verbos

consultar *to consult*
crecer *to grow*
encargar *to entrust*
evaluar *to evaluate, to assess*
explicar *to explain*
importar *to matter*
modernizar *to modernize*
perdonar *to forgive*
reorganizar *to reorganize*
representar *to represent*
salir[1] *to leave, to go out*
seguir (e:i) *to continue*
servir (e:i) *to serve*
sufrir *to suffer*
traer[2] *to bring*

Adjetivos

anterior *previous, former*
contable *accounting*
costoso(a) *costly*
financiero(a) *financial*

Otras palabras y expresiones

ayer *yesterday*
¿con quién? *with whom?*
Hizo bien. *You did the right thing.*
llevar la contabilidad *to keep the books*
perdone *excuse (me)*
tan pronto como *as soon as*
tomar una decisión *to make a decision*

[1]Irregular first person present indicative: **yo salgo**
[2]Irregular first person present indicative: **yo traigo**

Nombre ______________________ Sección ____________ Fecha ____________

VOCABULARIO ADICIONAL

Audio

a fondo *in depth*
a un tiempo *both,* at a time
cobro de impuestos *collecting taxes*
como fin primordial *as paramount objective*
deberían preocuparse *should pay attention*
desde ya *from now on*
economías emergentes *emerging economies*
estar al tanto *to be updated*
grave error *serious mistake*
hacer más confiable *to make more trustworthy*
han exigido *have required*
hasta hace poco *until recently*
hasta los gobiernos *even governments*
ni siquiera *not even*
no es ya el caso *is not the case any longer*
países desarrollados *developed countries*
países en vías de desarrollo *developing countiries*
países subdesarrollados *underdeveloped countries*
poner a tono to *syncronize*
se ha vuelto *has become*

Términos relacionados con la contabilidad

acreditar *to credit*
el (la) acreedor(a) *creditor*
el activo *assets*
adjunto(a) *attached*
el ajuste *adjustment, reconciliation*
el capital *capital*
conciliar, cuadrar *to reconcile*
el (la) contador(a) público(a) titulado(a) *certified public accountant (CPA)*
la cuenta a (por) cobrar *account receivable*
la cuenta a (por) pagar *account payable*
la cuenta acreedora *credit account*
la cuenta corriente *checking account*
la cuenta deudora *debit account*
el debe *debit*
debitar *to debit*
la deuda *debt*
el (la) deudor(a) *debtor*
el efectivo *cash*
el egreso *expenditure*
la fecha de cierre *closing date*
la fecha de vencimiento *due (expiration) date*
el folio *folio, page (i.e., accounting books)*
los fondos *funds, deposits*
el gasto *expense*
los gastos de representación *entertainment expenses*
los gastos generales *overhead expenses*
los gastos varios *miscellaneous expenses*
el haber *credit*
el inventario *inventory*
el libro de actas *minute book*
el libro de caja *cash book*
el libro de ventas *sales book*
liquidar *to liquidate, to pay off*
pasar al mayor *to enter in the ledger*
el pasivo *liabilities*
el saldo *balance*
el (la) tenedor(a) de libros *bookkeeper*

Nombre ______________________ Sección ____________ Fecha ____________

Search

iLrn

Notas Culturales

- During the last decade, large and medium sized enterprises in Hispanic America made sustained efforts to improve the quality of their accounting and auditing practices, adopt international standards, and modernize financial reporting procedures. However, the general weaknesses of regulatory regimes in most Latin American countries (and especially the lack of preparedness on the part of local accountants and auditors present in some countries) have drastically hindered the implementation of these standards. Consequently, small businesses continue to use outdated accounting practices.
- In small businesses in Spanish-speaking countries, the accounting work is often done by a bookkeeper who may be a graduate of a middle-level business school. The accounting and finances of large businesses and corporations are usually handled by accountants who are university graduates. The laws of some Spanish-speaking countries do not permit companies to hire people with degrees from foreign countries as accountants, but other countries do not regulate the employment of accountants. Many of the employees in charge of accounting have a practical, experiential knowledge of financial practices and procedures rather than knowledge gained through a course of study. Although the use of computers is increasing rapidly in Latin America, dependence on electronic media for accounting purposes such as spreadsheets, payroll programs, and other financial software remains in its infancy in most countries. Almost every country still requires that accounting information be recorded manually in books and/or ledger that are mandated by each country's laws. In general, these books are the daily ledger, the general ledger, inventory records, and the trial balance book. Commercial enterprises must also keep a minute book, and generally, companies keep books and/or records over and above those required by law. In these countries, the law also requires that a judge or a notary public examine and validate all accounting books before they can be used by a company. This authorization consists of certifying the number of pages that the books contain and marking each page with an official stamp.

Actividades

Dígame... Answer the following questions, basing your answers on the dialogue.

1. ¿Por qué tuvo que esperar el Sr. Villalba?

____

2. ¿Para qué compañía trabaja el Sr. Villalba?

____

3. ¿Por qué consulta la Sra. Artiles con la firma del Sr. Villalba?

____

4. ¿Qué arreglo tiene la compañía de la Sra. Artiles con su contador?

____

5. ¿Qué ocurrió con el negocio el año pasado?

____

6. ¿Qué está ocurriendo con los informes a los clientes en la compañía de la Sra. Artiles?

____

7. ¿Qué necesita hacer el Sr. Villalba?

____

8. ¿Qué no tiene que hacer Eva hoy? ¿Por qué?

____

9. ¿Qué van a hacer el Sr. Villalba y Eva?

____

10. ¿Qué le sirvió la Sra. Artiles al Sr Villalba? ¿Qué siguieron haciendo?

____

Hablemos

Interview a classmate, using the following questions. When you have finished, switch roles.

1. ¿Qué hace Ud. tan pronto como sale de la clase (*class*)?
2. ¿Hay un intercomunicador en esta clase? ¿Quién lo usa? ¿Para qué?
3. ¿Espera Ud. a alguien ahora?
4. ¿Hace mucho tiempo que Ud. está aquí?
5. ¿Creció mucho esta universidad el año pasado?
6. ¿Con quién consulta Ud. cuando no sabe qué hacer?
7. ¿Qué hace Ud. antes de decidir algo importante?
8. ¿Trajo Ud. su libro a clase hoy?

Quiz

Vamos a practicar

A With a partner, take turns asking and answering how long the following actions or circumstances have been going on.

Modelo the accountant / waiting
Pregunta: **¿Cuánto tiempo hace que el contador espera?**
Respuesta: **Hace unos minutos que espera.**

1. we / learning Spanish
2. you (**Ud.**) / are here
3. you (**tú**) / have your car
4. I / working here

Nombre ______________________ **Sección** __________ **Fecha** __________

B Rewrite the following sentences according to the given cues.

MODELO Ella prefiere consultar con un contador.
Last Thursday: **Ella prefirió consultar con un contador.**

1. Tengo una entrevista con el contador.

   Last Monday: ______________________________

2. Estoy en su oficina.

   Yesterday: ______________________________

3. No puedo explicarle las dificultades que tenemos.

   Last year: ______________________________

4. Hago los asientos de diario y los pases al mayor.

   Last month: ______________________________

5. El contador viene con los libros.

   Last week: ______________________________

6. ¿Qué dice el Sr. Villalba?

   The day before yesterday: ______________________________

7. ¿Quién trae el libro diario?

   Two days ago: ______________________________

8. ¿Por qué no quiere cambiar el sistema de contabilidad?

   Last Tuesday: ______________________________

9. Ella le sirve una taza de café.

   A few minutes ago: ______________________________

10. Uds. siguen conversando.

    Yesterday: ______________________________

Nombre ______________________ **Sección** ____________ **Fecha** ____________

C You and a colleague are working on the books for your company. Take turns asking each other what you should do, responding first affirmatively and then negatively. Use the **tú** command.

MODELO ¿Llamo al Sr. Villalba?
Sí, llámalo.
No, no lo llames.

1. ¿Traigo los libros?

______________________ ______________________

2. ¿Le digo al contador lo que pasó?

______________________ ______________________

3. ¿Hago los asientos en el diario?

______________________ ______________________

4. ¿Pongo los estados financieros en tu escritorio?

______________________ ______________________

5. ¿Te sirvo el café ahora?

______________________ ______________________

6. ¿Te explico mis problemas?

______________________ ______________________

7. ¿Lo consulto con el jefe?

______________________ ______________________

8. ¿Salgo de tu oficina?

______________________ ______________________

9. ¿Les encargo la contabilidad a los empleados de la oficina?

______________________ ______________________

Nombre ______________________ Sección ______________ Fecha ______________

Sirva usted de intérprete

With two classmates, play the roles of Sra. Pérez, an accountant, and the interpreter who helps them communicate. Switch roles until each of you has played the interpreter's role.

Sra. Pérez —Mi nombre es Sonia Pérez. Tengo un restaurante y necesito modernizar la contabilidad de mi negocio.

Intérprete —______________________

Contador(a) —*Who keeps the books for your business now?*

Intérprete —______________________

Sra. Pérez —Una de las empleadas de la oficina, pero el negocio creció mucho el año pasado y ahora necesito un contador.

Intérprete —______________________

Contador(a) —*What books did the employee keep?*

Intérprete —______________________

Sra. Pérez —Un libro diario y un mayor.

Intérprete —______________________

Contador(a) —*What financial statements did she do?*

Intérprete —______________________

Sra. Pérez —Solamente el estado de pérdidas y ganancias que necesitamos para pagar los impuestos.

Intérprete —______________________

Contador(a) —*I need to see the books and the profit and loss statements for past years. I would like to determine what your needs are.*

Intérprete —______________________

Sra. Pérez —Los libros no están aquí. Los tengo en mi casa.

Intérprete —______________________

Contador(a) —*The books must always be in the place of business or in the office of the company accountant.*

Intérprete —______________________

Sra. Pérez —Lo sé, pero necesitamos preparar las cuentas del mes anterior y algunas del mes actual.

Intérprete —______________________

Contador(a) —*Fine, when can I see the books?*

Intérprete —______________________

Nombre ______________________ Sección ____________ Fecha ____________

Sra. Pérez —Mañana, después de las cinco, se los llevo a su oficina. También le voy a llevar las cuentas del mes actual.

Intérprete —____

Contador(a) —*Sorry. We close at four-thirty.*

Intérprete —____

Sra. Pérez —Entonces voy a llevárselos a las cuatro menos cuarto, más o menos.

Sirva usted de traductor(a)

Your company's sales representative in the Dominican Republic sent the following report on the status of his company account for the month of March. Review the **Vocabulario adicional** in this lesson and then translate the report into English so your boss can review it. Use regular stationery to present your work.

Reporte del movimiento de fondos durante el mes de marzo

Saldo en febrero 28		$7.912,90
Ingresos:		
Cuentas a cobrar cobradas	$76.123,52	
Intereses acreditados	54,00	76.177,52
Egresos:		
Mi sueldo	3.750,00	
Pago de cuentas a pagar	500,00	
Gastos de viajes	245,80	
Gastos de representación	181,45	
Gastos varios	45,96	
Ajuste en cuenta del banco	85,43	4.808,64
Saldo		71.368,88
Cheque adjunto	$70.000,00	
Saldo en marzo 31		$1.368,88

Notas:
1. El banco nos acreditó $54 por intereses de la cuenta corriente, y nos debitó $85,43 por cheque sin fondo recibido de un deudor.
2. La firma López y Compañía me informó que no tiene el efectivo necesario para liquidar su deuda en la fecha de vencimiento. Su pasivo excede a su activo.

Importante:
1. Necesito contratar a un contador público o un tenedor de libros para que me ayude con la contabilidad.
2. Necesito aumentar el inventario de muestras para los clientes.

Nombre ______________________ Sección ____________ Fecha ____________

En estas situaciones

With a partner, act out the following situations in Spanish.

1. Your company has sent you to Panama in order to modernize the accounting system of a local firm. Introduce yourself. Ask the manager who is in charge of keeping the company books now, what books they presently keep, and what difficulties they're having with their current accounting system. Say that they must think about using computers with their new system, but you need to evaluate the needs of the company before making a final decision. Ask where the company books are and if their accountant can work with you for a week.
2. You are a Spanish-speaking business owner, interviewing an accountant about handling your company's affairs. Ask where the accountant worked before and what type of accounting work he/she has done. Explain that your business is experiencing delays and errors in its reports, and that is why you want to hand over (entrust) the firm's accounting to another accountant. Say that you urgently need a profit-and-loss statement, although you have already prepared the trial balance. Use the intercom to ask one of your employees to bring the balance sheet to your office.

Casos

With you and a partner playing the roles, work through the following scenarios.

1. An accountant and the administrator of a company discuss the modernization of the company's accounting system.
2. A business owner discusses concerns about problems in client reports with an employee.
3. Two employees work on their company's books together.

Un paso más

A You are the accountant for a large company, and your boss would like a brief report of the month's income and expenses. Review the **Vocabulario adicional** in this lesson and use it and other vocabulary to prepare the report. Use a separate sheet of paper and create your own letterhead to present your work.

B Your company is hiring an accountant and a bookkeeper. Review the **Vocabulario adicional** from this lesson and use it and other vocabulary you have learned to write two brief help-wanted ads describing your company's needs and each job's responsibilities. Use a separate sheet of paper and create your own letterhead to present your work.

Nombre ______________________ Sección ____________ Fecha ____________

Lectura

After reading this **lectura**, get together with a partner and take turns answering the following questions.

La globalización es uno de los tópicos candentes° de la actualidad. Unos° la ven como la gran oportunidad para los países en desarrollo°, otros creen que es una nueva forma de explotación de los países y de la gente° pobre. Lo cierto es que la globalización es un producto de las nuevas tecnologías, y es un hecho° irreversible. Si los países desarrollados no eliminan° los subsidios al sector agrícola° y a la industria manufacturera que requiere mano de obra intensiva,° los países en desarrollo van a sufrir las consecuencias. Pero si se eliminan esos subsidios y otras barreras° que cierran° o limitan el acceso a los mercados de los países ricos,° los países en desarrollo van a vender muchísimos más productos y a obtener muchas más divisas.°

tópicos... *burning topics*
Some
países... *developing countries*
people
fact, event
remove
agricultural
mano... *intensive labor*
barriers / close
rich
hard currency

1. ¿Qué es la globalización?
2. ¿Qué dicen los que defienden la globalización?
3. ¿Qué dicen los que atacan la globalización?
4. ¿Qué va a suceder (*happen*) si los países desarrollados no eliminan los subsidios?

Y usted...

1. ¿Cree que la globalización beneficia a los países pobres o a los ricos? ¿Por qué?
2. La globalización, ¿es un hecho irreversible? ¿Por qué?

Un dicho

El que no se arriesga ni gana ni pierde. *If you don't take risks, you neither win nor lose.*

Trivia

Many learners of Spanish make the mistake of assuming that **billón** is a cognate for *billion* in English; it is not. In the United States, one billion is written as 1,000,000,000. In Spain and Latin America, this number is **mil millones** (literally, a thousand millions), or a **millardo.** A **billón** in the Spanish-speaking world is written as 1.000.000.000.000, but this is a *trillion* in the United States.

LECCIÓN 12

LA CONTABILIDAD DE LA EMPRESA (II)

OBJECTIVES

Structures

- **En** and **a** as equivalents of ***at***
- The imperfect tense
- The past progressive
- The preterit contrasted with the imperfect

Business Communication

- Dealing with accounting and accountants

El Sr. Villalba está de nuevo en la Compañía Pérez y Hno. Hoy rinde informe de su gestión.

Sr. Villalba —Sra. Artiles, no vine ayer porque todavía estaba trabajando en el informe. Por cierto, la ayuda de la Sra. Pérez fue más valiosa de lo que esperaba.

Sra. Artiles —Muy bien. ¿En qué consiste el informe?

Sr. Villalba —Pues, Ud. necesita automatizar la contabilidad de su negocio.

Sra. Artiles —¿Cómo?

Sr. Villalba —Mediante el uso de computadoras.

Sra. Artiles —¿Cómo funciona el sistema?

Sr. Villalba —Primero, Ud. necesita hacer un inventario de toda la mercancía disponible y registrarlo en la computadora. Luego Ud. registra todos los pedidos según se reciben y la computadora rebaja las ventas automáticamente.

Sra. Artiles —¿Cómo es posible eso?

Sr. Villalba —Fácilmente. Cada caja registradora se conecta a la computadora. Entonces, cada vez que se hace una venta, la computadora lee el código de barras[1] de la etiqueta con la unidad óptica y registra la venta.

Sra. Artiles —¿Cómo se preparan los estados financieros?

Sr. Villalba —La computadora los prepara automáticamente. Ud. «alimenta» la computadora con datos como el alquiler, el importe de la nómina, la electricidad, el teléfono, los impuestos, los gastos bancarios, etc. y la máquina hace la computación necesaria.

---

[1] *bar code*

Sra. Artiles —¿Y cómo se prepara la nómina?

Sr. Villalba —Basta con conectar el reloj que marca las entradas y salidas de los empleados con la computadora. Ésta registra las asistencias, hace los descuentos por ausencias y los descuentos por concepto de retiro, impuestos, seguro social, etc.

Sra. Artiles —¿Podemos hacer todo eso con las computadoras que tenemos ahora en servicio?

Sr. Villalba —Me[2] temo que no. Uds. van a necesitar un equipo de computación más sofisticado y varias estaciones de trabajo. Además, van a necesitar algunos programas especialmente diseñados para trabajos contables, de nóminas, etc.

Sra. Artiles —¿Nos va Ud. a recomendar los equipos y programas que necesitamos?

Sr. Villalba —Sí, señora. Aquí tiene Ud. una lista y un presupuesto de la inversión.

Sra. Artiles —(*Leyendo la lista*) ¿Necesitamos otros dos programas para la computadora? ¿No le dijo la Sra. Pérez que ya teníamos un programa de composición de textos?

Sr. Villalba —Sí, señora, pero es muy rudimentario y ya está obsoleto. Con este nuevo programa Ud. va a poder, entre otras cosas, automatizar los cobros y enviarles a sus clientes y a sus proveedores circulares personalizadas, es decir, circulares que parecen cartas personales.

Sra. Artiles —Y con el programa de hoja de cálculo, ¿qué podemos hacer?

Sr. Villalba —Con ese programa sus computadoras les van a preparar las hojas de análisis de los estados financieros.

Sra. Artiles —Bien, ahora vamos a hablar de los costos de inversión y de operación del nuevo sistema. Ya le dije que no deseaba gastar mucho.

Sr. Villalba —Yo le aseguro que sus ahorros en gastos de operación van a compensar el costo de la inversión inicial.

Sra. Artiles —Sí, ya sé que estábamos gastando demasiado.

¡Escuchemos!

While listening to the dialogue, circle **V (verdadero)** if the statement is true or **F (falso)** if it is false.

1. El Sr. Villalba fue ayer a la oficina de la Sra. Artiles para rendirle informe de su gestión. V F
2. La Sra. Pérez no pudo ayudar al Sr. Villalba. V F
3. La Sra. Artiles necesita computadoras para automatizar la contabilidad de su empresa. V F
4. Los empleados registran los pedidos según se reciben. V F
5. La computadora debe estar conectada a las cajas registradoras. V F
6. Los empleados de la Sra. Artiles marcan las horas de entrada y salida de sus trabajos. V F
7. La Sra. Artiles descuenta el Seguro Social y los impuestos de los sueldos de sus empleados. V F
8. La Sra. Artiles tiene un programa moderno de composición de textos. V F

[2] Superfluous object pronoun commonly used in Spanish to show interest; i.e., **Me regreso a casa.**

Nombre ________________ Sección ________ Fecha ________

9. El programa de hoja de cálculo prepara circulares personalizadas para los clientes y proveedores. V F

10. El contador piensa que los ahorros en los gastos de operación no van a compensar el costo de la inversión inicial. V F

VOCABULARIO

Audio

Cognados

automáticamente
la circular
la computación
el concepto
la electricidad
necesario(a)
obsoleto(a)
la operación
personal
personalizado(a)
posible
rudimentario(a)
el Seguro Social
sofisticado(a)
el uso

Nombres

el alquiler *rent*
la asistencia *attendance*
la ausencia *absence*
la ayuda *help, assistance*
la caja registradora *cash register*
el cobro *collection (of debts)*
el descuento *deduction, reduction*
la entrada *arrival, entry*
el equipo *equipment*
el equipo de computación *computer hardware*
la etiqueta *label*
la gestión *the work or action someone has to do, management*
la hoja de cálculo (análisis) *spreadsheet*
el importe *amount, price*
la inversión *investment*
la máquina *machine*
el presupuesto *estimate, budget*
la unidad óptica *scanner, optic unit*
la vez *time*

Verbos

alimentar *to feed*
automatizar *to automate*
conectar *to connect*
gastar *to spend*
parecer[1] *to look like, to seem*
rebajar *to reduce, to diminish*
registrar *to record, to key into (a computer)*

Adjetivos

diseñado(a) *designed*
valioso(a) *valuable*

Otras palabras y expresiones

código de barras *UPC (Universal Price Code), bar code*
de nuevo, otra vez *again*
demasiado *too much*
es decir *that is to say, in other words*
fácilmente *easily*
mediante *through, by means of*
(me) temo que... *I am afraid that . . .*
por cierto *by the way*

[1]Irregular first person present indicative: **yo parezco**

Nombre ______________________ Sección ____________ Fecha ____________

por concepto (de) *referring to (a specific item), regarding*
rendir (e:i) informe *to report, to give an account*
según *as*
según se reciben *as they are received, as they come in*

VOCABULARIO ADICIONAL

Audio

amortizar, reducir el valor to *write-down*
anualidad, la renta vitalicia *annuity*
agotamiento de recursos naturales *depletion of natural resources*
ajuste contable *accounting adjustment*
activo realizable *liquid assets*
activos devengados *accrued assets*
balance (estado) constructivo *constructive balance*
balance de inventarios y balances *inventory and balance sheet (book)*
base contable *accounting principles (bases)*
base imponible *taxable income*
bienes pignorados *pledged assets*
caja chica *petty cash*
capital de riesgo *venture capital*
cartera de inversiones *portfolio*
cierre de libros *closing of accounting books/records*
cierre del balance *year-end balance sheet/ closing balance sheet*
cifra de ingresos *revenue*
código de comercio *commercial code*
coeficiente de liquidez a corto plazo *acid-test ratio*
compensación excesiva por despido *golden parachute*
costo de mercaderías vendidas *cost of goods sold*
declaración jurada *affidavit*
descubierto, sobregirado, en rojo *overdrawn*
desgaste natural (normal), el deterioro por el uso *wear and tear*
dinero ocioso *barren money*
impuestos atrasados *back taxes*
impuestos diferidos activos *current deferred taxes*
incentivar *to incite, to stimulate*
fideicomisario(a) *trustee*
indemnización por despido *severance pay*
ingreso derivado de la actividad laboral *earned income*
mora, el atraso *delay*
punto de referencia *benchmark*
reducción del precio de venta *markdown*
registrar datos falsos en los estados contables *to cook the books*
relación precio-ganancia *P/E (price-to-earnings) ratio*
rendimiento al vencimiento *yield to maturity*
servicios varios *various services*
subproducto *by-product*

Nombre ______________________ Sección ______________ Fecha ______________

valor nominal *face value*
valor residual *scrap value*
valores en cartera *holdings*
venta en subasta *auction sale*
venta judicial, la ejecución forzosa *compulsory sale*

Términos relacionados con la computadora

analógico *analog*
el cable USB *USB cable*
el componente *component*
descargar de la Internet *download*
digital *digital*
el disco, el disco de programación, el disquete *computer disk*
el disco duro *hard disc*
el escáner, el escanógrafo *scanner*
la generación *generation*
el gráfico *graphic*
la informática *computer science*
el manual del usuario (dueño) *user's (owner's) manual*
el módem *modem*
navegar la red *to surf the Web*
la página de la Web *Web page*
la pantalla *screen*
la pastilla *microchip*
el periférico *peripheral (device)*
poderoso(a) *powerful*
el (la) programador(a) *programmer*
la red *Web, Internet*
el ratón *mouse*
el salvapantallas *screensaver*
el soporte físico, el equipo *hardware*
el soporte lógico, los programas *software*
la tecla *key*
el teclado *keyboard*
la velocidad *speed*
la versión *version*

Search

iLrn

Notas Culturales

- **Las compañías o empresas de negocios en los países de habla hispana** (*Types of Companies in Spanish-speaking Countries*) Businesses are organized according to the laws of the country where these are established. The several types of business organizations in Spanish-speaking countries are generally similar among themselves, but they differ considerably from those in the United States.
- **Sociedad Anónima (S.A.)** or **Compañía Anónima (C.A.) [de Capital Variable (de C.V.)]** This is the business organization that resembles a U.S. corporation the most. The company capital is in the form of stocks. In the case of losses, stockholders are only responsible for the worth of the stocks they share. The abbreviation S.A. should follow the name of the company. The **Sociedad Anónima de Capital Variable (S.A. de C.V.)** is common in Mexico.

Nombre ______________________ **Sección** ______________ **Fecha** ______________

- **Sociedad Limitada (S.L.)** or **Sociedad de Responsabilidad Limitada (S. de R.L.)** This is a type of company in which partners are responsible for losses up to the total capital subscribed by them. The name of the company should be followed by the abbreviations **S.L.** or **S. de R.L.,** depending on the case.
- **Sociedad Regular Colectiva** or **Sociedad en Nombre Colectivo** This is a type of company created by two or more partners that agree to do business under a common name. The name of such company is formed by the surnames of the principal partners; for example: **Rodríguez, Sánchez y Cía.**[1] Partners are collectively and individually responsible for the debts of the company up to the total of all their assets.
- **Sociedad en Comandita (S. en C.)** There are two types of partners in **sociedades en comandita: socios solidarios** (*joint liable partners*) or **socios comanditarios** (*silent or nominal partners*). The partners of the first kind are responsible for losses up to the total of all their assets; the second kind, only up to the total capital they contributed. The abbreviation **S. en C.** should follow the company name.
- **Sociedad Cooperativa** There are two kinds of cooperatives: that of producers and that of consumers. The first kind consists of associations of small producers who contribute their labor and a little capital. In Spanish-speaking countries, there are many cooperatives of farm workers and of fishermen. The second kind consists of consumer associations that are able to purchase goods wholesale, therefore acquiring the merchandise at lower prices.
- **Sociedad de Beneficio Mutuo** or **Sociedad Mutualista** These organizations are created for the mutual benefit of their members or for the pursuit of a common interest. These are generally not-for-profit organizations in which the benefits consist of the services provided to their members.

Actividades

Dígame... Answer the following questions, basing your answers on the dialogue.

1. ¿Por qué no vino ayer el Sr. Villalba?

   ____

2. La ayuda de la Sra. Pérez, ¿fue menos valiosa de lo que el Sr. Villalba esperaba?

   ____

3. ¿Cómo puede la Sra. Artiles automatizar la contabilidad de su negocio?

   ____

[1]**Cía.** is the abbreviation for **Compañía.**

4. ¿Qué hace la computadora después de que los empleados registran los pedidos?

____

5. ¿Cómo "sabe" la computadora qué artículos se vendieron?

____

6. ¿Qué hay que hacer para preparar la nómina usando la computadora?

____

7. ¿Puede la empresa de la Sra. Artiles usar las computadoras que ya tiene? ¿Por qué o por qué no?

____

8. ¿Qué tipos de programas va a necesitar?

____

9. ¿Por qué necesita la Sra. Artiles otro programa de composición de textos?

____

10. ¿Qué otro programa necesita la Sra. Artiles?

____

Hablemos Interview a classmate, using the following questions. When you have finished, switch roles.

1. ¿Sabe Ud. usar una computadora?
2. ¿Usa Ud. una computadora en su trabajo o en la universidad?
3. ¿Sabe Ud. «alimentar» una computadora con datos?
4. ¿Sabe Ud. preparar una nómina?
5. ¿Está su nombre en alguna nómina? ¿En cuál?
6. ¿Cuánto por ciento de su sueldo le descuentan? ¿Para qué?
7. ¿Usa Ud. algunos programas diseñados para trabajos contables? ¿Los usa en su trabajo o en su casa?
8. ¿Sabe Ud. trabajar con un programa de hoja de cálculo? ¿Con cuál?
9. Mi programa de composición de textos es rudimentario y está obsoleto. ¿Me puede recomendar uno nuevo? ¿Cuál?
10. ¿Cree Ud. que el uso de las computadoras ahorra tiempo y trabajo? ¿Por qué o por qué no?

Nombre ______________________________ Sección ____________ Fecha ____________

Quiz

VAMOS A PRACTICAR

A Fill in the blanks with the preterit or the imperfect forms of the Spanish equivalents of the verbs in parentheses.

MODELO El contador le __________ (*told*) a la Sra. Artiles que __________ (she had) que hacer un inventario.
El contador le **dijo** a la Sra. Artiles que **tenía** que hacer un inventario.

1. Ella no __________ (*was*) aquí cuando él __________ (*came*) anoche.
2. __________ (*It was*) las ocho de la mañana cuando el contador __________ (*arrived*) a la oficina.
3. Cuando el Sr. García __________ (*left*), la recepcionista __________ (*called*) a la Sra. Artiles por el intercomunicador, y le __________ (*told*) que el Sr. Villalba la __________ (*was waiting*).
4. El contador le __________ (*told*) a la Sra. Artiles que __________ (*needed*) un equipo de computación más sofisticado.
5. La Sra. Artiles __________ (*said*) que el contador __________ (*was going*) a venir hoy.
6. El Sr. Villalba no __________ (*could*) terminar el informe porque la Sra. Pérez le __________ (*told*) que no __________ (*could*) ayudarlo.
7. La Sra. Artiles __________ (*bought*) un programa de hoja de cálculo cuando el contador le __________ (*told*) que ella __________ (*needed*) automatizar la contabilidad de la empresa.

B Give the Spanish equivalents of the following. Be aware that *at* may translate to mean either **a** or **en.**

MODELO She was at work at three.
Ella estaba en su trabajo a las tres.

1. Mrs. Pérez lives at 456 Riverside Street.

____

2. We are going to see her at lunchtime.

____

3. I am going to be at the gate at that time.

____

4. We are going to talk with Mrs. Artiles at the hotel.

____

Nombre ______________________ Sección ______________ Fecha ______________

Sirva usted de intérprete

With two classmates, play the roles of the accountant, the client, and the interpreter who helps them communicate. Switch roles until each of you has played the interpreter's role.

Contador(a) —*I didn't come yesterday because I was preparing the report.*

Intérprete —______________________

Cliente —¿Consultó con la Sra. Rodríguez sobre nuestro sistema contable actual?

Intérprete —______________________

Contador(a) —*Yes, and her help was very valuable.*

Intérprete —______________________

Cliente —Bien, ¿qué cree Ud. que debo hacer?

Intérprete —______________________

Contador(a) —*You should automate your accounting system by using computers.*

Intérprete —______________________

Cliente —¿Cómo funciona el sistema?

Intérprete —______________________

Contador(a) —*First, you need to take inventory of all merchandise in the store and "feed" all this data into the computer.*

Intérprete —______________________

Cliente —Sí, y después registro los pedidos según llegan, pero ¿cómo registro las ventas?

Intérprete —______________________

Contador(a) —*Sales are registered automatically each time a salesperson uses a scanner to read the UPC on the label of a product.*

Intérprete —______________________

Cliente —Sí, ya lo sé; ese sistema se usa en los supermercados (*supermarkets*).

Intérprete —______________________

Contador(a) —*Also, using other programs, you can prepare the financial statements.*

Intérprete —______________________

Cliente —Para eso necesito «alimentar» la computadora con los gastos, ¿verdad?

Intérprete —______________________

Contador(a) —*Yes, and if you connect a time clock to the computer, it can prepare the payroll.*

Intérprete —______________________

Cliente —¿Qué programmas necesito para preparar los estados financieros?

Intérprete —______________________

Nombre ______________________ Sección ____________ Fecha ____________

Contador(a) —*A spreadsheet and a database program.*

Intérprete —____

Sirva usted de traductor(a)

You are the executive assistant to the national sales manager of a relatively new computer company. In sorting through your boss's mail, you found the following letter of inquiry written in Spanish. Translate it into English on a separate sheet of paper so your boss can read it.

EdP

Sucre, 54
Quito, Ecuador

19 de octubre de 2010

Sr. Jefe de Ventas
Smart Computers, Inc.
4200 Danvers Street
Chicago, IL 60211

Estimado señor:

La firma que represento está interesada en la distribución y venta en Ecuador de las computadoras fabricadas por Smart Computers. Tenemos muestras de sus catálogos y folletos de propaganda en que leímos, con mucho interés, las descripciones de varios tipos de sus computadoras y entendemos que nuestro mercado está en condiciones de absorber una cantidad apreciable de esos equipos. Nos interesan principalmente sus computadoras pequeñas y económicas, pero suficientemente poderosas para resolver dificultades en fábricas, establecimientos comerciales y oficinas públicas.

Nuestra firma distribuye actualmente equipos eléctricos y electrónicos de varias compañías americanas y japonesas. Si Uds. se interesan en esta oferta, estamos en condiciones de ofrecerles las referencias y garantías necesarias.

De usted respetuosamente,

Rafael Suárez
Gerente
Electrónica del Pacífico, S.A.

Nombre ______________________ Sección ____________ Fecha ____________

En estas situaciones With a partner, act out the following situations in Spanish.

1. You have evaluated the accounting needs of a corporation in Mexico. Tell the manager that the business needs to modernize its accounting system. Recommend that it be done using computers because they can end costly errors. Also explain that a computer can read the UPCs on the company's products with scanners and in doing so can help the business with managing inventory, sales, and orders.
2. You are the sales manager of a company. Ask the computer programmer if your staff can prepare invoices and orders to suppliers using a computer. Tell him/her that you want the invoices and orders to be personalized. Ask what software programs you will need and find out how much they might cost.

Casos With you and a partner playing the roles, work through the following scenarios.

1. An accountant and a company manager speak about automating the company's accounting system.
2. An outside consultant familiarizes employees with their company's new accounting system.

Un paso más

A Review the **Vocabulario adicional** in this lesson and computer vocabulary in previous lessons, and label the following parts of the computers and its peripherals.

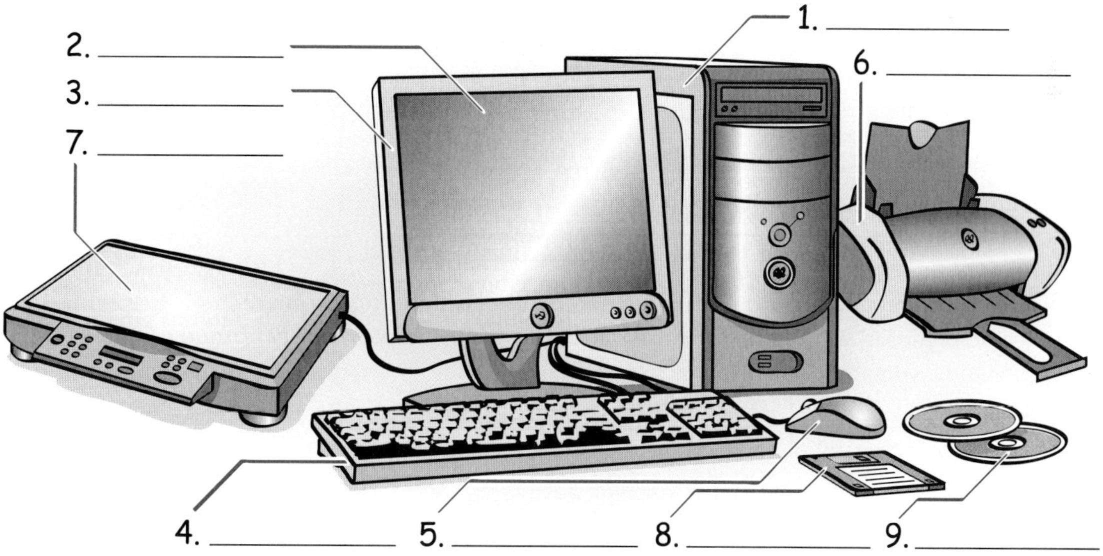

Nombre ______________________ **Sección** ____________ **Fecha** ____________

B You are looking for a computer for your personal use. Review the **Vocabulario adicional** in this lesson, and use it and other vocabulary you have learned to formulate ten questions for the salespersons at local computer stores. Use a separate sheet of paper.

C Now play the role of the computer store clerk to whom you asked the questions in exercise B. Answer those questions on a separate sheet of paper.

Lectura

After reading this **lectura,** get together with a partner and take turns answering the questions that follow.

Un sistema de contabilidad moderno y ajustado a las normas° internacionales es vital para la operación y el éxito de una empresa. Con un sistema de contabilidad rudimentario es casi imposible evitar el riesgo de enfrentar° problemas de flujo de caja, malgastar° su dinero y desperdiciar° oportunidades de ampliación° del negocio. La contabilidad le ayuda a administrar su negocio.

rules

encounter / waste

squander / enlargement

Por otra parte, la contabilidad de una empresa hace posible que las autoridades tributarias° evalúen sus operaciones —a lo que están autorizados por ley— y, si su contabilidad es clara y sencilla°, la auditoría puede y debe ser un proceso sencillo.

tributary

simple

Actualmente, los propietarios de pequeñas empresas usan programas de computación para llevar su contabilidad y otros aspectos de su negocio. ¿Cuál es el mejor programa? El que le ahorre tiempo para concentrarse en la administración de su negocio. Desde luego, si el negocio es pequeño, no pierda tiempo ni gaste dinero en implantar una contabilidad automática que podría ser más fácil si la hace con lápiz y papel°. La Corporación Financiera Internacional (IFC, por sus siglas en inglés) ofrece a las pequeñas y medianas empresas (PyME) información gratuita sobre la gestión empresarial y capacitación en las áreas de planificación empresarial, contabilidad, finanzas, recursos humanos, publicidad, ventas y tecnología informática. La Corporación también ofrece software empresarial, formularios profesionales e información general para ayudar a los hombres y mujeres de negocios o que aspiren a serlo a financiar, formalizar y hacer crecer sus negocios o a emprender° nuevos negocios.

paper

undertake

Source: Corporación Financiera Internacional

1. ¿Qué riesgos tiene usar un sistema de contabilidad rudimentario?
2. Para las autoridades tributarias, ¿qué ventajas tiene el uso de un sistema de contabilidad claro y sencillo?
3. ¿Cuál es el mejor programa de contabilidad computarizado?
4. ¿Qué quiere decir la sigla PyME?
5. ¿Qué ofrece la Corporación Financiera Internacional?

Y en su país...

1. ¿Qué autoridades tributarias están autorizadas para auditar la contabilidad de las empresas?
2. ¿Qué título universitario deben tener los encargados de llevar la contabilidad de las empresas?

Un dicho

Cuentas claras conservan amistades. *Clear accounts maintain friendships.*

Trivia

Updating Accounting in Latin America

In August 2007, the Dominican Republic hosted the first regional conference on accounting and auditing ever held in Latin America. The conference (known in Spanish as CReCER or **Contabilidad y Responsabilidad para el Crecimiento Económico Regional**) was organized by the World Bank, the Inter-American Development Bank and Multilateral Investment Fund, and the International Federation of Accountants. Its main purpose was to create greater awareness of the importance of sound accounting for the economic development of the region.

In regards to the corporate sector, it was decided that sound accounting and auditing significantly contribute to economic development. Since then, the World Bank and the Inter-American Development Bank have regularly supported and promoted policy reforms, but it is too early to evaluate results.

Lección 13

El impuesto sobre la renta

Objectives

Structures

- Changes in meaning with the imperfect and preterit of **conocer, saber,** and **querer**
- **Hace** meaning ***ago***
- Uses of **se**
- **¿Qué?** and **¿cuál?** used with **ser**

Business Communication

- Preparing an income tax return for a Spanish speaker with limited or no knowledge of English

La Sra. Rivas y su contador preparan la declaración de impuestos sobre la renta.

Los ingresos:

Contador —¿Cuál es su nombre completo, señora?
Sra. Rivas —María Inés Rivas.
Contador —Ud. es cabeza de familia, ¿verdad, señora?
Sra. Rivas —Sí, soy viuda y tengo dos hijos que viven conmigo.
Contador —¿Sus hijos son menores de edad?
Sra. Rivas —Mi hija es mayor de edad, pero estuvo estudiando en la universidad hasta que se graduó hace un mes.
Contador —Si el año pasado estudió cinco meses o más puede aparecer como dependiente suya. ¿Su hijo trabaja?
Sra. Rivas —Tiene un trabajo de medio tiempo en la universidad donde estudia.
Contador —Eso no cuenta, pero si ganó más de $4.600[1], debe hacer su propia declaración de impuestos. ¿Recibe Ud. un sueldo o trabaja por cuenta propia?
Sra. Rivas —Soy una de las socias de un negocio. Recibo un sueldo y, además, parte de las utilidades a fin de año, si las hay.
Contador —¿Trajo el comprobante de su sueldo y de los descuentos que le hicieron?
Sra. Rivas —Sí, aquí está.

---

[1]This amount varies from year to year.

Contador —¿Cobra Ud. alguna pensión?
Sra. Rivas —Sí, desde que murió mi esposo recibo una pensión de la compañía donde él trabajaba.
Contador —Bien, ¿trajo el documento que acredita los beneficios recibidos por ese concepto?
Sra. Rivas —Sí, señor.
Contador —¿Recibe Ud. rentas, comisiones o intereses de cuentas bancarias?
Sra. Rivas —Éstos son los intereses de mi cuenta de ahorros y de un certificado de depósito a plazo fijo.
Contador —¿Tiene bonos, acciones...?
Sra. Rivas —Tengo bonos municipales, pero están exentos de impuestos.
Contador —¿Tuvo ganancias en su negocio el año pasado?
Sra. Rivas —Sí, recibí doce mil setecientos dólares con cincuenta centavos por mi parte de las utilidades del negocio.
Contador —¿Algún otro ingreso? ¿Recibió regalos, premios, donaciones, legados, herencias?
Sra. Rivas —No, nada de eso.
Contador —¿Obtuvo alguna ganancia por la venta de su casa o de otros bienes muebles o inmuebles?
Sra. Rivas —Bueno, obtuve seiscientos dólares en la venta de muebles y otros artículos usados.
Contador —Si los vendió por menos de lo que le costaron no tiene que pagar impuestos.
Sra. Rivas —No sabía eso, y no sé cuánto costaron algunos de los muebles que vendí. Figúrese, eran de una abuela a la que nunca conocí.

Las deducciones:

Contador —Ahora vamos a hablar de las deducciones.
Sra. Rivas —Puedo deducir los intereses de la hipoteca de mi casa, ¿verdad?
Contador —Sí, y también los intereses de préstamos sobre la diferencia entre el valor de su casa y lo que debe de la hipoteca.
Sra. Rivas —¿Puedo deducir los gastos médicos?
Contador —Solamente si exceden del siete y medio por ciento de su ingreso bruto ajustado.
Sra. Rivas —¿Y las contribuciones a la iglesia y a las instituciones de caridad?
Contador —Sí, como Ud. usa la forma 1040, puede deducirlas, pero necesita los recibos de las donaciones de más de $250.
Sra. Rivas —Tengo los cheques cancelados.
Contador —Necesito los recibos. Para el Servicio de Rentas Internas los cheques cancelados no son prueba suficiente.
Sra. Rivas —Yo quería traerlos, pero mi hija no quiso buscarlos, y yo no tuve tiempo. ¿Qué más puedo descontar?
Contador —El dinero que depositó en un Keogh, y en una cuenta individual de retiro (IRA), porque Ud. no tiene 70 años y medio todavía.
Sra. Rivas —¿Qué es un Keogh?
Contador —Es una cuenta de retiro en la cual el empleado y el empleador depositan dinero.
Sra. Rivas —¿Se puede descontar algo más?
Contador —Sí, ¡lo que me va a pagar a mí por prepararle la declaración de impuestos!
Sra. Rivas —Bien. Mañana le traigo el documento que me faltó. ¿A qué hora se abre la oficina?
Contador —A las nueve.

Nombre ______________________ Sección ____________ Fecha ____________

¡Escuchemos! While listening to the dialogue, circle **V (verdadero)** if the statement is true or **F (falso)** if it is false.

1. La Sra. María Inés Rivas es cabeza de familia. V F
2. Los dos hijos de la Sra. Rivas son mayores de edad. V F
3. El hijo de la Sra. Rivas tiene un trabajo de tiempo completo. V F
4. La Sra. Rivas no trajo el comprobante de su sueldo. V F
5. Los intereses de las cuentas de ahorro no están exentos de impuestos. V F
6. La Sra. Rivas recibió $12.700 de herencia de una abuela a la que nunca conoció. V F
7. Los intereses de la hipoteca son deducibles. V F
8. Todos los gastos médicos son deducibles. V F
9. Para deducir las donaciones de caridad de más de $250 necesita los recibos. V F
10. La Sra. Rivas no puede deducir depósitos en una cuenta individual de retiro (IRA). V F

Audio VOCABULARIO

Cognados

el certificado de depósito
la comisión
completo(a)
la contribución
conveniente
la deducción
el (la) dependiente
la donación, el donativo
el fondo mutuo
la institución
la invitación
médico(a) (*adj.*)
municipal
la pensión
tradicional
la universidad

Nombres

el (la) abuelo(a) *grandfather, grandmother*
la acción *stock, share*
los bienes inmuebles, los inmuebles, los bienes raíces *real estate*
los bienes muebles *personal property*
el bono *bond*
el (la) cabeza de familia *head of household, head of the family*
la caridad *charity*
la cuenta *account*
la cuenta de ahorros *savings account*
la cuenta individual de retiro *individual retirement account (IRA)*
la declaración de impuestos, la planilla de contribución sobre ingresos (*P. Rico*) *tax return*

el (la) empleador(a), el (la) patrón(ona) *employer*
el (la) esposo(a) *husband, wife*
el fin *end*
la forma, la planilla *form*
la herencia *inheritance*
los hijos[1] *children*
la hipoteca *mortgage*
la iglesia *church*
el impuesto sobre la renta *income tax*
el ingreso bruto ajustado, ingreso neto *adjusted gross income*
el legado *bequest*
los muebles[2] *furniture*
el premio *prize*
el préstamo *loan*
la prueba *proof*
el recibo *receipt*
el regalo *gift*
la renta *revenue, income*
el (la) socio(a) *partner*
la utilidad, la ganancia *profit*
el (la) viudo(a) *widower, widow*

Verbos

acreditar *to accredit, to give official authorization*
aparecer[3] *to appear*
conocer *to meet (for the first time), to know*
contar (o:ue) *to count*
deber *to owe*
deducir[4] *to deduct*
depositar *to deposit*
estudiar *to study*
figurarse *to imagine*
graduarse *to graduate*
morir (o:ue), morirse (o:ue), fallecer *to die*
obtener, conseguir (e:i) *to obtain, to get*
vivir *to live*

Adjetivos

cancelado(a) *canceled*
recibido(a) *received*
suficiente *sufficient, enough*
usado(a), de uso *used*

Otras palabras y expresiones

a plazo fijo *fixed rate, fixed term (deposit)*
el comprobante del sueldo y de los descuentos *wage and tax statement (W-2)*
el (la) cual *which, what*
desde que *since*
mayor de edad *of age*
medio tiempo, media jornada *part-time*
menor de edad *minor*
ni tampoco *not either, neither*
sobre *on*
trabajar por cuenta propia *to be self-employed*

Audio VOCABULARIO ADICIONAL

a ser puesto en práctica *when they are acted*
al alcanzar el poder *after accessing to power*
andar mal *to go wrong*
argumentar *to argue*
cumplir *to comply*
cuyos *whose*

---

[1]The plural form **hijos** may mean *sons* or it may mean *children* if it refers to son(s) and daughter(s).
[2]Used in the plural form to mean the collective *furniture;* the singular form refers to a specific piece of furniture.
[3]First person, present indicative: **yo aparezco**
[4]First person, present indicative: **yo deduzco**

Nombre ______________________ Sección ____________ Fecha ____________

defensor(a) *defender*
disminuir *to decrease*
en conjunto *in its totality*
en este campo *in this field*
fuente de ingresos *income source*
hacer realidad *to become true*
han prometido *have promised*
han sido *have been*
no ha ocurrido *has not happened*
petróleo *oil*
pobre *poor*
políticos *politicians*
porción *part,* portion, 13.
Producto Interno Bruto (PIB) *Gross Domestic Product (GDP)*
se ven obligados *are pushed*
siglo pasado *past century*
un mayor porcentaje *a large percent*

Términos relacionados con la declaración de impuestos

alquilar, arrendar *to rent, to lease*
conjunto(a) joint
el (la) contribuyente *taxpayer*
debido(a), vencido(a) *due*
deducible *deductible*
la deducción general *standard deduction*
el desempleo *unemployment*
el dividendo *dividend*
en exceso (de) *in excess (of)*
la escala de impuestos *tax rate table*
la evasión fiscal *tax evasion*
la exclusión *exclusion*
la exención *exemption*
la forma corta (larga) *short (long) form*
el impuesto a la propiedad, la contribución *property tax*
el impuesto estatal, el impuesto del estado *state tax*
el impuesto sobre la venta *sales tax*
los ingresos sujetos a impuestos *taxable income*
la miscelánea *miscellany*
la multa *penalty, fine*
la pensión alimenticia *alimony*
el recargo adicional *additional charge*
el reembolso *refund, reimbursement*
registrar *to file*
el renglón *line (on a paper); item*
reportar *to report*
separado(a) *separate*
el subtotal *subtotal*

Search

iLrn

Notas Culturales

- The majority of the countries in the Hispanic world, including Spain, have tax systems very different from that of the United States. Most Spanish-speaking nations do impose some sort of income tax upon their residents. However, these governments obtain most of their income through assessed taxes, property taxes, and customs duties. Both Spain and Mexico also collect funds from the **I.V.A. (el impuesto al valor agregado),** or value-added tax (V.A.T.), which is an indirect tax added to the value of products and services in the various phases of production.
- It is interesting to note that while the number of Spanish-speaking citizens is growing rapidly in the United States, many governmental agencies are slow to become bilingual. The Internal Revenue Service provides a number of helpful publications in both Spanish and English. It does not, however, provide tax forms in Spanish. Tax payers who speak only Spanish may have to find a bilingual friend, family member, or accountant to help them file their tax returns. Another source of help lies in volunteer organizations, such as VITA/TCE (Volunteer Income Tax Assistance/Tax Counseling for the Elderly) and AARP (American Association of Retired Persons), which often provide bilingual assistance at no cost to qualified taxpayers.
- Using the Internet to file tax forms has become popular in the Hispanic community. At first, some people were attracted to the system because they expected to receive rebates, and this way they would receive them earlier. Then many realized that it was easy to file taxes electronically using any of the many programs available, and that it was safe and less expensive than using a tax preparer.

Nombre ______________________ Sección ____________ Fecha ____________

Actividades

Dígame... Answer the following questions, basing your answers on the dialogue.

1. ¿Cuántos dependientes tiene la Sra. Rivas?

2. ¿Todavía estudia la hija de la Sra. Rivas en la universidad?

3. ¿La Sra. Rivas es empleada o trabaja por cuenta propia?

4. El hijo de la Sra. Rivas, ¿trabaja o estudia?

5. ¿Desde cuándo recibe una pensión la Sra. Rivas?

6. ¿Qué tipos de cuentas bancarias tiene la Sra. Rivas?

7. ¿Debe pagar impuestos la Sra. Rivas por el dinero que recibió de la venta de sus muebles viejos? ¿Por qué o por qué no?

8. ¿De quién eran algunos de los muebles viejos que vendió la Sra. Rivas?

9. ¿Por qué puede descontar la Sra. Rivas el dinero que puede poner en su cuenta individual de retiro?

10. Los cheques cancelados, ¿son prueba suficiente de las donaciones de más de $250?

Nombre ______________________ Sección __________ Fecha __________

Hablemos Interview a classmate, using the following questions. When you have finished, switch roles.

1. ¿Es Ud. cabeza de familia?
2. ¿Es Ud. mayor de edad?
3. ¿Trabaja Ud. en la universidad donde estudia?
4. ¿En qué banco(s) tiene Ud. su(s) cuenta(s)?
5. ¿Qué tipos de cuentas tiene?
6. ¿Tiene alguna cuenta de retiro?
7. ¿Sabe Ud. qué es un Keogh?
8. ¿Vende Ud. a veces sus muebles viejos?
9. ¿Tiene Ud. casa propia? ¿Tiene que pagar la hipoteca de la casa?
10. ¿Tiene Ud. bonos o acciones?

Quiz

VAMOS A PRACTICAR

A Fill in the blank with the appropriate forms of **querer, saber,** or **conocer.**

MODELO Ayer __________ a tu hija. Yo no __________ que era contadora. Lo __________ ayer.
Ayer **conocí** a tu hija. Yo no **sabía** que era contadora. Lo **supe** ayer.

1. Hace dos días que ella __________ a la Sra. Rivas en la oficina del contador.
2. Yo no __________ que ella __________ al contador. Lo __________ el jueves.
3. Yo __________ depositar más dinero en mi cuenta de retiro, pero mi esposo no __________.
4. ¿__________ Ud. que hay dos tipos de IRA?
5. Ella __________ mandar a su hijo a una universidad local, pero él no __________.

B Fill in the blanks with **qué** or **cuál** as needed.

1. ¿__________ es un Keogh?
2. ¿__________ es mejor, la cuenta IRA Roth tradicional o la nueva?
3. ¿__________ es su dirección?
4. ¿__________ es un bien inmueble?
5. ¿__________ son sus gastos médicos?
6. ¿__________ es una cuenta IRA?

Nombre ______________________ **Sección** __________ **Fecha** __________

C Write complete sentences that indicate when the following events happened, using the cue provided and following the model.

Modelo ella / graduarse / (*six years ago*)
Ella se graduó hace seis años.
Hace seis años que ella se graduó.

1. nosotros / conocer al contador / (*two months ago*)

____

____

2. mi hermano / morirse / (*four years ago*)

____

____

3. yo / conseguir un buen empleo / (*three days ago*)

____

____

4. la Sra. Roque / depositar el dinero / (*ten minutes ago*)

____

____

5. Aurora / ver a Pedro / (*six weeks ago*)

____

____

Sirva usted de intérprete With three classmates, play the roles of Sr. Valle, Sra. Valle, the accountant, and the interpreter who helps them communicate. Switch roles until each of you has played the interpreter's role.

Contador(a) —*Let's talk first about your income. Do you receive a salary or are you self-employed?*

Intérprete —____

Sr. Valle —Yo trabajo para una compañía grande, pero mi esposa trabaja por cuenta propia.

Intérprete —____

Contador(a) —*Did you bring your W-2 (wage and tax statement)?*

Intérprete —____

Sra. Valle —Sí, aquí está. También tengo aquí los ingresos netos de mi esposo.

Intérprete —____

Nombre ______________________ **Sección** ____________ **Fecha** ____________

Contador(a) —*Mr. Valle, how do you earn your income?*

Intérprete —____

Sr. Valle —Yo vendo automóviles y recibo una comisión sobre las ventas.

Intérprete —____

Contador(a) —*Fine. Do you have any other income?*

Intérprete —____

Sr. Valle —Sí. Tenemos una casa que alquilamos por $1.500 mensuales.

Intérprete —____

Contador(a) —*Did you receive the rent for twelve months?*

Intérprete —____

Sr. Valle —Sí, pero tuvimos algunos gastos. Aquí están los comprobantes.

Intérprete —____

Contador(a) —*Do you have any other investments besides the house you now rent?*

Intérprete —____

Sra. Valle —Tenemos $4.000 en bonos de los Estados Unidos.

Intérprete —____

Contador(a) —*You have to pay taxes on these bonds when collecting them. Do you own any stocks?*

Intérprete —____

Sr. Valle —No, no tenemos ninguna.

Intérprete —____

Contador(a) —*Did you receive any retirement income, a pension, or interest from bank accounts?*

Intérprete —____

Sra. Valle —Tampoco.

Intérprete —____

Contador(a) —*Did you put money into an individual retirement account or a Keogh plan, Mr. Valle?*

Intérprete —____

Sr. Valle —Sí, yo dejo el 7% de mi sueldo en una cuenta de retiro 401k.

Intérprete —____

Contador(a) —*Did you receive any inheritance or donations?*

Intérprete —____

Sra. Valle —No. Ésos son todos nuestros ingresos.

Nombre ______________________ **Sección** ____________ **Fecha** ____________

Intérprete —____

Contador(a) —*Okay, now we're going to talk about your deductions.*

Intérprete —____

Sirva usted de traductor(a) Mr. Pulido does not speak English, and he needs to give the following information to the person who is going to help him prepare his tax return. On a separate sheet of paper, translate Mr. Pulido's notes so that he can give your translation to his English-speaking tax preparer.

Datos

Nombre: Francisco Pulido Romero
Domicilio (calle, número, ciudad, estado, zona postal):
Calle Palma, 32, Miami, Florida 33165
Estado civil: casado
Nombre de la esposa: Luz María Valle de Pulido
Número de hijos: tres; todos son menores de edad, y viven en mi casa.

Ingresos

- Trabajo en una tienda en un centro comercial y gané $28.500 el año pasado. Ver el W-2, adjunto.
- Mi esposa trabaja por cuenta propia. Vende mercancía de casa en casa. El año pasado ganó $22.341,76 de comisión.
- Nos hicieron los descuentos correspondientes a los impuestos, el seguro social y el Medicare.
- Adjunto envío los comprobantes de las cantidades recibidas mensualmente.
- Mi esposa depositó $500 en su cuenta individual de retiro.

Egresos

- Pagamos $2.412,87 de intereses en la hipoteca de la casa.
- Pagamos $1.456,00 de impuestos a la propiedad.
- Nuestros gastos médicos fueron $567.
- Mi esposa pagó $2.785,50 por la gasolina y otros gastos del carro que usa para su trabajo.
- Ella les hizo regalos a clientes por un total de $431.

Nombre ______________________ **Sección** __________ **Fecha** __________

En estas situaciones

With a partner, act out the following situations in Spanish.

1. You work in an accounting office preparing tax returns. Help a client who doesn't speak English. Ask who is the head of the household, if there are any minor children in the home, and if any of the children who are of age are studying full time. Say that children can be declared as dependents only until the date when they finish schooling. Ask if your client receives a salary or is self-employed and if he/she brought a W-2 form. Also, find out if he/she received any inheritances, donations, bequests, prizes, gifts, pensions, revenues, or commissions of any type. If so, ask for written verification(s).
2. One of your Spanish-speaking clients returned today to the tax preparation office where you work to talk about possible income tax deductions. Ask your client how much was paid in interest on the home mortgage and if there is a second mortgage on the house. Ask how much state and municipal tax was paid, and if any contributions to charities or churches were made. Ask for the total of business entertainment expenses. Say that the interest paid on installment purchases and credit card bills cannot be deducted.

Casos

With you and a partner playing the roles, work through the following scenarios.

1. A tax preparer and a client are working on a tax return form.
2. A husband and wife discuss documents needed to take to the tax preparer's office.

Nombre ______________________ Sección ____________ Fecha ____________

Un paso más

A Review the **Vocabulario adicional** in this lesson, and use it and other vocabulary you have learned to translate and fill in the following excerpt from a U.S. 1040 form with Spanish equivalents.

Income ______________________

1. Wages, tips ______________________
2. Interest income ______________________
3. Total dividends, no exclusion ______________________
4. Capital gains (losses) ______________________
5. Social Security subject to tax ______________________
6. All unemployment insurance ______________________
7. State tax refund ______________________
8. Alimony received, taxable pensions ______________________
9. Other income ______________________
10. Total gross income ______________________

Adjustments to income ______________________

11. Retirement plans deductions ______________________
12. Alimony paid ______________________
13. Total adjustments ______________________
14. Adjusted gross income (line 10 less line 13) ______________________

Itemized deductions ______________________

15. Medical expenses in excess of 7.5% of adjusted gross income ______________________

    ____

16. State and local taxes ______________________
17. Home-mortgage interest ______________________
18. Charitable contributions ______________________
19. Miscellaneous deductions in excess of 2% of adjusted gross income ______________________

    ____

20. Subtotal itemized deductions ______________________
21. Personal exemption(s) ______________________
22. Standard deduction (if more than line 20) ______________________
23. Total deductions (lines 20 and 21 or line 22) ______________________
24. Taxable income (line 14 less line 23) ______________________
25. Income tax due (see tax rate table) ______________________

Nombre ______________________ Sección ______________ Fecha ______________

B A self-employed friend of yours has asked whether you can recommend a tax preparer. When you tell him that you have seen the following ad in the paper, he asks you several questions. How would you answer them?

© Cengage Learning

1. ¿Dónde trabajó antes el Sr. Raúl Armendáriz?

____

2. ¿Dónde está situada la oficina del Sr. Armendáriz?

____

3. Además de la preparación de impuestos, ¿qué otros servicios ofrece Armendáriz Tax Service?

____

4. ¿Cuánto tiempo de experiencia tiene el Sr. Armendáriz?

____

5. ¿Cuánto cobra el Sr. Armendáriz por la primera consulta?

____

6. ¿A qué hora se puede llamar por teléfono a Armendáriz Tax Service? ¿Por qué?

____

[1]colloquial in the United States for **Ministerio de Hacienda**

Nombre ______________________ **Sección** __________ **Fecha** __________

Lectura After reading this **lectura**, get together with a partner and take turns answering the following questions.

El sistema tributario° de los países hispanos es muy distinto del usado en los Estados Unidos. Al igual° que aquí, los hispanos en sus países pagan impuestos sobre sus sueldos, que sus empleadores les descuentan automáticamente, y los negociantes° tienen que declarar sus utilidades a fin de año, y pagan impuestos sobre ellas. Sin embargo,° en la mayoría de esos países, el resto de la población no tiene que llenar todos los años declaraciones de ingresos, ni calcular sus propios° impuestos. Estos países no recaudan° la mayor parte de sus ingresos mediante un impuesto a la renta, sino mediante impuestos a la producción o a la venta. El consumidor los paga como parte del precio de los artículos que compra, en la misma forma° que aquí pagamos los impuestos a la gasolina. Por ese motivo,° los hispanos necesitan mucha ayuda a la hora de preparar sus impuestos.

sistema... *tax system*
Al... *In the same way*
business people
Sin... *Nevertheless*
own
collect
misma... *same way*
Por... *That is why*

1. ¿Qué impuestos pagan los latinoamericanos?
2. ¿Qué no tienen que hacer los latinoamericanos para pagar sus impuestos?
3. ¿Cómo recaudan la mayor parte de los impuestos los gobiernos latinoamericanos?
4. ¿Cómo pagamos en los Estados Unidos los impuestos a la gasolina?

Y usted...

1. ¿Necesita ayuda para preparar su declaración de impuestos? ¿Por qué o por qué no?
2. ¿Qué sistema tributario considera más justo, el que grava (*taxes*) los ingresos o el que grava el consumo? ¿Por qué?

Un dicho

El que paga lo que debe, sabe lo que tiene. *He who pays his debts, knows what he has.*

Trivia

Revenues for most Latin American governments are generated from taxes on goods and services (including value-added, sales, and excise taxes), and not from income taxes. In this way, the tax burden on consumed goods is identical for all income levels. Although this appears to be fair at first glance, it is not. Indeed, lower-income individuals end up paying a higher share of their income in taxes than higher-income individuals do.

Lección 14

En la agencia de publicidad

Objectives

Structures

- The past participle
- The present perfect tense
- The past perfect (pluperfect) tense

Business Communication

- Determining a client's advertising needs
- Working in sales at a department store

El Sr. Sosa, copropietario del Bazar Quisqueya, visita una agencia de publicidad.

Sr. Sosa —Mi socia y yo estamos interesados en hacerle propaganda a nuestro negocio.
Agente —¿Cuál es su giro?
Sr. Sosa —Somos importadores y distribuidores de ropa, y de carteras y otros accesorios de cuero.
Agente —¿Quieren hacerles publicidad a todas sus importaciones o solamente a algunos artículos?
Sr. Sosa —Principalmente a la ropa de niños, porque es un nuevo renglón que hemos agregado.
Agente —¿No quieren hacerle publicidad a la ropa para adultos?
Sr. Sosa —No, la ropa para hombres y para mujeres se vende bien todo el año.
Agente —¿Cuánto tiempo hace que introdujeron en el mercado este nuevo renglón?
Sr. Sosa —Hace más de seis meses, pero no hemos tenido suerte, a pesar de que nuestras confecciones son de primera calidad.
Agente —¿Qué prendas de vestir para niños distribuyen Uds.?
Sr. Sosa —Para las niñas, vestidos, blusas y faldas. Para los niños, camisas y pantalones. Para todos, pantalones de vaquero y, en el invierno, chaquetas y abrigos.
Agente —Sus prendas de vestir, ¿son fabricadas exclusivamente para Uds.?
Sr. Sosa —Sí, señor. Tenemos un contrato con una fábrica que nos confecciona artículos diseñados por nosotros, y que llevan nuestra marca.
Agente —¿Tienen la marca registrada?
Sr. Sosa —Ya hicimos la solicitud a la Oficina de Marcas y Patentes, pero todavía no hemos recibido respuesta.

Agente —¿Cuál es el volumen de ventas actual?

Sr. Sosa —Nuestras ventas varían notablemente con la estación. Durante el verano pasado las ventas no sobrepasaron los $100.000 mensuales.

Agente —La fábrica que produce para Uds., ¿tiene capacidad instalada para poder servir grandes pedidos?

Sr. Sosa —Sí, señor. Ésta es una industria manufacturera típica, y la mano de obra es barata en la República Dominicana.

Agente —Bien, mi consejo es empezar por mejorar la apariencia de sus productos y hacer resaltar sus características especiales.

Sr. Sosa —Nuestros productos son de magnífica calidad, pero hay mucha competencia. Nunca había visto tantas marcas nuevas en el mercado.

Agente —Señor, como Ud. ha visto, la calidad sola no vende. Hacen falta calidad, presentación y publicidad.

Sr. Sosa —¿Cómo puedo mejorar la presentación?

Agente —Por ejemplo, puede presentar los artículos envueltos en bolsas de plástico transparente. Y... ¿cómo son las etiquetas?

Sr. Sosa —Generalmente son de tela, con la marca, el país de origen y otras indicaciones que exige la ley.

Agente —Bien. Hay que cambiarlas; hay que agregarles un logo y un lema. Después, necesita hacer una buena campaña publicitaria.

Sr. Sosa —Yo había pensado en contratar anuncios en los periódicos y revistas de circulación local.

Agente —Pues yo pienso que debemos organizar una campaña de promoción en varias tiendas, precedida de anuncios en la radio y la televisión.

Sr. Sosa —La publicidad por televisión es muy efectiva, pero es muy cara.

Agente —No es tan cara si se hace a través de la compañía de cable local. Y el cable llega a hogares con poder adquisitivo.

Sr. Sosa —Sí, es verdad.

Agente —Nosotros podemos diseñar para Uds. una campaña masiva, con varias opciones en cuanto al costo.

Sr. Sosa —Me parece una magnífica idea.

¡Escuchemos!

While listening to the dialogue, circle **V (verdadero)** if the statement is true or **F (falso)** if it is false.

1. El Sr. Sosa es uno de los dueños del Bazar Quisqueya.	V	F
2. El Bazar Quisqueya es un negocio de exportación de ropa y de accesorios de cuero.	V	F
3. Los accesorios de cuero son un renglón nuevo del Bazar.	V	F
4. La ropa para adultos se vende bien todo el año.	V	F
5. Las confecciones para niños son de primera calidad.	V	F
6. Hace seis meses que venden ropa para niños.	V	F
7. Las ventas del Bazar Quisqueya no varían mucho con la estación.	V	F
8. La mano de obra es cara en la República Dominicana.	V	F

Nombre ______________________ **Sección** __________ **Fecha** __________

9. Las etiquetas indican el país de origen de las mercancías. V F

10. La publicidad por la televisión por cable es muy cara. V F

VOCABULARIO

Audio

Cognados

el agente
la apariencia
el bazar
la blusa
efectivo(a)
exclusivamente
la idea
la industria
el logo(grama)
masivo(a)
el origen
la patente
el plástico
la presentación
principalmente
la radio
la República Dominicana
transparente

Nombres

el abrigo *coat, sweater*
el anuncio *ad*
la bolsa *bag*
la camisa *shirt*
la campaña de promoción *ad campaign*
la capacidad *means, capacity*
la característica *feature*
la cartera *handbag, purse*
la chaqueta, la chamarra (*Méx.*) *jacket*
la circulación, la tirada *circulation*
la competencia *competition*
el (la) copropietario(a) *co-owner*
el consejo *advice*
la estación *season*
la falda, la saya *skirt*
la indicación *specification*
el invierno *winter*
el lema *slogan*
la marca registrada *registered brand, trademark*
los pantalones *trousers, pants, slacks*
los pantalones vaqueros, los pantalones de mezclilla *jeans*
la publicidad, la propaganda *advertising, publicity*
el renglón, la línea *line* (*of merchandise*) *item*
el verano *summer*
el vestido *dress*

Verbos

agregar *to add*
confeccionar *to make, to prepare, to put together*
diseñar *to design*
distribuir[1] *to distribute*
exigir[2] *to require, to demand*
introducir[3] *to introduce*
mejorar *to improve*
organizar *to organize*

---

[1]Present indicative forms: **distribuyo, distribuyes, distribuye, distribuimos, distribuyen**
[2]First person singular: **yo exijo**
[3]Irregular first person singular: **yo introduzco**

Nombre ______________________ Sección ____________ Fecha ____________

presentar *to present*
sobrepasar *to surpass*
variar[1] *to change, to vary*

Adjetivos

envuelto(a) *wrapped*
instalado(a) *installed, available*
mensual, al mes *monthly*
precedido(a) *preceded*
solo(a) *alone*
tanto(a) *as (so) much*
tantos(as) *so many*

Otras palabras y expresiones

a pesar de (que) *in spite of (the fact that)*
la capacidad instalada *productive capacity*
generalmente, por lo general *generally, usually*
hacer resaltar *to emphasize*
notablemente *notably*
nunca *never*
por ejemplo *for example*
tener suerte *to be lucky*
únicamente *only*
venderse bien *to sell well*

Audio VOCABULARIO ADICIONAL

acertar *to conjecture right*
analfabeto(a) *illiterate*
ante *before*
cobrizo *brown*
¿Cómo lo dice(s)? *How do you say it?*
conservar *to preserve*
dejar claro *to (make it) clear*
forma de vida *way of life*
lengua franca *common language, lingua franca*
localismo *localism*
locutor(a) *(tv, radio) announcer, speaker*
los que llamamos *those we identify as*
millardo *billion*
orgullo latino *Latino pride*
perdurar *to last*
poder adquisitivo *purchasing power*
que hacen publicidad *advertisers*
reconocimiento *recognition, acceptance*
seguir empeñado *to insist on*
sentirse bien *to feel well / fine*
tener en cuenta *to realize*

Términos relacionados con la publicidad

a toda plana *full-page*
anunciar *to advertise*
la autopista *expressway, freeway*
el cartel *poster*
la demostración *show*
el día de semana, el día de trabajo, el día hábil, el día laborable *weekday, workday*
el dibujo *drawing, design*
la edición *edition, issue*
el ejemplar *copy, sample*
en blanco y negro *in black and white*
en colores *in color*
el éxito *success*
filmar *to film*
el fin de semana *weekend*
el medio publicitario *advertising media*
las páginas amarillas *Yellow Pages*
la película, el filme *film*

[1]Present indicative forms: **varío, varías, varía, variamos, varían**

Nombre ______________________ Sección ____________ Fecha ____________

publicar *to publish*
el sondeo de opinión pública, la encuesta *poll, survey*
sugestivo(a), sugerente *catchy, suggestive*
el texto *text*
la valla, el anuncio panorámico *billboard*

Search

iLrn

Notas Culturales

- The growing number of homes in the United States in which Spanish is spoken as the first language has given rise to more communication and advertising delivered in Spanish through various media. Today, cities with significant Latino populations offer newspapers and magazines in Spanish. Among the newspapers with the greatest circulation and popular online editons are Miami's *El Nuevo Herald* (www.elherald.com), Los Angeles' *La Opinión* (www.laopinion.com), New York City's *El Diario*, Washington D.C. based *La Nación* (lanacionusa.com), and Toronto's *El Popular* (www.diarioelpopular.com).
- As a reflection of the growing importance of Spanish-speaking markets in North America and Latin America, companies frequently produce translated versions of their products. *The Wall Street Journal*, for example, provides a Spanish edition of its newspaper, replete with advertisements for North American companies and products in addition to its customary business and financial articles. Other examples include: the English magazine *Ladies Home Journal*, which for many years has also published a Spanish version and *People* which produces a successful Latin-orientated version of its magazine called ***People en Español***.
- Television is also mindful of the already substantial and rapidly growing markets of Spanish speakers. In the United States, four major channels broadcast in Spanish: **Univision, Telemundo, Azteca América,** and **Telefutura.** Some American channels such as CNN, FOX, The History Channel, and The Discovery Channel also broadcast in Spanish for their respective audiences in the U.S. as well as in Latin America. All these publications have their own websites. The most frequently visited web pages are **Google Español, Terra.com, Univision.com,** and **Hispaniconline.com.**
- During the last decade as the consumer power of Hispanic Americans began to represent tens of billions of dollars, many advertising agencies in the United States, particularly those in the Northeast, Southeast, Southwest, and on the West Coast, created departments to cater exclusively to Spanish-speaking consumers.

Actividades

Dígame... Answer the following questions, basing your answers on the dialogue.

1. ¿Quién es el Sr. Sosa?

____

2. ¿Por qué va el Sr. Sosa a una agencia de publicidad?

____

3. ¿Qué ha hecho recientemente (*recently*) la empresa del Sr. Sosa?

____

4. ¿Por qué no les va a hacer publicidad a los otros artículos?

____

5. ¿Por qué no tiene ya registrada su marca el Sr. Sosa?

____

Nombre ______________________________ Sección ______________ Fecha ______________

6. ¿Por qué dice el Sr. Sosa que no han tenido suerte?

____

7. ¿A cuánto alcanzaron las ventas durante el verano?

____

8. ¿Qué artículos distribuyen el Sr. Sosa y su socia?

____

9. ¿Qué tipo de industria es la industria de confecciones?

____

10. ¿Por qué es la República Dominicana un buen país para poner una industria manufacturera?

____

11. ¿Qué cree el agente que debe hacer el Sr. Sosa?

____

12. ¿Qué cree el agente que necesita un producto para tener éxito en el mercado?

____

13. ¿En qué tipos de anuncios había pensado el Sr. Sosa?

____

14. ¿Qué dice el agente de la publicidad por televisión?

____

Hablemos Interview a classmate, using the following questions. When you have finished, switch roles.

1. ¿Cree Ud. que la publicidad ayuda más a los productos de buena calidad o a los de mala calidad?
2. ¿Cree Ud. que la publicidad beneficia al cliente? ¿Por qué o por qué no?
3. ¿Cuál cree Ud. que es la publicidad más efectiva? ¿Por qué?
4. ¿Compra Ud. los artículos que ve anunciados por televisión? ¿Por qué o por qué no?
5. ¿Qué anuncio de television le gusta más? ¿Por qué?
6. ¿Cuál le parece más efectivo? ¿Por qué?
7. ¿Qué le parece la idea de tener programas de televisión sin anuncios?
8. Los anuncios, ¿dicen la verdad acerca de la calidad de los productos?
9. ¿Cree Ud. lo que dicen las etiquetas de los productos? ¿Por qué o por qué no?

10. ¿Prefiere Ud. comprar productos de marcas registradas? ¿Por qué o por qué no?
11. ¿Qué productos ha comprado Ud. después de verlos anunciados en la televisión?
12. ¿Cree Ud. que deben prohibirse los anuncios en los programas para niños? ¿Por qué o por qué no?

Quiz

Vamos a practicar

A Complete the following sentences with the past participles of the verbs given, using them as adjectives.

anunciar

1. Las prendas de vestir ____________ en la revista no son de cuero.
2. La campaña de promoción está ____________ en el periódico de hoy.
3. Los precios ____________ por televisión comienzan mañana.
4. El plástico ____________ no es transparente.

diseñar

5. La etiqueta fue ____________ por la Srta. Martínez.
6. El logo va a ser ____________ por mí.
7. No me gustan las prendas de vestir ____________ por ella.
8. Los zapatos ____________ por él son muy caros.

escribir

9. El texto del anuncio ____________ por él es muy bueno.
10. Las cartas ____________ por la Sra. López vinieron de Puerto Rico.
11. No he leído los libros ____________ por ella.
12. La revista está ____________ en español.

B Complete the following sentences with the present perfect or the pluperfect of the verbs in parentheses, as required.

1. Ellos todavía no ____________ (anunciar) la nueva marca de fábrica.
2. Hasta el año pasado nosotros ____________ (importar) solamente carteras y botas.
3. En este verano las ventas no ____________ (sobrepasar) los $4.000 dólares al día.

Nombre ________________ **Sección** ________ **Fecha** ________

4. La Sra. Vargas no __________ (tener) tiempo de leer el informe todavía.

5. Hasta ayer, la Srta. Rojas no __________ (decir) que necesitaba ayuda.

6. Él me va a enviar las muestras que yo le __________ (pedir) hoy.

7. Quiero comprar las botas que (yo) __________ (ver).

8. Yo __________ (poner) las chaquetas nuevas aquí ayer.

Sirva usted de intérprete

With two classmates, play the roles of Sr. Gutiérrez, the advertising agent, and the interpreter who helps them communicate. Switch roles until each of you has played the interpreter's role.

Sr. Gutiérrez —Vengo a verlo porque he decidido hacer alguna publicidad para mi negocio.

Intérprete —______________________________

Agente —*What is your line of business?*

Intérprete —______________________________

Sr. Gutiérrez —Tengo una tienda de ropa de hombre.

Intérprete —______________________________

Agente —*In that line of business there's a lot of competition.*

Intérprete —______________________________

Sr. Gutiérrez —Sí, mucha. En el centro comercial donde estamos han abierto varias tiendas de ropa de hombre este año.

Intérprete —______________________________

Agente —*Do your ready-made clothes have any special features?*

Intérprete —______________________________

Sr. Gutiérrez —Sí, vendemos una línea de ropa con diseños exclusivos.

Intérprete —______________________________

Agente —*It's expensive clothing, right?*

Intérprete —______________________________

Sr. Gutiérrez —Bueno, la ropa con diseños exclusivos es cara por lo general.

Intérprete —______________________________

Agente —*Have you advertised your store?*

Intérprete —______________________________

Sr. Gutiérrez —Sí, en los periódicos y revistas locales, pero generalmente los hombres no leen los anuncios de las tiendas.

Intérprete —______________________________

Agente —*Have you thought of an ad in the university newspaper?*

Intérprete —______________________________

Sr. Gutiérrez —No, no había pensado en eso.

Intérprete —______________________________

Agente —*And a TV ad?*

Intérprete —______________________________

Sr. Gutiérrez —Eso sí, pero me han dicho que un anuncio por televisión cuesta mucho.

Intérprete —______________________________

Agente —*Quite a bit, but TV publicity is the most effective.*

Intérprete —______________________________

Sirva usted de traductor(a) Your firm has just begun to export its products to a Spanish-speaking country, and you want to advertise them. These are the options that a local advertising agency offers. Review the **Vocabulario adicional** in this lesson, and then translate these options into English on a separate sheet of paper.

Publicidad Progreso

Gran variedad de medios publicitarios para el mundo hispano

PERIÓDICOS:
- Anuncios a toda plana, en blanco y negro, para publicar en la edición de fin de semana de los periódicos locales.
- Creamos anuncios sugerentes exclusivos para su firma. (No deben tratar de traducir al español sus anuncios en inglés.)

REVISTAS:
- Anuncios en colores en revistas semanales, quincenales y mensuales. (Un sondeo de la opinión pública encontró que los consumidores leen más los anuncios en las revistas que en los periódicos.)

TELEVISIÓN:
- Más costosa, pero muy efectiva.
- Filmamos películas y anuncios cortos.

OTROS:
- Vallas en las autopistas que van al centro.
- Demostraciones en los centros comerciales.
- Anuncios en las páginas amarillas.

Nombre ______________________ **Sección** __________ **Fecha** __________

En estas situaciones

With a partner, act out the following situations in Spanish.

1. Your boss at the advertising agency where you work has just assigned you a new client. He/She is a native Spanish speaker who is a partner in a clothing store. Ask the client about the brand of clothing he/she sells and find out where it is made, if it is for men or women, and if it is of good quality. Say that price and appearance are not enough. Ask what the sales volume is at the present time. Advise your client to put an ad in the local papers and an ad on TV, even though television costs a lot.
2. You are in the business of exporting beans to Venezuela. You are now in Venezuela talking with an advertising executive. Say that you have been exporting beans to Venezuela for two years, but that you haven't been lucky because there's a lot of competition. Say that until now, you have never advertised your product. Say that the beans come in small packages with a very attractive logo because the competition demands a good presentation. Ask which newspaper in Venezuela has the highest circulation, and what that daily circulation is.

Casos

With you and a partner playing the roles, work through the following scenarios.

1. An advertising agent speaks to a client who wants to advertise his/her business.
2. A client discusses with an advertising agent his/her dissatisfaction with the new promotional campaign for his/her business.

Un paso más

Review the **Vocabulario adicional** in this lesson, and match the terms in column **A** with their English equivalents in column **B**.

	A	B
______	1. la demostración	a. *biweekly*
______	2. la valla	b. *issue*
______	3. el cartel	c. *full-page*
______	4. las páginas amarillas	d. *poster*
______	5. el ejemplar	e. *advertisement*
______	6. quincenal	f. *Yellow Pages*
______	7. el sondeo de opinión pública	g. *show*
______	8. a toda plana	h. *sample*
______	9. la edición	i. *drawing*
______	10. el dibujo	j. *expressway*
______	11. el anuncio	k. *billboard*
______	12. la autopista	l. *poll*

Nombre ______________________ Sección ____________ Fecha ____________

Lectura After reading this **lectura**, get together with a partner and take turns answering the following questions.

Las confecciones requieren° gran cantidad de mano de obra. Cuando la diferencia de salarios entre los obreros° de los países ricos° y los de los países pobres se hizo notable, las grandes empresas productoras de ropa hecha° trasladaron sus talleres a lo que entonces se conocía como países del **tercer mundo.**[1] En casi° todos los países de la América Latina se establecieron° talleres° de confecciones que pagan salarios muy bajos° pero que los países aceptan porque resuelven,° en parte, el problema del desempleo° y, porque si les exigen que paguen° salarios más altos, las compañías trasladan sus talleres a otros países aún° más pobres.°	*require* *workers / wealthy* **ropa...** *ready-made clothes* *almost* **se...** *were established / workshops* *low* *solve* *unemployment / pay* *even /* **más...** *poorer*

1. ¿Cuándo comenzaron las grandes empresas a trasladar sus talleres a los países pobres?
2. Los talleres de confecciones fueron de los (*some of the*) primeros en trasladarse a los países pobres. ¿Por qué?
3. ¿Por qué aceptan los países pobres los talleres de confecciones que pagan salarios bajos?
4. ¿Qué nombre se les da a los países pobres?

Y usted...

1. ¿Compra ropa confeccionada en países del **tercer mundo?** ¿Por qué o por qué no?
2. ¿Qué cree que pueden hacer los países ricos para ayudar a los trabajadores del **tercer mundo?**

Un dicho

Las arañas hacen su tela en la caja registradora de los negocios que no se anuncian.

Spiders build their webs in the cash register of those businesses that do not advertise.

---

[1]Hasta que el bloque de países socialistas se desintegró con la caída de la Unión Soviética, se llamaba **primer mundo** a las naciones altamente industrializadas, **segundo mundo** a las naciones del mundo socialista y **tercer mundo,** a los países poco desarrollados de occidente. Aunque estos nombres ya son obsoletos, todavía se oye hablar del **tercer mundo.** Actualmente, los políticos y los economistas se refieren a ellos como **países en vías de desarrollo.**

Nombre ______________________ Sección ____________ Fecha ____________

Trivia

- For a long time, U.S.-based advertisers produced Spanish TV ads in the U.S. for both U.S. and Canadian viewers. Eventually, these firms realized the advertisements had to be adapted to Hispanic American culture. Most notably, these changes included the use of well known Latin American actors and regional sport stars, most of whom were brown-skinned and dark-haired.
- Since the PAS satellite's launch in 1988, advertisers have been taking advantage of its cost-effectiveness by showing commercials throughout Hispanic America despite some differences from country to country.
- Besides the standard local channels, Hispanic America TV broadcasts now include international networks such as **Televisa, Sur, TVE** (from Spain), and multiple U.S. channels.
- Latin American Internet advertising is a flourishing enterprise. ZenithOptimedia, a London-based advertising agency, described the region as having "the world's second-highest growth rate" of 2008. This observance could be attributed to the overall rapid rate of growth in regional Internet usage. According to the Internet World Stats (www.internetworldstats.com), the number of Internet users in Latin America grew from less than 20 million in 2000 to about 174 million in 2008. Unsurprisingly, this rapid growth is not ubiquitous across Latin American countries. For example, while more than half of Chileans enjoy Internet access, less than 3% of Nicaraguans have this luxury.

LECCIÓN 15

ABRIENDO CUENTAS

OBJECTIVES

Structures

- The future tense
- The conditional tense
- Some uses of the prepositions **a, de,** and **en**

Business Communication

- Helping customers at the bank

El Sr. Santana habla con un oficial del Banco Popular de Hialeah, FL, porque quiere abrir una cuenta corriente.

Sr. Santana —Buenos días. Deseo abrir una cuenta corriente.
Empleada —Siéntese, por favor. ¿Tiene Ud. alguna otra cuenta en este banco?
Sr. Santana —No, tengo mi cuenta en el Trust Bank de West Palm Beach, donde yo vivía, pero me mudé a este barrio ayer.
Empleada —¿Quiere abrir una cuenta individual o una cuenta conjunta?
Sr. Santana —Una cuenta individual, pero me gustaría poner como beneficiarios a mis hijos.
Empleada —Bien. Entonces, llene esta planilla y firme estas dos tarjetas, por favor. ¿Cuánto va a depositar?
Sr. Santana —Ahora voy a depositar $500 en efectivo y mañana, después de cerrar mi cuenta en el otro banco, depositaré un cheque de caja por el saldo de esa cuenta.
Empleada —Ud. sabe que pagamos intereses sobre el saldo de las cuentas corrientes, ¿verdad?
Sr. Santana —Sí, ya lo sé. Pero también cobran cuarenta centavos por cada cheque girado.
Empleada —Sí, señor, y también cobramos por la impresión de los cheques, pero ambos servicios son gratuitos si mantiene un saldo promedio de más de $1.000.
Sr. Santana —Me gustaría ver los modelos de cheques personalizados. Quiero seleccionar un modelo.
Empleada —En seguida se los mostraré. Ud. tendrá sus cheques en dos semanas.

Nombre ______________________ Sección ____________ Fecha ____________

La Sra. Díaz está en el mismo banco para abrir una cuenta de ahorros.

Sra. Díaz	—Mi banco quebró y necesito abrir una cuenta de ahorros.
Empleado	—¿Ud. tenía su cuenta en el Center Bank que se declaró en quiebra?
Sra. Díaz	—Sí, pero no perdí nada.
Empleado	—Claro, las cuentas de hasta $100.000 están aseguradas por una agencia del gobierno federal. Bien. ¿Qué tipo de cuenta quiere abrir?
Sra. Díaz	—Una cuenta conjunta, a nombre mío y de mi hija.
Empleado	—Debe llenar estas formas, y después Ud. y su hija deberán firmar estas tarjetas.
Sra. Díaz	—Mi hija vendrá a firmarlas más tarde. Por favor, ¿qué interés están pagando en las cuentas del mercado de dinero?
Empleado	—El dos y un cuarto por ciento y el tres por ciento en los certificados de depósito a plazo fijo, por dieciocho meses o más.
Sra. Díaz	—Un banco electrónico está ofreciendo el 4,25%, pero todavía no me hago a la idea de manejar mi dinero por Internet.
Empleado	—Es el sistema del futuro, pero todavía está dando sus primeros pasos.
Sra. Díaz	—Por otra parte, no me convendría tener todo mi dinero inmovilizado en un CD (ce-de).
Empleado	—Entonces necesitará abrir dos cuentas.

¡Escuchemos!

While listening to the dialogue, circle **V (verdadero)** if the statement is true or **F (falso)** if it is false.

1. El Sr. Santana quiere abrir una cuenta de ahorros en el Banco Popular de Hialeah, FL. V F
2. El Sr. Santana se mudó para Hialeah ayer. V F
3. Al Sr. Santana le gustaría poner como beneficiaria a su esposa. V F
4. El Sr. Santana depositará un cheque de caja por el saldo de su cuenta en otro banco. V F
5. El Banco Popular no cobra por los cheques girados si el cliente mantiene un saldo de más de $1.000. V F
6. El Sr. Santana tendrá sus cheques personalizados en dos semanas. V F
7. El Banco de la Sra. Díaz se declaró en quiebra pero ella no perderá su dinero. V F
8. La Sra. Díaz abrirá una cuenta conjunta a nombre suyo y de su esposo. V F
9. El Banco de Hialeah no paga intereses en las cuentas del mercado de dinero. V F
10. La Sra. Díaz depositará su dinero en un certificado de depósito porque recibirá un interés más alto. V F

Nombre ______________________ Sección ____________ Fecha ____________

VOCABULARIO

Audio

Cognados

el (la) beneficiario(a)
federal
individual

Nombres

el barrio, el vecindario, la colonia (*Méx.*) *neighborhood*
el cheque de caja *cashier's check*
la cuenta conjunta *joint account*
la cuenta corriente, la cuenta de cheques (*Méx.*) *checking account*
la cuenta del mercado de dinero *money market account*
la impresión *printing*
el promedio *average*
la quiebra, la bancarrota, la insolvencia *bankruptcy, insolvency*

Verbos

declararse *to declare oneself*
mantener[1] *to keep*
mudarse[2] *to move (relocate)*
perder (e:ie) *to lose*
quebrar (e:ie), declararse en quiebra *to go bankrupt, to declare bankruptcy*
sentarse (e:ie) *to sit down*

Adjetivos

asegurado(a) *insured*
girado(a) *drawn*
inmovilizado(a) *tied up, locked*
mismo(a) *same*

Otras palabras y expresiones

claro, por supuesto *of course*
convenirle a uno *to be to one's advantage*
ya lo sé *I know*

VOCABULARIO ADICIONAL

Audio

bajos ingresos *low income*
brusca *rough, brusque*
clase media *the middle class*
congelación *freezing*
como efecto *as a result*
confianza *trust, confidence*
cuentacorrentista *one having a current account in a bank*
cuentahabiente *one having an account in a bank*
estatal *state (adj.)*
guardar *to keep, to save*
han ido a parar a *have gone to*
Hispanoamérica *Spanish-speaking countries from the Mexican border to Argentina and Chile*
Latinoamérica *All countries from the Mexican border to Argentina and Chile (except guayanas)*
lo mismo *the samething*
miseria *misery, poverty*
monto *summation*
mundial *world (adj.)*
ocasionar *to cause*

---

[1]Conjugated like **traer**
[2]The substitution of **moverse** for **mudarse** is frequent in U.S. Spanish, but not admitted by the ***Real Academia Española***.

paraguayo(a) *from Paraguay*
predominar *to predominate, to exceed*
significar *to mean*
variar *to vary, to change*

Para hacer transacciones bancarias

a nombre mío, en mi nombre *in my name*
el (la) banquero(a) *banker*
el billete (de banco) *bill, bank note*
el billete falso *counterfeit bill*
el cajero automático *automatic teller machine (ATM)*
la casa matriz, la oficina principal (*P. Rico*) *main office*
el cheque al portador *check to the bearer*
el cheque sin fondos *bounced check, overdrawn check*
la chequera, el talonario de cheques *checkbook*
cobrar (cambiar) un cheque *to cash a check*
el (la) depositante *depositor*
el depositario *depositary, receiver*
el estado de cuenta *statement of account*
extender (e:ie) (girar) un cheque *to write a check*
la moneda fraccionaria, el suelto, la calderilla, el menudo (*Cuba, P. Rico*) **la morralla** (*Méx.*) *small change*
la moneda falsa *counterfeit coin*
el retiro, la extracción (de dinero) *withdrawal*
sacar, retirar, extraer[1] **dinero** *to withdraw money*
el sobregiro *overdraft*
el (la) solicitante *applicant*
la sucursal *branch*

Search

iLrn

Notas Culturales

- Each Latin American country has a central bank authorized to issue currency (bills and coins) and to control the activities of commercial banks. In addition to commercial banks, almost all countries have other types of financial institutions, such as development banks, mortgage banks, and savings banks. Development banks are created by the government to service specialized areas of the economy, such as public works, agriculture, and industry. Mortgage banks, created to help families purchase homes, and savings banks are generally private.
- Opening a bank account in Latin America is not as easy as in the United States, especially if it is a checking account. In fact, banking in many Latin American countries is limited to the middle and upper classes. Poor people who earn enough money to save generally deposit their money in the **Caja Postal de Ahorros,** a savings service provided by the post offices in some countries.
- Some Hispanics do not feel comfortable banking electronically. They prefer going to the bank, talking with a person, and leaving the bank with proof of their transactions in black and white. In their countries of origin, the law gives importance to written documents with signatures and seals.

Actividades

Dígame... Answer the following questions, basing your answers on the dialogues.

1. ¿Para qué va al banco el Sr. Santana?

____

[1]Conjugated like **traer**

2. ¿Por qué quiere el Sr. Santana abrir una cuenta en ese banco?

____

3. ¿Qué tipo de cuenta quiere abrir el Sr. Santana?

____

4. ¿A quiénes va a poner como beneficiarios el Sr. Santana?

____

5. ¿Dónde tiene el Sr. Santana otra cuenta y qué va a hacer con ella?

____

6. ¿Cuánto tendrá que pagar el Sr. Santana por cada cheque girado?

____

7. ¿Cuándo tendrá sus cheques el Sr. Santana?

____

8. ¿Qué está haciendo la Sra. Díaz en ese mismo banco?

____

9. ¿Dónde tenía la Sra. Díaz su cuenta de ahorros?

____

10. ¿Perdió la Sra. Díaz el dinero que tenía en el otro banco? ¿Por qué o por qué no?

____

11. ¿Qué deben hacer la Sra. Díaz y su hija?

____

12. ¿Qué interés paga el banco en las cuentas del mercado de dinero?

____

Hablemos Interview a classmate, using the following questions. When you have finished, switch roles.

1. ¿Tiene Ud. una cuenta en algún banco? ¿En cuál?
2. ¿Está su dinero asegurado por el gobierno federal? ¿Por qué o por qué no?
3. ¿Qué tipo(s) de cuenta tiene?
4. ¿Gana interés el dinero que tiene en el banco?
5. ¿Paga interés su banco en las cuentas corrientes?

6. ¿Cuánto cobra su banco por imprimir los cheques personalizados?
7. ¿Tiene Ud. más dinero en su cuenta de ahorros o en su cuenta corriente?
8. ¿Cree Ud. que es buena idea tener el dinero en una cuenta conjunta? ¿Por qué o por qué no?

Quiz

VAMOS A PRACTICAR

A Rewrite the following sentences, substituting the future tense of the verbs for the **ir a** + *infinitive* form.

MODELO El banco *va a pagarme* intereses sobre el saldo.
El banco **me pagará** intereses sobre el saldo.

1. El Sr. Santana *va a abrir* una cuenta corriente.

 ____

2. Yo *voy a mudarme* para este barrio.

 ____

3. Mis hijos *van a llenar y a firmar* las tarjetas.

 ____

4. Después *vamos a cerrar* la cuenta en el otro banco.

 ____

5. Ud. *va a tener* sus cheques en dos semanas.

 ____

6. Tú no *vas a poder* ganar un interés del ocho por ciento.

 ____

7. ¿Quién *va a venir* con el dinero?

 ____

8. No les *va a convenir* tener todo el dinero inmovilizado.

 ____

9. Ella *va a hacer* los modelos.

 ____

10. Les *vamos a decir* la verdad (*truth*).

 ____

Nombre ______________________ **Sección** __________ **Fecha** __________

B Report what the following people said.

MODELO Sra. Alba —Abriré una cuenta en este banco.
¿Qué dijo? —**La Sra. Alba dijo que abriría una cuenta en este banco.**

1. Ella —Llenaré la planilla hoy mismo.
   ¿Qué dijo? —______________________________
2. Yo —Volveré mañana por la tarde.
   ¿Qué dije? —______________________________
3. Tú —No me convendrá tener todo mi dinero inmovilizado.
   ¿Qué dijiste? —______________________________
4. Nosotras —Iremos a otro banco.
   ¿Qué dijimos? —______________________________
5. Ud. —María no podrá firmar hoy.
   ¿Qué dijo? —______________________________
6. Ana y Silvia —Estamos seguras de que no nos gustarán los modelos.
   ¿Qué dijeron? —______________________________

C Complete the following dialogues using **a, de,** or **en.**

1. —¿__________ qué hora regresa la Srta. Varela?
   —__________ las dos __________ la tarde.
   —¿Está __________ el banco?
2. —¿Cuándo viene el Sr. Vega __________ Lima?
   —El trece de marzo.
   —¿Viene __________ avión?
   —No, viene __________ autobús.
   —¿Va __________ visitar a sus hijos?
   —No, no va __________ visitarlos.

Nombre ______________________ Sección ____________ Fecha ____________

Sirva usted de intérprete

With two classmates, play the roles of Srta. Lara, the bank employee, and the interpreter who helps them communicate. Switch roles until each of you has played the interpreter's role.

Srta. Lara —Buenas tardes. Quiero abrir una cuenta de ahorros.

Intérprete —________________________________

Empleado —*Sit down, please. You have another account at this bank, right?*

Intérprete —________________________________

Srta. Lara —Yo tenía una cuenta del mercado de dinero pero la cerré hace tres meses.

Intérprete —________________________________

Empleado —*Do you want to open an individual account or a joint account?*

Intérprete —________________________________

Srta. Lara —Una cuenta individual, pero quiero poner a mi hijo como beneficiario.

Intérprete —________________________________

Empleado —*Fine. Please fill out this form and sign these two cards.*

Intérprete —________________________________

Srta. Lara —Voy a depositar $450 en efectivo y un cheque de caja por $500.

Intérprete —________________________________

Empleado —*We are now paying two percent on the balance of savings accounts.*

Intérprete —________________________________

Srta. Lara —Yo leí que pagaban el dos y medio por ciento.

Intérprete —________________________________

Empleado —*That was last week. Interest rates are going down almost every week.*

Intérprete —________________________________

Now play the roles of Sr. and Sra. Madrigal, who want to open a checking account, the bank employee, and the interpreter who helps them communicate.

Empleado —*What type of account do you want to open?*

Intérprete —________________________________

Sr. Madrigal —Una cuenta corriente a nombre mío y de mi esposa.

Intérprete —________________________________

Nombre ______________________ **Sección** ____________ **Fecha** ____________

Empleado —*Very well, a joint account. How much are you going to deposit?*

Intérprete —______________________________

Sr. Madrigal —Setecientos cincuenta dólares en cheques y $250 en efectivo.

Intérprete —______________________________

Sr. Madrigal —¿Cuánto cuesta la impresión de los cheques?

Intérprete —______________________________

Empleado —*Sixteen dollars for five hundred checks.*

Intérprete —______________________________

Sra. Madrigal —¿Cobran por cada cheque girado o cargan una cantidad mensual?

Intérprete —______________________________

Empleado —*We charge thirty-five cents for each check drawn.*

Intérprete —______________________________

Sra. Madrigal —¿Cuándo estarán listos nuestros cheques?

Intérprete —______________________________

Empleado —*In two weeks. Now you must fill out these forms.*

Intérprete —______________________________

Sr. Madrigal —¿Qué interés ganaremos en el depósito?

Intérprete —______________________________

Empleado —*We don't pay interest on checking accounts.*

Intérprete —______________________________

Sra. Madrigal —Entonces lo mejor sería abrir dos cuentas: una cuenta corriente y una cuenta del mercado de dinero.

Intérprete —______________________________

Empleado —*Very well. How much are you going to deposit in each account?*

Intérprete —______________________________

Sra. Madrigal —Depositaremos $300 en la cuenta corriente y $700 en la cuenta del mercado de dinero.

Intérprete —______________________________

Nombre ______________________ Sección ____________ Fecha ____________

Sirva Ud. de traductor(a) You work at a bank in Asunción, Paraguay. A colleague has made you a list of phrases that he would like to be able to say to English-speaking business people and tourists. Review the **Vocabulario adicional** and then translate the list into English.

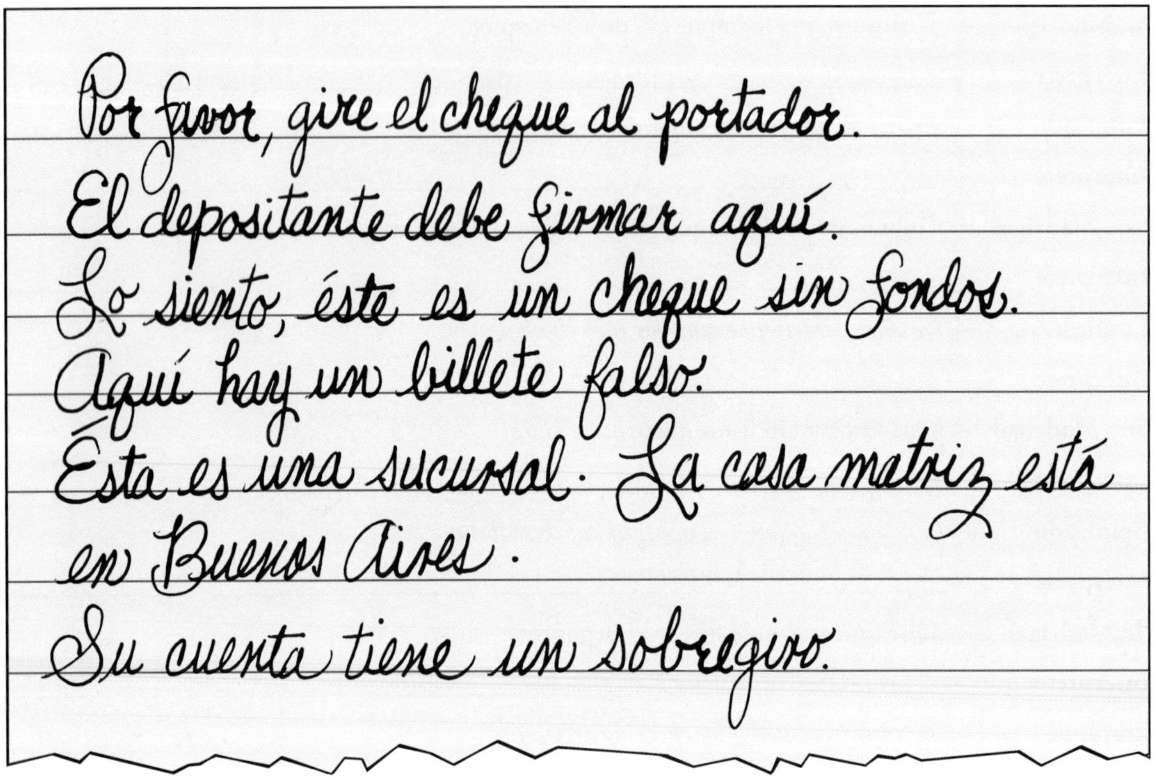
Por favor, gire el cheque al portador.
El depositante debe firmar aquí.
Lo siento, éste es un cheque sin fondos.
Aquí hay un billete falso.
Ésta es una sucursal. La casa matriz está en Buenos Aires.
Su cuenta tiene un sobregiro.

En estas situaciones

With a partner, act out the following situations in Spanish.

1. You are a bank employee. Wait on a customer who wants to open an account. Ask what type of account the customer wants to open and how much the deposit will be. The customer must fill out two cards. Say that the bank doesn't charge for each check processed, but it charges a $10 monthly service fee. Also add that the bank doesn't pay interest on checking accounts, but that it pays three percent on money market accounts. Tell your customer that his/her personalized checks will arrive in two or three weeks.
2. You are opening a savings account in Santiago, Chile. Tell the employee that you want to open a savings account and that you will deposit 15,800 pesos. Ask how much interest the bank pays. Say that you want to include your parents as beneficiaries, and that you are going to have the money there for nine months. Ask if you can put the money in a fixed-term certificate of deposit to earn more interest. Say that you left your passport at home, but you will bring it tomorrow and will fill out the forms then.

Nombre ______________________________ Sección ____________ Fecha ____________

Casos

With you and a partner playing the roles, work through the following scenarios.

1. A bank employee speaks to a customer who wants to open an account.
2. A newly married couple discusses opening a savings account together.

Un paso más

A You are an advertising executive with a large bank as your client. Review the **Vocabulario adicional** in this lesson and use it and other vocabulary to create a newspaper ad detailing the services offered by your client.

B Review the **Vocabulario adicional** in this lesson and act out the following dialogues in Spanish with a partner.

1. —Where can I cash this check?
   —Is the check in your name?
   —No, it's a check to the bearer.
   —At the bank's main office or at a branch, but they're closed now.
   —Does the branch have an ATM?
   —Yes.
2. —Can you lend me ten dollars?
   —I have ten dollars in coins . . .
   —Thanks, but I need a ten-dollar bill.
   —I can write you a check, if you want.
   —You wrote me an overdrawn check last time!

Lectura

After reading this **lectura,** get together with a partner and take turns answering the following questions.

La mayoría de los hispanos que llegan a este país son gente pobre que jamás° ha tenido cuenta en un banco. Como ya dijimos, en casi° todos los países hispanoamericanos los bancos son sólo para las clases media y alta. Cuando los hispanos llegan a este país continúan haciendo todas sus compras al contado,° y esto les hace muy difícil conseguir crédito e, incluso,° tarjetas de crédito. Además, les cuesta trabajo adaptarse° a nuestra forma de manejar° el dinero. En primer lugar,° muchos de ellos son inmigrantes indocumentados que, hasta hace poco, no podían abrir cuentas bancarias. En segundo lugar, muchos no hablan inglés,

never
almost
al... *cash*
even
les... *they find it difficult to adapt to our way of handling / to manage /* **En...** *In the first place*

o lo hablan con dificultad, y temen° no	*are afraid*
entender claramente° las explicaciones° que	*clearly / explanations*
les dan en inglés. Pero como los inmigrantes	
hispanos suman° ya 40 millones, los bancos	*add up*
están cada vez más interesados en tener	
personal bilingüe calificado.°	*qualified*

1. ¿A qué clase social pertenece la mayoría de los hispanos que llegan a este país?
2. ¿Qué clases sociales tienen acceso a los bancos en la mayoría de los países latinoamericanos?
3. Muchos inmigrantes hispanos hacen sus compras al contado. ¿Por qué?
4. ¿Por qué están interesados ahora los bancos en contratar personal bilingüe?

Y usted...

1. ¿Cree que es conveniente permitir que los inmigrantes indocumentados puedan abrir cuentas bancarias? ¿Por qué o por qué no?
2. ¿Qué le recomendaría a un inmigrante indocumentado que quiere conseguir una tarjeta de crédito?

Un dicho

Si quieres saber el valor del dinero, pídelo prestado.	*If you want to know the value of money, borrow it.*

Trivia

Online Banking

Most online banks offer the same services as traditional banks, including the ability to access your checking accounts, savings accounts, CDs, installment loans, mortgages, home equity loans, and lines of credit. Transferring funds, paying bills, and placing stop payments are other popular banking services that can easily be conducted online. Although online banking can offer higher returns on investments and other incentives, it can be risky endeavor if one fails to take the necessary precautions in deciding where to deposit or invest. Here are two general rules of thumb to avoid unpleasant surprises that people tend to experience while banking online. First, ensure the bank you initially select is a legitimate credited institution. Second, do not respond to requests for personal information such as Social Security number, ATM or debit card number, or PIN through text, voice, or e-mail messages.

Suplemento 3

Otras comunicaciones de negocios

- La carta circular
- El memorando o memorándum
- El informe o reporte
- El facsímil (fax)
- El correo electrónico (e-mail, correo-e, "emilio")
- La red informática (*Websites on the World Wide Web*)

La carta circular Circulars are form letters circulated to company clients or employees. They are most often used to inform vendors and existing or prospective clients of changes within the company, such as a new name or organizational structure, new management, or the addition of new products or services to the company line. Internal circulars often announce global changes in schedule, benefits, or other matters of importance to employees.

1. Your company needs to send a circular. Read the following two examples. Then, write your company's circular according to its purpose and audience.

Nombre ______________________ Sección ____________ Fecha ____________

Circular announcing the opening of a business

QUINTERO, LÓPEZ Y CÍA.

Compraventa de frutas al mayoreo[1] Juárez No. 647 Guadalajara, Jalisco

15 de junio de 2010

Estimados señores:

Les participamos[2] que ante el notario público de esta ciudad, Sr. Lic. Roberto Calderón García, hemos constituido una Sociedad Regular Colectiva[3], que se dedicará a la compraventa de frutas al mayoreo, la cual girará bajo la razón social[4] de

QUINTERO, LÓPEZ Y CÍA.

Por nuestra experiencia en el giro, estamos seguros de poder ofrecer a nuestros clientes la mayor eficiencia y rapidez en la atención de sus pedidos.

Atentamente,
QUINTERO, LÓPEZ Y CÍA.
Pedro Quintero
Pedro Quintero
Administrador General

[1] **al...** *wholesale* [2] *give notice* [3] **Sociedad...** *General Partnership* [4] **razón...** *trade name*

Nombre ______________________ Sección ____________ Fecha ____________

Circular from a business to potential clients

Bancosur

Avenida Universidad 1500 México, D.F. 03339

24 de octubre de 2010

Estimado cliente:

Tenemos el agrado[1] de comunicarle que Bancosur, a partir de esta fecha, le ofrece una alternativa más para invertir[2] su dinero, con la garantía de intereses fijos mayores a los actuales. Este nuevo instrumento de inversión se puede establecer a plazos de 3, 6, 9 y 12 meses para que Ud. elija el que mejor se adapte a sus necesidades.

Le agradecemos su preferencia y esperamos seguir contando con su confianza. Visite Ud. la oficina de su agrado donde nuestros asesores de inversiones[3] tendrán mucho gusto en ampliar esta información.

Atentamente,
BANCOSUR
Div. Promoción de Inversiones

[1]*pleasure* [2]*to invest* [3]**asesores...** *investment officers*

Nombre ______________________ **Sección** ____________ **Fecha** ____________

El memorando Memorandums (memos) are used for internal communication within a company. As shown in the models, their format is simpler than that of a business letter or circular.

2. You need to send a memo to a coworker in Mexico City. Read the following examples. Then, write your memo. Use regular stationery.

MEMORANDO

Fecha: 15 de febrero 2010

Hora: 10:30

Asunto: Solicitud de informe

De: Jefe de Ventas

A: Jefe de Contabilidad

Por favor, envíeme el saldo de la cuenta del Sr. Juan López.

MEMORANDO

A: Fermín Domínguez

De: Alberto González A.G.

Fecha: 7 de mayo de 2010

Asunto: Mal uso de los vehículos de la empresa

Las cuentas por reparación de vehículos de la empresa durante los primeros cuatro meses del presente año se elevaron un 17% sobre las de igual período del año anterior. El jefe del taller de reparaciones[1] informa que el exceso de reparaciones se debe a que los vehículos no están recibiendo el mantenimiento adecuado.[2]

Sírvase[3] notificar a todos los choferes la obligación que tienen de cumplir las disposiciones de la empresa en relación al mantenimiento de sus equipos. La administración impondrá sanciones a aquéllos que no cumplan dichas disposiciones.

[1]taller... *mechanic's shop* [2]mantenimiento... *adequate maintenance* [3]*Please*

Nombre ______________________ **Sección** ____________ **Fecha** ____________

El informe o reporte

Reports generally are used to inform one's boss of the result or progress of an action.

3. You must write a report for your boss. Read the following example. Then, write your report. Use regular stationery.

LIBRERÍA MINERVA

Santurce, Puerto Rico

A: Carmen Bernal, Gerente 6 de julio, 2010

De: Dora León, J. de Personal

ASUNTO: Compra de un equipo de oficina.

PROPOSICIÓN: Comprar una fotocopiadora para el Departamento de Personal, con un costo de $4.000.

EXPLICACIÓN: Actualmente el Departamento de Personal utiliza la fotocopiadora del Departamento de Contabilidad para hacer copias de sus cartas y documentos. Nuestras necesidades son ahora mucho mayores que las que teníamos cuando se dispuso[1] el sistema actual.

La pérdida de tiempo de trabajo de los empleados que deben ir de uno a otro departamento para hacer las copias es superior a la inversión.

CONCLUSIÓN: Recomendamos la compra del equipo.

Atentamente,

Dora León

Dora León

Jefa de Personal

[1]**se...** *was set*

Nombre ______________________ Sección ____________ Fecha ____________

El facsímil (*Fax*) Technological advances have made possible two quicker ways of transmitting information: the fax machine and electronic mail via the computer. Faxes allow us to instantly transmit letters, contracts, and any other kinds of communication, including those with graphic elements or photographs. The transmitted documents are usually accompanied by a cover sheet that includes the name, telephone number, and fax number of both the sender and the addressee, the date, and the subject or purpose of the transmission.

4. Bancaribe lent you the money to pay for college. You need to send them a fax to let them know that they have billed you twice this month. Fill out the following fax cover sheet, and include the message that you want to send.

Bancaribe

Calle de San Francisco, 237

San Juan, PR 00901

NÚM. DE FACSÍMIL (787) 351-6040

FAX

NÚMERO DE FACSÍMIL AL QUE SE ENVÍA ESTA HOJA: ______________________

A: ______________________

____

____

____

____

____

DE: ______________________

____

____

FECHA: ______________________

NÚMERO DE PÁGINAS, INCLUIDA ESTA HOJA:

____

ASUNTO: ______________________

____

____

____

____

De haber cualquier problema o error en esta transmisión, favor de comunicarse con: ______________________, tel. (787) 351-6041.

APARTADO POSTAL 8431 SAN JUAN, PUERTO RICO 00901

Nombre ______________________ Sección ____________ Fecha ____________

El correo electrónico (E-mail, correo-e, "emilio")

E-mail communication is mainly used for sending messages of a more informal kind, and may be seen as the electronic counterpart to the note that was used as a means of more informal intra-office communication. However, the e-mail's range of communication also allows for follow-up communication after any kind of Internet transaction.

5. Write an e-mail to your supervisor requesting vacation time for the upcoming year. Read the following example; then write your e-mail.

> ***De:*** **Diego Santoro, Jefe de Ventas**
> ***Enviado el:*** **7 de febrero de 2010**
> ***Para:*** **Juan Álvarez, Jefe de Producción**
> ***Asunto:*** **Disminución[1] de la producción**
>
> **Explicación:** Las ventas de enero fueron un 10% menos que las del año anterior y, en consecuencia, tenemos un exceso de mercancía en almacén.
>
> **Recomendación:** Eliminar un día de trabajo a la semana hasta que el nivel de mercancía en almacén baje al nivel normal para esta fecha del año.

La red informática (*Websites on the World Wide Web*)

Websites and web pages allow both consumers and enterprises to quickly find information about business and merchandise, and to make transactions. Look at the example of a customer's order confirmation from an online purchase on page 220.

6. Using the Spanish setting in your search engine, do an internet search to learn more about news, business, or the economy of a Spanish-speaking country. Type in the name of a country, such as México, España, or Argentina, and the words "noticias," "finanza," or "economia." Then browse the same type of information for a different Spanish-speaking country. Are both countries dealing with similar issues?

7. With a partner . . .
   - Using your favorite search engine, do an internet search in Spanish.
   - Type **ideas de negocios.**
   - Read ideas from several pages.
   - Select the idea each of you likes best and defend your selections.
   - Do you have any innovative ideas for a new business? Brainstorm possibilities with your partner to come up with a new business and company name.

[1] *Decrease*

Nombre ______________________ **Sección** ____________ **Fecha** ____________

Subj: **Registro de pedido LIBROS Y MÁS**
Date: 12/3/10 1:06:29 PM Pacific Standard Time
From: clientes@libros.es
To: LuisK@email.com
Sent from the Internet

www.libros.es

De: Libros y más / Comercio Electrónico
Enviado el: 3 de diciembre de 2010 a las 22:4
Para: LUIS LEBREDO
Asunto: Recepción de su pedido n° 20011203220449

Estimado Sr. **LEBREDO:**
El Departamento de Comercio Electrónico de Libros y más le quiere agradecer la confianza que ha depositado en nuestra organización y aprovechar esta ocasión para confirmarle que **la tramitación y el envío de su pedido ya ha sido registrado en nuestros sistemas informáticos,** siendo los datos del mismo los siguientes:

PARA FACTURACIÓN:	**PARA ENVÍO:**
LUIS LEBREDO	LUIS LEBREDO
CALLE PALOMA 510	CALLE PALOMA 510
REDLANDS - CALIFORNIA	REDLANDS - CALIFORNIA

ARTÍCULOS DEL PEDIDO	**UNIDADES**	**PRECIO**	**IMPORTE**
DICCIONARIO DE LA LENGUA ESPAÑOLA	1	39,68 EURO	39,68 EURO
GRATIS ESTE MARCAPÁGINAS METALIZADO EN PLATA	1	0,00 EURO	0,00 EURO
SUS PEDIDOS DE NAVIDAD ENVUELTOS PARA LA OCASIÓN	1	0,00 EURO	0,00 EURO
GASTOS DE ENVÍO			12,8 EURO
IMPORTE TOTAL PEDIDO			52,55 EURO

Atentamente,
Departamento de Atención al Cliente
Libros y más

Si quiere conocer la situación en la que se encuentra su pedido ahora mismo, haga clic aquí. Le recordamos que en todo momento podrá usted conocer la situación de su pedido pulsando sobre el ícono situado en la parte superior derecha de todas nuestras tiendas de comercio electrónico.

Nombre ______________________ Sección ____________ Fecha ____________

Lecciones 11-15 Repaso

Práctica de vocabulario

A Circle the word or phrase that does not belong in each group.

1. arreglo iguala caso
2. asiento de diario final contabilidad
3. paso ganancia pérdida
4. balance general contador reloj
5. esposo playa hijo
6. morir vivir evaluar
7. empresa circulación tirada
8. de nuevo por supuesto otra vez
9. máquina invierno verano
10. bazar tienda copropietario
11. fabricar producir mantener
12. empezar recomendar comenzar
13. modernizar reorganizar parecer
14. barrio saldo vecindario
15. nómina salario sueldo
16. planilla hijos forma
17. publicidad propaganda quiebra

B Circle the word or phrase that best completes each sentence.

1. Quiero (explicar / importar / modernizar) el sistema de contabilidad.
2. El contador va a preparar los balances de (problemas / ausencia / comprobación).
3. Tenemos errores (costosos / actuales / anteriores) en los informes a los clientes.
4. Los empleados de la oficina hacen los asientos de (casos / equipos / diario) y los pases al mayor.
5. Periódicamente ellos preparan los estados de pérdidas y (ganancias / entradas / herencias).
6. Ellos necesitan (alimentar / automatizar / imprimir) la contabilidad del negocio.
7. Me figuro que su ayuda es muy (valiosa / diseñada / segura) para ellos.
8. El (alquiler / gasto / reloj) marca las entradas y salidas de los empleados.
9. Con el sistema (cancelado / nuevo / solo) no van a ahorrar dinero tampoco.
10. Ellos tienen que hacer un (cobro / inventario / presupuesto) de toda la mercancía disponible.
11. Mis hijos son menores de (legado / bono / edad).
12. Ellos terminaron su (carrera / cabeza / caridad) el año pasado.
13. Mi esposa trabaja por cuenta (propia / cancelada / recibida).
14. Recibo una pensión de la compañía desde que se (vendió / acreditó / murió) mi esposo.
15. ¿Puedo deducir los intereses de la (abuela / hipoteca / acción) de mi casa?

16. A las etiquetas tiene que (organizarles / introducirles / agregarles) un logo y un lema.
17. Estas chaquetas se venden únicamente en (ley / invierno / país).
18. Las etiquetas con la marca son de (verano / vestido / tela).
19. Los artículos se venden (precedidos / envueltos / mensuales) en un plástico transparente.
20. Uds. necesitan organizar una (cartera / competencia / campaña) de promoción en varias tiendas.
21. ¿Quiere Ud. abrir una cuenta individual o una cuenta (actual / tradicional / conjunta)?
22. ¿Cuánto cobran Uds. por cada cheque (girado / inmovilizado / anterior)?
23. El banco se (mostró / gustó / declaró) en quiebra hace una semana.
24. ¿Cuánto va a depositar Ud. en (efectivo / gobierno / empresa)?
25. Su cuenta está (asegurada / diseñada / usada) por el gobierno federal.

C Match the questions in column **A** with the answers in column **B.**

A		B
1. ¿Quiénes llevan la contabilidad de la firma?	______	a. Ha crecido mucho.
2. ¿Qué ha pasado con el negocio?	______	b. No, es menor.
3. ¿Están aquí los libros?	______	c. Sí, y las ausencias.
4. ¿Qué vas a preparar?	______	d. No, viuda.
5. ¿El programa es sofisticado?	______	e. A mis hijos.
6. ¿Cómo se preparan los estados financieros?	______	f. No, hemos agregado un nuevo renglón.
7. ¿La computadora registra las asistencias?	______	g. Una cuenta de ahorros individual.
8. ¿Él es mayor de edad?	______	h. Sí, y parte de las utilidades.
9. ¿Es Ud. casada?	______	i. El próximo junio.
10. ¿Puedo deducir los intereses de la hipoteca?	______	j. No, es muy rudimentario.
11. ¿Tiene Ud. dependientes?	______	k. La nómina.
12. ¿Recibe Ud. un sueldo?	______	l. Sí, pienso que la he visto antes.
13. ¿Cómo están envueltos?	______	m. Sí, diez dólares por 200 cheques.
14. La mano de obra, ¿es barata?	______	n. La computadora los prepara automáticamente.
15. ¿En qué estación vende Ud. más?	______	o. No, es costosa.
16. ¿Cobran Uds. por la impresión de cheques?	______	p. Sí, y la de mujer también.
17. ¿Qué tipo de cuenta quiere abrir?	______	q. En invierno.
18. ¿A quiénes va a poner como beneficiarios?	______	r. Sí, y los gastos médicos.

A		B
19. ¿Cuándo se gradúa?	_______	**s.** En plástico transparente.
20. ¿Conoces a la Sra. Santana?	_______	**t.** Sí, dos.
21. ¿Siguen vendiendo los mismos artículos?	_______	**u.** Sí, yo los traje.
22. ¿Se vende bien la ropa de hombre?	_______	**v.** Los empleados.

Situaciones del mundo de las empresas

Review the **Notas culturales** and **Lecturas** of the past five lessons and then read the following scenarios. Find out what went wrong, and propose possible solutions in Spanish.

1. Total annual sales in our company were over $4,000,000,000 this year. In a marketing brochure to be distributed throughout Latin America, I wrote: **Nuestras ventas anuales superan (*exceed*) los cuatro billones de dólares.**
2. Enrique Mota does not speak English. He wants to file his federal tax form. I advised him that the Internal Revenue Service has forms available in Spanish.
3. My company wants to reach the Latino market. I told my supervisor that she would only need to contact Univision, Telemundo, or Telefutura because the main U.S. networks that broadcast in English do not have affiliates that broadcast their programs in Spanish.

Advanced Translation

The following translations include some words not presented yet. You may need to use a dictionary.

Translate into English

1. Necesitamos evaluar las nuevas leyes fiscales aprobadas recientemente.

   ____

2. La Internet ofrece oportunidades de negocios a los jóvenes creativos.

   ____

3. Vamos a tener una auditoría la semana próxima. Debemos tener terminados todos nuestros estados financieros.

   ____

4. Es posible que el país adopte sistemas tributarios similares a los de la Unión Europea.

   ____

5. Es difícil calcular los ingresos que he tenido en actividades ajenas a mi empleo.

   ____

Nombre ______________________ Sección ____________ Fecha ____________

Translate into Spanish

1. Before making a final decision I need to talk to my accountant.

___

2. The UPC on this label is not wrong, but this coat is on sale. You must enter the discount price into the computer.

___

3. Some Latin American countries do not require professional experience or the successful completion of professional qualification exams prior to registration as a public accountant.

___

4. You do not have to be a business giant to be able to have the financial benefits of operating a corporation.

___

5. Taxpayers who don't file a past due return are subject to penalties and interest will increase the amount of tax due.

___

Lección 16 Solicitando préstamos

Objectives

Structures

- The present subjunctive
- The subjunctive with verbs of volition
- The absolute superlative

Business Communication

- Informing bank customers about different types of loans

José, un estudiante de Puerto Rico, necesita que le den un préstamo para poder pagar sus estudios.

José —Necesito un préstamo para pagar la matrícula y los demás gastos de la universidad.
Empleado —¿Dónde estudia?
José —Estudio administración de empresas en la Universidad de Arizona, pero este año no me dieron beca.
Empleado —¿Cuánto ganan sus padres?
José —Mi padre murió el año pasado. Mi madre gana bastante, más de[1] $80.000 al año.
Empleado —Lo siento, pero Ud. no reúne los requisitos necesarios para recibir este tipo de préstamo.
José —Es que mi madre quiere que estudie aquí, en Puerto Rico, y no me quiere dar dinero para irme a Arizona.
Empleado —Yo le aconsejo que hable con su mamá para tratar de resolver el problema.

Elena, una joven recién graduada, pide un préstamo para poner un negocio.

Elena —Necesito un préstamo para abrir un pequeño negocio.
Oficial del banco —¿Conoce Ud. las disposiciones de la Administración de Pequeños Negocios?
Elena —Sí, y también he obtenido asesoramiento legal, económico y financiero.
Oficial del banco —¿Qué negocio piensa abrir?
Elena —Una tienda de ropa para niños.
Oficial del banco —¿Cuánto dinero necesita?

---

[1]**Más de** is used for *more than* when speaking of numbers.

Elena —Cincuenta mil dólares.
Oficial del banco —¿Necesitará muchos empleados su establecimiento?
Elena —No, por ahora solamente dos.

Evelia y su novio Carlos deciden comprar una casa porque van a casarse.

Carlos —Queremos financiar la compra de una casa. Necesitamos tomar $90.000 en hipoteca.
Oficial del banco —¿Es una casa nueva o ya fue habitada?
Carlos —Ya fue habitada. Los dueños viven allí ahora.
Oficial del banco —¿Uds. quieren asumir la hipoteca original?
Evelia —No, las tasas de interés están más bajas ahora que cuando los dueños la compraron.
Oficial del banco —¿Están interesados en una tasa de interés fija o variable?
Carlos —Fija, a treinta años. Queremos aprovechar que las tasas de interés están bajísimas.
Oficial del banco —¿Cuáles son sus ingresos?
Carlos —Yo trabajo en las oficinas del condado y gano $28.000 anuales. Ella tiene una tienda de ropa. Tiene un sueldo de $30.000, más las ganancias a fin de año.

La Sra. Sonia de la Rosa solicita un préstamo personal.

Sra. de la Rosa —Vengo a solicitar un préstamo personal. Necesito $2.000 para pagar algunas deudas.
Oficial del banco —¿Tiene Ud. casa propia?
Sra. de la Rosa —Sí, mi esposo y yo tenemos un condominio que estamos pagando.
Oficial del banco —Entonces le sugiero que pida un préstamo sobre la diferencia entre el valor del condominio y lo que debe de la hipoteca.
Sra. de la Rosa —¿Qué ventajas tiene ese tipo de préstamo?
Oficial del banco —Para Ud. tiene dos ventajas: paga una tasa de interés menor y puede deducir el interés pagado de los impuestos federal y estatal.
Sra. de la Rosa —El problema es que nosotros compramos el condominio hace tres meses, y el pago inicial fue sólo el 5% del precio.
Oficial del banco —Entonces tenemos que descartar esta opción. Llene esta planilla y ya le diremos si reúne los requisitos necesarios para obtener un préstamo personal.
Sra. de la Rosa —Para calificar[1] para el préstamo, ¿necesito un aval u otro tipo de garantía?
Oficial del banco —Eso no lo sabremos hasta después de estudiar su caso.

¡Escuchemos!

While listening to the dialogue, circle **V (verdadero)** if the statement is true or **F (falso)** if it is false.

1. José quiere que el banco le preste dinero para pagar la matrícula. V F
2. Él reúne los requisitos para ese tipo de préstamos. V F
3. La madre de José quiere que él estudie en Puerto Rico. V F
4. Su padre también prefiere que él estudie allí. V F

[1]**Calificar** has not been accepted by the ***Academia*** as an equivalent of **reunir los requisitos,** but it is commonly used to express this concept.

Nombre ______________________ Sección ____________ Fecha ____________

5. El oficial del banco le aconseja a Elena que lea las disposiciones de la Administración de Pequeños Negocios. V F
6. Evelia y Carlos quieren comprar una casa que ya fue habitada. V F
7. El oficial del banco les sugiere que tomen una hipoteca a quince años. V F
8. La Sra. de la Rosa y su esposo compraron un condominio hace tres meses. V F
9. Los esposos de la Rosa pagaron solamente el 20% del precio del condominio. V F
10. El oficial no sabe si la Sra. de la Rosa va a necesitar un aval. V F

Audio VOCABULARIO

Cognados

el condominio
económico(a)
el estudiante
la garantía
legal
variable

Nombres

la administración de empresas (negocios) *business administration*
la Administración de Pequeños Negocios *Small Business Administration*
el asesoramiento *advice, consulting*
el aval *collateral*
la beca *scholarship*
el condado *county*
el (la) dueño(a), el (la) propietario(a) *owner*
la madre *mother*
la matrícula *registration, registration fees*
el (la) novio(a) *boyfriend (girlfriend)*
el (la) oficial del banco *bank officer*
el padre *father*
los padres *parents*
el pago *payment*
el pago (la cuota) inicial, la entrada, el enganche (*Méx.*) *down payment*
la tasa de interés, el interés *interest rate*
la ventaja *advantage*

Verbos

aconsejar *to advise*
aprobar (o:ue) *to approve*
asumir *to assume*
casarse *to get married*
descartar *to rule out*
esperar *to hope*
financiar *to finance*
negar (e:ie) *to deny*
reunir (los requisitos), "calificar" *to qualify*
sugerir (e:ie) *to suggest*

Adjetivos

fijo(a) *fixed*
habitado(a) *occupied (i.e., a house)*

Otras palabras y expresiones

allí *there*
poner (abrir) un negocio *to set up a business*
recién, recientemente *recently*
tener casa propia *to own a house*

Nombre ____________________ Sección ____________ Fecha ____________

Audio

VOCABULARIO ADICIONAL

actualmente *nowadays*
apenas alcanza *barely reaches*
aseguró tener *assured to have*
bien merecido *well deserved*
bienestar social *social welfare*
con el objeto de medir *to find out how large*
disfrutar *to enjoy*
disparidad *disparity*
entrenamiento *training*
estabilidad *stability*
han fallado *have failed*
hipotecario(a) *mortgage (adj.)*
incertidumbre *uncertitude*
medios de publicidad *advertising media*
odio *hate*
orientar *to orientate*
pequeñas y medianas empresas (PYMEs) *small and medium-size enterprises (SMEs)*
prestatario(a) *borrower*
realizar *to make*
terminar con *to put an end to*

Vocabulario relacionado con los préstamos

la aprobación *approval*
la identificación *identification, I.D.*
insolvente *insolvent*
el interés simple (compuesto) *simple (compound) interest*
la liquidez *liquidity*
el (la) prestamista *lender, pawnbroker*
el presupuesto *budget*
el rendimiento *yield*
tasar *to value, to appraise*
el (la) testigo *witness*

Search

iLrn

Notas Culturales

- Standard & Poor's (S&P), a well known enterprise that publishes financial research and analysis on stocks and bonds, recently reviewed Latin American banking entities' direct exposure to U.S. subprime mortgage-related instruments. S&P ultimately rated their effect as negligible. This is primarily because Latin American banks invest mainly in local government securities. Alternatively, it was local regulatory requirements, risk management practices, and the general dynamics of Latin American markets that kept the banks safe.
- Latin American banks pay high interest rates on savings accounts, but they also charge high interest rates on loans and credit cards. The high cost of credit impedes the development of new businesses and in some countries, such as Argentina, may drive existing companies with outstanding loans into bankruptcy. Latin American companies must also compete with foreign firms, which can obtain loans in their own countries and are thus at an advantage for establishing and expanding businesses. While this situation is unfair to domestic investors, these countries need foreign investment, and thus maintain in effect policies that favor international business interests. This strategy has met with mixed results, however, since serious investors seek more stable economic and financial conditions than many Latin American countries have to offer.

Actividades

Dígame... Answer the following questions, basing your answers on the dialogues.

1. ¿Quién es José y qué necesita?

____

2. ¿Qué estudia José?

______

3. ¿Por qué no reúne José los requisitos necesarios para recibir un préstamo?

______

4. ¿Qué tipo de tienda va a abrir Elena? ¿Cuántos empleados necesitará?

______

5. ¿Dónde trabajan Evelia y su novio?

______

6. ¿Cuánto dinero ganan Evelia y Carlos juntos?

______

7. ¿Van a asumir Carlos y Evelia la hipoteca original? ¿Por qué o por qué no?

______

8. ¿Por qué quiere la Sra. de la Rosa un préstamo personal?

______

9. ¿Qué tipo de préstamo le sugiere el oficial del banco?

______

Hablemos Interview a classmate, using the following questions. When you have finished, switch roles.

1. ¿Pide Ud. un préstamo todos los años para pagar su matrícula? ¿Por qué o por qué no?
2. ¿Qué carrera estudia Ud.?
3. ¿Le ayuda alguien a pagar los gastos de la universidad?
4. ¿Ud. reúne los requisitos para recibir un préstamo para pagar la matrícula?
5. ¿Piensa Ud. abrir algún negocio en el futuro (*future*)?
6. ¿Qué tipo de negocio le gustaría abrir?
7. ¿Tiene dinero para abrir el negocio que desea?
8. Si no tiene el dinero, ¿cómo podría conseguirlo? ¿Necesitaría un aval?
9. ¿Es suya la casa o el condominio donde vive?
10. ¿Cuándo es conveniente asumir la hipoteca original de una casa o de un condominio?

Nombre ______________________ Sección ____________ Fecha ____________

VAMOS A PRACTICAR

Quiz

A Rewrite the following sentences according to the new cue.

MODELO Yo asumo la hipoteca.
El banco no quiere **que yo asuma la hipoteca.**

1. José pide un préstamo para pagar la matrícula.
   La madre de José quiere ______________________.
2. Carlos no ha decidido qué va a estudiar.
   Su novia quiere que ______________________.
3. Yo estudio aquí.
   Mis padres me sugieren que ______________________.
4. Elena pone una tienda de ropa para niños.
   Su esposo prefiere que ______________________.
5. El banco me presta $5.000.
   Necesito que ______________________.
6. Tú tomas $50.000 en hipoteca sobre tu casa.
   Te aconsejo que ______________________.
7. Ellos asumen la hipoteca original.
   Nosotros les recomendamos que ______________________.

B Rewrite the following sentences using the absolute superlative of the underlined adjectives.

MODELO Aquí, la ropa es *barata.*
Aquí la ropa es **muy barata.** / Aquí, la ropa es **baratísima.**

1. Las tasas de interés están *bajas.*
   ______________________ / ______________________
2. Ella está *interesada* en asumir la hipoteca.
   ______________________ / ______________________
3. Es un trabajo *original.*
   ______________________ / ______________________
4. La tienda necesita *muchos* empleados.
   ______________________ / ______________________

Nombre ______________________ **Sección** __________ **Fecha** __________

5. Mis ingresos son *pequeños.*
______________________ / ______________________

6. Los problemas son difíciles.
______________________ / ______________________

Sirva usted de intérprete

With two classmates, play the roles of Alberto, a student from Uruguay; the bank officer; and the interpreter who helps them communicate. Switch roles until each of you has played the interpreter's role.

Alberto	—Necesito un préstamo para pagar la matrícula de la universidad.
Intérprete	—______________________
Oficial del banco	—*Are you an American citizen?*
Intérprete	—______________________
Alberto	—Sí, soy americano. No hablo muy bien el inglés porque mis padres se mudaron para Uruguay cuando era muy pequeño.
Intérprete	—______________________
Oficial del banco	—*Where are you studying?*
Intérprete	—______________________
Alberto	—Aquí, en la Universidad de California en San Diego.
Intérprete	—______________________
Oficial del banco	—*How much do your parents earn?*
Intérprete	—______________________
Alberto	—Muy poco, si se cambia a dólares.
Intérprete	—______________________
Oficial del banco	—*I understand. You must fill out this form and sign it.*
Intérprete	—______________________

Sirva usted de traductor(a)

You are working for a branch of Banco Nacional in Bogotá. Review the **Vocabulario adicional** in this lesson, and then translate the following instructions into English for an American coworker who is not fluent in Spanish.

1. Quiero que les pida una identificación a las personas que deseen cambiar cheques de viajero.
____

2. No cambie cheques personales de más de $100 sin la aprobación de su jefe.
____

3. Dígales a los clientes que pueden cambiar sus cheques en dólares o en moneda nacional.
____

4. Dígales que pueden ganar hasta un 8% de interés compuesto en depósitos a plazo fijo.

____

5. Dígales que el rendimiento es de más de un 9%.

____

En estas situaciones

With a partner, act out the following situations in Spanish.

You are a bank officer. Take care of the following customers.

1. A couple needs a loan to buy a house. Ask how much money they need to buy the house, if it is new or already occupied, and if they are going to assume the existing mortgage. Say that interest rates are low now. Ask if they're interested in a fixed or variable interest rate. Find out what their income is, where they work, and the address of the house they want to buy.
2. A client needs a personal loan. Ask for the amount the client wants to borrow. Find out about the client's income and place of employment. Ask about any real estate and debts he/she has. Say that a home equity loan can be considered, but that if the house was bought only a few months ago, that option must be ruled out. Point out that collateral or another guarantee will be needed.

Casos

With you and a partner playing the roles, work through the following scenarios.

1. A bank officer speaks to a student who needs a loan to pay for schooling.
2. A bank officer speaks to a customer who needs a loan to start a business.
3. A couple discusses their options for a home loan.

Un paso más

A good friend approaches you about a loan. Review the **Vocabulario adicional** in this lesson and use it and other vocabulary to discuss the proposition, as well as other options for your friend's needs. Don't forget to be thorough, and be sure to clearly define the terms of the loan.

Lectura

After reading this **lectura,** get together with a partner and take turns answering the following questions.

Desde que los hispanos son un factor importante a la hora de las elecciones, los políticos han comenzado a preocuparse° de ellos, y a facilitar su acceso a beneficios a los que siempre tuvieron derecho de acuerdo con nuestras leyes, pero de los que apenas se les informaba. Entre esos beneficios está el acceso a préstamos para estudiantes universitarios y para los pequeños negocios. Hoy el gobierno federal y los gobiernos estatales les hacen propaganda en español a estos programas, y los hispanos están empezando a hacer buen uso de ellos.

° *worry*

Nombre ______________________ Sección ____________ Fecha ____________

1. ¿Por qué han comenzado a preocuparse los políticos por los derechos de los inmigrantes hispanos?
2. ¿Por qué no disfrutaban muchos hispanos de beneficios a los que tenían derecho?
3. ¿Cuáles son algunos de estos beneficios?
4. ¿Qué hacen actualmente el gobierno federal y los gobiernos estatales para que los hispanos conozcan sus derechos?

Y usted...

1. ¿Cree que es justo que los inmigrantes hispanos tengan los mismos derechos que los ciudadanos americanos? ¿Por qué o por qué no?
2. ¿Piensa que el gobierno debe hacer publicaciones en los idiomas de los inmigrantes o que los inmigrantes deben aprender inglés?

Un dicho

Los bancos no prestan dinero a quienes lo necesitan, sino a quienes pueden devolvérselo con intereses.

Banks do not lend money to those who need it, but to those who are able to repay it with interest.

Trivia

Urbanization: A New Challenge for Latin America

Less than five decades ago, more than one in every two Hispanic Americans were farmers. Today, three out of four of these individuals live in cities or towns. Even though Hispanic America is the most urbanized region of the developing world, this transition has differed from country to country. In Uruguay and Argentina, for example, urban dwellers comprise of more than 90% of total population. On the other end of the spectrum, only 40% of Guatemalans live in cities or towns.

Unlike the migration patterns of the last century, immigration from European countries to Hispanic America hardly exists today. In fact, almost all new urban dwellers originate from the rural areas of their own countries. Every year for the last four decades, about five million Hispanic-Americans have migrated from rural to urban areas.

Most of rural migrants are poorly educated and thus unfit for the higher wage jobs. Consequently, most are forced to work in the short-term service sector, seek informal forms of employment from private citizens, or find a means to become self employed.

Source: UN Common Database

Lección 17

Comprando una casa

Objectives

Structures

- The subjunctive to express emotion
- The subjunctive with some impersonal expressions
- Formation of adverbs

Business Communication

- Advising clients about the purchase or sale of real estate
- Refinancing properties

La Sra. Bernal, corredora de bienes raíces, habla con la Sra. Abreu, que está interesada en comprar una casa.

Sra. Abreu —Estoy interesada en esta casa que anuncian en el periódico de hoy.
Sra. Bernal —¿Quiere que la lleve a verla?
Sra. Abreu —Sí, ya la vi por fuera y me gustó mucho, pero temo que sea demasiado cara para mí.
Sra. Bernal —El dueño pide $320.000 por ella. Dice que no está dispuesto a rebajarla, pero si le gusta, ¿por qué no le hace una oferta?
Sra. Abreu —Para comprarla, tengo que vender mi casa. ¿Cree Ud. que el dueño acepte iniciar los trámites de la venta con tal condición?
Sra. Bernal —Sí, señora. La mayor parte de las transacciones de bienes raíces dependen de esa contingencia.
Sra. Abreu —Uds. pueden encargarse de la venta de mi casa, ¿verdad?
Sra. Bernal —Desde luego. ¿Cuánto piensa pedir por su casa?
Sra. Abreu —Según el tasador, la propiedad vale unos $220.000, y todavía debo unos $86.000.
Sra. Bernal —Bien. Le aconsejo que pida $225.000, para que Ud. pueda negociar el precio que desea.
Sra. Abreu —Me parece una buena idea. ¿A cuánto llegarían los gastos relacionados con la venta de mi casa?
Sra. Bernal —Si la vende en $220.000 nuestra comisión será de $13.200, y los gastos de cierre serán unos $1.200, incluidos los gastos legales y el traspaso de la escritura.
Sra. Abreu —Entonces quedará un saldo a mi favor de poco más de $119.000. Bien, ¿cuándo puedo ver la otra casa?
Sra. Bernal —Siento no poder llevarla ahora mismo, pero puedo llevarla esta tarde.

Nombre ______________________ **Sección** ____________ **Fecha** ____________

En la casa:

Sra. Bernal —Como Ud. ve, la casa está situada en un barrio muy elegante. La mayor parte de sus vecinos serán profesionales y ejecutivos de empresas.

Sra. Abreu —La fachada es muy bonita y el jardín está muy bien cuidado.

Sra. Bernal —Me alegro de que le guste. La casa está construida en varios niveles. La sala y el comedor están hundidos.

Sra. Abreu —Me gusta mucho la chimenea de piedra en la sala de estar.

Sra. Bernal —Esta casa fue construida a la orden, sin sacrificar la calidad al ahorro.

Sra. Abreu —Sí, las alfombras son de primera, y el piso de la cocina y de los baños es de losas de cerámica, ¿verdad?

Sra. Bernal —Sí, lo único de linóleo en la casa es el piso del cuarto de lavar.

Sra. Abreu —Es una lástima que las cortinas del comedor estén manchadas. ¿Cómo está el techo?

Sra. Bernal —Estos techos de tejas duran muchísimo, pero de todos modos, el propietario ordenó recientemente una inspección del techo y de comején.

Sra. Abreu —Está recién pintada, ¿verdad?

Sra. Bernal —Sí, y también remodelaron la cocina. Ahora tiene una cocina eléctrica y tiene dos hornos: uno convencional y otro de microondas.

Sra. Abreu —La lavadora de platos también es nueva, ¿no?

Sra. Bernal —Sí, señora.

Dos días después, en la oficina de la Sra. Bernal:

Sra. Abreu —Bien, quiero comprar la casa. ¿Qué entrada tendría que dar para comprarla?

Sra. Bernal —El banco generalmente requiere un mínimo de veinte por ciento. Si el dueño acepta su oferta de $310.000, entonces la entrada sería de $62.000.

Sra. Abreu —Ya consulté con mi banco y «califico» para un préstamo de hasta $265.000. ¿Cuánto tendría que pagar mensualmente si la hipoteca es de $200.000?

Sra. Bernal —A ver... al siete y tres cuartos por ciento, por treinta años... serían $1.366,05, más los gastos de seguro y contribuciones.

Sra. Abreu —¡Ojalá que acepten la oferta!

VENTA DE CASAS
Se vende: $245.000
(o la mejor oferta)
3 recámaras, 2 baños, sala de estar, garaje para dos carros. Calefacción y aire acondicionado. Muy bien situada. Cerca de escuelas. Hipoteca asumible, al 7%

Teléfono: (213) 406-5249

Nombre ______________________________ **Sección** ____________ **Fecha** ____________

¡Escuchemos!

While listening to the dialogue, circle **V (verdadero)** if the statement is true or **F (falso)** if it is false.

1.	La Sra. Bernal vende casas y condominios.	V	F
2.	La Sra. Abreu quiere comprar un condominio.	V	F
3.	La Sra. Abreu no vio la casa por fuera.	V	F
4.	Ella teme que la casa sea muy cara para ella.	V	F
5.	Para comprar esa casa no es necesario que venda la suya.	V	F
6.	La Sra. Abreu siente que la corredora no pueda llevarla a ver la casa hoy.	V	F
7.	La corredora se alegra de que la casa le guste a la Sra. Abreu.	V	F
8.	No remodelaron la cocina recientemente.	V	F
9.	Generalmente los bancos requieren un mínimo del 20% del precio.	V	F
10.	La Sra. Abreu no sabe si «califica» para un préstamo de más de $200.000.	V	F

VOCABULARIO

Audio

Cognados

asumible
la contingencia
eléctrico(a)
elegante
el garaje
la inspección
el linóleo
el mínimo
el (la) profesional, el (la) profesionista (*Méx.*)
recientemente
la transacción

Nombres

la alfombra *carpet*
la chimenea *fireplace*
la cocina *kitchen, stove*
el comedor *dining room*
el comején, la termita *termite*
el (la) corredor(a) de bienes raíces *real estate agent, realtor*
el cuarto de lavar *laundry room*
la escritura *deed*
la escuela *school*
la fachada *façade*
los gastos de cierre *closing costs*
el horno *oven*
el jardín *garden*
la lavadora de platos, el lavaplatos *dishwasher*
la losa, la baldosa *tile*
el microondas *microwave*
el nivel *level*
la piedra *stone*
la propiedad *property*

Nombre ______________________ **Sección** ______________ **Fecha** ______________

la sala *living room*
la sala (el salón) de estar *family room*
el (la) tasador(a) *appraiser*
el techo *roof*
la teja *roof tile*
el traspaso *transfer*
el (la) vecino(a) *neighbor*

Adjetivos

bonito(a), lindo(a) *beautiful*
construido(a) *built*
cuidado(a) *cared (for), kept*
hundido(a) *sunken*
manchado(a) *stained*
mil *one thousand*
pintado(a) *painted*
tal *such*

Verbos

alegrarse *to be happy, to be glad*
durar *to last*
negociar *to negotiate*
remodelar *to remodel*
sacrificar *to sacrifice*
sentir (e:ie), lamentar *to regret, to be sorry*
temer *to fear, to be afraid of*
valer[1] *to be worth*

Otras palabras y expresiones

ahora mismo *right now*
cerca (de) *near*
construido(a) [hecho(a)] a la orden *custom built*
demasiado *too*
es (una) lástima *it's a pity*
estar dispuesto(a) *to be willing*
hasta *up to*
lo único *the only thing*
mensualmente, al mes *monthly*
¡Ojalá! *I hope . . . , If only . . .*
poner a la venta *to put up for sale*
por fuera *from (the) outside*
se vende *for sale*

VOCABULARIO ADICIONAL

Audio

a través *through*
a la hora de *when it was the right time for*
agente de bienes inmuebles (raíces) *realtor*
alentar *to encourage*
burbuja inmobiliaria *the housing bubble*
capacidad de pago *ability to pay*
conceder *to grant*
cuyo(a) *whose*
facilitar *to make it easier*
estallar *to burst*
hipoteca de alto riesgo *subprime morgage*
latinos con vivienda propia *Latino homeowners*
línea roja *red-lining*
lo que podían pagar *what they were able to afford*
mensualidad *monthly payment*
pesadilla *nightmare*
prohibir *to prohibit*
puntuación de crédito *credit scoring*
se mantuvieron altos y subiendo *were high and were increasing*
solvencia *solvency*
sueño americano *American dream*

[1]Irregular first-person indicative: **yo valgo**

Nombre ______________________ Sección ____________ Fecha ____________

Para hablar de la vivienda (*Housing*)

El exterior

los árboles frutales *fruit trees*
el césped, la hierba, la yerba, el zacate (*Méx.*), **el pasto** *lawn, grass*
la entrada para vehículos *driveway*
el estuco *stucco*
el ladrillo *brick*
la madera *wood*
el patio *patio*
la piscina, la alberca (*Méx.*) *swimming pool*
el sistema de riego automático *automatic sprinkler system*
el tejamanil (*Méx.*), **tejamaní** (*Antillas*) *shingle*

El interior

el apartamento, el departamento *apartment*
la conexión para el cable *cable outlet*
el cuarto (el dormitorio, la habitación, la recámara) principal *master bedroom*
los electrodomésticos *appliances*
el enchufe *electrical outlet, socket*
el gabinete, el estante *cabinet, shelf*
el granito *granite*
la lámpara *light*
la lavadora *washing machine*
el mármol *marble*
el refrigerador (empotrado), la nevera (*P. Rico*) *(built in) refrigerator*
la secadora *dryer*

Más palabras y frases útiles para los corredores de bienes raíces

la Administración Federal de Hipotecas *Federal Housing Authority (FHA)*
el inmueble *building, real estate*
inspeccionar *to inspect*
los puntos *points*
se alquila *for rent*
traspasar *to transfer*

Search

iLrn

Notas Culturales

The American dream is also the immigrants' dream, though immigrants additionally regard purchasing a home as the ultimate benchmark of success. According to the U.S. Census Bureau, the years between 2000 and 2007 saw a drastic increase in Hispanic homeownership from 4.1 million to 6.1 million. But when the national housing bubble exploded during 2008 and 2009, Hispanic borrowers were hit hard, especially those who owned properties in Southern California, Nevada, and Florida.

Purchasing real estate in Latin American countries is not easy, unless the buyer is paying cash. In general, banks do not grant long-term loans to individuals, and they are not always willing to finance more than 50% of the cost of the property. The process by which real estate is acquired is very different from that required in the United States. A purchase is usually made through the intervention of a notary public, who in Latin American countries, must be a lawyer. The notary draws up a purchase and sale agreement that must be signed, in his or her presence, by the buyer, the seller, and a certain number of witnesses. The document is then filed in an office called the Registry of Property.

Nombre ______________________ **Sección** __________ **Fecha** __________

Actividades

Dígame... Answer the following questions, basing your answers on the dialogue.

1. ¿Con quién habla la Sra. Abreu?

____

2. ¿En qué casa está interesada?

____

3. ¿Cuánto pide el dueño por la casa?

____

4. ¿Qué tiene que hacer la Sra. Abreu para poder comprar esa casa?

____

5. ¿Cuánto debe todavía la Sra. Abreu de la hipoteca de su casa?

____

6. ¿Cuánto vale su casa? ¿Está dispuesta a rebajar el precio?

____

7. ¿Qué gastos relacionados con la venta de su casa tendría que pagar?

____

8. ¿Qué partes de la casa le gustan a la Sra. Abreu?

____

9. ¿Qué partes de la casa tienen pisos de losas de cerámica?

____

10. ¿Cuál es la única habitación que tiene piso de linóleo?

____

11. ¿Qué ordenó el dueño de la casa recientemente?

____

12. ¿Cómo es la cocina de la casa?

____

Nombre ______________________ Sección ____________ Fecha ____________

Hablemos

Interview a classmate, using the following questions. When you have finished, switch roles.

1. ¿Es Ud. propietario de su casa?
2. ¿Cómo es el barrio donde Ud. vive?
3. ¿Cuántos dormitorios tiene su casa o apartamento? ¿Cuántos baños?
4. El piso de su casa, ¿es de losas, linóleo, madera o tiene alfombra?
5. ¿Le gustan más los techos de tejamanil o los de tejas?
6. ¿Cuánto tiempo hace que pintaron su casa?
7. ¿Remodelaron su casa alguna vez? ¿Qué le hicieron?
8. Cuando Ud. compra algo, ¿sacrifica la calidad por el ahorro?

Vamos a practicar

Quiz

A Rewrite the following sentences according to the new cue.

MODELO Los gastos de cierre *son* unos $1.500.
Es posible que **los gastos de cierre sean unos $1.500.**

1. La alfombra *está* manchada.

   Es una lástima que ______________________________.

2. El techo *tiene* comején.

   Temo que ______________________________.

3. Ud. *rebaja* el precio de la casa.

   Espero que ______________________________.

4. Esta casa *tiene* termitas.

   Puede ser que ______________________________.

5. El corredor de bienes raíces *va* a ver el condominio.

   Es necesario que ______________________________.

6. El dueño *ordena* una inspección del techo.

   ¡Ojalá que ______________________________!

Nombre ______________________ **Sección** ____________ **Fecha** ____________

7. Ellos *ponen* hornos convencionales en las cocinas.

   Es posible que ____.

8. Estas tejas *duran* muchísimo.

   Es imposible que ____.

9. Esa compañía *sacrifica* la calidad por el ahorro.

   Siento que ____.

10. *Se queda* con un beneficio de $500.

   Es probable que ____.

B Complete the following sentences with the adverb forms of the words in parentheses.

MODELO Ella no había ido __________ a la oficina. (inmediato)
Ella no había ido **inmediatamente** a la oficina.

1. Ellos pintaron la casa __________. (reciente)
2. __________ van a comprar la casa. (probable)
3. Pago la hipoteca __________. (mensual)
4. El tasador inspeccionó el techo __________ y __________. (lento, cuidadoso)
5. Tiene __________ un baño. (sólo)

Sirva usted de intérprete

With two classmates, play the roles of Sr. Mendoza, the real estate agent, and the interpreter who helps them communicate. Switch roles until each of you has played the interpreter's role.

Corredora —*The owner is asking $99,900 for the house.*

Intérprete —____

Sr. Mendoza —Bien, vamos a verla.

Intérprete —____

Corredora —*You own a house, right?*

Intérprete —____

Sr. Mendoza —Sí, y quiero venderla para comprar otra en un vecindario mejor.

Intérprete —____

Corredora —*How much are you asking for your house?*

Intérprete —____

Sr. Mendoza —Setenta mil dólares. En el barrio han vendido otras similares por $75.000.

Intérprete —____

Corredora —*How much do you still owe on the mortgage?*

Intérprete —______________________________

Sr. Mendoza —Veintidós mil dólares. Yo compré la casa cuando estaban más baratas.

Intérprete —______________________________

Corredora —*We can sell your house and you will be left with a balance in your favor of $45,000.*

Intérprete —______________________________

Sr. Mendoza —Con eso puedo dar la entrada de la nueva casa, y me queda algún dinero disponible para comprar muebles.

Intérprete —______________________________

Corredora —*If you make the minimum down payment, the monthly payments will be bigger.*

Intérprete —______________________________

Sirva usted de traductor(a)

An executive in your company is being transferred to Mexico and is looking for a house to rent. Review the **Vocabulario adicional** in this lesson, and, on a separate sheet of paper, translate the following fax that has just arrived from a Mexican realtor.

26/6 CASAMEX 9:48 FAX

26 de junio, 2010

Atención: Sr. Daniel Soyer

Distinguido Sr. Soyer:

Creo que he encontrado el tipo de casa que Ud. busca. Tiene una sala grande, cuatro recámaras y dos baños. La cocina es grande y tiene cocina eléctrica, lavaplatos, microondas y refrigerador. El jardín tiene un sistema de riego automático y en el patio hay muchos árboles frutales. La casa también tiene alberca. La fachada es de ladrillos rojos y la casa tiene un garaje para un coche.

Si le interesa esta casa, podré darle más información sobre las condiciones de alquiler la próxima semana.

Marta Ruiz
INMUEBLES CASAMEX

Nombre ______________________ **Sección** __________ **Fecha** __________

En estas situaciones

With a partner, act out the following situations in Spanish.

You are a real estate agent talking with a client. Discuss how a house appears from the outside. Say that the owner is asking $86,000 and that you don't know if he/she'll go down in price, but that, in any case, an offer can be made. Find out if the client needs to sell his/her house in order to buy the other one. Find out how much is still owed on the mortgage, how much the client plans to ask for the house, and if less will be accepted. Mention that with a 20% down payment, the monthly payments would be $917. Point out that the neighborhood is ten minutes away from downtown, that the living room carpet is stained but that the owner is going to change it, and that the fireplace is very pretty. Say that there will be a termite inspection very soon, and that you can sell the client's current house if he/she wants to buy this one.

Casos

With you and a partner playing the roles, work through the following scenarios.

1. A real estate agent is talking with a prospective buyer.
2. Two friends discuss their options regarding buying a new house.

Un paso más

You have found a house you want to buy! Review the **Vocabulario adicional** in this lesson and use it and other vocabulary to formulate a list of ten questions to ask the real estate agent about it.

Lectura

After reading this **lectura**, get together with a partner and take turns answering the following questions.

Hasta hace poco,° la mayor parte de los hispanos que emigraban a los Estados Unidos lo hacían con la idea de regresar a sus países de origen tan pronto como cambiaran° las circunstancias políticas o económicas que los habían obligado a emigrar. La idea de que su estancia° aquí sería transitoria hacía que pocos pensaran en° tener casa propia. En las últimas décadas, sin embargo, la gran mayoría de los inmigrantes hispanos vienen para quedarse,° porque han perdido la esperanza de que sus naciones puedan superar° sus crisis económicas o políticas a corto plazo° y lograr° un estándar de vida similar al de este país. Por eso están comprando casas y, ya hoy, el 48% de todos los hispanos en los Estados Unidos son propietarios de sus viviendas.

Hasta... *Until recently*
changed
stay
pensaran... *thought about*
vienen... *come to stay*
puedan... *may overcome*
a... *in a short term*
attain

1. En general, ¿qué obliga a muchos hispanos a emigrar a los Estados Unidos?
2. Hasta hace poco, ¿con qué idea venían los inmigrantes hispanos?
3. ¿Con qué idea vienen ahora? ¿Por qué?
4. Como resultado de esta nueva realidad, ¿qué están haciendo los hispanos inmigrantes?

Nombre ______________________ Sección ____________ Fecha ____________

Y usted...

1. ¿Cree que los inmigrantes son un beneficio o una carga (*burden*) para este país? ¿Por qué?
2. ¿Piensa que el inglés debería ser el idioma oficial de los Estados Unidos? ¿Por qué o por qué no?

Un dicho

La peor gestión es la que no se hace. *The worst effort is that which is not made.*

Trivia

Latin America has morphed into a dream destination for retirees. Since the region has some of the world's most undervalued real estate, many foreigners are now retiring in countries such as Mexico, Costa Rica, Panama, and the Dominican Republic. These areas offer retirees the chance to purchase a spacious home in a beautiful setting that costs a mere fraction of what it could potentially sell for back home.

LECCIÓN 18

ALQUILANDO UN LOCAL COMERCIAL

OBJECTIVES

Structures

- The subjunctive to express doubt, disbelief, and denial
- The subjunctive to express indefiniteness and nonexistence
- Diminutive suffixes

Business Communication

- Renting commercial space

Roberto y Anita alquilan un local para su negocio.

Roberto —Señorita, venimos por el anuncio de los locales de negocio en un centro comercial de la calle Ocho.
Corredora —¿Ya han visto los locales? ¿Cuál les interesa?
Roberto —Estamos interesados en el número 27 de la planta baja.
Corredora —Ése ya está alquilado. ¿Les interesaría el 127? Está en el primer piso, exactamente sobre el que Uds. quieren.
Roberto —No creo que nos convenga. ¿No tiene otro que esté en la planta baja?
Corredora —El número 18 está vacío, pero es mucho más grande y más caro.
Anita —¿Cuánto mide ese local?
Corredora —Veinte por treinta; es decir, seiscientos pies cuadrados.
Anita —¿Cuánto piden de alquiler?
Corredora —Tres dólares y veinticinco centavos por pie cuadrado con un contrato por un mínimo de tres años.
Roberto —Anita, por favor, préstame tu calculadora.
Corredora —No se moleste en sacar la cuenta; son $1.950 mensuales.
Anita —(*A Roberto*) ¿Qué te parece?
Roberto —Anita, recuerda que no queremos pagar más de $1.500 de alquiler.
Anita —Sí, pero dudo que encontremos un lugar mejor para la tienda.
Roberto —(*A la corredora*) ¿Podemos ir a verlo?
Corredora —Sí, cómo no. Voy a buscar la llave.

En el centro comercial:

Roberto —¿Cuál es el número 18?
Anita —Es aquél, a la derecha. ¡Qué bien situado está! Cerca de la salida de una de las escaleras mecánicas.
Corredora —Sí, y de este lado van a poner una juguetería y del otro una tienda de galletas. Esos son dos lugares que todos los niños quieren visitar.
Roberto —Dudo que esa proximidad nos convenga. Son muchos los padres que evitan esas tiendas cuando traen a sus hijos.
Anita —Sí, pero acuérdate de que la mayoría de los regalos para niños son juguetes, ropa y dulces. Así lo encuentran todo en un solo lugar.
Roberto —Quizás tengas razón.

Otra vez en la oficina:

Roberto —Nos quedamos con el local. ¿Cuáles son las condiciones?
Corredora —Las de costumbre: tres meses de depósito y los pagos por adelantado.
Roberto —¿Cuándo podemos firmar el contrato?
Corredora —Primero deben llenar esta planilla. Necesitamos que nos autoricen para investigar su crédito.
Anita —Podemos adaptar el espacio a nuestras necesidades, ¿verdad?
Corredora —Sí, claro, si no afectan la estructura del edificio.
Anita —Solamente necesitamos probadores, escaparates y estantes de exhibición y algunos anaqueles.

¡Escuchemos!

While listening to the dialogue, circle **V (verdadero)** if the statement is true or **F (falso)** if it is false.

1.	Roberto y Anita están interesados en un local de la planta alta.	V	F
2.	El local de la planta baja no está alquilado todavía.	V	F
3.	Ellos no creen que les convenga un local en la planta alta.	V	F
4.	El local que está vacío es mucho más pequeño.	V	F
5.	Roberto duda que la proximidad a una juguetería les convenga.	V	F
6.	Sin embargo, Anita cree que esa proximidad les conviene.	V	F
7.	Roberto dice que quizás Anita tenga razón.	V	F
8.	La corredora no necesita que Roberto y Anita la autoricen para investigar su crédito.	V	F
9.	El dueño no les permite que adapten el local a sus necesidades.	V	F
10.	Pueden modificar el local si no afectan la estructura del edificio.	V	F

Nombre ______________________ Sección ____________ Fecha ____________

VOCABULARIO

Audio

Cognados

la estructura
exactamente
la proximidad

Nombres

el anaquel, el entrepaño *shelf*
el centro comercial *shopping center*
los dulces *sweets, confections*
el edificio *building*
la escalera rodante, la escalera mecánica *escalator*
el escaparate, la vidriera *shop window, display window*
el estante *open cabinet with shelves*
el fondo *down payment*
la galleta, la galletica, la galletita *cookie*
la juguetería *toy shop*
el lado *side*
el local, el espacio comercial *space*
el lugar *place*
la mayoría, la mayor parte *majority*
el pie (cuadrado) *(square) foot*
el probador *fitting room*

Verbos

acordarse (o:ue) *to remember*
adaptar *to adapt*
afectar *to affect*
autorizar *to authorize*
convenir[1] *to suit, to be good for*
dudar *to doubt*
interesar *to interest*
investigar *to investigate*
molestar(se) *to bother*
prestar *to lend*
quedarse con *to take, to keep*

Adjetivos

alquilado(a) *rented*
cuadrado(a) *square*
vacío(a), desocupado(a) *vacant, empty*

Otras palabras y expresiones

aquél *that (over there)*
en fondo, en depósito, de enganche *(Méx.)* *(in) deposit (down payment)*
por adelantado *in advance*
¡Qué...! *How . . . !*
sacar la cuenta, calcular *to add up*
sobre *above, over*
tener razón *to be right*

VOCABULARIO ADICIONAL

Audio

acreedor(a) hipotecario(a) *mortgagee*
amortización *repayment of loan*
avalúo *appraisal*
casa individual *detached home*
casa semiadosada *semi detached home*
cesionario(a) *grantee*
cobertizos/casetas independientes *free standing sheds*
colindante *adjoining*
cocina integrada *open plan kitchen*

---

[1]Conjugated like **venir.**

Nombre ______________________ Sección ______________ Fecha ______________

colocación de título de propiedad en poder de un tercero, hasta que se ejecute la compraventa *escrow*
contrato de compraventa de vivienda *private property sales contract*
corredor(a) *broker*
cuota de trámite de préstamo *loan origination fee*
derecho del gobierno a adquirir propiedades *eminent domain*
deudor(a) hipotecario(a) *mortgator*
ejecución hipotecaria *foreclosure*
financiamiento directo *seller carry-back*
gravamen *lien*
impedimentos (sobre una propiedad) *encumbrances*
inquilino(a) *tenant*
La ubicación lo es todo. *It's location, location, location.*
limitación por escritura *deed restriction*
medidas y colindancias *metes and bounds*
mejoras efectuadas por el arrendatario *tenant owned improvements*
ordenanza de uso de terrenos *zoning ordinance*
otorgante *grantor*
préstamo de segunda hipoteca *second trust deed loan*
préstamo hipotecario *lien mortgage loan*
prorrateo *apportionment*
tasación *independent valuation of property*
título de propiedad *deeds*
valor de catastro *assessed value*

Para alquilar un local

el arrendamiento, el arriendo *lease*
el (la) arrendatario(a) *lessee*
la constancia *proof*
convenir en *to agree on*

Establecimientos comerciales (*Businesses*)

la barbería *barber shop*
la carnicería *meat market*
la casa de empeño(s), el monte de piedad, el Montepío *pawnshop*
la dulcería *candy store*
la farmacia *drugstore*
la ferretería *hardware store*
la florería, la floristería (*España*) *flower shop*
los (grandes) almacenes, la tienda por departamentos *department store*
la joyería *jewelry store*
la lavandería *laundry*
la mueblería *furniture factory or store*
la panadería *bakery*
la peluquería, el salón de belleza *beauty parlor, salon*
la perfumería *perfume store* (*department*)
la pescadería *fish market*
el supermercado *supermarket*
el taller de mecánica, el taller mecánico *auto shop*
la tintorería *dry cleaning shop*
la zapatería *shoe store*

Search

iLrn

Notas Culturales

- Due to the difficulties of obtaining mortgage loans in their own countries, most Latin Americans live in rented dwellings. Since eviction laws in most Spanish-speaking countries favor owners over tenants, many investors choose real estate investments as a guaranteed way to make money. This practice reduces the amount of capital available to business and industry, augmenting already high interest rates.

Nombre ______________________ Sección ____________ Fecha ____________

- Since most real estate transactions have to be made in cash, many Latin Americans try to pay for their homes in full. Many of them participate in capitalization plans, which are modified insurance policies at fixed term. The subscriber pays a monthly premium in order to have the right, at the end of the term, to withdraw all the money stipulated in the policy. If a subscriber dies before the end of the term, his or her heirs receive the sum. These policies allow Latin Americans a long-term, stable way to save for major cash purchases.

Actividades

Dígame... Answer the following questions, basing your answers on the dialogue.

1. ¿Qué local les interesa a Roberto y a Anita?

   ____

2. ¿Por qué no pueden alquilar ese local?

   ____

3. ¿Qué otros espacios están disponibles?

   ____

4. ¿Cuánto mide el local número dieciocho?

   ____

5. ¿Qué le recuerda Roberto a Anita?

   ____

6. ¿Qué duda Anita?

   ____

7. ¿Por cuánto tiempo les ofrecen el contrato?

   ____

8. ¿Qué negocios van a abrir a uno y otro lado del local?

   ____

9. ¿Por qué cree Anita que esa proximidad les conviene?

   ____

10. ¿Cuánto deben dejar de depósito para alquilar el local?

    ____

Nombre ______________________ Sección ____________ Fecha ____________

11. ¿Por qué deben llenar una planilla antes de firmar el contrato?

____

12. Anita y Roberto pueden adaptar el local con una condición. ¿Cuál es esa condición?

____

13. ¿Qué necesitan hacer en el local?

____

Hablemos

Interview a classmate, using the following questions. When you have finished, switch roles.

1. ¿Hay algún centro comercial cerca de su casa? ¿Cómo se llama?
2. ¿Le gustaría abrir una tienda algún día? ¿Qué tipo de tienda?
3. ¿Estaría su tienda en la planta baja?
4. ¿Qué otras tiendas le gustaría tener al lado de la suya?
5. Cuando va a una tienda, ¿utiliza el elevador o prefiere subir por la escalera rodante?
6. ¿Le gusta mirar los escaparates de las tiendas?

Quiz

Vamos a practicar

Rewrite the following sentences according to the cue.

MODELO Se acuerda **de eso.**
No hay nadie que **se acuerde de eso.**

1. La proximidad de una juguetería nos conviene.

   Dudo que _______________________________.

2. Los padres evitan las tiendas de galleticas y dulces.

   No creo que _______________________________.

3. Ella quiere pagar más de mil dólares de alquiler mensual.

   No estoy seguro de que _______________________________.

4. Necesitamos afectar la estructura del local.

   No es verdad que _______________________________.

Nombre ______________________ **Sección** __________ **Fecha** __________

5. Hay un espacio que se adapta a nuestras necesidades.

Buscamos un espacio que ______________________________.

6. Uds. nos autorizan a investigar su crédito.

¿Hay alguien que ______________________________?

7. El local mide 800 pies cuadrados.

No hay ningún local que ______________________________.

8. Le interesa alquilar un espacio más grande.

¿Conoces a alguien a quien ______________________________?

9. Quiere poner una juguetería.

¿Sabes de alguien que ______________________________?

10. Tú puedes ir a hacer el depósito hoy.

Dudo que ______________________________.

Sirva usted de intérprete

With two classmates, play the roles of Sra. Álvarez, the real estate agent, and the interpreter who helps them communicate. Switch roles until each of you has played the interpreter's role.

Sra. Álvarez —Estoy interesada en alquilar un local en el centro comercial de la calle Magnolia.

Intérprete —______________________________

Corredor —*Which one? We have three vacant spaces there.*

Intérprete —______________________________

Sra. Álvarez —El local que yo quiero está en la planta baja, al lado de una joyería.

Intérprete —______________________________

Corredor —*That one is already rented, but we have another one on the second floor, next to a toy shop.*

Intérprete —______________________________

Sra. Álvarez —Sí, lo vi, pero creo que es demasiado grande.

Intérprete —______________________________

Corredor —*It is only five feet longer than the other one.*

Intérprete —______________________________

Sra. Álvarez —¿Cuánto piden de alquiler?

Nombre ______________________ **Sección** ____________ **Fecha** ____________

Intérprete —______________________________

Corredor —*Seven dollars per square foot, with a minimum lease period of four years.*

Intérprete —______________________________

Sra. Álvarez —Lo siento, pero yo no creo que pueda pagar un alquiler tan alto.

Intérprete —______________________________

Corredor —*Well, that's okay, but I doubt you'll find a place like this for less money.*

Intérprete —______________________________

Sirva usted de traductor(a)

Mr. Richard Elliot, an American in Panama, needs to sign the following leasing contract. Review the **Vocabulario adicional** in this lesson, and then translate the contract for him on a separate sheet of paper.

CONTRATO DE ARRENDAMIENTO

De una parte el Sr. José Zamora Sosa, propietario del Edificio Zamora, situado en Alcalá número 125, en la ciudad de Panamá, y de la otra parte el Sr. Richard Elliot como arrendatario, convienen en:

1. El propietario alquila al arrendatario el local número 101 del edificio antes mencionado.
2. El arrendatario debe pagar un alquiler de cuatrocientos dólares mensuales ($400.00) por el local mencionado.
3. El arrendatario debe pagar los alquileres por adelantado y entregar el alquiler de un mes en depósito.
4. El arrendatario debe usar el local para oficina.
5. El presente contrato es válido por cinco años a partir de la fecha de su firma.

Y, para constancia, el arrendatario y el propietario firman el presente contrato en Panamá, a 4 de noviembre de 20—.

______________________ Propietario

______________________ Arrendatario

En estas situaciones

With a partner, act out the following situations in Spanish.

You are a real estate agent, talking with a client who wants to rent commercial space. The space he/she is interested in is rented, but you have a similar one on the ground floor. Tell him/her that the place on the ground floor is more expensive because it is six hundred and eighty square feet; it is next to a toy shop, and you doubt a better place can be found. Mention that the place has display windows and counters, but it doesn't have fitting rooms. Modifications can be made if they do not affect the structure of the building. Say that you need to investigate his/her credit, but first you need him/her to sign a form to authorize the investigation.

Nombre ______________________ **Sección** ____________ **Fecha** ____________

Casos With you and a partner playing the roles, work through the following scenarios.

1. An employee from the rental office of a shopping center takes care of a potential customer, who wants to rent commercial space.
2. Two business partners discuss a space for rent for their new shopping center.

Un paso más You are a real estate broker. What listings would you recommend to clients who are looking for the following types of commercial space?

ALQUILER DE LOCALES COMERCIALES

Anaheim

SEA SU PROPIO JEFE

900-3600 pies^2, tienda–oficina para alquilar. Excelente local, buen alquiler y contrato. No espere más. Vea: 9300–9386 Katella Ave.
(800) 426–2971
(310) 947–1686

Bell Gardens

LOCALES COMERCIALES

Se renta, esquina de Florence y Garfield, adecuados para florería, renta de video, autopartes, carnicería, panadería o cualquier otro negocio. Alquileres empiezan desde $500. Para más informes llamar al (310) 923–2788.

Los Ángeles

ESTACIÓN DE ALQUILER

Excelente negocio para estilistas, cuidado de piel, etc. Un mes de alquiler gratis. Mes a mes. Llame en inglés a Alvina, (818) 702–0343.

Los Ángeles

LOCALES EN EXCELENTE ÁREA

Beverly Blvd. y W estern. 600 p^2, mucho tráfico. (213) 654–1464

Los Ángeles

PARA TIENDA U OFICINA

$850 mensuales. 3071 W. Pico Blvd., cerca de Western y Pico Blvd. Nuevo edificio.
(213) 737–1333
Preguntar por Norma.

1. space suitable for opening a video rental shop
2. space with at least two thousand and five hundred square feet
3. space in a new building
4. space that comes rent free for the first month.
5. space suitable for a store, on a corner lot of a busy street

Lectura After reading this **lectura,** get together with a partner and take turns answering the following questions.

Muchos inmigrantes hispanos, cuando ganan lo suficiente para invertir, piensan en tener su propio° negocio. Su sueño° es "independizarse",° esto es, ser sus propios jefes. En sus países no es común° que la clase media invierta en la bolsa,° compre bonos o fondos mutuos. Aquí siguen pensando igual; por eso hoy hay miles de pequeños negocios hispanos en los Estados Unidos. Los negocios que más les atraen,° o que se sienten° más preparados° para dirigir, son restaurantes, tiendas de comestibles° o de ropa, mercados de productos agrícolas, guarderías infantiles,° periódicos y estaciones de radio, jardines y todos los negocios relacionados con la agricultura. En California, Texas y Florida los negocios hispanos representan un alto porcentaje de las economías estatales, y proporcionan trabajo a miles de obreros.

own / dream / to be independent
usual / stock exchange
attract / feel
qualified
tiendas... *grocery stores*
guarderías... *children's nurseries*

1. ¿Qué deseo tienen muchos inmigrantes hispanos cuando ganan lo suficiente para invertir? ¿Para qué?
2. Normalmente, ¿en qué no invierte la clase media en los países hispanos? ¿Qué pasa cuando miembros de esa clase están en este país?
3. ¿Qué tipos de negocios se sienten preparados para dirigir?
4. ¿En qué estados hay un alto porcentaje de negocios hispanos?

Y usted...

1. ¿Le interesaría más invertir su dinero en la bolsa o abrir un negocio?
2. ¿Qué tipo de negocio le interesaría? ¿Por qué?

Nombre ______________________ Sección ____________ Fecha ____________

Un dicho

El cliente siempre tiene la razón. *The customer is always right.*

Trivia

Generally, if you plan to live at a property for only a few years, renting is a financially smarter decision than buying. There are, however, other situations in which it is better to buy than to rent a property. If you are unsure about which decision is better for you, you can find several buy vs. rent calculators online.

Lección 19

Vendiendo y comprando seguros

Objectives

Structures

- The subjunctive after certain conjunctions
- The present perfect subjunctive
- Uses of the present perfect subjunctive

Business Communication

- Selling insurance to a prospective Spanish-speaking client

Una agente visita a la Sra. Aguirre para venderle un seguro de vida.

Agente	—¿Tiene Ud. hijos, Sra. Aguirre?
Sra. Aguirre	—Sí, tengo dos hijos.
Agente	—Espero que haya pensado qué será de ellos cuando Ud. les falte.
Sra. Aguirre	—No creo que haya pensado mucho en esa eventualidad. Soy bastante joven todavía.
Agente	—Pero cuando Ud. sea mayor, el seguro de vida le costará más.
Sra. Aguirre	—Tengo cuarenta y cinco años. ¿Cuánto me costaría el seguro ahora?
Agente	—Por cada mil dólares de cobertura, pagaría una prima de un dólar y noventa centavos.
Sra. Aguirre	—¿La cobertura incluye la muerte por cualquier motivo?
Agente	—Sí, excepto por suicidio durante los dos años después de la firma de la póliza.
Sra. Aguirre	—Déjeme una copia de la póliza y literatura. Tan pronto como las lea la llamaré.

El Sr. Caro compra un seguro de automóviles.

Sr. Caro	—Necesito un seguro para mi coche.
Agente	—¿Quiere un seguro contra todo riesgo o uno que cubra solamente la responsabilidad civil?
Sr. Caro	—Uno que cubra lo que exige la ley. El coche es muy viejo y no vale la pena asegurarlo contra robos o contra los daños que sufra.
Agente	—En este estado, una póliza que cubra la responsabilidad civil es suficiente.
Sr. Caro	—¿Qué cubre la póliza más barata de ese tipo?

Agente —Hasta $15.000 por daños a las personas, con un máximo de $30.000 por accidente, y $5.000 por daños a la propiedad. Esta póliza sólo cubre al conductor y a los pasajeros del otro coche.

Sr. Caro —¿Y qué pasa en caso de que mi seguro no alcance para pagar los gastos médicos?

Agente —Entonces Ud. es responsable por la diferencia; por eso le recomiendo que compre una póliza con mayor cobertura, por si hay que pagar atención médica y hospitalaria.

Sr. Caro —¿Cuánto me costaría una cobertura de responsabilidad civil de $50.000 por persona?

Agente —¿Quién va a manejar el coche?

Sr. Caro —Solamente yo. Bueno, mi novia lo maneja algunas veces.

Agente —¿Cuántos años hace que Uds. tienen licencia de conducir?

Sr. Caro —Yo, cuatro años, y mi novia, tres.

Agente —¿Han tenido Uds. algún accidente?

Sr. Caro —Yo choqué hace dos meses, pero el juez declaró culpable al otro chofer.

Agente —¿Han pagado multas por violaciones de las leyes del tránsito?

Sr. Caro —Mi novia ha pagado dos por no hacer caso a las señales de parada, y yo una por pasar con la luz roja y otra por exceso de velocidad.

Agente —Lo siento. No podemos venderle una póliza. Uds. tienen demasiadas violaciones y esto es un riesgo para nosotros.

Sr. Caro —¿Qué puedo hacer? No debo conducir sin seguro.

Agente —Ud. tendrá que llamar a la agencia del estado que se encarga de los conductores que están en su situación para que lo aseguren.

La Sra. Llano quiere comprar un seguro para su negocio.

Agente —¿Es suyo el edificio?

Sra. Llano —No, yo solamente soy una de las propietarias del negocio.

Agente —En ese caso puede comprar un seguro que cubra los equipos, los muebles y enseres, y la mercancía de su negocio.

Sra. Llano —Me interesa un seguro contra robos y contra incendios.

Agente —Yo le aconsejo que asegure su negocio contra todo riesgo.

Sra. Llano —¿Qué cubre la póliza contra todo riesgo?

Agente —Tenemos un seguro comprensivo que incluye la restitución de pérdidas por daños causados por robos, fuegos, motines, inundaciones y otros fenómenos naturales como nevadas, tornados, huracanes, etc.

Sra. Llano —¿No incluye terremotos?

Agente —No, señora. Ése es un seguro aparte, y nuestra compañía no lo ofrece ahora.

Sra. Llano —Y si un trabajador o un cliente sufre lesiones u otros daños en nuestro establecimiento, ¿está nuestra responsabilidad civil cubierta por esa póliza?

Agente —Sí, señora.

Nombre ______________________ Sección ____________ Fecha ____________

¡Escuchemos! While listening to the dialogue, circle **V (verdadero)** if the statement is true or **F (falso)** if it is false.

1. El agente espera que la Sra. Aguirre haya pensado qué será de sus hijos cuando ella les falte. V F
2. Cuando la Sra. Aguirre sea mayor, el seguro le costará menos. V F
3. La Sra. Aguirre quiere que el agente le deje una copia de la póliza. V F
4. Ella llamará al agente cuando haya leído la póliza. V F
5. El Sr. Caro quiere un seguro contra todo riesgo. V F
6. La póliza más barata sólo cubre al conductor y a los pasajeros del coche del Sr. Caro. V F
7. El Sr. Caro no cree que su novia haya pagado multas por exceso de velocidad. V F
8. El agente no le vende una póliza al Sr. Caro porque él y su novia tienen demasiadas violaciones. V F
9. La Sra. Llano es la dueña del edificio. V F
10. La póliza que le ofrece el agente cubre la responsabilidad civil en caso de que un cliente sufra un accidente. V F

VOCABULARIO

Audio

Cognados

el accidente
comprensivo(a)
la eventualidad
excepto
el huracán
la literatura
la póliza
precisamente
responsable
la restitución
el suicidio
el tornado
la violación

Nombres

la cobertura *coverage*
los enseres *fixtures*
el exceso de velocidad *speeding*
el fenómeno natural, la fuerza mayor *natural phenomenon, act of God*
el fuego, el incendio *fire*
la inundación *flood*
la lesión *injury*
la luz *light*
el motín *riot*
el motivo *cause, reason*
la muerte *death*
la multa *fine, ticket*

la nevada *snowstorm*
la prima *premium*
la responsabilidad civil *liability*
el robo *theft, burglary, robbery*
el seguro, la aseguranza (*coll.*) *insurance*
el seguro de vida *life insurance*
la señal de parada *stop sign*
el terremoto, el temblor de tierra *earthquake*
el (la) trabajador(a) *worker*
el tránsito *traffic*
la vida *life*

Verbos

aconsejar *to advise*
alcanzar *to be enough, to reach*
asegurar *to insure*
chocar *to collide, to have a collision*
faltar *to be lacking*
incluir *to include*

Adjetivos

causado(a) *caused*
cubierto(a) *covered*
culpable *at fault, guilty*
joven *young*
mayor *older*
rojo(a) *red*

Otras palabras y expresiones

algunas veces *sometimes*
la atención médica y hospitalaria *medical and hospital care*
bastante *quite*
contra *against*
declarar culpable *to declare at fault*
en caso de que *in case* (*that*)
en cuanto *as soon as*
hacer caso *to pay attention*
hay que *one must, it is necessary to*
para que, a fin de que *so that*
por cualquier motivo *for any reason*
¿Qué será de...? *What will become of . . . ?*
valer la pena *to be worth it*

Audio VOCABULARIO ADICIONAL

acontecimiento imprevisto *unforeseen occurrence*
anterior *foregoing*
anulación *cancelation*
atribuible a *attributable to*
cláusulas a *provisions*
cobertura *(insurance) cover*
comienzo de la cobertura *inception of the cover*
conforme a *in accordance with*
conformidad con sus instrucciones *as instructed by you*
conmoción civil *civil unrest*
daños por agua (vapores, olores) *damage by water (vapours, smells)*
dependiendo de *subject to*
desde la fecha en que causara el suceso *as from the event giving rise thereto*
derivado(a) de *arising from*
emitidos a favor del asegurado *issued on behalf of the insured*
en adelante *hereafter, hereunder*
en caso de muerte (fallecimiento) *in the event of death*
en vigor *in force*
estando involucrado(a) en *being engaged in*
falta de notificación *failure to notify*
fecha de efecto *inception date*
fecha límite *deadline*
estipulado(a) en *defined in*

Nombre ______________________ Sección ______________ Fecha ______________

explosión *explosion*
historial personal de reclamos *personal claims record*
impago *financial default*
huelga *strike*
incumplimiento por parte de *non-compliance on the part of*
indemnización fijada por arbitraje *arbitration award*
indemnizar *to indemnify, to compensate*
independientemente de *regardless of*
interrupción *curtailment*
invalidez permanente (incapacidad permanente) *permanent disability*
ley consuetudinaria de contratos *common contract law*
leyes y normativas *laws and regulations*
límite de indemnización $_____ *up to _____*
línea directa de atención al cliente *customer help-line*
motín *riot*
nota de cotización *quote sheet*
pagadero(a) *payable*
pendiente *impending*
pérdida de equipaje *personal baggage and property loss*
póliza se rige bajo *the policy is governed by*
ponemos en su conocimiento *we draw your attention to*
preceptos de *the provisions of*
proceder *to proceed*
rechazo *non-acceptance, rejection*
reembolsar *to reimburse*
reemplazar *to supersede, to replace*
responsable de *liable for*
resumen de las coberturas y los costos *summary of covers and costs*
rogamos contacten *please notify*
se compromete *undertakes*
sea cual sea su naturaleza *whatsoever their nature*
sede social *headquarters*
si desea alguna aclaración *if you need any clarification*
so pena de suspensión de cobertura *on pain of forfeiture of the cover*
siempre y cuando *providing*
suplementos *endorsements*
validez legal *legayl enforced*
rogamos contacten *please notify*
se compromete *undertakes*
sea cual sea su naturaleza *whatsoever their nature*
sede social *headquarters*
si desea alguna aclaración *if you need any clarification*
so pena de suspensión de cobertura *on pain of forfeiture of the cover*
siempre y cuando *providing*
suplementos *endorsements*
validez legal *legayl enforced*

Para hablar de los seguros

a favor de *on behalf of*
el (la) asegurado(a), el (la) subscriptor(a) *policyholder*
el (la) asegurador(a) *insurer, insurance company*
la indemnización *compensation, indemnification*
la invalidez *disability, disablement*
la probabilidad de vida, la expectativa de vida *life expectancy*
la reclamación *claim*
la renta vitalicia *life annuity*
el rescate *surrender value*
el seguro de accidentes de trabajo *workers' compensation insurance*
el seguro de grupo, el seguro colectivo *group insurance*
el seguro de salud *health insurance*
el seguro dotal *endowment insurance*
la tercera persona, el tercero *third party*

Nombre ______________ Sección ______________ Fecha ______________

Search

Notas Culturales

- Taking out insurance is not a widespread practice among Latinos. Even though property insurance and life insurance are the types of insurance most frequently bought in Latin America, much more property is uninsured than insured, and only a small percentage of Latin Americans buy life insurance. In some countries, there is a growing availability of very inexpensive life insurance policies whose benefits barely cover funeral expenses.
- Auto insurance is not mandatory in most countries, and consequently is not considered essential by many. Health insurance is not provided through a workplace-based system similar to that of the United States; instead, Latin Americans who can afford it purchase coverage for their families themselves. Long before there were HMOs in the United States, Spanish-speaking countries had similar organizations called **asociaciones mutualistas** that offered their members doctor's visits, prescription drugs, and hospital care for a modest monthly fee. Middle-class families generally join one of these "clinics"; the poor rely on public hospitals and clinics, which are usually free of charge, for their health care.

Actividades

Dígame... Answer the following questions, basing your answers on the dialogues.

1. ¿Cree que la Sra. Aguirre necesita un seguro de vida? ¿Por qué o por qué no?

   ____

2. ¿Qué edad tiene la Sra. Aguirre?

   ____

3. ¿Cuánto va a pagar por el seguro si lo compra ahora?

   ____

4. ¿Qué motivo de muerte no cubre el seguro?

   ____

5. ¿Para qué quiere la Sra. Aguirre una copia de la póliza y literatura?

   ____

6. ¿Qué tipos de seguro de carros le ofrece la agente al Sr. Caro?

   ____

7. ¿Por qué no está interesado el Sr. Caro en un seguro contra todo riesgo?

   ____

8. ¿Cuánto paga la póliza que cubre la responsabilidad civil?

______

9. ¿Qué ocurre si el seguro no cubre el total de los gastos médicos?

______

10. ¿Qué le recomienda la agente al Sr. Caro?

______

11. ¿Por qué no asegura la Sra. Llano el edificio de su negocio?

______

12. ¿Qué riesgos cubre el seguro comprensivo?

______

Hablemos Interview a classmate, using the following questions. When you have finished, switch roles.

1. ¿Tiene Ud. algún seguro? ¿Cuál(es)?
2. ¿Ha pensado Ud. qué será de su familia cuando Ud. les falte?
3. ¿Quién paga su seguro médico?
4. ¿Qué cubre su seguro de salud?
5. ¿Cuánto tiempo de atención hospitalaria cubre su seguro?
6. ¿Exigen las leyes de su estado que se tenga seguros contra todo riesgo?
7. ¿Ha tenido Ud. un accidente de automóvil alguna vez?
8. ¿Pagó su compañía de seguro todos los daños?
9. ¿Maneja otra persona su coche algunas veces?
10. ¿Ud. siempre para su coche cuando el semáforo (*traffic light*) está en rojo?
11. ¿Ha pagado Ud. alguna multa por exceso de velocidad?
12. ¿Vale la pena asegurar su auto contra robos? ¿Por qué o por qué no?

Nombre ______________________ Sección ____________ Fecha ____________

Quiz

Vamos a practicar

A Combine the following sentences, using the cues given.

MODELO ¿A quién llamo? / Él tiene un accidente. (en caso de que)
¿A quién llamo en caso de que él tenga un accidente?

1. ¿Qué será de ellos? / Yo les falto. (cuando)

____

2. No pagará los daños. / El juez lo declara culpable. (hasta que)

____

3. Lo llamaré. / Leo la póliza. (tan pronto como)

____

4. Van a pagar la prima. / Tienen dinero. (en cuanto)

____

5. No compraré el seguro. / Cubre los daños por inundación. (a menos que)

____

B Rewrite the following sentences to indicate that the events to which they refer took place in the past. Follow the model.

MODELO Ojalá que ella *compre* el seguro.
Ojalá que ella haya comprado el seguro.

1. Espero que la póliza *cubra* el total de la atención médica.

____

2. Dudo que ella *asegure* los enseres contra inundaciones.

____

3. No creo que le *pongan* una multa por exceso de velocidad.

____

4. Es posible que el seguro no *alcance* para la atención hospitalaria.

____

5. Temo que *choque* el coche nuevo.

____

Nombre ______________________ Sección ______________ Fecha ______________

Sirva usted de intérprete

With two classmates, play the roles of Sr. Alonso, the insurance agent, and the interpreter who helps them communicate. Switch roles until each of you has played the interpreter's role.

Sr. Alonso —Deseo asegurar mi negocio contra fuego y contra robos.

Intérprete —______________________________

Agente —*What type of business do you have?*

Intérprete —______________________________

Sr. Alonso —Yo importo vegetales.

Intérprete —______________________________

Agente —*Do you want to insure the building or the merchandise and the fixtures?*

Intérprete —______________________________

Sr. Alonso —El edificio no es mío. Deseo asegurar solamente lo que está dentro del edificio: los equipos, los muebles y enseres, y la mercancía.

Intérprete —______________________________

Agente —*Where is your business located?*

Intérprete —______________________________

Sr. Alonso —Cerca de Malibú.

Intérprete —______________________________

Agente —*In that case, I think that you must buy flood insurance also.*

Intérprete —______________________________

Sr. Alonso —No, no lo necesito. Mi negocio está situado en un lugar alto.

Intérprete —______________________________

Sirva usted de traductor(a)

You are helping set up an office for your company in a Spanish-speaking country. While you were out to lunch, an insurance broker called to answer several questions you had about his company's services. Review the **Vocabulario adicional** in this lesson, and then translate the notes your assistant took so that you can fax them to your boss in the United States. Use a separate sheet of paper.

Nombre ______________________ Sección ____________ Fecha ____________

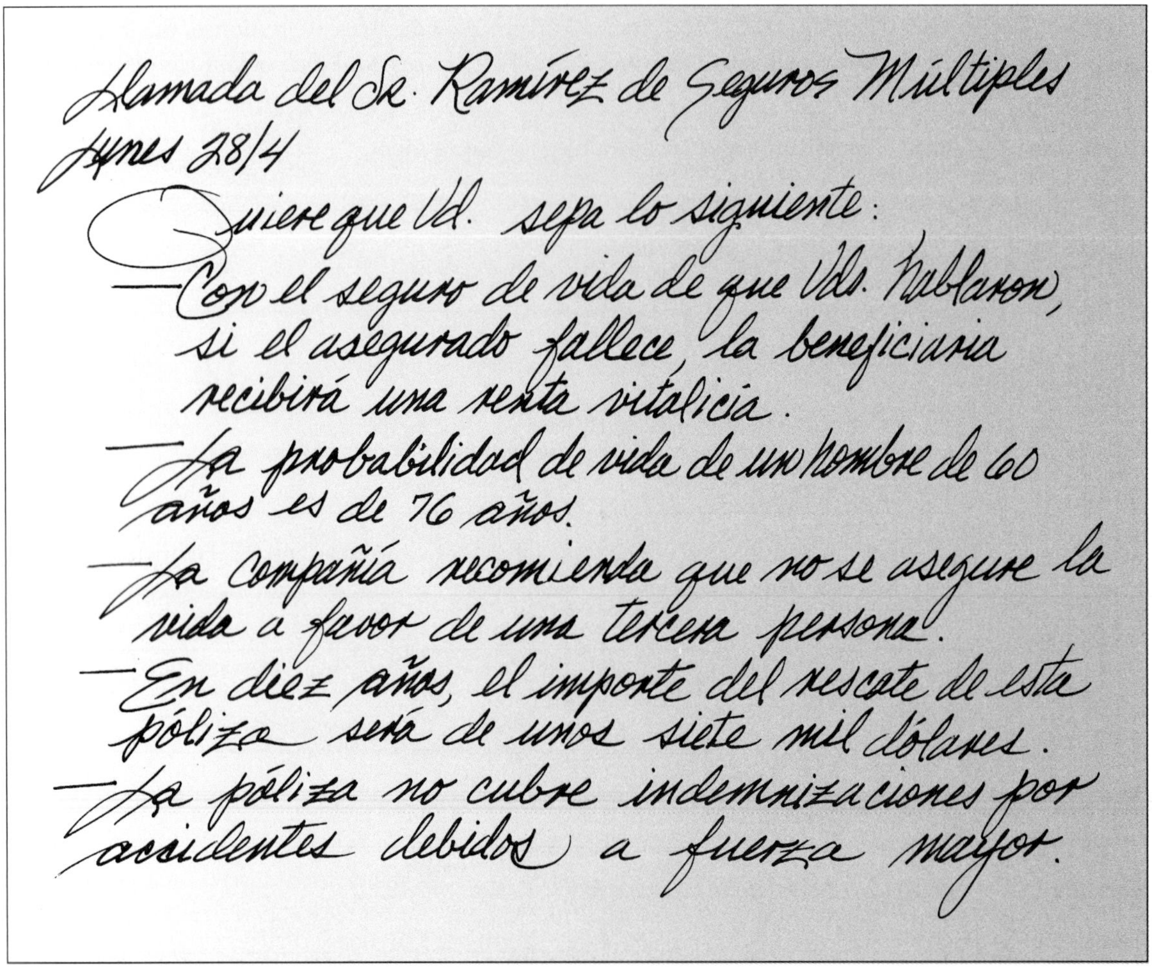

Llamada del Sr. Ramírez de Seguros Múltiples
Lunes 28/4

Quiere que Ud. sepa lo siguiente:

—Con el seguro de vida de que Uds. hablaron, si el asegurado fallece, la beneficiaria recibirá una renta vitalicia.

—La probabilidad de vida de un hombre de 60 años es de 76 años.

—La compañía recomienda que no se asegure la vida a favor de una tercera persona.

—En diez años, el importe del rescate de esta póliza será de unos siete mil dólares.

—La póliza no cubre indemnizaciones por accidentes debidos a fuerza mayor.

En estas situaciones

With a partner, act out the following situations in Spanish.

1. You are an insurance agent meeting with a customer who doesn't speak English. Ask if the client has a life insurance policy. Find out the customer's age and let him/her know that, for that age, the premium is one dollar and fifty cents for every thousand dollars of coverage. Say that, in case of accidental death, the company pays double, that the policy doesn't cover suicide during the first two years after the signing, and that you can provide a copy of the policy to be read later.
2. You are in Mexico. Buy a local automobile insurance policy. Tell the agent that you're going to be driving in Mexico for two weeks. Ask what type of car insurance is required by law in Mexico. Say that you do not want insurance that covers all risks. Say that you have decided to buy only the required insurance.

Casos

With you and a partner playing the roles, work through the following scenarios.

1. An insurance agent discusses life insurance with a client.
2. An insurance agent sells car insurance to a young couple.
3. A person interested in buying insurance for his/her business talks about it with an agent.

Nombre ______________________ Sección ____________ Fecha ____________

Un paso más You need to find a new insurance company for your employees. Review the **Vocabulario adicional** in this lesson and use it and other vocabulary to formulate a list of ten questions for agents of prospective providers on a separate sheet of paper.

Lectura After reading this **lectura,** get together with a partner and take turns answering the following questions.

Venderles seguros a los hispanos no es fácil. La mayoría de ellos nunca tuvo seguro de ningún tipo en su país de origen, excepto quizás el seguro social, al que pertenecen automáticamente cuando empiezan a trabajar. Hay que recordar° que muchos inmigrantes hispanos que viven en este país son campesinos° y obreros no calificados° que llegaron buscando el trabajo que allá les faltaba. Quizás° lo primero que debería hacer un agente de seguros antes de tratar con un cliente hispano, es averiguar sutilmente° por qué está aquí, y cuál era su situación económica en su país. Los que provienen° de la clase media o de la alta, que ya conocían los beneficios de los seguros, los compran tan pronto su economía se lo permite.°

remember
farmers / **obreros...** *unqualified workers*
Maybe
subtly
come from
allows

1. ¿Por qué no es fácil venderles seguros a los hispanos?
2. En sus países, ¿cuándo tienen derecho los hispanos al seguro social?
3. ¿Qué tipos de trabajos desempeñan la mayoría de los hispanos en este país?
4. ¿Qué es lo primero que un agente de seguros debería averiguar?
5. ¿Qué hacen los hispanos que provienen de las clases media o alta?

Y usted...

1. ¿Qué tipo de seguro considera indispensable o muy importante? ¿Por qué?
2. ¿Cree que, a veces, es mejor ahorrar dinero para afrontar (*to face*) ciertos riesgos? ¿Por qué o por qué no?

Un dicho

Nunca compres pesos a peseta. *If an offer looks too good to be true, it is probably not true.*

Trivia

The term *insurance* is defined as the transfer of a certain small loss (what you pay for premium) for a possible devastating loss (the total value of the insured asset). It is a form of risk management that was first practiced by the Chinese, and dates back to as early as the third millennium B.C.E.

LECCIÓN 20 LIBRE COMERCIO CON HISPANOAMÉRICA

OBJECTIVES

Structures

- The imperfect subjunctive
- Uses of the imperfect subjunctive
- *If* clauses

Business Communication

- Talking about Latin American business partners
- Debating free trade agreements
- Using facts to support your arguments

La semana pasada, el profesor Carrillo, de la Universidad Internacional de la Florida[1], les pidió a sus estudiantes que se prepararan para un debate sobre los tratados de libre comercio entre Estados Unidos y varios países latinoamericanos. Hoy comienza el debate. Participan Eva, Juan, Carlos, María y Andrés, estudiantes hispanoamericanos de un curso de verano en la Universidad Internacional de la Florida.

Profesor —Bien, vamos a dedicar los últimos minutos de la clase de hoy para iniciar el debate sobre los tratados de libre comercio.

Eva —Yo soy mexicana y leí sobre el TLCAN[2], el NAFTA[3], como decimos aquí. Entró en vigor el 1 de enero de 1994. Entonces, la mayor parte de los mexicanos dudábamos de que el tratado trajera beneficios para México.

Juan —Las cifras parecen decir lo contrario: de 1995 a 2007, el INBP[4] de los mexicanos pasó de $3.800 a $8.000 dólares anuales.

Carlos —Sí, pero los obreros norteamericanos perdieron miles de trabajos cuando muchas empresas norteamericanas trasladaron parte de sus procesos industriales a México. Lo que aquí llaman "*outsourcing*".

María —Bueno, también en México miles de campesinos lo perdieron todo, porque sus cosechas no podían competir con los productos subsidiados que llegaban de Estados Unidos.

---

[1]Florida International University
[2]Tratado de Libre Comercio de América del Norte
[3]North America Free Trade Agreement
[4]Ingreso Nacional Bruto Per Cápita

Eva —El problema no es simple. En realidad, si las fábricas norteamericanas no aprovecharan la mano de obra barata de México, muchos productos fabricados aquí tendrían precios no competitivos. Las empresas irían a la bancarrota y todos, los de aquí y los de allá, se quedarían sin empleos.

Andrés —Y el proteccionismo tiene una cara bastante fea. Aquí, en el sur de la Florida, hemos visto cómo el cultivo de la caña de azúcar ha dañado gravemente el ecosistema de los Everglades.

Eva —Y la producción de azúcar de caña en esta zona, protegida por altos impuestos aduaneros, hace que todos tengamos que pagar el azúcar a precios altísimos.

Carlos —Y que los países del Caribe, que podrían vendernos azúcar a bajo precio, no reciban las divisas que necesitan para comprar productos nuestros.

Profesor —Lamentablemente, se nos terminó el tiempo. Les sugiero que mañana hablemos de los demás tratados de libre comercio con países latinoamericanos.

Llegó mañana.

Profesor —Hoy también tenemos tiempo para debatir. Les sugiero que dediquemos esta sesión al tratado de libre comercio con Chile, pues los otros tratados son tan recientes que no podríamos analizar sus efectos.

Juan —Yo leí sobre los tratados de libre comercio de Chile. Chile tiene 57 tratados de libre comercio. Si es que no firmó otro ayer.

Eva —Eso quiere decir que Chile apuesta por la globalización.

Andrés —Definitivamente, y parece que le va muy bien. Aunque generalmente son los obreros los que más se oponen al libre comercio, son las empresas nacionales de productos caros y de baja calidad las que más sufren con dichos tratados.

Carlos —Y los consumidores, los que más se benefician.

María —No, yo creo que son las grandes empresas transnacionales las que más se benefician. Frecuentemente abusan de su poder, y los países pequeños pocas veces pueden evitar que lleven a la quiebra a las pequeñas y medianas empresas, PyME[5], como se les llama en español.

Eva —Pero el tratado contiene acuerdos que me parecen muy buenos. Además de eliminar derechos de aduana, se ocupa de la protección del medio ambiente y establece medidas sanitarias y fitosanitarias...

Juan —Sí, es un tratado amplio que también incluye la protección de los derechos de autor y regula el intercambio sobre las telecomunicaciones, entre otras muchas cosas.

Profesor —Bien, pero, ¿qué beneficios y perjuicios trajo para Estados Unidos y para Chile el Tratado de Libre Comercio entre ambos países?

Juan —El Tratado de Libre Comercio entre el Gobierno de la República de Chile y los Estados Unidos de América entró en vigor el 1 de enero de 2004, y desde su firma hasta el 2008, el comercio entre los dos países aumentó en un 154%.

Andrés —Bueno, el gobierno chileno estima que el verdadero aumento del comercio entre los dos países sería sólo del 60%, si se tuviera en cuenta la inflación y el alto precio alcanzado por el cobre en esos años.

Eva —¿Y qué otros productos nos llegan de Chile, además del cobre?

Carlos —Algunos los comes todos los días: pescado y frutas. Y, si no fueras abstemia, seguramente habrías probado los excelentes vinos chilenos.

---

[5]Pequeñas y Medianas Empresas

Nombre ______________________ **Sección** ____________ **Fecha** ____________

¡Escuchemos!

While listening to the dialogue, circle **V (verdadero)** if the statement is true or **F (falso)** if it is false.

1.	El profesor Carrillo trabaja en la Universidad Internacional de la Florida.	V	F
2.	Eva leyó sobre el tratado de libre comercio con Chile.	V	F
3.	María cree que los consumidores son los más beneficiados con los tratados de libre comercio.	V	F
4.	Muchas empresas americanas trasladaron algunos procesos industriales a México	V	F
5.	El proteccionismo aumenta los precios de los productos a los consumidores.	V	F
6.	Chile es partidario de la globalización.	V	F
7.	Generalmente los obreros apoyan los tratados de libre comercio.	V	F
8.	Los países pequeños siempre pueden evitar que las compañías transnacionales abusen de las pequeñas empresas nacionales.	V	F
9.	El tratado de libre comercio con Chile se ocupa de la protección del medio ambiente.	V	F
10.	A Eva le gusta el vino.	V	F

VOCABULARIO

Audio

Cognados

amplio (a)
el beneficio
Caribe
el comercio
el debate
definitivamente
el ecosistema
el efecto
excelente
fitosanitario(a)
frecuentemente
la globalización
la inflación
el proceso
la producción
el proteccionismo
reciente
la República de Chile
sanitaria
la sesión
simple
las transnacionales, las multinacionales

Nombres

el (la) abstemio(a) *non-drinker*
el acuerdo *agreement*
el (la) azúcar *sugar*
la bancarrota, la quiebra *bankruptcy*
la caña de azúcar *sugar cane*

la cifra *number, figure*
el cobre *copper*
la cosecha *crop*
el cultivo *cultivation, farming*
los derechos aduanales (de aduana) *customs duty*
los derechos de autor *copyright*
el perjuicio *damage*
el proteccionismo *protectionism*

Verbos

abusar de *to abuse*
analizar *to analyze*
apostar (o:ue) *to bet*
beneficiar *to benefit, to do good*
dañar *to harm, to damage*
debatir *to debate*
dedicar *to dedicate*
establecer *to establish*
estimar *to estimate, to think*
iniciar *to initiate, to commence*
ocuparse de *to deal with*
poner en vigor *to enact*
probar (o:ue) *to taste*
proteger[1] *to protect*
quedarse sin empleo (trabajo) *to lose your job*
subsidiar *to subsidize*

Adjetivos

libre *free*

Otras palabras y expresiones

gravemente *seriously*
lamentablemente *regrettably*
lo contrario *just the opposite*
los (las) de aquí *those here*
los (las) de allá *those over there*
los (las) otros(as) *the others*
los (las) que más se oponen *those who most vigorously oppose*
me parece *it looks to me*
protección del medio ambiente (f.) *environmental protection*

VOCABULARIO ADICIONAL

Audio

arbitraje *arbitration*
la ampliación *expansion*
apoyar *to favor*
la barrera *barrier*
Banco Interamericano de Desarrollo (BID) *Inter-American Development Bank*
Banco Mundial *World Bank* WB
brutal *brutal*

[1]First person singular, present indicative: yo **protejo**

buque de transporte de carga sólida a granel *bulk carrier*
cadena de suministro *supply chain*
el (la) capitalista *capitalist*
carta de crédito *letter of credit*
catálogo *brochure catalogue*
cheque bancario *bank draft*
comercio exterior *foreign trade, international business*
Comunidad Andina *Andean Community*
Conferencia de las Naciones Unidas sobre Comercio y Desarrollo *United Nations Conference on Trade and Development*
consejo de administración *board of directors*
dedicado(a) *dedicated*
desarrollar *to develop*
director ejecutivo *chief executive officer C.E.O.*
disfrazado(a) *disguised*
el (la) economista *economist*
eficientemente *efficiently*
la explotación *exploitation*
filial *branch*
fusiones y adquisiciones *mergers and acquisitions*
gestión *management*
los hacen *make them*
huso horario *time zone*
índice de precios al consumidor *consumer price index*
la infraestructura *infrastructure*
licitaciones *tenders*
logística *logistics*
el Manifiesto Comunista *Communist Manifesto*
Mercado Común del Sur (Mercosur) *Southern Common Market (Mercosur)*
mercados emergentes *emerging markets*
Objetivos de Desarrollo del Milenio *Millennium Development Goals*
la oferta y la demanda *supply and demand*
oleoducto *pipeline (oil)*
el (la) opositor(a) *opponent*
Organización Mundial del Comercio *World Trade Organization* WTO
países del tercer mundo *third world countries*
paridad de poder adquisitivo *purchasing power parity*
persona jurídica *legal person*
planificación *planning*
pobreza *poverty*
posicionamiento *positioning*
promoción *promotion*
propiedad intelectual *intellectual property*
protocolo *protocol*
el punto de vista *point of view*
rentabilidad *profitability*
socialista *socialist*
sustituir *to substitute*
tendencias *trends*
transferencia bancaria *bank transfer*
Unión aduanera *Customs union*
Unión Europea (EU) *European Union*

Nombre ______________________ **Sección** ______________ **Fecha** ______________

Search

iLrn

Notas Culturales

Los Tratados de Libre Comercio

- **¿Qué dicen sus partidarios?** Los TLC, al eliminar las barreras fiscales, fomentan el acceso de los consumidores a productos extranjeros de mejor calidad o menor precio, pues los precios resultan del libre juego° de la oferta y la demanda. De este modo, el libre comercio contribuye a aumentar la producción nacional de los productos que cada país participante produce más eficientemente. Por otra parte, al extenderse los mercados a países extranjeros, se hace necesaria la creación o la ampliación y modernización de empresas productoras, lo que genera° más inversiones y más empleo. Así, los países pobres, atraen inversiones extranjeras que les ayudan a desarrollar sus infraestructuras.

  libre... *fair play*

  generates

- **¿Qué dicen sus opositores?** Los grupos anti-globalización dicen que los tratados de libre comercio generalmente no aumentan la libertad económica de los pobres, y frecuentemente los hace más pobres.
- Los socialistas creen que esos tratados promueven una mayor explotación de los trabajadores por parte de los capitalistas. Marx, en *El Manifiesto Comunista,* dice que "Comercio libre" es la palabra que "ha sustituido la explotación desnuda°, desvergonzada°, directa y brutal."

  naked / shameless

- El conocido economista latinoamericano Manuel Ayau recuerda que la Constitución de los Estados Unidos necesitó sólo 54 palabras para establecer el comercio libre entre los estados de la Unión, mientras que el TLCAN (NAFTA) tiene 2.000 páginas, y que 900 de ellas están dedicadas a las tarifas.

Actividades

Dígame... Answer the following questions, basing your answers on the dialogues.

1. ¿Qué curso están tomando los estudiantes que participan en este debate? ¿Dónde?

   ____

2. ¿De dónde son los estudiantes? ¿Cuál es el tema del debate?

   ____

3. ¿Qué dudaba la mayor parte de los mexicanos antes de firmarse el TLC?

   ____

4. ¿En qué consiste el "*outsourcing*"?

   ____

5. ¿Qué tratan de aprovechar las empresas que trasladan algunas de sus operaciones a México?

   ____

6. ¿Qué pasaría si las empresas americanas no trasladaran algunas de sus operaciones a México?

   ____

Nombre ______________________ Sección ____________ Fecha ____________

7. ¿Quiénes cree Ud. que se benefician más con los tratados de libre comercio? ¿Los consumidores o las grandes empresas? Explique su opinión.

____

8. ¿Cuáles son algunos de los asuntos de que trata el tratado de libre comercio con Chile?

____

9. ¿Por qué estima el gobierno chileno que el aumento de su comercio con los Estados Unidos fue sólo de un 60%?

____

10. ¿Cuáles son algunos de los productos que Chile exporta a los Estados Unidos?

____

Hablemos

Interview a classmate, using the following questions. When you have finished, switch roles.

1. ¿Qué ventajas tiene el libre cambio de mercancías y productos?
2. ¿Qué inconvenientes tiene?
3. ¿Qué ventajas tiene el proteccionismo?
4. ¿Qué inconvenientes tiene?
5. ¿Cree usted que los tratados entre países poderosos y países débiles son convenientes para los dos países o sólo para los países poderosos? Justifique su posición dando ejemplos.
6. ¿Es usted partidario del proteccionismo o del libre intercambio de mercancías y servicios? Explique su posición.

Quiz

Vamos a practicar

A Rewrite the following sentences using the new cues.

MODELO No hay nada que pueda justificar ese tratado.
No había nada que pudiera justificar ese tratado.

1. Los obreros americanos exigen que los tratados incluyan esa cláusula.

   Los obreros americanos exigían que ______________________.

2. Es conveniente que el Congreso apruebe el Tratado de Libre Comercio con Colombia.

   Sería conveniente que ______________________.

3. Los camioneros mexicanos temen que los camiones americanos les quiten trabajo.

   Los camioneros mexicanos temían que ______________________.

4. Algunos políticos piden que se modifique el Tratado de Libre Comercio con México.

   Algunos políticos pidieron que ____.

5. La mayor parte de los economistas recomiendan que EE.UU. firme nuevos tratados de libre comercio.

   La mayor parte de los economistas recomendaron que ________________________________.

6. No creemos que Venezuela tenga un tratado de libre comercio con Argentina.

   No creíamos que ____.

B Combine the two sentences into one using the conditional **si**. Follow the model.

MODELO El Congreso no aprobará el tratado con Colombia. / Incluirán una cláusula que proteja a los obreros.
El Congreso no aprobará el tratado con Colombia si no incluyen una cláusula que proteja a los obreros.

1. Muchos obreros perderán su trabajo. / Aprobarán el tratado.

   ____

2. Los camiones mexicanos transportarán mercancías a los Estados Unidos y Canadá. / Implementarán los acuerdos del TLCAN.

   ____

3. El etanol será más barato. / Los Estados Unidos rebaja las tarifas al etanol de Brasil.

   ____

4. Venderíamos más productos a Cuba. / Cuba tiene dinero para pagarlos.

   ____

5. Los grupos anti-globalización apoyarían el tratado. / El tratado aumenta la libertad económica de los pobres.

   ____

6. Eva tomaría vino. / Es abstemia.

   ____

Sirva usted de intérprete

With two classmates, play the roles of Terry Thomson, a graduate student doing research for his/her dissertation, Daniel Guerra, a politician who favors NAFTA, and an interpreter who helps them to communicate.

Terry —*Good afternoon, Sr. Guerra, glad to meet you.*

Intérprete —____

Sr. Guerra —Buenas tardes. Supongo que usted sepa que yo apoyo el TLCAN.

Intérprete —______________________________________

Terry —*Yes, I know. Now tell me, why do you favor the treaty? I have read that it was very difficult for many Mexican factories to compete with American and Canadian products.*

Intérprete —______________________________________

Sr. Guerra —Cierto, porque la calidad de sus productos dejaba mucho que desear.

Intérprete —______________________________________

Terry —*And thousands of Mexican workers lost their jobs.*

Intérprete —______________________________________

Sr. Guerra —En realidad, la mayor parte de ellos pasó de trabajar en una fábrica ineficiente a hacerlo en una empresa moderna. Ahora trabajan en industrias más mexicanos que antes.

Intérprete —______________________________________

Terry —*But thousands of Mexicans continue to cross the border for a better job in the States or in Canada.*

Intérprete —______________________________________

Sr. Guerra —Eso es así porque todavía el producto bruto por cabeza de los mexicanos está muy debajo del producto bruto de los estadounidenses y de los canadienses.

Intérprete —______________________________________

Terry —*Do you think that the Treaty will help to increase Mexicans' per capita income?*

Intérprete —______________________________________

Sr. Guerra —Sí, claro. Lo está haciendo. Recuerde que el número de mexicanos pobres es ahora mucho menor que antes del Tratado.

Intérprete —______________________________________

Now, Terry interviews Antonia Sánchez, a Mexican politician who opposes NAFTA.

Terry —*Good morning, Sra. Sánchez, thank you very much for allowing me the opportunity to hear your point of view about NAFTA.*

Intérprete —______________________________________

Sra. Sánchez —Gracias a usted. Yo tengo mucho interés en que los norteamericanos sepan cómo el Tratado de Libre Comercio de América del Norte está dañando la economía mexicana.

Intérprete —______________________________________

Terry —*Which sectors of the economy are the most affected?*

Intérprete —______________________________________

Sra. Sánchez —El sector agrícola, principalmente. Mire. Los Estados Unidos ayudan a sus agricultores con grandes subsidios.

Nombre ______________________ Sección ____________ Fecha ____________

Intérprete —______________________________

Terry —*I know. I have learned that the U.S. government's subsidies to the corn sector surpass ten billion dollars a year.*

Intérprete —______________________________

Sra. Sánchez —Esa cantidad es cerca de diez veces el total del presupuesto mexicano para la agricultura. Por eso nuestros agricultores no pueden competir.

Intérprete —______________________________

Terry —*Until recently, that was a valid argument against the Treaty, but now since the U.S. uses corn to produce ethanol, the price of the American corn is much higher.*

Intérprete —______________________________

Sra. Sánchez —Sí, pero para los agricultores mexicanos ya es muy tarde. La mayor parte de ellos tuvieron que declararse en quiebra.

Intérprete —______________________________

Terry —*But, because of the large demand of produce and fruit both in the U.S. and Canada, many Mexican farmers have doubled their income.*

Intérprete —______________________________

Sra. Sánchez —Eso es cierto, pero el maíz es un alimento básico en México, y porque ahora tenemos que importar su maíz a altos precios, las tortillas son demasiado caras para los mexicanos de la clase baja.

Intérprete —______________________________

Sirva usted de traductor(a)

You are preparing yourself to participate in a debate about the proposed free-trade agreement with Colombia. You would like to quote from an article you found in a Colombian magazine.

Translate this section into English.

Comercio bilateral con los Estados Unidos

Lima, Perú. junio 16

En el mundo globalizado de hoy, el progreso económico de los países y la mejor calidad de vida de su gente depende de cómo logren incorporarse a la economía mundial para aprovechar las ventajas que ofrece el comercio libre.

Como el Perú tiene un pequeño mercado interno, sus industrias no pueden desarrollarse si no logran exportar buena parte de su producción. Es por eso que el Tratado de Libre Comercio (TLC) con los Estados Unidos era la oportunidad que el Perú necesitaba para la transformación de su producción industrial. Los Estados Unidos es el mayor mercado mundial, y más del 80% de sus importaciones son productos manufacturados.

Desde la firma del ATPA, en 1991, y del ATPDEA, en 2001, el Perú ha aumentado sus exportaciones hacia EE.UU. en un 15% anual y, desde la implementación del tratado de libre comercio bilateral, nuestras exportaciones han aumentado de tal forma que, actualmente, la balanza comercial nos es favorable.

Nombre ______________________ Sección ____________ Fecha ____________

En estas situaciones With a partner, act out the following situations in Spanish.

1. You are visiting Costa Rica and you are interested in finding out how the Free Trade Agreement between the U.S. and Central America has affected the country. Ask how the treaty has affected bilateral trade, which sector of the economy has benefitted from the trade and which sector has suffered from it, how the treaty has affected employment, and whether the country's economy has improved or worsened since the treaty was implemented.
2. You are a business person visiting La Vega, in the Dominican Republic. You are interested in importing vegetables to the U.S. Ask pertinent questions to find out which vegetables are grown there and the quality, amount, price, transporting procedures involved, etc. (This area grows cabbage, cauliflower, carrots, beans, and garlic.)

Casos With you and a partner playing the roles, work through the following scenarios.

1. You and a partner agree to learn more about outsourcing and improve each other's Spanish skills at the same time. One of you will read articles in favor of outsourcing and the other will read articles opposing it. You should find plenty of information concerning this topic on Google Español**.** After you have finished, get together and discuss what each of you read.
2. You and a partner agree to learn more about NAFTA and improve each other's Spanish skills at the same time. One of you will read articles in favor of NAFTA, the other will read articles opposing it. You should find plenty of information concerning this topic on Google Español. After you have finished, get together and discuss what each of you read.

Un paso más Make a list of the glossed words in the following **Lectura.** Think about everyday situations in which you may be able to use them. Write sentences using each word or phrase.

Lectura After reading this **lectura,** get together with a partner and take turns answering the following questions.

Hemos llegado al final de la última lección. Su profesor(a) y los autores del libro confían[1] en que (1) dominen[2] el español a un nivel suficiente como para considerarse[3] bilingües, (2) que hayan adquirido[4] un vocabulario especializado sobre el lenguaje usado en los negocios que les permitan usar su nueva lengua como una herramienta[5] más en el curso de sus carreras y (3) que conozcan mejor a los países de habla hispana al sur del río Grande.

En esta última lección hemos querido presentarles distintos puntos de vista sobre los mismos temas. Y los hemos invitado[6], en *Casos*, a que debatan cada tema. Recuerden que quien lee sólo lo que está de acuerdo con sus propias ideas, está muy mal informado. Y recuerden también que nadie es dueño de la verdad, que todas las ideas e ideologías contienen dosis de verdad y de falsedad[7]; y que los problemas no tienen soluciones mágicas: son sólo los demagogos los que dicen tenerlas. Por tanto, hay que ser suficientemente curiosos[8] y tolerantes como para escuchar o leer con interés y respeto a los que piensan distinto. Lo dijo Benito Juárez: "El repeto al derecho ajeno[9] es la paz."

1. ¿Dónde está el río Grande?
2. ¿Qué le sucede a quien sólo lee lo que está de acuerdo con sus ideas?
3. ¿Qué contienen todas las ideologías?
4. ¿Quién fue Benito Juárez?

Y Ud. ...

1. ¿Domina el español a un nivel suficiente como para considerarse bilingüe?
2. ¿Qué título universitario deben tener los encargados de llevar la contabilidad de las empresas?

[1] *trust*
[2] *master*
[3] **para...** *see yourselves*
[4] *acquired*
[5] *tool*
[6] *invited*
[7] *untruth*
[8] *inquisitive*
[9] **derecho...** *another's right*

Un dicho

La economía es el estudio de la escasez (*scarcity*), y de los problemas que de ésta se derivan.

Trivia

Free Trade

Free trade refers to economic systems where governments do not interfere in the movement of goods between countries; that is, there are no taxes on imports. Presently, free trade tends to hold within economic groups such as NAFTA, the European Union (EU), Área de Libre Comercio de las Américas (ALCA), Mercado Común del Sur (Mercosur), Pacto Andino, etc., but since the General Agreement on Tariffs and Trade (GATT) of 1948, developed and undeveloped countries are trying to reduce tariffs to liberalize international trade.

In November 2001, the Fourth Ministerial Conference in Doha, Qatar, asked for negotiations on agriculture and services, but successive meetings in Cancún (2003), Geneva (2004), Hong Kong (2005), Geneva (2006, 2008) have been unable to reach a generally accepted agreement.

SUPLEMENTO 4

DOCUMENTOS DE NEGOCIOS

- Documentos mercantiles
- Instrumentos de crédito
- Contratos

DOCUMENTOS MERCANTILES (*BUSINESS DOCUMENTS*)

El recibo (*Receipt*)
Read the following receipts and answer the questions that follow.

1. Recibo de arrendamiento o subarrendamiento de inmueble

No. Reg. Fed. de Contribuyentes ______

NOMBRE Javier Gómez

(Arrendador o Subarrendador)

DOMICILIO Calle Doce 32

población ______ Entidad federativa ______

RECIBI DE María Monsalvo

DOMICILIO Calle de los Reyes 343, Nº 18

(Ubicación del inmueble y no. ext. e int.)

Seiscientos pesos

(cantidad con letra)

LA CANTIDAD DE $600

I.V.A. ______

RENTA DEL MES Y AÑO ______ **I.S.R.** ______

______ **TOTAL** $600

Lugar ______ Fecha 10/9 Firma JG

Nombre ______________________ Sección ______________ Fecha ______________

2. Recibo de pago de trabajo por cuenta propia

No. 45 *por $* 82 50/

Recibí de la *Sra.* Juana Osuna

la cantidad de Ochenta y dos 50/00 pesos

por la reparación de una caja registradora

4 *de* enero *del 20*10

Pedro Hernández

3. Recibo de pago de honorarios

No. Reg. Fed. de Contribuyentes ______ No. Reg. I.M.S.S. ______ Ced. o Reg. Correspondiente ______

NOMBRE Lic. Mariana García de León
apellido paterno, materno y nombre(s) o asociación o sociedad civil o profesional

DOMICILIO Calle de la Cuesta, 381 tel. 24-31-720

población ______ entidad federativa ______

RECIBI DE: Susana Reyes Hidalgo

Mil quinientos pesos
(cantidad con letra)

DOMICILIO Juárez, 38 **LA CANTIDAD DE** $1.500

I.S.R. —

CONCEPTO Servicios legales **I.V.A.** $150

TOTAL $1.650

lugar Puebla fecha 11/9 Firma M. García de León

Nombre ______________________ **Sección** ____________ **Fecha** ____________

Now, answer the following questions.

1. ¿Por qué recibió dinero el Sr. Gómez de la Srta. Monsalvo?

    ____

2. ¿Cuánto paga ella de alquiler al mes?

    ____

3. ¿Qué trabajo hizo el Sr. Hernández?

    ____

4. ¿Cuánto cobró el Sr. Hernández por su trabajo?

    ____

5. ¿Qué profesión tiene la Lic. García de León?

    ____

6. ¿Cuánto cobró la Lic. García de León en este caso?

    ____

Nombre ______________________ Sección ____________ Fecha ____________

El pedido (*Purchase order*)

Read the information in the purchase order and answer the questions that follow.

LIBRERÍA MINERVA
Calvo Sotelo No. 560
Madrid, España

PEDIDO No. 164

A: Editorial Austral

Fecha: 19 oct. 2010

Domicilio: Sarmiento, 645
Buenos Aires, Argentina

Entrega: 30 días fecha

Remitir por: Avión

Cantidad	Descripción	Encuadernación[1]	Precio/U.	Total
25	Borges: Ficciones	Rústica	$2,00	$50,00
10	Sarmiento: Facundo	"	1,75	17,50
5	Rodó: Ariel	"	2,50	12,50
			TOTAL	$80,.00

Favor enviar por expreso aéreo.

Instrucciones adicionales: Empacar correctamente

Nota: Precio US $ según catálogo
1 septiembre del 2010 .

Original: Proveedor

Departamento de Compras
Juan González
Jefe de Compras

[1]**encuadernación:** binding

1. ¿Cuántos libros se pidieron?

____

2. ¿Cómo van a enviarlos?

____

3. ¿En qué moneda debe pagar el cliente?

____

Nombre ________________ Sección ________ Fecha ________

La factura (*Invoice*) Read the invoices on the following pages and answer the questions that follow.

SERVICIO OFICIAL

SEAT

Talleres Bengoechea

LAVADO - ENGRASE - REPARACIÓN DE AUTOMOVILES
EXPOSICIÓN Y VENTA - SERVICIO GRÚA

MARIA DE LEZO, núm. 26

Taller autorizado núm. 05576

TELEFONOS 51 21 46 - 51 32 45

RENTERIA, 10 DE octubre DE 2010
(Gulpúzcoa)

D. Pablo Izurieta

REPARACION COCHE: Panda 1993

CONCEPTO	IMPORTE Euros	Cts.
MANO DE OBRA[1]	153	85
MATERIALES	269	23
ENGRASE Y CAMBIO DE ACEITE[2]		
SUMA	423	08
2,70 % I.G.T.E.	11	42
TOTAL EUROS	434	50

NOTA: Para evitar demoras, la factura de la reparación de su coche va en forma extractada.
Si desea una relación detallada de los trabajos realizados, le rogamos lo solicite a nuestro Cajero.
Muchas gracias **SEAT**

TALLERES BENGOECHEA

Ibepacón-60074 M

PAGAR DE CONTADO

CONFORME, N.º 26

Mario del Río

[1]**mano...** *labor* [2]**engrase...** *lube and oil change*

Nombre ____________ Sección ____________ Fecha ____________

Karpatos S.R.L.[1]

Fabricación - Importación

Equipajes - Mochilas - Bolsos Deportivos

Cerrito 274 Tel. 35-1970
(1010) Capital Federal
IVA RESPONSABLE INSCRIPTO

B

N° 0003- 00009632

Día	Mes	Año
18	8	10

C.U.I.T. 30-55568791-1
Ing. Brutos N° 195153-10
Caja Prev. C.N.P.S. Ind. y Com.
Inscripción N° 55568791

FACTURA

SEÑOR José Castillo TEL. 64-43-21

CALLE Ocho, 71 N° 341

LOCALIDAD ____________

IVA No Respon. ☐ Exento ☐ Cons. Final ☒ CUIT

CONDICIONES DE VENTA: Contado ☒ Cta. Cte. ☐ REMITO N°

ORIGINAL

CANTIDAD	DETALLE	PRECIO	TOTAL
3	Mochila[2] de cuero negro	$ 230.00	
	I.V.A	69.00	
		TOTAL $	299.00

Imprimió: *Cresingraf S.A.*
C.U.I.T.: 33-62540937-9
Fecha de impresión: Mayo 96

[1]**Sociedad de Responsabilidad Limitada** *Limited Liability Company* [2] *backpack*

Nombre ______________________ **Sección** ____________ **Fecha** ____________

1. ¿Por qué recibió el Sr. Uzurieta la factura de Talleres Bengochea?

____

2. ¿Cuánto costó la mano de obra?

____

3. ¿Cuál es el giro de Karpatos S.R.L.?

____

4. ¿Qué compró el Sr. Castillo?

____

5. ¿Cuánto costó cada mochila?

____

6. ¿Cuánto pagó de impuesto el Sr. Castillo?

____

Nombre ______________________ **Sección** __________ **Fecha** __________

Instrumentos de crédito (*Credit documents*)

La letra de cambio (*Bill of exchange*) The **letra de cambio** is the most common instrument of payment in both Spain and Latin America. It involves three parties, each of which can be either a person or a business: the **girador** (party that orders payment of a determined amount of money), the **girado** (party that will pay the amount indicated), and the **beneficiario** (person or business authorized to receive payment). In the model below, the **girador** is *Pedro Delgado Infante;* the **girado** is *Flores y Cía.;* and the **beneficiario** is *Fábrica de Muebles de Aluminio, S.A.*

The most common means of expressing the due date, or **vencimiento,** of the letter of credit are **a fecha fija** (by a certain date), **a la vista** (as soon as the bill of exchange is presented), or by a certain time after the bill of exchange is presented (for example, **a tres días vista**).

As a business document, the **letra de cambio** has been in use for centuries. Before it was possible to communicate easily between one place and another, it was customary to make several copies of the document, which were called **primera de cambio, segunda de cambio,** and so on. Today it is more common to make a single copy, called **única de cambio,** as in the model.

LETRA DE CAMBIO

No. 189 $ 50.000,00

Monterrey, N.L., 4 de enero de 20 10

A la vista Se servirá (n) Ud (s) mandar pagar incondicionalmente por ésta única Letra de Cambio en esta plaza a la orden de Fábrica de Muebles de Aluminio, S.A. la cantidad de

CINCUENTA MIL PESOS 00/100

Valor recibido en mercancías que sentarán[1] Ud(s) en cuenta # 7349260 según aviso[2] de

A Flores y Cía.
Aguila No. 285
Monterrey, Nueva León

S.S.S. Pedro Delgado Infante
Pedro Delgado Infante

SEGURIDAD 506

[1]**que sentarán** *should be entered* [2]**aviso** *notification*

Use the **letra de cambio** above to answer the following questions.

1. ¿Quiénes son el girador, el girado y el beneficiario en la letra de cambio?

____

2. ¿Cuánto dinero recibirá la fábrica de muebles de aluminio?

____

Nombre ______________________ Sección ____________ Fecha ____________

El pagaré (*Promissory note, I.O.U.*) Like a bill of exchange, a **pagaré** represents a written promise to pay a certain amount of money by a certain date. Laws in effect in Spanish-speaking countries make it easier to collect on debts guaranteed by a bill of exchange than by a **pagaré.**

PAGARE

PAGARE No. 185 **BUENO POR** $ 1000,00

Por el presente pagaré reconoceré ________ deber y estar obligado ________ a pagar en esta ciudad o en cualquier otra en que se me requiera de pago a Orlando Martínez Vega ________ o a su orden el día 18 de noviembre de 2010 ________ la cantidad de $1000

Mil pesos 00/100

Valor recibido en mercancías a mi entera satisfacción. La cantidad que ampara[1] este pagaré es parte de cantidad mayor, por la cual se otorgan[2] otros pagarés con vencimientos posteriores y queda expresamente convenido que si no es pagado este documento precisamente a su vencimiento, se darán por vencidos anticipadamente[3] los demás pagarés a que se refiere ésta cláusula.

Este pagaré mercantil está regido[4] por la Ley General de Títulos y Operaciones de Crédito en su artículo 173 parte final y artículos correlativos[5], por no ser pagaré domiciliado.

De no verificarse el pago de la cantidad que este pagaré expresa el día de su vencimiento abonaré,[6] en efectivo el rédito de 10 por ciento mensual por todo el tiempo que esté insoluto[7], sin perjuicio[8] al cobro más los gastos que se originen.

Otorgante Antonio García Prieto 10 de febrero de 20 10

Domicilio Av. Salinas 35 - Tecate Firma Antonio García Prieto

SEGURIDAD 507

[1] **ampara** *supports* [2] **se otorgan** *are issued* [3] **anticipadamente** *ahead of time* [4] **regido** *to be in force* [5] **correlativos** *related* [6] **abonaré** *I'll pay* [7] **insoluto** *unsolved* [8] **sin perjuicio** *not affecting*

1. ¿Quién debe pagar los mil pesos del pagaré?

   ____

2. ¿A quién se los debe pagar?

   ____

El vale (*Voucher*) The **vale** is used to order advance payment of small amounts of money. This is generally an advance on salary, or payment made for work not finished.

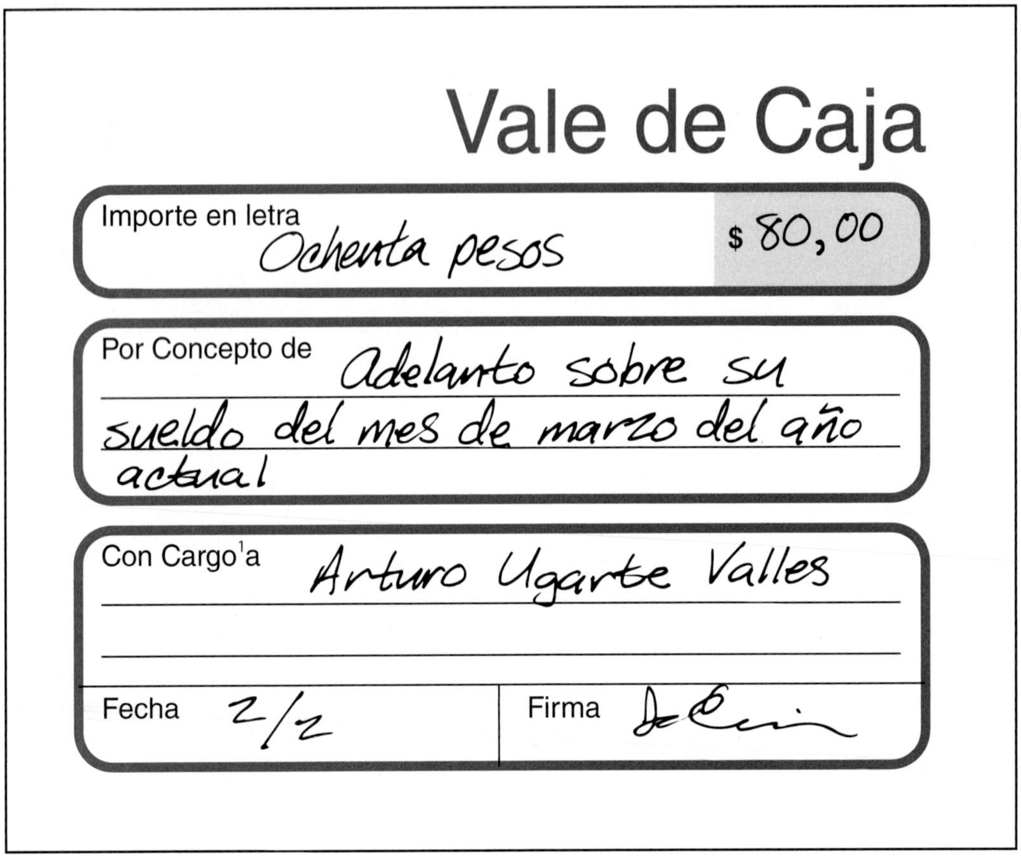

Vale de Caja

Importe en letra Ochenta pesos $ 80,00

Por Concepto de adelanto sobre su sueldo del mes de marzo del año actual

Con Cargo[1] a Arturo Ugarte Valles

Fecha 2/2 Firma

[1] **Con Cargo** *drawn on*

1. ¿Cuánto le debe entregar la caja (*petty cash*) al Sr. Ugarte?

____

2. ¿Del sueldo de qué mes le van a descontar el dinero al Sr. Ugarte?

____

Contratos Review each contract, circling cognates as you encounter them. Try to figure out from context the meaning of other unknown words, and answer the questions.

1. Si un mexicano compra esta póliza de seguro, ¿está asegurado su coche en los Estados Unidos?

____

2. El 2 por ciento de los daños sufridos por un coche es de $560. ¿Lo paga todo la compañía? ¿Por qué o por qué no?

____

Nombre ______________________ Sección ____________ Fecha ____________

Póliza de seguro de automóviles Aseguradora Cuauhtémoc S.A.

Gerencia Regional

Pasaje Alamos y Jalapa No. 1008-A
Centro Cívico Comercial
Tel. 57-15-24
Mexicali, B.C.

PÓLIZA No. ______________

La compañía mencionada, que en lo adelante[1] se llamará "La Compañía", asegura dentro de los límites de la República Mexicana, a favor del Asegurado: ______________________________

Dirección: ______________________________

____

llamado en adelante "El Asegurado", de conformidad con las condiciones de esta póliza, y durante el plazo establecido, contra aquellos riesgos de la especificación de riesgos que más adelante aparece que sufra o cause el vehículo descrito a continuación

Marca: ______________ Modelo: ______________

Año: ______________ Motor No. : ______________

La cantidad máxima a que asciende la cobertura que se otorga[2] mediante esta póliza, queda determinada en la especificación de riesgos siguiente :

Riesgo	Límite de responsabilidad
Vehículo asegurado	
Choque	$ ______________
Fuego, robo	$ ______________
Responsabilidad civil	
Daños a propiedad de terceros	$ ______________
Lesiones o muerte de terceros	
Cada persona	$ ______________
Cada accidente	$ ______________
Gastos médicos	
Ocupantes del vehículo	
Cada persona	$ ______________
Cada accidente	$ ______________

Deducibles

Choques, vuelcos[3], rotura de cristales, 2% de la suma asegurada o $500, la mayor de las dos cantidades. Fuego, robo, alborotos[4] populares, temblor, erupción volcánica, explosiones y derrumbes[5], 5% de la suma asegurada o $1.000, la mayor de las dos cantidades.

Plazo establecido para el seguro

Tiempo: ______________

De: ________ / ________ / ________ Hora: ________ ________ A.M.
día mes año

A: ________ / ________ / ________

Costo de la póliza

Prima: ________ Impuesto: ________ Total: ________

Conformes:

______________________________ ______________________________
Agente del asegurador Asegurado

[1]**en (lo) adelante** *from now on* [2]**se otorga** *is stipulated* [3]**vuelco** *overturning* [4]**alborotos...** *riots* [5]**derrumbe** *collapse*

Nombre ______________________ Sección ____________ Fecha ____________

CONTRATO INDIVIDUAL DE TRABAJO

CONTRATO INDIVIDUAL DE TRABAJO QUE CELEBRAN, POR UNA PARTE ______________________ A QUIEN EN LO SUCESIVO SE LE DENOMINARA "EL PATRÓN", Y POR LA OTRA ______________________ A QUIEN EN LO SUBSECUENTE SE DENOMINARA "EL TRABAJADOR" O "EMPLEADO", AL TENOR DE LAS SIGUIENTES DECLARACIONES Y CLÁUSULAS:

DECLARACIONES

I.-Declara "EL PATRÓN":
Estar constituido como ______________ conforme[1] a las leyes del país; nacionalidad ______________ ; edad ________ año ________ ; estado civil ______________ Registro Federal de Contribuyentes o Registro Patronal No. ______________ con domicilio en ______________

II.-Declara "EL TRABAJADOR" o "EMPLEADO":
Nacionalidad ______________ ; edad ________ años; sexo ________ ; estado civil ______________ ; Registro Federal de Contribuyentes ______________ ; con domicilio en ______________

CLÁUSULAS

1a.-El contrato se celebra por ______________ siendo sólo modificable, suspendido, rescindido o terminado conforme a la Ley Federal del Trabajo.

2a.-"EL TRABAJADOR" o "EMPLEADO" se compromete a realizar servicios personales bajo la supervisión y dependencia del "PATRÓN", como ______________ en el domicilio o área ______________

3a.-La jornada[2] diaria será de ________ horas por ser jornada ______________, quedando repartida de las ________ a las ________ y de ________ a ________ , y el día ________ de las ________ a ________ descansando el día ______________ conforme al artículo 69 de la Ley Federal del Trabajo.

4a.-Se conviene en que el salario o sueldo que se ofrecerá a cambio de los servicios especificados en el presentees el siguiente:
Salario o sueldo fijo por ______________ $ ______________
Salario o sueldo fijo por hora $ ______________
Salario o sueldo a destajo, conforme a la siguiente tarifa: ______________
sometiéndose a los descuentos exigidos por la Ley del Seguro Social, la Ley Impuesto sobre la Renta, ______________

El pago de éste se efectuará conforme a la ley monetaria, los días ______________ de cada ________ y en ______________

5a.-De acuerdo al artículo 74 de la Ley Federal del Trabajo serán días de descanso obligatorio[3]: el 1º de enero, 5 de febrero, 21 de marzo, 1º de mayo, 16 de septiembre, 20 de noviembre y el 1º de diciembre de cada 6 años, cuando corresponda a la Transmisión del Poder Ejecutivo Federal, el 25 de diciembre y aquellos en los que se comprendan las vacaciones a las que hace mención la cláusula sexta, el trabajador percibirá su salario o sueldo íntegro, promediándose las percepciones contenidas en los últimos días efectivamente trabajados si se calcula a destajo.

6a.-"EL TRABAJADOR" o "EMPLEADO" tendrá derecho a 6 días de vacaciones al año de servicios prestados, que aumentará a razón de dos días por año hasta sumar doce, por cada año posterior. Después del cuarto año éstas aumentarán en dos días, por cada cinco años de servicio. Las vacaciones comenzarán cada año el ______________

7a.-"EL TRABAJADOR" o "EMPLEADO" conviene en someterse a los chequeos médicos que el "PATRÓN" ordene periódicamente, en los términos de la fracción X del artículo 134 de la Ley Federal del Trabajo en el concepto de que el médico que los practique será designado y retribuido por "EL PATRÓN".

Seguridad 8601

[1]**conforme** *according to* [2]**jornada...** *working hours, day's work* [3]**dias...** *compulsory vacations*

Nombre ______________________ **Sección** __________ **Fecha** __________

8a.-En los casos de que "EL TRABAJADOR" o "EL EMPLEADO", hubiere[1] de laborar por mayor tiempo al establecido en la jornada máxima legal, el "PATRÓN" retribuirá las primeras 9 horas a la semana con un 100% y las ulteriores a un 200% más de salario por hora, sin perjuicio de las sanciones respectivas.

9a.-En el caso de que el "TRABAJADOR" sea mayor de 14 años, pero menor de 16, el presente contrato debe ser autorizado por los padres o tutores[2], o en su defecto por el Sindicato[3] al cual pertenezca[4], la Junta Local de Conciliación y Arbitraje, el Inspector del Trabajo o la Autoridad Política de acuerdo con el Art. 23 de la Ley Federal del Trabajo.

10a.-Las partes convienen que en caso de controversia se estará a lo establecido en el presente, y en lo que fuere omiso[5] se entenderá a lo dispuesto por la Ley Federal del Trabajo, o el Reglamento Interior de Trabajo del cual se entrega un ejemplar al "TRABAJADOR" o "EMPLEADO", bajo la jurisdicción de la Junta de Conciliación y Arbitraje del Distrito Federal.

LUGAR PARA CLÁUSULAS EXTRAORDINARIAS O ACLARACIONES

____

____

____

____

____

____

____

Leído que fue por las partes el documento ante los testigos que firman e impuestos contenido y conscientes de las obligaciones que se engendran, así como las que la ley les impone lo firman por ______________________ en __________ el __________ del mes de ______________ del 20 ______ quedando un ejemplar en poder del "TRABAJADOR" y __________ en poder del "PATRÓN".

FIRMA DEL "PATRÓN"

"TRABAJADOR" O "EMPLEADO" DECLARO QUE RECIBI COPIA DEL PRESENTE CONTRATO

______________________ ______________________

TESTIGO **TESTIGO**

______________________ ______________________

Seguridad

8601

[1]**hubiere...** *will work* [2]**tutor** *guardians* [3]**Sindicato** *Union* [4]**pertenezca** *belongs* [5]**omiso** *omitted*

Nombre ______________________ **Sección** ____________ **Fecha** ____________

Refer to the **Contrato individual de trabajo** on pages 290–291 to answer the following questions.

1. Una de las partes en un contrato de trabajo es "el trabajador"; ¿cuál es la otra?

   ____

2. ¿A cuántos días de vacaciones al año tendrá derecho el trabajador según el contrato?

   ____

3. ¿Quiénes deben autorizar los contratos de trabajadores menores de 16 años?

   ____

Nombre ______________________ **Sección** ____________ **Fecha** ____________

CONTRATO DE ARRENDAMIENTO[1]

CON FIADOR[2]

CONTRATO DE ARRENDAMIENTO DE ______________________________
vivenda o local

de la casa No. ____________ **de** ______________________________

que celebran, como arrendatario[3] ______________________________
inquilino[4] que declara ser mayor de edad

y como arrendador[5] ______________________________
propietario

con domicilio ______________________________

sujetándolo a las clásulas siguientes:

1a. El inquilino pagará al arrendador o a quien sus derechos represente la cantidad de $ ______________________________ por el arrendamiento mensual de la localidad mencionada arriba, que se cubrirá en moneda nacional con toda puntualidad por meses adelantados, en el despacho o domicilio del arrendador o de quien sus derechos represente, y que comenzará a contarse desde la fecha en que se firme este contrato.

2a. El término del arrendamiento será ______________________________

3a. Si al terminar el plazo fijado en la cláusula anterior, continúa el inquilino ocupando la localidad, a partir de entonces la duración del arrendamiento será voluntario y, por lo tanto cualquiera de los contratantes lo puede dar por concluído a su arbitrio. Cuando el arrendador lo dé por terminado notificará al inquilino que desocupe dentro del plazo[6] de ____________ a contar de la fecha en que le haga la notificación; en el cual caso no pagará el inquilino sino lo que está debiendo al desocupar, lo que deberá hacer dentro del plazo señalado, para el cual efecto renuncia al de dos meses que concede el Art. 2478 del Código Civil. Si el inquilino es quien decide desocupar la localidad, lo notificará al arrendador por escrito[7] con ____________ días de anticipación, que comenzarán a contarse a partir de la fecha en que el arrendador reciba dicha notificación quedando éste facultado para anunciar desde luego el alquiler de la localidad y ponerle cédulas.

4a. Toda mensualidad será pagada íntegra[8], aun cuando el inquilino sólo ocupe la localidad parte del mes.

5a. Aunque el arrendador reciba las rentas en fecha distinta de la estipulada, o admita abonos por cuenta de las mismas, no se entenderá novado este Contrato, ni en cuanto a los términos, ni en cuanto a la forma de pago.

6a. La Localidad se destinará exclusivamente para ______________________ y si el inquilino hace otro uso de ella, ésta será motivo suficiente para obligarlo a que la desocupe, aun cuando todavía esté corriendo el plazo fijado en la cláusula 2a. de este Contrato.

7a. No podrá el inquilino, sin consentimiento del arrendador dado por escrito ceder o subarrendar la localidad o parte de la misma.

8a. Tampoco, podrá el inquilino, sin consentimiento del arrendador por escrito, hacer obras en la localidad, y todas las que hiciere, sean de la clase que fueren, quedarán en beneficio de la finca. De una manera expresa queda convenido que se reputarán como obras las que deben quedar a beneficio de la casa, las instalaciones que el inquilino hiciera para alumbrado y calefacción eléctricos. En caso de que el inquilino falte al cumplimiento de esta cláusula, será responsable de los daños y perjuicios que se causen y deberá devolver la localidad en el estado en que la haya recibido.

9a. No podrá el inquilino retener la renta en ningún caso, ni bajo ningún título, ni judicial, ni extrajudicialmente ni por falta de composturas o reparaciones que el arrendador dejase de hacer, sino que pagará íntegramente la renta en la fecha estipulada para el cual efecto renuncia los beneficios que le conceden los Arts. 2412, 2413, 2414 y 2490 del Código Civil.

10a. El inquilino recibe la localidad aseada[9], con sus pisos en buen estado, las puertas y las vidrieras con su herraje y todo lo demás de acuerdo con el inventario que aparece al final de este Contrato; todo lo cual devolverá al terminarse el arrendamiento, con el deterioro natural del uso, siendo por su cuenta los gastos de reparación, y se obliga a indemnizar al arrendador de cualquier deterioro posterior que apreciare en la localidad arrendada causado por su culpa o negligencia. El inquilino conservará aseados y al corriente los fregaderos, caños y excusados de la localidad, y todas las composturas que requieran durante el tiempo que la ocupe, serán de su exclusiva cuenta.

11a. Si el inquilino estableciere en la localidad alguno de los negocios enumerados en el Art. 137 de la Ley de Hacienda vigente, quedará obligado a hacer su instalación directa de agua potable y pagará por su cuenta la cuota correspondiente, ya que la Ley sólo obliga al arrendador a proporcionar el referido líquido para usos domésticos.

12a. Si en la casa a que pertenece la localidad objeto de este Contrato, hay otros arrendatarios, no podrá hacer el inquilino uso de los patios, corredores, escaleras y azoteas si no es únicamente para el tránsito para el servicio indispensable de la localidad arrendada, en este caso, se le prohibe expresamente tener animales que molesten o perjudiquen a los demás inquilinos o maltraten la finca.

13a. Firma este Contrato ______________________________ como fiador solidario del inquilino y declara que es propietario de ______________________________

____

y señala como su domicilio ______________________________
Hace renuncia de los beneficios de orden y excusión, consignados en los Arts. 2812, 2814 y 2825 del Código Civil. Además de dichos artículos, el fiador renuncia los números 2818, 2820, 2823, 2825, 2820, 2845, 2847 y 2848 del propio ordenamiento y acepta las renuncias que en este Contrate hace el inquilino. No cesará la responsabilidad del fiador, sino hasta cuando el arrendador se dé por recibido de la localidad y de todo cuanto se le deba por virtud de este Contrato, aun cuando el arrendamiento dure más tiempo del fijado por el Art. 2478 del Código Civil por lo que, igualmente, renuncia el fiador este Art. ______________________________

INVENTARIO

Carraduras ____________ Vidrios ____________
Picaportes ____________ Llaves ____________
Instalación completa para alumbrado eléctrico compuesta de alambre, sockets, apagadores, etc. para ____________ lámparas,
Instalación de baño compuesta de ____________ ____________ de ____________ de 20___

ARRENDADOR ____________ **FIADOR** ____________ **ARRENDATARIO** ____________

[1]**arrendamiento** *lease, rent* [2]**fiador** *guarantor* [3]**arrendatario** *leasee, tenant* [4]**inquilino** *tenant (of a house)*
[5]**arrendador** *lessor, landlord* [6]**plazo** *term* [7]**por escrito** *in writing* [8]**integra** *entire, complete* [9]**aseado** *clean*

Nombre ______________________ **Sección** __________ **Fecha** __________

Refer to the **Contrato de arrendamiento** to answer the following questions.

1. ¿Cuáles son las dos partes en un contrato de arrendamiento?

____

2. ¿Cuál de las dos partes es el propietario de la vivienda o del local?

____

Nombre ______________________ Sección ____________ Fecha ____________

Lecciones 16-20 Repaso

Práctica de vocabulario

A Circle the word or phrase that does not belong in each group.

1. dueño condado propietario
2. beca madre padre
3. novio casarse ventaja
4. nivel techo teja
5. cocina tipo horno
6. entrada lavaplatos enganche
7. comején termita lugar
8. inspección losa baldosa
9. espacio local lado
10. escaparate jardín vidriera
11. galletitas probadores dulces
12. entrepaño estante amplio
13. cobertura huracán terremoto
14. fenómeno natural tornado enseres
15. muerte tránsito vida
16. nevada multa exceso de velocidad
17. la quiebra la inflación la bancarrota
18. el cobre el cultivo la cosecha
19. la demanda la deuda la oferta
20. beneficio perjuicio acuerdo
21. tan pronto como en cuanto a fin de que
22. graduarse terminar de estudiar empezar a estudiar

B Circle the word or phrase that best completes each sentence.

1. Ellos esperan (llenar los requisitos / abusar de / descartar) para un préstamo.
2. Este condominio es nuevo. Nunca fue (desocupado / establecido / habitado).
3. ¿La hipoteca tiene un interés (hundido / fijo / cuidado) o variable?
4. Mi padre quiere (sugerir / aprobar / asumir) la hipoteca original.
5. Para poner el negocio necesito (asesoramiento / aval / deuda) legal.
6. El propietario ordenó una inspección del techo y de (cuota inicial / comején / temblor).
7. La mayor parte de sus (incendios / vecinos / anaqueles) serán ejecutivos de empresas.
8. Necesito hablar con el corredor de (bienes / trabajadores / compañías) raíces.
9. Siento que las (alfombras / contribuciones / ofertas) estén manchadas.
10. Los techos son de (chimeneas / baños / tejas).
11. La (galletita / llave / fachada) del edificio es muy bonita.
12. El edificio no está vacío; está (cuadrado / pintado / alquilado).

Nombre ______________________ Sección ____________ Fecha ____________

13. Nos alegramos de que el local esté cerca de la escalera (rodante / hundida / cara).
14. Vamos a comprar dulces y (pies / entrepaños / galletitas) para los niños.
15. Ellos no pueden (adaptarnos / autorizarnos / afectarnos) para investigar su crédito.
16. ¿Cuánto tendría que pagar por cada mil dólares de (muerte / cobertura / sesión)?
17. Mi coche (chocó / financió / pasó) y no tengo seguro.
18. ¡Ojalá que declaren (cubierto / joven / culpable) al otro chofer!
19. El seguro incluye las pérdidas causadas por fenómenos naturales como (motines / robos / tornados).
20. Él se pasó la (lesión / luz / inundación) roja y le pusieron una multa.
21. Muchas empresas americanas (trasladaron / beneficiaron / analizaron) algunos procesos industriales a México.
22. Los tratados son tan (recientes / libres / simples) que no podríamos analizar sus efectos.
23. Sus cosechas no podían (debatir / establecer / competir) con los productos subsidiados.
24. Compraron una casa grande. (Resolvieron / Aconsejaron / Aprovecharon) que las tasas de interés estaban bajísimas.
25. La recién graduada pedirá un préstamo (en cuenta / es decir / en caso de) que no le den la beca.
26. El gobierno chileno estima que el verdadero aumento del (tratado / proceso / comercio) entre los dos países sería sólo del 60%.
27. Chile (apuesta / estima / dedica) por la globalización.

C Match the questions in column **A** with the answers in column **B**.

A		B
1. ¿Ud. quiere asumir la hipoteca original?	______	a. En un centro comercial.
2. ¿El condominio está habitado?	______	b. Sí, y gastos de cierre.
3. ¿Qué negocio piensa abrir?	______	c. Para sacar unas cuentas.
4. ¿De qué es la chimenea?	______	d. Cuatrocientos pies cuadrados.
5. ¿Tengo que pagar comisiones?	______	e. No, porque ahora las tasas de interés están más bajas.
6. ¿Cuánto debo dar de entrada?	______	f. Con el abogado.
7. ¿Quiénes serán mis vecinos?	______	g. Sí, los dueños viven allí.
8. ¿Dónde están situados los locales?	______	h. El 20%.
9. ¿Cuánto mide el local?	______	i. Veinte años.
10. ¿Adónde vas a llevar a los niños?	______	j. De piedra.
11. ¿Cuáles son las condiciones?	______	k. Su esposo y sus hijos.
12. ¿Necesitan tener probadores?	______	l. A la juguetería.

Nombre ______________________ Sección ____________ Fecha ____________

A		B
13. ¿Para qué necesitas la calculadora?	________	m. Sí, contra robos.
14. ¿Por qué le impusieron una multa?	________	n. Las de costumbre.
15. ¿Quiere asegurar su coche?	________	o. Profesionales y ejecutivos.
16. ¿Qué edad tiene Ud.?	________	p. Una tienda de ropa.
17. ¿Quiénes son sus herederos?	________	q. Por exceso de velocidad.
18. ¿Con quién hablaron Uds.?	________	r. Sí, y escaparates de exhibición.

Situaciones del mundo de las empresas

Review the **Notas culturales** and **Lecturas** of the past five lessons and then read the following scenarios. Find out what went wrong, and propose possible solutions in Spanish.

1. Elena wants to buy a condo by the ocean in Mexico. She needs to finance 80% of the total price. I advised her to get a loan from a Mexican bank because interest rates in Mexico are lower than in the United States.

____

____

____

____

2. A friend wants to open a business in Honduras. I told him he should carefully plan how to provide health insurance to his employees since in all Spanish-speaking countries companies are required to provide health insurance to their employees.

____

____

____

____

3. My friend, Florinda Pereyra, told me that in her country of origin she used to pay a monthly fee to a **clínica mutualista** that provided health care. I told her such a concept must derive from the HMO health care model of the United States.

____

____

____

____

4. My company has recently established business relations with Mexico. Since NAFTA is now in effect, I am confident that, should legal difficulties arise, I would be able to solve these through the U.S. justice system and solely in accordance with U.S. law.

5. While engaged in a casual conversation with a Cuban citizen, I said that there is no real justice when the defendant is not tried by a jury of his (her) peers.

Advanced Translation

Translate into English

1. Un usurero es un prestamista que cobra un interés mayor del permitido por la ley.

2. Una inspección puede ayudarle a evitar comprar una vivienda que necesita reparaciones mayores.

3. Las arañas hacen su tela en las cajas registradoras de los comerciantes que no se anuncian.

Translate into Spanish

1. Money can't buy happiness, but it can buy you the kind of misery you prefer.

2. I am grateful for the lawn that needs mowing, windows that need cleaning, and floors that need waxing because it means I have a home.

3. Insurance agents never retire, they just expire.

APPENDIX A

INTRODUCTION TO SPANISH SOUNDS AND THE ALPHABET

Sections marked with a Web-audio icon are recorded on the website that supplements this text. Repeat each Spanish word after the speaker, imitating as closely as possible the correct pronunciation.

THE ALPHABET

Letter	Name	Letter	Name	Letter	Name	Letter	Name
a	a	h	hache	ñ	eñe	t	te
b	be	i	i	o	o	u	u
c	ce	j	jota	p	pe	v	ve
d	de	k	ka	q	cu	w	doble ve
e	e	l	ele	r	ere	x	equis
f	efe	m	eme	rr	erre	y	i griega
g	ge	n	ene	s	ese	z	zeta

Audio

THE VOWELS

1. The Spanish **a** has a sound similar to the English *a* in the word *father.* Repeat:

Ana casa banana mala dama mata

2. The Spanish **e** is pronounced like the English *e* in the word *eight.* Repeat:

este René teme déme entre bebe

3. The Spanish **i** is pronounced like the English *ee* in the word *see.* Repeat:

sí difícil Mimí ir dividir Fifí

4. The Spanish **o** is similar to the English *o* in the word *no,* but without the glide. Repeat:

solo poco como toco con monólogo

5. The Spanish **u** is similar to the English *ue* sound in the word *Sue.* Repeat:

Lulú un su universo murciélago

The Consonants

Audio

1. The Spanish **p** is pronounced like the English *p* in the word *spot.* Repeat:

pan	papá	Pepe	pila	poco	pude

2. The Spanish **c** in front of **a, o, u, l,** or **r** sounds similar to the English *k.* Repeat:

casa	como	cuna	clima	crimen	cromo

3. The Spanish **q** is only used in the combinations **que** and **qui,** in which the **u** is silent, and also has a sound similar to the English *k.* Repeat:

que	queso	Quique	quinto	quema	quiso

4. The Spanish **t** is pronounced like the English *t* in the word *stop.* Repeat:

toma	mata	tela	tipo	atún	Tito

5. The Spanish **d** at the beginning of an utterance or after **n** or **l** sounds somewhat similar to the English *d* in the word *David.* Repeat:

día	dedo	duelo	anda	Aldo

In all other positions, the **d** has a sound similar to the English *th* in the word *they.* Repeat:

medida	todo	nada	Ana dice	Eva duda

6. The Spanish **g** also has two sounds. At the beginning of an utterance and in all other positions, except before **e** or **i,** the Spanish **g** sounds similar to the English *g* in the word *sugar.* Repeat:

goma	gato	tengo	lago	algo	aguja

In the combinations **gue** and **gui,** the **u** is silent. Repeat:

Águeda	guineo	guiso	ligue	la guía

7. The Spanish **j,** and **g** before **e** or **i,** sounds similar to the English *h* in the word *home.* Repeat:

jamás	juego	jota	Julio	gente	Genaro	gime

8. The Spanish **b** and the **v** have no difference in sound. Both are pronounced alike. At the beginning of the utterance or after **m** or **n,** they sound similar to the English *b* in the word *obey.* Repeat:

Beto	vaga	bote	vela	también	un vaso

Between vowels, they are pronounced with the lips barely closed. Repeat:

sábado	yo voy	sabe	Ávalos	Eso vale

9. In most Spanish-speaking countries, the **y** and the **ll** are similar to the English *y* in the word *yet.* Repeat:

yo	llama	yema	lleno	ya	lluvia	llega

10. The Spanish **r (ere)** is pronounced like the English *tt* in the word *gutter.* Repeat:

cara	pero	arena	carie	Laredo	Aruba

The Spanish **r** in an initial position and after **l, n,** or **s,** and **rr (erre)** in the middle of a word are pronounced with a strong trill. Repeat:

Rita	Rosa	torre	ruina	Enrique	Israel
perro	parra	rubio	alrededor	derrama	

11. The Spanish **s** sound is represented in most of the Spanish-speaking world by the letters **s, z,** and **c** before **e** or **i.** The sound is very similar to the English sibilant *s* in the word *sink.* Repeat:

sale	sitio	solo	seda	suelo
zapato	cerveza	ciudad	cena	

In most of Spain, the **z,** and **c** before **e** or **i,** is pronounced like the English *th* in the word *think.* Repeat:

zarzuela	cielo	docena

12. The letter **h** is silent in Spanish. Repeat:

hilo	Hugo	ahora	Hilda	almohada	hermano

13. The Spanish **ch** is pronounced like the English *ch* in the word *chief.* Repeat:

muchacho	chico	coche	chueco	chaparro

14. The Spanish **f** is identical in sound to the English *f.* Repeat:

famoso	feo	difícil	fuego	foto

15. The Spanish **l** is pronounced like the English *l* in the word *lean.* Repeat:

dolor	ángel	fácil	sueldo	salgo	chaval

16. The Spanish **m** is pronounced like the English *m* in the word *mother.* Repeat:

mamá	moda	multa	médico	mima

17. In most cases, the Spanish **n** has a sound similar to the English *n.* Repeat:

nada	norte	nunca	entra	nene

The sound of the Spanish **n** is often affected by the sounds that occur around it. When it appears before **b, v,** or **p,** it is pronounced like the English *m.* Repeat:

invierno	tan bueno	un vaso	un bebé	un perro

18. The Spanish **ñ (eñe)** has a sound similar to the English *ny* in the word *canyon.* Repeat:

muñeca	leña	año	señorita	piña	señor

19. The Spanish **x** has two pronunciations, depending on its position. Between vowels, the sound is similar to the English *ks.* Repeat:

examen	boxeo	exigente	éxito

Before a consonant, the Spanish **x** sounds like the English *s.* Repeat:

expreso	excusa	exquisito	extraño

Audio

Linking

In spoken Spanish, the various words in a phrase or sentence are not pronounced as isolated elements, but they are combined. This is called *linking.*

1. The final consonant of a word is pronounced together with the initial vowel of the following word. Repeat:

Carlos‿anda	un‿ángel	el‿otoño	unos‿estudiantes

2. The final vowel of a word is pronounced together with the initial vowel of the following word. Repeat:

su‿esposo	la‿hermana	ardua‿empresa	la‿invita

3. When the final vowel of a word and the initial vowel of the following word are identical, they are pronounced slightly longer than one vowel. Repeat:

Ana‿alcanza	me‿espera	mi‿hijo	lo‿olvida

The same rule applies when two identical vowels appear within a word. Repeat:

cooperación	crees	leemos	coordinación

4. When the final consonant of a word and the initial consonant of the following word are the same, they are pronounced as one consonant with slightly longer-than-normal duration. Repeat:

el‿lado	un‿novio	Carlos‿salta	tienes‿sed	al‿leer

Rhythm

Rhythm is the variation of sound intensity that we usually associate with music. Spanish and English each regulate these variations in speech differently, because they have different patterns of syllable length. In Spanish the length of the stressed and unstressed syllables remains almost the same, while in English stressed syllables are considerably longer than unstressed ones. Pronounce the following Spanish words, enunciating each syllable clearly.

es-tu-dian-te	bue-no	Úr-su-la
com-po-si-ción	di-fí-cil	ki-ló-me-tro
po-li-cí-a	Pa-ra-guay	

Because the length of the Spanish syllables remains constant, the greater the number of syllables in a given word or phrase, the longer the phrase will be.

Intonation

Intonation is the rise and fall of pitch in the delivery of a phrase or a sentence. In general, Spanish pitch tends to change less than English, giving the impression that the language is less emphatic.

As a rule, the intonation for normal statements in Spanish starts in a low tone, raises to a higher one on the first stressed syllable, maintains that tone until the last stressed syllable, and then goes back to the initial low tone, with still another drop at the very end.

Tu amigo viene mañana.	José come pan.
Ada está en casa.	Carlos toma café.

Syllable Formation in Spanish

General rules for dividing words into syllables are as follows.

Vowels

1. A vowel or a vowel combination can constitute a syllable.

   a-lum-no a-bue-la Eu-ro-pa

2. Diphthongs and triphthongs are considered single vowels and cannot be divided.

   bai-le puen-te Dia-na es-tu-diáis an-ti-guo

3. Two strong vowels (**a, e, o**) do not form a diphthong and are separated into two syllables.

   em-ple-ar vol-te-ar lo-a

4. A written accent on a weak vowel (**i** or **u**) breaks the diphthong, thus the vowels are separated into two syllables.

   trí-o dú-o Ma-rí-a

Consonants

1. A single consonant forms a syllable with the vowel that follows it.

   po-der ma-no mi-nu-to

   NOTE: **rr** is considered a single consonant: **pe-rro.**

2. When two consonants appear between two vowels, they are separated into two syllables.

   al-fa-be-to cam-pe-ón me-ter-se mo-les-tia

   EXCEPTION: When a consonant cluster composed of **b, c, d, f, g, p,** or **t** with **l** or **r** appears between two vowels, the cluster joins the following vowel: **so-bre, o-tros, ca-ble, te-lé-gra-fo.**

3. When three consonants appear between two vowels, only the last one goes with the following vowel.

ins-pec-tor trans-por-te trans-for-mar

EXCEPTION: When there is a cluster of three consonants in the combinations described in rule 2, the first consonant joins the preceding vowel, and the cluster joins the following vowel: **es-cri-bir, ex-tran-je-ro, im-plo-rar, es-tre-cho.**

Accentuation

In Spanish, all words are stressed according to specific rules. Words that do not follow the rules must have a written accent to indicate the change of stress. The basic rules for accentuation are as follows.

1. Words ending in a vowel, **n,** or **s** are stressed on the next-to-the-last syllable.

hi-jo	**ca**-lle	**me**-sa	fa-**mo**-sos
flo-**re**-cen	**pla**-ya	**ve**-ces	

2. Words ending in a consonant, except **n** or **s,** are stressed on the last syllable.

ma-**yor** a-**mor** tro-pi-**cal** na-**riz** re-**loj** co-rre-**dor**

3. All words that do not follow these rules must have the written accent.

ca-**fé**	**lá**-piz	**mú**-si-ca	sa-**lón**
án-gel	**lí**-qui-do	fran-**cés**	**Víc**-tor
sim-**pá**-ti-co	rin-**cón**	a-**zú**-car	**dár**-se-lo
sa-**lió**	**dé**-bil	e-**xá**-me-nes	**dí**-me-lo

4. Pronouns and adverbs of interrogation and exclamation have a written accent to distinguish them from relative pronouns.

—¿**Qué** comes?	*"What are you eating?"*
—La pera que él no comió.	*"The pear that he did not eat."*
—¿**Quién** está ahí?	*"Who is there?"*
—El hombre a quien tú llamaste.	*"The man whom you called."*
—¿**Dónde** está?	*"Where is he?"*
—En el lugar donde trabaja.	*"At the place where he works."*

5. Words that have the same spelling but different meanings take a written accent to differentiate one from the other.

el	*the*	**él**	*he, him*	**te**	*you*	**té**	*tea*
mi	*my*	**mí**	*me*	**si**	*if*	**sí**	*yes*
tu	*your*	**tú**	*you*	**mas**	*but*	**más**	*more*

APPENDIX B

VERBS

REGULAR VERBS

Model -ar, -er, -ir *verbs*

	INFINITIVE	
amar (*to love*)	**comer** (*to eat*)	**vivir** (*to live*)
	GERUND	
amando (*loving*)	**comiendo** (*eating*)	**viviendo** (*living*)
	PAST PARTICIPLE	
amado (*loved*)	**comido** (*eaten*)	**vivido** (*lived*)

SIMPLE TENSES

Indicative Mood

	PRESENT	
(*I love*)	(*I eat*)	(*I live*)
am**o**	com**o**	viv**o**
am**as**	com**es**	viv**es**
am**a**	com**e**	viv**e**
am**amos**	com**emos**	viv**imos**
am**áis**[1]	com**éis**	viv**ís**
am**an**	com**en**	viv**en**
	IMPERFECT	
(*I used to love*)	(*I used to eat*)	(*I used to live*)
am**aba**	com**ía**	viv**ía**
am**abas**	com**ías**	viv**ías**
am**aba**	com**ía**	viv**ía**
am**ábamos**	com**íamos**	viv**íamos**
am**abais**	com**íais**	viv**íais**
am**aban**	com**ían**	viv**ían**

[1]**Vosotros amáis:** The **vosotros** form of the verb is used primarily in Spain. This form has not been used in this text.

	PRETERIT	
(I loved)	*(I ate)*	*(I lived)*
am**é**	com**í**	viv**í**
am**aste**	com**iste**	viv**iste**
am**ó**	com**ió**	viv**ió**
am**amos**	com**imos**	viv**imos**
am**asteis**	com**isteis**	viv**isteis**
am**aron**	com**ieron**	viv**ieron**

	FUTURE	
(I will love)	*(I will eat)*	*(I will live)*
amar**é**	comer**é**	vivir**é**
amar**ás**	comer**ás**	vivir**ás**
amar**á**	comer**á**	vivir**á**
amar**emos**	comer**emos**	vivir**emos**
amar**éis**	comer**éis**	vivir**éis**
amar**án**	comer**án**	vivir**án**

	CONDITIONAL	
(I would love)	*(I would eat)*	*(I would live)*
amar**ía**	comer**ía**	vivir**ía**
amar**ías**	comer**ías**	vivir**ías**
amar**ía**	comer**ía**	vivir**ía**
amar**íamos**	comer**íamos**	vivir**íamos**
amar**íais**	comer**íais**	vivir**íais**
amar**ían**	comer**ían**	vivir**ían**

Subjunctive Mood

	PRESENT	
([*that*] *I* [*may*] *love*)	([*that*] *I* [*may*] *eat*)	([*that*] *I* [*may*] *live*)
am**e**	com**a**	viv**a**
am**es**	com**as**	viv**as**
am**e**	com**a**	viv**a**
am**emos**	com**amos**	viv**amos**
am**éis**	com**áis**	viv**áis**
am**en**	com**an**	viv**an**

	IMPERFECT (two forms: **-ra**, **-se**)	
(*[that] I [might] love*)	(*[that] I [might] eat*)	(*[that] I [might] live*)
am**ara(-ase)**	com**iera(-iese)**	viv**iera(-iese)**
am**aras(-ases)**	com**ieras(-ieses)**	viv**ieras(-ieses)**
am**ara(-ase)**	com**iera(-iese)**	viv**iera(-iese)**
am**áramos (-ásemos)**	com**iéramos (-iésemos)**	viv**iéramos (-iésemos)**
am**arais(-aseis)**	com**ierais(-ieseis)**	viv**ierais(-ieseis)**
am**aran(-asen)**	com**ieran(-iesen)**	viv**ieran(-iesen)**

Imperative Mood (Command Forms)

(*love*)	(*eat*)	(*live*)
am**a** (tú)	com**e** (tú)	viv**e** (tú)
am**e** (Ud.)	com**a** (Ud.)	viv**a** (Ud.)
am**emos** (nosotros)	com**amos** (nosotros)	viv**amos** (nosotros)
am**ad** (vosotros)	com**ed** (vosotros)	viv**id** (vosotros)
am**en** (Uds.)	com**an** (Uds.)	viv**an** (Uds.)

COMPOUND TENSES

	PERFECT INFINITIVE	
haber amado	**haber comido**	**haber vivido**

	PERFECT PARTICIPLE	
habiendo amado	**habiendo comido**	**habiendo vivido**

Indicative Mood

	PRESENT PERFECT	
(*I have loved*)	(*I have eaten*)	(*I have lived*)
he amado	he comido	he vivido
has amado	has comido	has vivido
ha amado	ha comido	ha vivido
hemos amado	hemos comido	hemos vivido
habéis amado	habéis comido	habéis vivido
han amado	han comido	han vivido

	PLUPERFECT	
(*I had loved*)	(*I had eaten*)	(*I had lived*)
había amado	había comido	había vivido
habías amado	habías comido	habías vivido
había amado	había comido	había vivido
habíamos amado	habíamos comido	habíamos vivido
habíais amado	habíais comido	habíais vivido
habían amado	habían comido	habían vivido

	FUTURE PERFECT	
(*I will have loved*)	(*I will have eaten*)	(*I will have lived*)
habré amado	habré comido	habré vivido
habrás amado	habrás comido	habrás vivido
habrá amado	habrá comido	habrá vivido
habremos amado	habremos comido	habremos vivido
habréis amado	habréis comido	habréis vivido
habrán amado	habrán comido	habrán vivido

	CONDITIONAL PERFECT	
(*I would have loved*)	(*I would have eaten*)	(*I would have lived*)
habría amado	habría comido	habría vivido
habrías amado	habrías comido	habrías vivido
habría amado	habría comido	habría vivido
habríamos amado	habríamos comido	habríamos vivido
habríais amado	habríais comido	habríais vivido
habrían amado	habrían comido	habrían vivido

Subjunctive Mood

	PRESENT PERFECT	
([*that*] *I* [*may*] *have loved*)	([*that*] *I* [*may*] *have eaten*)	([*that*] *I* [*may*] *have lived*)
haya amado	haya comido	haya vivido
hayas amado	hayas comido	hayas vivido
haya amado	haya comido	haya vivido
hayamos amado	hayamos comido	hayamos vivido
hayáis amado	hayáis comido	hayáis vivido
hayan amado	hayan comido	hayan vivido

PLUPERFECT (two forms: **-ra, -se**)		
([*that*] *I* [*might*] *have loved*)	([*that*] *I* [*might*] *have eaten*)	([*that*] *I* [*might*] *have lived*)
hubiera(-iese) amado	hubiera(-iese) comido	hubiera(-iese) vivido
hubieras(-ieses) amado	hubieras(-ieses) comido	hubieras(-ieses) vivido
hubiera(-iese) amado	hubiera(-iese) comido	hubiera(-iese) vivido
hubiéramos(-iésemos) amado	hubiéramos(-iésemos) comido	hubiéramos(-iésemos) vivido
hubierais(-ieseis) amado	hubierais(-ieseis) comido	hubierais(-ieseis) vivido
hubieran(-iesen) amado	hubieran(-iesen) comido	hubieran(-iesen) vivido

Stem-Changing Verbs

The -ar *and* -er *stem-changing verbs*

Stem-changing verbs are those that have a change in the root of the verb. Verbs that end in **-ar** and **-er** change the stressed vowel **e** to **ie** and the stressed **o** to **ue.** These changes occur in all persons, except the first and second persons plural of the present indicative, present subjunctive, and command.

INFINITIVE	PRESENT INDICATIVE	IMPERATIVE	PRESENT SUBJUNCTIVE
cerrar (*to close*)	ci**e**rro	—	ci**e**rre
	ci**e**rras	ci**e**rra	ci**e**rres
	ci**e**rra	(Ud.) ci**e**rre	ci**e**rre
	cerramos	cerremos	cerremos
	cerráis	cerrad	cerréis
	ci**e**rran	(Uds.) ci**e**rren	ci**e**rren

INFINITIVE	PRESENT INDICATIVE	IMPERATIVE	PRESENT SUBJUNCTIVE
perder (*to lose*)	**pier**do	—	**pier**da
	pierdes	**pier**de	**pier**das
	pierde	(Ud.) **pier**da	**pier**da
	perdemos	perdamos	perdamos
	perdéis	perded	perdáis
	pierden	(Uds.) **pier**dan	**pier**dan
contar (*to count, to tell*)	**cue**nto	—	**cue**nte
	cuentas	**cue**nta	**cue**ntes
	cuenta	(Ud.) **cue**nte	**cue**nte
	contamos	contemos	contemos
	contáis	contad	contéis
	cuentan	(Uds.) **cue**nten	**cue**nten
volver (*to return*)	**vue**lvo	—	**vue**lva
	vuelves	**vue**lve	**vue**lvas
	vuelve	(Ud.) **vue**lva	**vue**lva
	volvemos	volvamos	volvamos
	volvéis	volved	volváis
	vuelven	(Uds.) **vue**lvan	**vue**lvan

Verbs that follow the same pattern include the following.

acertar *to guess right*
acordarse *to remember*
acostar(se) *to go to bed*
almorzar *to have lunch*
atravesar *to go through*
cegar *to blind*
cocer *to cook*
colgar *to hang*
comenzar *to begin*
confesar *to confess*
costar *to cost*
demostrar *to demonstrate, to show*
despertar(se) *to wake up*
empezar *to begin*
encender *to light, to turn on*
encontrar *to find*
entender *to understand*
llover *to rain*
mostrar *to show*
mover *to move*
negar *to deny*
nevar *to snow*
pensar *to think, to plan*
probar *to prove, to taste*
recordar *to remember*
resolver *to decide on*
rogar *to beg*
sentar(se) *to sit down*
soler *to be in the habit of*
soñar *to dream*
tender *to stretch, to unfold*
torcer *to twist*

The -ir *stem-changing verbs*

There are two types of stem-changing verbs that end in **-ir:** one type changes stressed **e** to **ie** in some tenses and to **i** in others and stressed **o** to **ue** or **u;** the second type always changes stressed **e** to **i** in the irregular forms of the verb.

Type I		**e:ie**	or	**i**
	-ir:			
		o:ue	or	**u**

These changes occur as follows.

Present Indicative: all persons except the first and second plural change **e** to **ie** and **o** to **ue.** *Preterit:* third person, singular and plural, changes **e** to **i** and **o** to **u.** *Present Subjunctive:* all persons change **e** to **ie** and **o** to **ue,** except the first and second persons plural, which change **e** to **i** and **o** to **u.** *Imperfect Subjunctive:* all persons change **e** to **i** and **o** to **u.** *Imperative:* all persons except the second person plural change **e** to **ie** and **o** to **ue;** first person plural changes **e** to **i** and **o** to **u.** *Present Participle:* changes **e** to **i** and **o** to **u.**

	Indicative		*Imperative*	*Subjunctive*	
INFINITIVE	PRESENT	PRETERIT		PRESENT	IMPERFECT
sentir	siento	sentí	—	sienta	sintiera(-iese)
(*to feel*)	sientes	sentiste	siente	sientas	sintieras
	siente	sintió	(Ud.) sienta	sienta	sintiera
PRESENT	sentimos	sentimos	sintamos	sintamos	sintiéramos
PARTICIPLE	sentís	sentisteis	sentid	sintáis	sintierais
sintiendo	sienten	sintieron	(Uds.) sientan	sientan	sintieran
dormir	duermo	dormí	—	duerma	durmiera(-iese)
(*to sleep*)	duermes	dormiste	duerme	duermas	durmieras
	duerme	durmió	(Ud.) duerma	duerma	durmiera
PRESENT	dormimos	dormimos	durmamos	durmamos	durmiéramos
PARTICIPLE	dormís	dormisteis	dormid	durmáis	durmierais
durmiendo	duermen	durmieron	(Uds.) duerman	duerman	durmieran

Other verbs that follow the same pattern include the following.

advertir	*to warn*	**herir**	*to wound, to hurt*
arrepentir(se)	*to repent*	**mentir**	*to lie*
consentir	*to consent, to pamper*	**morir**	*to die*
convertir(se)	*to turn into*	**preferir**	*to prefer*
discernir	*to discern*	**referir**	*to refer*
divertir(se)	*to amuse oneself*	**sugerir**	*to suggest*

Type II **-ir:** **e:i**

The verbs in this second category are irregular in the same tenses as those of the first type. The only difference is that they only have one change: **e:i** in all irregular persons.

	Indicative		*Imperative*	*Subjunctive*	
INFINITIVE	PRESENT	PRETERIT		PRESENT	IMPERFECT
pedir	pido	pedí	—	pida	pidiera(-iese)
(*to ask for,*	pides	pediste	pide	pidas	pidieras
to request)	pide	pidió	(Ud.) pida	pida	pidiera
PRESENT	pedimos	pedimos	pidamos	pidamos	pidiéramos
PARTICIPLE	pedís	pedisteis	pedid	pidáis	pidierais
pidiendo	piden	pidieron	(Uds.) pidan	pidan	pidieran

Verbs that follow this pattern include the following.

competir	*to compete*	**reír(se)**	*to laugh*
concebir	*to conceive*	**reñir**	*to fight*
despedir(se)	*to say good-bye*	**repetir**	*to repeat*
elegir	*to choose*	**seguir**	*to follow*
impedir	*to prevent*	**servir**	*to serve*
perseguir	*to pursue*	**vestir(se)**	*to dress*

Orthographic-Changing Verbs

Some verbs undergo a change in the spelling of the stem in certain tenses in order to maintain the original sound of the final consonant. The most common verbs of this type are those with the consonants **g** and **c.** Remember that **g** and **c** have a soft sound in front of **e** or **i** and a hard sound in front of **a, o,** or **u.** In order to maintain the soft sound in front of **a, o,** and **u, g** and **c** change to **j** and **z,** respectively. And in order to maintain the hard sound of **g** and **c** in front of **e** and **i, u** is added to the **g** (**gu**) and **c** changes to **qu.**

The following important verbs undergo spelling changes in the tenses listed below.

1. Verbs ending in **-gar** change **g** to **gu** before **e** in the first person of the preterit and in all persons of the present subjunctive.

pagar (*to pay*)
Preterit: pa**gu**é, pagaste, pagó, etc.
Pres. Subj.: pa**gu**e, pa**gu**es, pa**gu**e, pa**gu**emos, pa**gu**éis, pa**gu**en

Verbs that follow the same pattern: **colgar, jugar, llegar, navegar, negar, regar, rogar.**

2. Verbs ending in **-ger** and **-gir** change **g** to **j** before **o** and **a** in the first person of the present indicative and in all persons of the present subjunctive.

proteger (*to protect*)
Pres. Ind.: prote**j**o, proteges, protege, etc.
Pres. Subj.: prote**j**a, prote**j**as, prote**j**a, prote**j**amos, prote**j**áis, prote**j**an

Verbs that follow the same pattern: **coger, corregir, dirigir, elegir, escoger, exigir, recoger.**

3. Verbs ending in **-guar** change **gu** to **gü** before **e** in the first person of the preterit and in all persons of the present subjunctive.

averiguar (*to find out*)
Preterit: averi**gü**é, averiguaste, averiguó, etc.
Pres. Subj.: averi**gü**e, averi**gü**es, averi**güe,** averi**güemos,** averi**gü**éis, averi**güe**n

The verb **apaciguar** follows the same pattern.

4. Verbs ending in **-guir** change **gu** to **g** before **o** and **a** in the first person of the present indicative and in all persons of the present subjunctive.

conseguir (*to get*)
Pres. Ind.: consi**g**o, consigues, consigue, etc.
Pres. Subj.: consi**g**a, consi**g**as, consi**g**a, consi**g**amos, consi**g**áis, consi**g**an

Verbs that follow the same pattern: **distinguir, perseguir, proseguir, seguir.**

5. Verbs ending in **-car** change **c** to **qu** before **e** in the first person of the preterit and in all persons of the present subjunctive.

tocar (*to touch, to play* [*a musical instrument*])
Preterit: to**qu**é, tocaste, tocó, etc.
Pres. Subj.: to**qu**e, to**qu**es, to**qu**e, to**qu**emos, to**qu**éis, to**qu**en

Verbs that follow the same pattern: **atacar, buscar, comunicar, explicar, indicar, pescar, sacar.**

6. Verbs ending in **-cer** and **-cir** preceded by a consonant change **c** to **z** before **o** and **a** in the first person of the present indicative and in all persons of the present subjunctive.

torcer (*to twist*)
Pres. Ind.: tuer**z**o, tuerces, tuerce, etc.
Pres. Subj.: tuer**z**a, tuer**z**as, tuer**z**a, tor**z**amos, tor**z**áis, tuer**z**an

Verbs that follow the same pattern: **convencer, esparcir, vencer.**

7. Verbs ending in **-cer** and **-cir** preceded by a vowel change **c** to **zc** before **o** and **a** in the first person of the present indicative and in all persons of the present subjunctive.

conocer (*to know, to be acquainted with*)
Pres. Ind.: cono**zc**o, conoces, conoce, etc.
Pres. Subj.: cono**zc**a, cono**zc**as, cono**zc**a, cono**zc**amos, cono**zc**áis, cono**zc**an

Verbs that follow the same pattern: **agradecer, aparecer, carecer, entristecer, establecer, lucir, nacer, obedecer, ofrecer, padecer, parecer, pertenecer, reconocer, relucir.**

8. Verbs ending in **-zar** change **z** to **c** before **e** in the first person of the preterit and in all persons of the present subjunctive.

rezar (*to pray*)
Preterit: re**c**é, rezaste, rezó, etc.
Pres. Subj.: re**c**e, re**c**es, re**c**e, re**c**emos, re**c**éis, re**c**en

Verbs that follow the same pattern: **abrazar, alcanzar, almorzar, comenzar, cruzar, empezar, forzar, gozar.**

9. Verbs ending in **-eer** change the unstressed **i** to **y** between vowels in the third person singular and plural of the preterit, in all persons of the imperfect subjunctive, and in the present participle.

creer (*to believe*)
Preterit: creí, creíste, cre**y**ó, creímos, creísteis, cre**y**eron
Imp. Subj.: cre**y**era(ese), cre**y**eras, cre**y**era, cre**y**éramos, cre**y**erais, cre**y**eran
Pres. Part.: cre**y**endo

Leer and **poseer** follow the same pattern.

10. Verbs ending in **-uir** change the unstressed **i** to **y** between vowels (except **-quir,** which has the silent **u**) in the following tenses and persons.

huir (*to escape, to flee*)
Pres. Part.: hu**y**endo
Past Part.: huido
Pres. Ind.: hu**y**o, hu**y**es, hu**y**e, huimos, huís, hu**y**en
Preterit: huí, huiste, hu**y**ó, huimos, huisteis, hu**y**eron
Imperative: hu**y**e, hu**y**a, hu**y**amos, huid, hu**y**an

Pres. Subj.: hu**y**a, hu**y**as, hu**y**a, hu**y**amos, hu**y**áis, hu**y**an
Imp. Subj.: hu**y**era(ese), hu**y**eras, hu**y**era, hu**y**éramos, hu**y**erais, hu**y**eran

Verbs that follow the same pattern: **atribuir, concluir, constituir, construir, contribuir, destituir, destruir, disminuir, distribuir, excluir, incluir, influir, instruir, restituir, sustituir.**

11. Verbs ending in **-eír** lose one **e** in the third person singular and plural of the preterit, in all persons of the imperfect subjunctive, and in the present participle.

reír(se) (*to laugh*)
Preterit: reí, reíste, **r**ió, reímos, reísteis, **r**ieron
Imp. Subj.: **r**iera(ese), **r**ieras, **r**iera, **r**iéramos, **r**ierais, **r**ieran
Pres. Part.: **r**iendo

Freír and **sonreír** follow the same pattern.

12. Verbs ending in **-iar** add a written accent to the **i,** except in the first and second persons plural of the present indicative and subjunctive.

fiar(se) (*to trust*)
Pres. Ind.: fío, fías, fía, fiamos, fiáis, fían
Pres. Subj.: fíe, fíes, fíe, fiemos, fiéis, fíen

Verbs that follow the same pattern: **ampliar, criar, desviar, enfriar, enviar, esquiar, guiar, telegrafiar, vaciar, variar.**

13. Verbs ending in **-uar** (except **-guar**) add a written accent to the **u,** except in the first and second persons plural of the present indicative and subjunctive.

actuar (*to act*)
Pres. Ind.: act**ú**o, act**ú**as, act**ú**a, actuamos, actuáis, act**ú**an
Pres. Subj.: act**ú**e, act**ú**es, act**ú**e, actuemos, actuéis, act**ú**en

Verbs that follow the same pattern: **acentuar, continuar, efectuar, exceptuar, graduar, habituar, insinuar, situar.**

14. Verbs ending in **-ñir** remove the **i** of the diphthongs **ie** and **ió** in the third person singular and plural of the preterit and in all persons of the imperfect subjunctive. They also change the **e** of the stem to **i** in the same persons.

teñir (*to dye*)
Preterit: teñí, teñiste, **tiñó,** teñimos, teñisteis, **tiñeron**
Imp. Subj.: **tiñe**ra(ese), **tiñe**ras, **tiñe**ra, **tiñé**ramos, **tiñe**rais, **tiñe**ran

Verbs that follow the same pattern: **ceñir, constreñir, desteñir, estreñir, reñir.**

Some Common Irregular Verbs

Only those tenses with irregular forms are given below.

adquirir (*to acquire*)

Pres. Ind.: adquiero, adquieres, adquiere, adquirimos, adquirís, adquieren
Pres. Subj.: adquiera, adquieras, adquiera, adquiramos, adquiráis, adquieran
Imperative: adquiere, adquiera, adquiramos, adquirid, adquieran

andar (*to walk*)

Preterit: anduve, anduviste, anduvo, anduvimos, anduvisteis, anduvieron
Imp. Subj.: anduviera (anduviese), anduvieras, anduviera, anduviéramos, anduvierais, anduvieran

avergonzarse (*to be ashamed, to be embarrassed*)

Pres. Ind.: me avergüenzo, te avergüenzas, se avergüenza, nos avergonzamos, os avergonzáis, se avergüenzan
Pres. Subj.: me avergüence, te avergüences, se avergüence, nos avergoncemos, os avergoncéis, se avergüencen
Imperative: avergüénzate, avergüéncese, avergoncémonos, avergonzaos, avergüéncense

caber (*to fit, to have enough room*)

Pres. Ind.: quepo, cabes, cabe, cabemos, cabéis, caben
Preterit: cupe, cupiste, cupo, cupimos, cupisteis, cupieron
Future: cabré, cabrás, cabrá, cabremos, cabréis, cabrán
Conditional: cabría, cabrías, cabría, cabríamos, cabríais, cabrían
Imperative: cabe, quepa, quepamos, cabed, quepan
Pres. Subj.: quepa, quepas, quepa, quepamos, quepáis, quepan
Imp. Subj.: cupiera (cupiese), cupieras, cupiera, cupiéramos, cupierais, cupieran

caer (*to fall*)

Pres. Ind.: caigo, caes, cae, caemos, caéis, caen
Preterit: caí, caíste, cayó, caímos, caísteis, cayeron
Imperative: cae, caiga, caigamos, caed, caigan
Pres. Subj.: caiga, caigas, caiga, caigamos, caigáis, caigan
Imp. Subj.: cayera (cayese), cayeras, cayera, cayéramos, cayerais, cayeran
Past Part.: caído

conducir (*to guide, to drive*)

Pres. Ind.: conduzco, conduces, conduce, conducimos, conducís, conducen
Preterit: conduje, condujiste, condujo, condujimos, condujisteis, condujeron
Imperative: conduce, conduzca, conduzcamos, conducid, conduzcan
Pres. Subj.: conduzca, conduzcas, conduzca, conduzcamos, conduzcáis, conduzcan
Imp. Subj.: condujera (condujese), condujeras, condujera, condujéramos, condujerais, condujeran

(All verbs ending in **-ducir** follow this pattern.)

convenir (*to agree*) See **venir.**

dar (*to give*)

Pres. Ind.: doy, das, da, damos, dais, dan
Preterit: di, diste, dio, dimos, disteis, dieron
Imperative: da, dé, demos, dad, den

Pres. Subj.: dé, des, dé, demos, deis, den
Imp. Subj.: diera (diese), dieras, diera, diéramos, dierais, dieran

decir (*to say, to tell*)
Pres. Ind.: digo, dices, dice, decimos, decís, dicen
Preterit: dije, dijiste, dijo, dijimos, dijisteis, dijeron
Future: diré, dirás, dirá, diremos, diréis, dirán
Conditional: diría, dirías, diría, diríamos, diríais, dirían
Imperative: di, diga, digamos, decid, digan
Pres. Subj.: diga, digas, diga, digamos, digáis, digan
Imp. Subj.: dijera (dijese), dijeras, dijera, dijéramos, dijerais, dijeran
Pres. Part.: diciendo
Past Part.: dicho

detener (*to stop, to hold, to arrest*) See **tener.**

entretener (*to entertain, to amuse*) See **tener.**

errar (*to err, to miss*)
Pres. Ind.: yerro, yerras, yerra, erramos, erráis, yerran
Imperative: yerra, yerre, erremos, errad, yerren
Pres. Subj.: yerre, yerres, yerre, erremos, erréis, yerren

estar (*to be*)
Pres. Ind.: estoy, estás, está, estamos, estáis, están
Preterit: estuve, estuviste, estuvo, estuvimos, estuvisteis, estuvieron

Imperative: está, esté, estemos, estad, estén
Pres. Subj.: esté, estés, esté, estemos, estéis, estén
Imp. Subj.: estuviera (estuviese), estuvieras, estuviera, estuviéramos, estuvierais, estuvieran

haber (*to have*)
Pres. Ind.: he, has, ha, hemos, habéis, han
Preterit: hube, hubiste, hubo, hubimos, hubisteis, hubieron
Future: habré, habrás, habrá, habremos, habréis, habrán
Conditional: habría, habrías, habría, habríamos, habríais, habrían
Imperative: he, haya, hayamos, habed, hayan
Pres. Subj.: haya, hayas, haya, hayamos, hayáis, hayan
Imp. Subj.: hubiera (hubiese), hubieras, hubiera, hubiéramos, hubierais, hubieran

hacer (*to do, to make*)
Pres. Ind.: hago, haces, hace, hacemos, hacéis, hacen
Preterit: hice, hiciste, hizo, hicimos, hicisteis, hicieron
Future: haré, harás, hará, haremos, haréis, harán
Conditional: haría, harías, haría, haríamos, haríais, harían
Imperative: haz, haga, hagamos, haced, hagan
Pres. Subj.: haga, hagas, haga, hagamos, hagáis, hagan
Imp. Subj.: hiciera (hiciese), hicieras, hiciera, hiciéramos, hicierais, hicieran
Past Part.: hecho

imponer (*to impose, to deposit*) See **poner.**

introducir (*to introduce, to insert, to gain access*) See **conducir.**

ir (*to go*)

Pres. Ind.:	voy, vas, va, vamos, vais, van
Imp. Ind.:	iba, ibas, iba, íbamos, ibais, iban
Preterit:	fui, fuiste, fue, fuimos, fuisteis, fueron
Imperative:	ve, vaya, vayamos, id, vayan
Pres. Subj.:	vaya, vayas, vaya, vayamos, vayáis, vayan
Imp. Subj.:	fuera (fuese), fueras, fuera, fuéramos, fuerais, fueran

jugar (*to play*)

Pres. Ind.:	juego, juegas, juega, jugamos, jugáis, juegan
Imperative:	juega, juegue, juguemos, jugad, jueguen
Pres. Subj.:	juegue, juegues, juegue, juguemos, juguéis, jueguen

obtener (*to obtain*) See **tener.**

oír (*to hear*)

Pres. Ind.:	oigo, oyes, oye, oímos, oís, oyen
Preterit:	oí, oíste, oyó, oímos, oísteis, oyeron
Imperative:	oye, oiga, oigamos, oíd, oigan
Pres. Subj.:	oiga, oigas, oiga, oigamos, oigáis, oigan
Imp. Subj.:	oyera (oyese), oyeras, oyera, oyéramos, oyerais, oyeran
Pres. Part.:	oyendo
Past Part.:	oído

oler (*to smell*)

Pres. Ind.:	huelo, hueles, huele, olemos, oléis, huelen
Imperative:	huele, huela, olamos, oled, huelan
Pres. Subj.:	huela, huelas, huela, olamos, oláis, huelan

poder (*to be able*)

Pres. Ind.:	puedo, puedes, puede, podemos, podéis, pueden
Preterit:	pude, pudiste, pudo, pudimos, pudisteis, pudieron
Future:	podré, podrás, podrá, podremos, podréis, podrán
Conditional:	podría, podrías, podría, podríamos, podríais, podrían
Imperative:	puede, pueda, podamos, poded, puedan
Pres. Subj.:	pueda, puedas, pueda, podamos, podáis, puedan
Imp. Subj.:	pudiera (pudiese), pudieras, pudiera, pudiéramos, pudierais, pudieran
Pres. Part.:	pudiendo

poner (*to place, to put*)

Pres. Ind.:	pongo, pones, pone, ponemos, ponéis, ponen
Preterit:	puse, pusiste, puso, pusimos, pusisteis, pusieron
Future:	pondré, pondrás, pondrá, pondremos, pondréis, pondrán
Conditional:	pondría, pondrías, pondría, pondríamos, pondríais, pondrían
Imperative:	pon, ponga, pongamos, poned, pongan

Pres. Subj.:	ponga, pongas, ponga, pongamos, pongáis, pongan
Imp. Subj.:	pusiera (pusiese), pusieras, pusiera, pusiéramos, pusierais, pusieran
Past Part.:	puesto

querer (*to want, to wish, to like*)

Pres. Ind.:	quiero, quieres, quiere, queremos, queréis, quieren
Preterit:	quise, quisiste, quiso, quisimos, quisisteis, quisieron
Future:	querré, querrás, querrá, querremos, querréis, querrán
Conditional:	querría, querrías, querría, querríamos, querríais, querrían
Imperative:	quiere, quiera, queramos, quered, quieran
Pres. Subj.:	quiera, quieras, quiera, queramos, queráis, quieran
Imp. Subj.:	quisiera (quisiese), quisieras, quisiera, quisiéramos, quisierais, quisieran

resolver (*to decide on*)

Past Part.:	resuelto

saber (*to know*)

Pres. Ind.:	sé, sabes, sabe, sabemos, sabéis, saben
Preterit:	supe, supiste, supo, supimos, supisteis, supieron
Future:	sabré, sabrás, sabrá, sabremos, sabréis, sabrán
Conditional:	sabría, sabrías, sabría, sabríamos, sabríais, sabrían
Imperative:	sabe, sepa, sepamos, sabed, sepan
Pres. Subj.:	sepa, sepas, sepa, sepamos, sepáis, sepan
Imp. Subj.:	supiera (supiese), supieras, supiera, supiéramos, supierais, supieran

salir (*to leave, to go out*)

Pres. Ind.:	salgo, sales, sale, salimos, salís, salen
Future:	saldré, saldrás, saldrá, saldremos, saldréis, saldrán
Conditional:	saldría, saldrías, saldría, saldríamos, saldríais, saldrían
Imperative:	sal, salga, salgamos, salid, salgan
Pres. Subj.:	salga, salgas, salga, salgamos, salgáis, salgan

ser (*to be*)

Pres. Ind.:	soy, eres, es, somos, sois, son
Imp. Ind.:	era, eras, era, éramos, erais, eran
Preterit:	fui, fuiste, fue, fuimos, fuisteis, fueron
Imperative:	sé, sea, seamos, sed, sean
Pres. Subj.:	sea, seas, sea, seamos, seáis, sean
Imp. Subj.:	fuera (fuese), fueras, fuera, fuéramos, fuerais, fueran

suponer (*to assume*) See **poner.**

tener (*to have*)

Pres. Ind.:	tengo, tienes, tiene, tenemos, tenéis, tienen
Preterit:	tuve, tuviste, tuvo, tuvimos, tuvisteis, tuvieron
Future:	tendré, tendrás, tendrá, tendremos, tendréis, tendrán
Conditional:	tendría, tendrías, tendría, tendríamos, tendríais, tendrían
Imperative:	ten, tenga, tengamos, tened, tengan
Pres. Subj.:	tenga, tengas, tenga, tengamos, tengáis, tengan
Imp. Subj.:	tuviera (tuviese), tuvieras, tuviera, tuviéramos, tuvierais, tuvieran

traducir (*to translate*) See **conducir.**

traer (*to bring*)

Pres. Ind.:	traigo, traes, trae, traemos, traéis, traen
Preterit:	traje, trajiste, trajo, trajimos, trajisteis, trajeron
Imperative:	trae, traiga, traigamos, traed, traigan
Pres. Subj.:	traiga, traigas, traiga, traigamos, traigáis, traigan
Imp. Subj.:	trajera (trajese), trajeras, trajera, trajéramos, trajerais, trajeran
Pres. Part.:	trayendo
Past Part.:	traído

valer (*to be worth*)

Pres. Ind.:	valgo, vales, vale, valemos, valéis, valen
Future:	valdré, valdrás, valdrá, valdremos, valdréis, valdrán
Conditional:	valdría, valdrías, valdría, valdríamos, valdríais, valdrían
Imperative:	vale, valga, valgamos, valed, valgan
Pres. Subj.:	valga, valgas, valga, valgamos, valgáis, valgan

venir (*to come*)

Pres. Ind.:	vengo, vienes, viene, venimos, venís, vienen
Preterit:	vine, viniste, vino, vinimos, vinisteis, vinieron
Future:	vendré, vendrás, vendrá, vendremos, vendréis, vendrán
Conditional:	vendría, vendrías, vendría, vendríamos, vendríais, vendrían
Imperative:	ven, venga, vengamos, venid, vengan
Pres. Subj.:	venga, vengas, venga, vengamos, vengáis, vengan
Imp. Subj.:	viniera (viniese), vinieras, viniera, viniéramos, vinierais, vinieran
Pres. Part.:	viniendo

ver (*to see*)

Pres. Ind.:	veo, ves, ve, vemos, veis, ven
Imp. Ind.:	veía, veías, veía, veíamos, veíais, veían
Preterit:	vi, viste, vio, vimos, visteis, vieron
Imperative:	ve, vea, veamos, ved, vean
Pres. Subj.:	vea, veas, vea, veamos, veáis, vean
Imp. Subj.:	viera (viese), vieras, viera, viéramos, vierais, vieran
Past. Part.:	visto

volver (*to return*)

Past Part.:	vuelto

APPENDIX C

MÁS SOBRE EL TEMA

Lección 1

EL VIAJE DE NEGOCIOS

Más sobre el tema

Algunos avisos para viajeros en el Aeropuerto Internacional de la Ciudad de México

RECOMENDACIONES AL PASAJERO (*PASSENGER RECOMMENDATIONS*)

Peso permitido de equipaje documentado *Permitted Weight of Checked Baggage*
Equipaje clase premier: 2 maletas de 23 kgs *Baggage, First Class: 2 suitcases, 23 kgs.*
Equipaje clase turista: 1 maleta de 23 kgs *Baggage, Tourist Class: 1 suitcase, 23 kgs.*

Artículos prohibidos en equipaje de mano *Forbidden Items in Hand Luggage*

Armas de fuego o réplicas, incluyendo las de juguete. *Firearms or imitation firearms, including toys.*

Explosivos o pirotécnicos de cualquier especie. *Explosives or pyrotechnics of any kind.*

Objetos punzantes, punzocortantes, contundentes y cortocontundentes. *Sharp, stabbing, heavy or blunt objects.*

Tijeras mayores de 6 cm. *Scissors of at least 6 cm or larger.*

Sustancias químicas, biológicas y radiológicas tóxicas e infecciosas. *Chemical, biological or radioactive substances that are toxic and infectious*

Venenos, sangre y otros fluidos corporales infectados, biopsias, isótopos medicinales o comerciales. *Poisons, infected blood or other bodily fluids, biopsies, medical or commercial isotopes.*

Bebidas alcohólicas: vinos, licores, cervezas, tequilas, etcétera. *Alcoholic beverages:* wines, liqueurs, beer, tequila, etc.

Líquidos en cantidades mayores de 100 ml (3.4 oz.). *All liquids in amounts greater than 100 ml (3.4 oz.).*

Palabras y frases clave (*Key Words and Phrases*)

el arma de fuego *firearm*
la cantidad *amount*
la carretilla *cart*
la clase económica *economy (tourist) class*
el control de seguridad *security check*
el equipaje documentado (facturado) *checked baggage*
mayores de *greater than*
el mostrador de facturación *check-in desk*
permitido (a) *permitted, allowed*
la puerta *gate*
la recogida de equipajes *baggage claim*

la recomendación *recommendation*
la sangre *blood*
la terminal de llegadas *arrivals*
la terminal de salidas *departures*
la tienda libre de impuestos *duty-free store*
las tijeras *scissors*
el veneno *poison*

Lección 2

Más avisos para viajeros en el Aeropuerto Internacional de la Ciudad de México

Más sobre el tema

Pasajeros con necesidades médicas especiales (*Passengers with special medical needs*)

Medicamentos *Medication*
Están permitidos medicamentos, leche y alimentos para bebé, así como para necesidades dietéticas especiales. *Medication, and baby food and milk are allowed, as well as any special diet needs.*

Tanques de oxígeno *Oxygen Tanks*
Solo están permitidos los cilindros de oxígeno de uso medicinal. *Only medical use oxygen gas cylinders are allowed.*

Personas con discapacidades motrices *Persons with Motor Disabilities*
Se permite el ingreso con silla de ruedas, muletas, bastones, etcétera. *The use of wheelchairs, crutches, canes, etc. is allowed.*

Personas con marcapasos y mujeres embarazadas *Persons with Pacemakers and Pregnant Women*
La radiación emitida por el arco detector de metales es menor a la de un teléfono móvil, por tal razón no afecta a las personas con marcapasos ni a las mujeres embarazadas; sin embargo los pasajeros pueden elegir una revisión manual. *The radiation emitted by the metal detector arch is lower than that of cellular phones, and therefore it does not affect people with pacemakers or pregnant women; however, passengers may choose a manual check.*

Personas con diabetes *Persons with Diabetes*
Las personas diabéticas podrán ingresar con los medicamentos y jeringas necesarios para el viaje; no es necesario mostrar la receta. Es recomendable portar su credencial de paciente diabético. *People with diabetes may enter with the medications and syringes necessary for the flight; it is not necessary to show a medical prescription. We recommend that you travel with your diabetes patient credential.*

Palabras y frases clave

los alimentos para bebé *baby food*
elegir *to choose*
emitir *to emit*
es menor de *is lower than*
ingresar *to enter, to come in*
el ingreso *entry*

la jeringa, la jeringuilla *syringe*
el marcapasos *pacemaker*
las mujeres embarazadas *pregnant women*
el (la) paciente *patient*
poder *to be able to, can*
por tal razón *therefore*
portar *to travel with*
la receta (medicine) *prescription*
la silla de ruedas *wheelchair*
sin embargo *however*

Lección 3

En un hotel

Más sobre el tema

Preguntas frecuentes y probables respuestas (*Frequent questions and probable answers*)
¿El hotel cuenta con personal bilingüe inglés - español? *Does the hotel have bilingual English – Spanish employees?*
¿Aceptan tarjetas de crédito? ¿Cuáles? *Do you accept credit cards? Which ones?*
El hotel, ¿tiene ascensor (*elevador*)? *Is there an elevator in the hotel?*
¿Tiene servicio de habitaciones? ¿Horario limitado? ¿De qué hora a qué hora? *Do you have room service? Limited hours? From what time to what time?*
¿Tiene servicio de transporte desde y/o hasta el aeropuerto? ¿Cuánto cuesta? *Do you have shuttle service from / or to the airport? How much does it cost?*
¿Tiene acceso y otras facilidades para discapacitados? *Do you have access and other facilities for the disabled?*
¿Tiene conexión a Internet? *Do you have Internet access?*
¿Hay restaurante o cafetería en el hotel? *Is there a restaurant or a cafeteria in the hotel?*
¿El precio de las habitaciones incluye los impuestos? *Are taxes included in the price?*

Top of Form

Bottom of Form

Los 5 servicios más importantes para los viajeros de hable hispana

Servicios más importantes	**Huéspedes**
1. Desayuno incluido en la reserva	88%
2. Acceso Wi-Fi a Internet	71%
3. Restaurante	65%
4. Transporte al aeropuerto o lugares de interés	62%
5. Piscina	59%

Servicios menos importantes	**Huéspedes**
1. Mascotas permitidas	92%
2. Centro de Negocios	92%
3. Acceso a un Club Ejecutivo	91%
4. Gimnasio	89%
5. Preparación de cama	84%

Palabras y frases clave

cuenta con *has*
desde .... hasta, de.....a... *from.... to...*
el (la) discapacitado(a), minusválido(a) *disabled person*
el horario limitado *limited hours*
el servicio de habitaciones *room service*
el transporte *shuttle*

Lección 4

Las comidas de negocios

Más sobre el tema

Frecuentemente, después de una reunión de negocios, una de las partes invita a la otra a cenar. En los países de habla hispana, las comidas, tanto en un restaurante como en una casa, requieren vestimentas más formales que en los EEUU o Canadá. Además, los hispanos cuidan mucho las reglas de etiqueta en la mesa. Pero los hispanos, por lo general, no son muy puntuales. Si algún invitado a la comida llega tarde, es correcto esperarlo por más de unos pocos minutos.

Si usted es quien invita debe encargarse de todos los trámites: a usted le toca elegir el restaurante, reservar la mesa y pagar la cuenta. Antes, desde luego, debe averiguar, discretamente, cuáles son las preferencias gastronómicas de su(s) invitado(s).

Si usted es el invitado debe evitar pedir los platos caros. Una comida de negocios no debe convertirse en un banquete.

La cuenta la paga quien invita. Si usted es el invitado, no trate de pagar la cuenta. Evite la típica escena de varias personas intentando pagar la cuenta.

Aunque la comida sea una extensión de una reunión de negocios, si usted es el invitado, deje que sea la otra parte la que inicie la conversación de negocios. Una charla de asuntos ligeros es una buena introducción para los temas serios de los negocios.

Si es necesario hacer presentaciones o intercambiar tarjetas, trate de hacerlo antes de sentarse a la mesa. La mesa, salvo situaciones excepcionales, no es el sitio adecuado para esas formalidades.

Y recuerde, los móviles deben estar apagados durante la comida.

Palabras y frases clave

apagado *off*
cuidar mucho las reglas de etiqueta *to pay a lot of attention to the rules of ettiquete*
la paga *is paid by*
le toca elegir *you must decide(choose)*
llegar tarde *to be late*
no son muy puntuales *are not very punctual*
la reunión de negocios *business meeting*
salvo *except*

tanto en .... como *both at .... as in (on, at)*
una de las partes invita a la otra *one party invites the other*
unos pocos *a few*
usted es quien *you are the one who*
la vestimenta más formal *more formal dress*

Lección 5

Comprando para importar

Más sobre el tema

Reglas de etiqueta para hacer negocios con empresas de países hispanos

La cita:

Debe programar sus citas con dos o tres semanas de anticipación, pero no dependa del servicio de correo electrónico para programar sus citas; es más recomendable usar el teléfono o el fax.

La forma de escribir la fecha en los países hispanos es: primero el día, luego el mes y después el año. Evite confusiones. Es mejor no usar números para indicar el mes.

El horario de las oficinas públicas y de negocios varía de unos países a otros. Averígüelo.

Usted debe llegar puntual, aunque sus colegas hispanos no lo hagan.

Reglas de vestir:

Infórmese con anticipación sobre la forma apropiada de vestir para los negocios en el lugar que visita. Los hispanos consideran la ropa como un símbolo de estatus social.

Los hombres deben vestir trajes de colores oscuros, corbatas conservadoras y zapatos de vestir. Por lo general, los hispanos sólo usan zapatos deportivos cuando hacen ejercicio.

El atuendo apropiado para las mujeres es un traje o vestido para los negocios, y un vestido tipo coctel para las ocasiones sociales.

Consejos sobre reglas de conducta en países hispanos:

- Si usted va a oficinas estatales o de negocios, salude al empleado antes de hacerle cualquier tipo de pregunta. Recuerde, los hispanos usan "Hola" solamente entre amigos. Diga "Buenos días", "Buenas tardes", etcétera.
- Un abrazo, una palmada en la espalda e incluso un beso en la mejilla entre mujeres es normal.
- Es muy probable que sus anfitriones lo inviten a tomar café o, en Argentina y Uruguay, mate. Tenga cuidado, el café es muy fuerte, y el mate tiene un sabor muy especial.
- Si quiere halagar a sus anfitriones pidiendo una bebida o comida típica, recuerde que:
  1. prácticamente todos los países de la región están orgullosos de la calidad de sus cervezas.
  2. el tequila mexicano y los vinos chilenos y argentinos son excelentes. Perú y Chile reclaman cada uno para sí el origen del *pisco*.
  3. algunas comidas incluyen ingredientes que quizá no sean de su agrado. El menudo es un platillo tradicional mexicano a base de panza de res. La parrillada argentina, uruguaya y paraguaya incluye riñones, tripa y morcilla. La paella valenciana tradicional no lleva pescado. Su ingrediente principal es el conejo.
- Muchos hispanos critican sus propios países, pero usted no debe hacerlo.

Palabras y frases clave

el (la) anfitrión(ona) *host(ess)*
el conejo *rabbit*
la corbata *necktie*
halagar *to flatter*
el menudo *traditional Mexican dish*
la morcilla *blood sausage*
no sean de su agrado *are not to your liking*
oscuro(a) *dark*
la panza de res *beef tripe*
puntual *on time*
reclamar *to claim*
el riñón *kidney*
saludar *to say hello, to greet*
el traje *suit*

Lección 6

Vendiendo para exportar

Más sobre el tema

Cómo dirigirse a otros de manera respetuosa

La mayoría de los hispanos usan el apellido materno y el paterno. Sin embargo, al dirigirse a alguien, usted debe usar solamente el apellido paterno (que es el primero), por ejemplo: Manuel García López será llamado "Señor García".

Debe dirigirse a la mayoría de las personas por el título y el apellido (Doctor Lamas, Licenciado Rosas, Sr. Gómez, Sra. Juárez, Srta. Recio).

En la mayoría de los países hispanos, cuando una mujer se casa, no adopta el apellido del esposo, pero generalmente añade al suyo el apellido del esposo, precedido de "de". Ana Pérez, la esposa de José Díaz, se llamará Ana Pérez de Díaz.

Obsequios apropiados:

Plumas u otros accesorios de oficina
Algo propio de su país
Vinos y otras bebidas alcohólicas (whiskey, vodka o ginebra) (para los hombres)
Perfumes (para las mujeres)
Cuando lo inviten a cenar en un hogar hispano, puede llevar flores, dulces, chocolates, frutos secos o frutas.

Palabras y frases clave

alguien *someone*
añadir *to add*
dirigirse *to address*

la mayoría de *most of*
los frutos secos *dried fruits*
el obsequio *present*
la pluma *pen*
respetuoso(a) *respectful*
se casa *gets married*

Algunas unidades de medida

Medidas de peso

la onza *ounce*
la arroba, @[1]
el quintal *100 pounds*

Medidas de longitud

la pulgada *inch*
el pie *foot*

Medidas de capacidad

el litro *liter*
la botella *bottle (0.725 liter)*
el barril *barrel (36 gallons)*

Medidas de superficie

la hectárea *2.47 acres*
la vara *0.,836 meters*
la manzana (medida de tierra) *10 000 square "varas",* 6 989 m^2 *(land)*
la manzana (en una ciudad) *space limited by four streets*

---

[1]In Spanish, @ is the short form of "arroba"; that is why Spanish speakers translate the @ sign as "arroba".

Lección 7

Comunicaciones

Más sobre el tema

Internet en América Latina

El uso de Internet en Latinoamérica y el Caribe creció más de un 900% en la última década, pero las pequeñas y medianas empresas (PYMES) todavía no aprovechan todas sus ventajas. Aunque más de un 80% de ellas está en la red, solo la usan para anunciarse. Solamente el 18% permite hacer transacciones en línea.

Los sectores que más usan la red son: servicios generales, manufactura y ventas minoristas; pero los servicios financieros, el comercio electrónico y la agricultura apenas la usan.

Los empresarios latinoamericanos deberían comprender:

- que el comercio electrónico es un negocio nuevo que no necesita una nueva inversión.
- que es como abrir una tienda más: una nueva sucursal, a un costo mínimo.
- que es la manera más fácil de llegar a sus clientes y de ganar otros nuevos.
- y que si no lo hacen ahora, sus competidores llegarán primero.

Existen grandes oportunidades de crecimiento para las empresas con productos para vender en línea a clientes en otras regiones de su país o en el extranjero.

Palabras y frases clave

base de retención de datos *retention base*
brecha digital *digital divide*
buscador *search engine*
centro de asistencia técnica *helpdesk*
compatibilidad con sistemas anteriores *backward compatibility*
comprender *to understand*
datos de inicio de sesión *login information*
desactivar *to disable*
desbloquear *to release*
descarga de canción en MP3 sin protección de derechos de autor *DRM-free MP3 song download*
diseñar una estrategia electrónica *to craft an e-strategy*
dominio público *public domain*
el (la) competidor(a) *the competition*
el (la) empresario(a) *entrepreneur*
eliminar de la lista de amigos *to unfriend*
en línea *on line*
enlace externo a la página *external link to the page*
los enlaces de entrada *inbound link*
el estacionamiento de nombre de dominio *domain name parking*
la galería de imágenes *photowall*
incluir en favoritos *to bookmark page*
el informe de actividad reciente *recent activity feed*
introduzca la contraseña *enter password*
el juego en red *hosted game*
la página de inicio de sesión *login screen*
la página de recuperación de contraseña *password-recovery page*
la pista (supercarretera) de la información *information (super) highway*
el portal de acceso mundial *global gateway*
los proveedores independientes de contenidos *third party content providers*
los rastreadores automatizados *automated spiders*
la redacción de textos publicitarios *marketing copywriting*
el rendimiento del sistema de registro de datos *data logging engine performance*
el sitio (la página) web en construcción *website under construction*
la suplantación de correo electrónico *email spoofing*
el tablero *dashboard*

la tecnología líder en su categoría/clase *best of breed technology*
las tendencias del usuario *searchers' behaviour*
la tienda virtual *online store*
el uso desautorizado *unauthorized use*
la velocidad de carga *upload speed*
la velocidad de descarga *download speed*
la violación de la seguridad *breach of security*
visitado(a) *accessed*

Lección 8

Transporte de pasajeros

Más sobre el tema

Para viajar por tren *To travel by train*

En España, Argentina y otros países de habla hispana, viajar por tren puede ser la mejor opción. *In Spain, Argentina and a few other Spanish-speaking countries, traveling by train may be the best option.*

Preguntas frecuentes y posibles respuestas

P. ¿Dónde está la estación del tren? *Where's the train station?*
R. A _________ cuadras de aquí. Siga derecho. _________ *blocks ahead. Continue straight ahead.*

P. ¿A qué hora sale el tren? *What time does the train leave?*
R. A la(s) _________. *At* _________.

P. ¿De qué andén sale? *What platform does it leave from?*
R. Del andén número _________. *From platform number* _________.

P. ¿Con qué anticipación puedo reservar un pasaje por tren? *How far in advance can I book a train ticket?*
R. Puede hacer su reservación hasta con tres meses de anticipación. *You may make the reservation up to three months in advance.*

P. ¿Cuántas maletas/bolsos se pueden llevar en el tren? *How many items of luggage can I carry on-board?*
R. Cada pasajero puede llevar dos maletas y un bolso de mano. *Each passenger may carry two suitcases and a handbag.*

P. ¿Hay vagones comedor en todos los trenes? *Are there dining cars in all trains?*
R. La mayoría de los trenes de larga distancia tienen vagón comedor. *Most of the long distance trains have dining cars.*

P. ¿Hay sanitarios en los trenes? *Are there restrooms in the trains?*
R. Todos los trenes cuentan con servicios de fácil acceso. En España están identificados con las letras "WC"; en América, "Baños"; también como "Caballeros" y "Damas/Señoras". *All trains have easily accessible restrooms. In Spain they are identified with the letters "WC"; in America, "Baños"; also as "Caballeros"y "Damas/Señoras".*

P. ¿Qué tipos de compartimentos dormitorio hay en los trenes nocturnos? *Which types of sleeping facilities are there on night trains?*
R. Los compartimentos dormitorio pueden ser individuales, dobles o para cuatro o seis personas. *Sleeping facilities may consist of individual rooms, double rooms or rooms for four or six people.*

P. ¿Desde qué edad se aplica la tarifa *Senior* en los trenes? *What is the minimum age to get a senior rate on the train?*
R. A los 60 años. *At sixty years of age*

P. ¿Hay descuentos para estudiantes? *Do students receive any discount?*
R. No, pero hay descuentos para viajeros menores de 25 años. *No, but there are discounts for people under 25 years of age.*

Palabras y frases clave

un boleto para ________, por favor. *One ticket for ________, please.*
el coche dormitorio *sleeping car*
el compartimento dormitorio para 4 ó 6 pasajeros *sleeping facility for 4 or 6 passengers*
el (la) jefe(a) de estación *station master*
la sala de espera *waiting room*
va a llegar a su hora *is arriving on time*
va a llegar adelantado *is coming early*
va a llegar atrasado, está atrasado *is running late*
el vagón, el carro (Méx.) *train car*

Lección 9

Transporte de carga

Más sobre el tema

Transporte de mercancías en el Área de Libre Comercio de las Américas (ALCA)

Convención Interamericana sobre Contrato de Transporte Internacional de Mercadería por Carretera

Responsabilidad de los transportistas:

El porteador responde a los hechos y omisiones de sus agentes, empleados y dependientes o de los terceros a los cuales se encomienda la totalidad o parte de los servicios; el convenio no puede excluir su responsabilidad o limitar cuantitativamente la indemnización.

Casos frecuentes:

- Pérdida
- Daño o avería
- Retraso o falta de entrega de la mercancía

"En ningún caso, la responsabilidad del porteador excederá del valor de la mercancía" .

Ámbito TLCAN o NAFTA
Prácticas Uniformes de Transporte de América del Norte.
Los camiones de México a los Estados Unidos y a Canadá pueden operar libremente, pero para que los camiones mexicanos transiten en los Estados Unidos necesitan un certificado de registro de la ICC (Interstate Commerce Comission).

Las tres cuartas partes de las exportaciones mexicanas van hacia los Estados Unidos.

La mayoría del transporte de mercancías se realiza por vía terrestre.

Palabras y frases clave

afianzado(a) y asegurado(a) *bonded and insured*
altura restringida *low clearance*
la carga líquida *wet bulk*
el cargador a granel *bulk loader*
los carriles adyacentes a la acera *curbside bus lanes*
consignado a la orden *consigned to order*
los contenedores sellados y de refrigerados *sealed and refrigerated containers*
el convenio *convention, agreement*
la cuneta *roll curb*
el empaque (de calidad) industrial *industrial crating*
encomendar *to entrust*
la entrega a domicilio sin cargo *free house delivery*
la estación de peaje *mainline toll*
la estadía *lay time*
la falta de entrega *non-delivery*
la garantía limitada *cost-ceiling warranty*
la merma en transporte (tránsito) *transit loss*
el (la) porteador(a) *carrier*
prevalecer *to prevail, to predominate*
realizarse *to take place*
el retraso *delay*
la señal de paso a nivel *crossbuck*
el servicio de mensajería aérea *air courier service provider*
el servicio de puerta a puerta *first and last mile*
el servicio de punta a punta *end-to-end service*
el servicio de transporte nocturno *trucking overnight service*
el sobrecupo *overcrowding*
las tarifas de fletamento *charter rates*
el transporte de contenedores *container shipping*
el (la) transportista *transporter*
el viaje de retorno (regreso) *backhaul*

Lección 10

Las Multilatinas

Más sobre el tema

Las empresas multinacionales latinoamericanas (o Multilatinas) son empresas multinacionales con sede en algún país latinoamericano, que producen artículos y/o prestan servicios en varios países.

Las Multilatinas han asimilado la crisis de los últimos años con buenos resultados en relación al manejo de los recursos humanos. A diferencia de lo que sucede en Asia, donde las empresas enfrentan serias dificultades en cuanto a la atracción y retención de sus empleados, en Latinoamérica este tipo de problemas es relativamente menor. La razón es el buen nivel de cualificaciones del capital humano local, sumado a una relativa falta de interés en la región por parte de las multinacionales extranjeras. Esto ha permitido que las Multilatinas –a pesar de sus bajos niveles de acceso directo al capital– sacaran ventaja de la crisis y lograran un fuerte crecimiento.

El hecho de que Latinoamérica tenga una importante fuente de talento cada vez más cualificado hace que los problemas de atracción y retención de personal cualificado se parezcan más a los de las empresas europeas y estadounidenses que a los de los mercados emergentes.

El talento latinoamericano es muy versátil y flexible, con un importante grado de movilidad entre industrias. Más aún, en lugar de buscar talento especializado dentro de la industria o entre el personal de la competencia, las Multilatinas parecen desarrollar y adaptar gran parte de su capital humano a las necesidades de la empresa recurriendo a la capacitación interna durante el horario laboral.

Palabras y frases clave

cada vez más *increasingly*
con sede en *based in*
el conocimiento de embarque *bill of lading*
en cuanto a *related to*
en lugar de *instead of*
enfrentar *to face*
la falta de *lack of*
la fuente de talento *source of talent*
el grado *degree*
el manejo *management, handling*
el manifiesto *manifest (a document listing and describing the cargo contents)*
el margen *margin (the difference between the cost of goods sold and the sales price)*
la nación más favorecida *most favored nation*
el país de origen *country of origin*
prestan servicios *render services*
la retención *keeping back*
sumado(a) *added*

Lección 11

La contabilidad en América Latina

Más sobre el tema

El conocimiento de los sistemas de contabilidad en América Latina se ha vuelto importante debido al papel que los países en vías de desarrollo están jugando en la actual economía global. Sin embargo, a pesar de la importancia que sus economías han ganado, todavía la mayoría de los contadores de los países desarrollados, no se han preocupado por conocer a fondo ni siquiera los sistemas contables de los países latinoamericanos más desarrollados.

En general, se tiene la idea de que los sistemas contables latinoamericanos son de menor calidad que los del mundo capitalista desarrollado. Eso es un grave error. Es cierto que, hasta hace poco, la mayor parte de los sistemas contables de los países latinoamericanos tenía, como fin primordial, cumplir con las regulaciones gubernamentales, destinadas en su mayoría a facilitar y hacer más confiable el cobro de impuestos. Pero este no es ya el caso.

Las empresas interesadas en hacer negocios con América Latina deberían preocuparse de que sus contadores estuvieran al tanto de la evolución que las prácticas contables latinoamericanas han tenido en años recientes. En este momento, todo lo relacionado con la economía cambia rápidamente en América Latina: 1) las universidades han actualizado sus cursos para ponerlos a tono con las prácticas internacionales; 2) las empresas multinacionales han exigido que los informes de sus contadores cumplan a un tiempo con los requisitos exigidos por las leyes locales y los estándares internacionales de la contabilidad global; 3) las empresas nacionales y hasta los gobiernos han entendido las ventajas de modernizar sus sistemas contables siguiendo normas internacionales. Como resultado, Latinoamérica tiene sistemas contables cada vez más eficientes y confiables.

Palabras y frases clave

a fondo *in depth*
a un tiempo *both (at the same time)*
como fin primordial *as paramount objective*
deberían preocuparse *should pay attention*
desde ya *from now on*
el cobro de impuestos *tax collection*
las economías emergentes *emerging economies*
estar al tanto *to be updated*
hacer más confiable *to make more trustworthy*
han exigido *have required*
hasta hace poco *until recently*
hasta los gobiernos *even governments*
ni siquiera *not even*
no es ya el caso *is not the case any longer*
los países desarrollados *developed countries*
los países en vías de desarrollo *developing countiries*
los países subdesarrollados *underdeveloped countries*
poner a tono *synchronize*
se ha vuelto *has become*
un grave error *a serious mistake*

Lección 12

América Latina comienza a adoptar estándares internacionales en contabilidad

Más sobre el tema

La globalización ha incentivado a los países de América Latina a adoptar los estándares internacionales en la contabilidad de sus empresas. Desde mediados de la década pasada, la República Dominicana, El Salvador y Uruguay adoptaron en su totalidad las normas IFRS (International Finantial Reporting

Standards), pero los países más grandes continuaron desarrollando sus propios estándares. Pronto, sin embargo, se dieron cuenta de que, aunque sus sistemas contables eran sofisticados y eficientes, no eran fáciles de comprender por los contadores de los países más desarrollados del mundo que sí habían adoptado las normas IFRS. En consecuencia, Brasil, México, Argentina y Chile han adoptado ya las normas IFRS, y otros países van siguiendo su ejemplo.

La adopción de normas internacionales de contabilidad y auditoría es la base para el establecimiento de una información financiera transparente y confiable que facilita el comercio y el acceso a los créditos internacionales, fundamentales para el desarrollo económico de la región.

Palabras y frases clave

el activo realizable *liquid assets*
los activos devengados *accrued assets*
el agotamiento de recursos naturales *depletion of natural resources*
el ajuste contable *accounting adjustment*
amortizar, reducir el valor *to write-down*
la anualidad, la renta vitalicia *annuity*
el balance (estado) constructivo *constructive balance*
el balance de inventarios y balances *inventory and balance sheet (book)*
la base contable *accounting principles (bases)*
la base imponible *taxable income*
los bienes pignorados *pledged assets*
la caja chica *petty cash*
el capital de riesgo *venture capital*
la cartera de inversiones *portfolio*
el cierre de libros *closing of accounting books/records*
el cierre del balance *year-end balance sheet/closing balance sheet*
la cifra de ingresos *revenue*
el código de comercio *commercial code*
el coeficiente de liquidez a corto plazo *acid-test ratio*
compensación excesiva por despido *golden parachute*
el costo de mercaderías vendidas *cost of goods sold*
la declaración jurada *affidavit*
el desgaste natural, el deterioro por el uso *wear and tear*
el dinero ocioso *barren money*
en descubierto, sobregirado, en rojo *overdrawn*
el (la) fideicomisario(a) *trustee*
los impuestos atrasados *back taxes*
los impuestos diferidos activos *current deferred taxes*
incentivar *to incite, to stimulate*
la indemnización por despido *severance pay*
el ingreso derivado de la actividad laboral *earned income*
la mora, el atraso *delay*
el punto de referencia *benchmark*
la reducción del precio de venta *markdown*
registrar datos falsos en los estados contables *cook the books*

la relación precio-ganancia *P/E (price-to-earnings) ratio*
el rendimiento al vencimiento *yield to maturity*
los servicios varios *various services*
el subproducto *by-product*
el valor nominal *face value*
el valor residual *scrap value*
los valores en cartera *holdings*
la venta en subasta *auction sale*
la venta judicial, la ejecución forzosa *compulsory sale*

Lección 13

Los impuestos en América Latina

Más sobre el tema

Desde las últimas décadas del siglo pasado, ha habido numerosos intentos de reformar los sistemas de impuestos de casi todos los países latinoamericanos. Reiteradamente, los políticos han prometido que, al alcanzar el poder, reformarían los sistemas de impuestos para hacerlos más justos y hacer más fácil cumplir con sus disposiciones. Sin embargo, una vez en el poder, ninguno ha querido, o podido, hacer realidad sus más o menos radicales promesas electorales. No obstante, gradualmente han ido ocurriendo cambios importantes en este campo.

Las principales reformas han sido:

1. Introducir el impuesto al valor agregado (IVA).
2. Reducir los trámites y los gastos necesarios para que los contribuyentes paguen sus impuestos.
3. Hacer más fáciles y menos costosos para los gobiernos los trámites necesarios para cobrar los impuestos.
4. Aumentar de manera significativa la porción del Producto Interno Bruto (PIB) que el gobierno recauda en concepto de impuestos. Desde luego, esto no ha ocurrido en los países cuyos presupuestos obtienen la mayor parte de sus ingresos de la exportación de productos parcial o totalmente estatales. Por ejemplo, la exportación de petróleo en Venezuela.
5. Reducir las tarifas a la importación y a la exportación para facilitar el comercio internacional.

De todas estas reformas, la más importante ha sido la introducción del impuesto al valor agregado. El IVA, importado de Europa, comenzó a ser puesto en práctica en América Latina en la década de los 70, y hoy forma parte de los sistemas de impuestos de todos los países latinoamericanos. En realidad, todos los países de América, de Canadá al Cono Sur, excepto los Estados Unidos, tienen al IVA como su principal fuente de ingresos.

Los defensores del IVA argumentan que el impuesto al valor agregado es un sistema de impuestos progresivo, porque las personas con más ingresos gastan más y, por tanto, pagan más. Sus críticos consideran que el IVA es un sistema de impuestos regresivo, porque los pobres pagan un mayor porcentaje de sus ingresos que los ricos.

No hay duda de que el impuesto a los ingresos hace posible cobrar un mayor porcentaje de sus ingresos a los ricos que a los pobres pero, como todas las cosas, tiene también sus inconvenientes. Los ricos, en conjunto, reciben la mayor parte de sus ingresos de sus negocios. Cuando la economía anda mal, los ingresos de los ricos disminuyen extraordinariamente. Así, los ingresos del estado son muy inestables.

Al contrario, como los ricos no se ven obligados a gastar menos en tiempos de crisis, con el IVA pagarían los mismos impuestos que en tiempos de bonanza y, como el ingreso de los pobres depende principalmente de los sueldos, y estos generalmente no disminuyen en tiempos malos para la economía, los ingresos del estado son menos inestables con el IVA. Quizás es por eso que muchos países han optado por mantener los dos sistemas de impuestos al mismo tiempo.

Palabras y frases clave

puesto en práctica *put into practice*
al alcanzar el poder *after being elected*
andar mal *to go wrong*
argumentar *to argue*
cumplir *to comply*
cuyos *whose*
el (la) defensor(a) *defender, advocate*
disminuir *to decrease*
en conjunto *in its totality*
en este campo *in this field*
la fuente de ingresos *source of income*
hacer realidad *to become true*
han prometido *have promised*
han sido *have been*
no ha ocurrido *has not happened*
el petróleo *oil*
los políticos *politicians*
la porción *the part*
Producto Interno Bruto (PIB) *Gross Domestic Product (GDP)*
se ven obligados *are pushed*
el siglo pasado *past century*
un mayor porcentaje *a larger percentage*

Lección 14

Publicidad para hispanohablantes de los Estados Unidos y Canadá

Más sobre el tema

Desde hace varios años, el poder adquisitivo de los hispanohablantes sobrepasó el billón de dólares (*one trillion* en inglés). Si los hispanohablantes de los Estados Unidos fueran una nación, esta sería una de las primeras diez economías del mundo.

Son numerosas las empresas anglosajonas que están pidiendo a sus agencias de publicidad que les preparen anuncios en español. Estas agencias han acertado en algunos casos. McDonald's, por ejemplo, tiene un sitio web en español, **meEncanta.com,** con una página llamada **Orgullo latino,** una de cuyas secciones, bajo el título **Cómo lo dices** presenta los localismos con que en diferentes países llaman un mismo artículo. En general, los medios de publicidad en español tratan de usar un lenguaje lo más neutro posible, que entiendan todos los hispanohablantes de cualquier país, aunque predominan los mexicanismos por motivos obvios. Los inmigrantes de otros países se sienten bien ante el reconocimiento que McDonald's hace de sus localismos.

Por el contrario, hay anunciantes que piden a las agencias que los locutores y artistas que participan en sus anuncios usen el *spanglish*. Esto es un grave error. Muchos hispanos se sienten ofendidos porque saben que esos locutores y artistas hablan bien el español, pero que les han pedido que hablen *spanglish* porque las empresas parecen tener en sus mentes el estereotipo del inmigrante latino indocumentado que no habla bien ni el español ni el inglés.

No se entiende que hay una gran diversidad entre los que seguimos empeñados en identificar como "latinos" o "hispanos". Los que llamamos en inglés "*Hispanics*" no son un grupo homogéneo: los hay blancos, negros, cobrizos, ricos, de clase media, pobres, cultos, analfabetos... Y hay algo que deberían empezar a tener en cuenta los que hacen publicidad. Un informe de *The Pew Hispanic Center* dejó bien claro que la mayor parte de los hispanohablantes no se identifican como "latinos" ni como "hispanos", y solamente los unen el idioma y ciertos rasgos culturales.

Según el estudio citado, la lengua franca de los hispanos y su identidad nacional cambian radicalmente de la primera a la tercera generación de inmigrantes.

1. El 80% de la primera generación piensa en español, mientras que el 80% de la tercera generación piensa en inglés.
2. Dos terceras partes de los inmigrantes de primera generación, los nacidos en el extranjero, dicen ser muy diferentes de los americanos típicos... pero dos terceras partes de los de la segunda y tercera generación se sienten como americanos típicos.
3. Todos, sin embargo, conservan ciertos valores culturales. En primer lugar, la importancia que para ellos tiene la familia. Cuando se les pidió que compararan las formas de vida de sus países de origen y las de los Estados Unidos, lo único que señalaron como mejor en sus países de origen fue los estrechos lazos familiares.
4. Aunque los inmigrantes van adoptando el modo de vida americano, todo parece indicar que los últimos rasgos de identidad que más perdurarán serán sus valores tradicionales.

Si los anunciantes tuvieran más en cuenta todo esto, a la hora de anunciar un producto para hispanohablantes deberían determinar qué anuncios hacer en inglés y cuáles en español y, en todos ellos, poner el mayor énfasis en los rasgos culturales que los unen a todos.

Palabras y frases clave

acertar *to guess correctly*
analfabeto(a) *illiterate*
ante *before*
cobrizo *brown*
¿Cómo lo dice(s)? *How do you say it?*
conservar *to preserve*
dejar claro *to make it clear*

la forma de vida *way of life*
la lengua franca *common language, lingua franca*
el localismo *localism*
el (la) locutor(a) *(tv, radio) announcer, speaker*
los que hacen publicidad *advertisers*
los que llamamos *those we identify as*
el orgullo latino *Latin pride*
perdurar *to last*
el poder adquisitivo *purchasing power*
el reconocimiento *recognition, acceptance*
seguir empeñado *to insist on*
sentirse bien *to feel well/fine*
tener en cuenta *to take into account*

Lección 15

Los bancos en América Latina

Más sobre el tema

Según un informe de The World Bank Group (Financial Access 2010—Latin America and the Caribbean Factsheet) en los países de Latinoamérica y el Caribe hay unas 865 cuentas por cada 1000 adultos. Esto no significa que más de un 86% de los adultos tengan cuentas bancarias, sino que las instituciones públicas y privadas y una minoría de la población tiene más de una cuenta. Además, el informe se refiere a Latinoamérica, no a Hispanoamérica.

En Latinoamérica, el 75% de la población no tiene acceso a los bancos: no tienen cuentas bancarias ni consiguen préstamos, pero la situación varía mucho de país a país. Mientras más de un 80% de los chilenos tiene cuentas bancarias, solo poco más del 10% de los paraguayos las tiene.

También hay mucha diferencia entre las instituciones financieras existentes en cada país. En casi todos los países latinoamericanos hay bancos comerciales, pero en Chile la mayor parte de los depósitos están en instituciones financieras estatales, y lo mismo sucede con buena parte de los depósitos en Perú y en Panamá. En Costa Rica, Ecuador y Bolivia una buena cantidad de los depósitos están en cooperativas de crédito.

Solo en los países en que predominan las instituciones financieras estatales, una buena parte de los créditos ha ido a parar a personas de bajos ingresos. Esto es especialmente notable en Bolivia y Perú donde se han creado instituciones específicamente orientadas hacia los microcréditos.

Sin embargo, lo cierto es que el acceso de los latinoamericanos a los créditos bancarios ha mejorado. En la década anterior, los préstamos se elevaron hasta 341 por cada 1000 adultos, aunque, como efecto de la crisis financiera mundial, el monto de los préstamos bajó un promedio de un 18% en relación con el Producto Interno Bruto de la región.

Muchos latinoamericanos todavía comercian y guardan sus ahorros en efectivo. Esto se explica por la falta de protección al consumidor que ha ocasionado grandes pérdidas a los cuentahabientes. El caso más notable y reciente fue el de Argentina en 2001. Una congelación de los depósitos y una brusca devaluación de la moneda nacional llevaron a la bancarrota a numerosos bancos y a la miseria a gran parte de la clase media del país. Desde entonces, el sistema bancario argentino no ha podido recuperar la confianza del pueblo.

Palabras y frases clave

los bajos ingresos *low income*
brusca *rough, sudden*
la clase media *the middle class*
como efecto *as a result*
la confianza *trust, confidence*
la congelación *freezing*
el (la) cuentacorrentista *one having a current account in a bank*
el (la) cuentahabiente *one having an account in a bank*
estatal *state (adj.)*
guardar *to keep, to save*
han ido a parar a *have gone to*
Hispanoamérica *Spanish-speaking countries from the Mexican border to Argentina and Chile*
Latinoamérica *all countries from the Mexican border to Argentina and Chile(?).*
lo mismo *the same thing*
la miseria *misery, poverty*
el monto *summation*
mundial *world (adj.)*
ocasionar *to cause*
paraguayo(a) *from Paraguay*
predominar *to predominate, to exceed*
significar *to mean*
variar *to vary, to change*

Lección 16

Los bancos latinoamericanos y las PYME

Más sobre el tema

Tanto en los países desarrollados como en aquellos en vías de desarrollo, las pequeñas y medianas empresas representan las bases más firmes del desarrollo económico de cada país. Actualmente, tras la globalización, las grandes empresas no tienen patria, son multinacionales y, en muchos casos, son más grandes y poderosas que los países en los que hacen algunos de sus negocios. Lo peor es que, a veces, usan su poder para competir con ventaja sobre las pequeñas y medianas empresas nacionales. El odio que se han ganado en algunos países está bien merecido.

Según una investigación realizada por *The Inter-American Investment Corporation (IIC), the Multilateral Investment Fund (MIF), and the Latin American Federation of Banks (FELABAN)* con el objeto de medir la disposición de los bancos latinoamericanos de financiar las pequeñas y medianas empresas (PYME), los bancos de la región ven a las PYME de manera muy positiva, como agentes del desarrollo y progreso de la región.

Un alto porcentaje de los bancos investigados aseguró tener políticas favorables a la financiación de las pequeñas y medianas empresas. A tal efecto, la gran mayoría de ellos ha creado departamentos con personal cualificado en el análisis y procesamiento de pequeños préstamos, en las relaciones con los medios de publicidad, y en el uso de Internet para llegar a los posibles clientes. Además, algunos bancos ofrecen servicios de entrenamiento a personal de las PYME.

Sin embargo, según Augusto de la Torre, economista jefe del departamento latinoamericano del Banco Mundial, los bancos han fallado en cuanto a su contribución al crecimiento económico y al bienestar social de Latinoamérica. Según afirma, el monto de los préstamos a las PYME es mucho menor que el de las grandes empresas y, además, esos préstamos les cuestan más, y tienen que pagar más por todo tipo de servicios bancarios. Por otra parte, los bancos orientan la mayoría de sus préstamos al sector de consumo, principalmente a la emisión de tarjetas de crédito, mientras que los préstamos hipotecarios, que hacen tanta falta en la región, apenas alcanzan el 14% de todos sus préstamos, mientras que en los países desarrollados representan un 47% del total.

Las causas de estas disparidades son varias, pero quizá la más notable es la falta de estabilidad legal.

A veces faltan leyes que establezcan claramente los derechos y deberes de prestamistas y prestatarios; a veces las leyes existen, pero es difícil o imposible hacerlas cumplir. Mientras América Latina no termine con este clima de incertidumbre legal, no puede aspirar a disfrutar las enormes ventajas de un sistema financiero eficiente y justo.

Palabras y frases clave

actualmente *nowadays*
apenas alcanza *barely reaches*
aseguró tener *claimed to have*
bien merecido *well deserved*
el bienestar social *social welfare*
con el objeto de medir *to find out how large*
disfrutar *to enjoy*
la disparidad *disparity*
el entrenamiento *training*
la estabilidad *stability*
han fallado *have failed*
hipotecario(a) *mortgage (adj.)*
la incertidumbre *uncertainty*
medios de publicidad *advertising media*
el odio *hate*
orientar *to orientate*
las pequeñas y medianas empresas (PYME) *small and medium-size enterprises (SMEs)*
el (la) prestatario(a) *borrower*
realizar *to make*
terminar con *to put an end to*

Lección 17

Los latinoamericanos compran casas... y las pierden

Más sobre el tema

Durante muchos años, para la mayoría de los inmigrantes latinoamericanos, la compra de una vivienda era el punto de referencia que marcaba su éxito. Pero lograr "el sueño americano" no ha sido fácil para los latinos. Durante mucho tiempo, los préstamos de los bancos estaban limitados por las llamadas "líneas rojas" que establecían zonas geográficas, generalmente barrios latinos y de otras minorías, en las que los bancos se negaban a prestar.

Después de mucho tiempo sufriendo discriminación a la hora de conseguir hipotecas, una ley prohibió que los bancos discriminaran, y otra facilitó la compra de viviendas con poca o ninguna entrada (*enganche*). Los bancos se vieron obligados a prestar a las minorías. Entre los años 2000 a 2007, el número de hipotecas concedidas a los latinos aumentó casi un 30% y el número de latinos con vivienda propia pasó de 4 a 6 millones.

Normalmente, los bancos no hacían préstamos a individuos con una puntuación de crédito tan baja que hacía dudar de su capacidad de pago pero, aceptando como buenas las garantías que les ofrecía el gobierno a través de instituciones semi-oficiales como *Fannie Mae* y *Freddie Mac,* dejaron de preocuparse por la solvencia de los compradores y comenzaron a firmar miles de hipotecas de alto riesgo.

Los agentes de bienes inmuebles y los bancos alentaron a las minorías a comprar viviendas caras, con hipotecas cuyas mensualidades eran más altas de lo que podían pagar... Mientras los precios de las casas se mantuvieron altos y subiendo, no hubo problemas. Cuando no podían pagar las mensualidades de las hipotecas, los prestatarios vendían rápidamente las casas, ganaban dinero en las operaciones, y con eso compraban otras casas dando una entrada mayor. Pero estalló la burbuja inmobiliaria: las casas bajaron de precio y miles y miles de compradores se quedaron con casas que valían menos de lo que debían. No podían venderlas ni podían seguir pagando las hipotecas. Miles tuvieron que declararse en bancarrota... y el sueño americano se convirtió en pesadilla.

Palabras y frases clave

a la hora de *when the time came to*
a través *through*
el (la) agente de bienes inmuebles (raíces) *realtor*
alentar *to encourage*
la burbuja inmobiliaria *the housing bubble*
la capacidad de pago *ability to pay*
conceder *to grant*
cuyo(a) *whose*
estallar *to burst*
facilitar *to make it easier, to facilitate*
la hipoteca de alto riesgo *subprime mortgage*
los latinos con vivienda propia *Latino homeowners*
la línea roja *red line*
lo que podían pagar *what they were able to afford*

la mensualidad *monthly payment*
la pesadilla *nightmare*
prohibir *to prohibit*
la puntuación de crédito *credit scoring*
se mantuvieron altos y subiendo *were high and were increasing*
la solvencia *solvency*
el sueño americano *the American dream*

Lección 18

Bienes inmuebles

Más sobre el tema

Palabras y frases clave

el (la) acreedor(a) hipotecario(a) *mortgagee*
la amortización *loan repayment*
el avalúo *appraisal*
la casa individual *detached home*
la casa semiadosada *semi detached home*
el (la) cesionario(a) *grantee*
los cobertizos/las casetas independientes *free standing sheds*
la cocina integrada *open plan kitchen*
colindante *adjoining*
la colocación de título de propiedad en poder de un tercero, hasta que se ejecute la compra-venta *escrow*
el contrato de compraventa de vivienda *private property sales contract*
el (la) corredor(a) *broker*
la cuota de trámite de préstamo *loan origination fee*
el derecho del gobierno a adquirir propiedades *eminent domain*
el (la) deudor(a) hipotecario(a) *mortgator*
la ejecución hipotecaria *foreclosure*
el financiamiento directo *seller carry-back*
el gravamen *lien*
la hipoteca con un pago final global *variable-rate mortgage, adjustable-rate mortgage (ARM)*
los impedimentos (sobre una propiedad) *encumbrances*
el (la) inquilino(a) *tenant*
la limitación por escritura *deed restriction*
las medidas y colindancias *metes and bounds*
las mejoras efectuadas por el arrendatario *tenant owned improvements*
la ordenanza de uso de terrenos *zoning ordinance*
el (la) otorgante *grantor*
el préstamo hipotecario *lien mortgage loan*

el préstamo de segunda hipoteca *second trust deed loan*
el prorrateo *apportionment*
tasación *independent valuation of property*
el título de propiedad *deeds*
La ubicación lo es todo. *it's location, location, location*
el valor de catastro *assessed value*

Lección 19

Seguros

Más sobre el tema

Palabras y frases clave

el acontecimiento imprevisto *unforeseen occurrence*
anterior *foregoing*
la anulación *cancelation*
atribuible a *attributable to*
las cláusulas *provisions*
la cobertura *(insurance) cover*
el comienzo de la cobertura *inception of the cover*
conforme a *in accordance with*
la conmoción civil *civil unrest*
los daños por agua (vapores, olores) *damage by water (vapors, smells)*
de conformidad con sus instrucciones *as instructed by you*
dependiendo de *subject to*
derivada de *arising from*
desde la fecha en que causara el suceso *as from the event giving rise thereto*
emitidos a favor del asegurado *issued on behalf of the insured*
en adelante *hereafter, hereunder*
en caso de muerte (fallecimiento) *in the event of death*
en vigor *in force*
estando involucrado en *being engaged in*
estipulado(a) en *defined in*
la explosión *explosion*
la falta de notificación *failure to notify*
la fecha de efecto *inception date*
la fecha límite *deadline*
el historial personal de reclamos *personal claims record*
la huelga *strike*
impago *financial default*
el incumplimiento por parte de *non-compliance on the part of*
la indemnización fijada por arbitraje *arbitration award*
independientemente de *regardless of*
la interrupción *curtailment*

la invalidez (la incapacidad) permanente *permanent disability*
la ley consuetudinaria de contratos *common contract law*
las leyes y normativas *laws and regulations*
el límite de indemnización $_____ *compensation up to $______*
la línea directa de atención al cliente *customer help-line*
el motín *riot*
la nota de cotización *quote sheet*
pagadero(a) *payable*
pendiente *impending*
la pérdida de equipaje *personal baggage and property loss*
la póliza se rige bajo *the policy is governed by*
ponemos en su conocimiento *we draw your attention to*
los preceptos de *the provisions of*
proceder *to proceed*
el rechazo *non-acceptance*
reembolsar *to reimburse*
reemplazar *to supersede*
responsable de *liable for*
el resumen de las coberturas y los costos *summary of covers and costs*
rogamos contacten *please notify*
se compromete *undertakes*
sea cual sea su naturaleza *whatsoever their nature*
la sede social *headquarters*
el seguro colectivo *group insurance*
el seguro contra accidentes *casualty insurance*
el seguro contra neglicencia médica *malpractice insurance*
si desea alguna aclaración *if you need any clarification*
siempre y cuando *providing*
so pena de suspensión de cobertura *on pain of forfeiture of the cover*
los suplementos *endorsements*
la validez legal *legally enforced*

Lección 20

Comercio internacional

Más sobre el tema

Palabras y frases clave

el arbitraje *arbitration*
el buque de transporte de carga sólida a granel *bulk carrier*
la cadena de suministro *supply chain*
la carta de crédito *letter of credit*
el catálogo *brochure*

el comercio exterior *foreign trade, international business*
el consejo de administración *board of directors*
el director ejecutivo *chief executive officer C.E.O.*
la filial *branch*
las fusiones y adquisiciones *mergers and acquisitions*
la gestión *management*
el huso horario *time zone*
el índice de precios al consumidor *consumer price index*
las licitaciones *tenders*
la logística *logistics*
los mercados emergentes *emerging markets*
los Objetivos de Desarrollo del Milenio *Millennium Development Goals*
el oleoducto *pipeline (oil)*
los países del tercer mundo *third world countries*
la paridad de poder adquisitivo *purchasing power parity*
la persona jurídica *legal person*
la pobreza *poverty*
la planificación *planning*
el posicionamiento *positioning*
la propiedad intelectual *intellectual property*
la promoción *promotion*
el protocolo *protocol*
la rentabilidad *profitability*
las tendencias *trends*
la transferencia bancaria *bank transfer*

Algunas organizaciones internacionales

Banco Interamericano de Desarrollo *Inter-American Development Bank*
Banco Mundial *World Bank* WB
Comunidad Andina *Andean Community*
Mercado Común del Sur (Mercosur) *Southern Common Market (Mercosur)*
Organización Mundial del Comercio *World Trade Organization* WTO
Unión Europea *European Union*

Algunas regulaciones internacionales

Acuerdo general sobre comercio y aranceles *General Agreement on Tariffs and Trade*
Conferencia de las Naciones Unidas sobre Comercio y Desarrollo *United Nations Conference on Trade and Development*
Unión aduanera *Customs union*

Appendix D

Weights and Measures

Length

la pulgada = *inch*
el pie = *foot*
la yarda = *yard*
la milla = *mile*

1 centímetro (cm) = .3937 pulgadas (*less than 1/2 inch*)
1 metro (m) = 39.37 pulgadas (*1 yard, 3 inches*)
1 kilómetro (km) (1.000 metros) = .6214 millas (*5/8 mile*)

Weight

la onza = *ounce*
la libra = *pound*
la tonelada = *ton*

1 gramo (g) = .03527 onzas
100 gramos = 3.527 onzas (*less than 1/4 pound*)
1 kilogramo (kg) (1.000 gramos) = 2.2 libras

Liquid Measure

la pinta = pint
el cuarto (de galón) = quart
el galón = gallon

1 litro (l) = 1.0567 cuartos (de galón) (*slightly more than a quart*)

Surface

el acre = *acre*
1 hectárea = 2.471 acres

Temperature

°C = Celsius (*Celsius*) or centigrade (*centígrado*); °F = Fahrenheit (*Fahrenheit*)
0° C = 32° F (*freezing point of water*)
37° C = 98.6° F (*normal body temperature*)
100° C = 212° F (*boiling point of water*)

Conversión de grados Fahrenheit a grados centígrados °C = 5/9 (°F −32)
Conversión de grados centígrados a grados Fahrenheit °F = 9/5 (°C) + 32

Spanish-English Vocabulary

The Spanish-English and English-Spanish vocabularies contain all active and passive vocabulary that appears in the manual. Active vocabulary includes words and expressions appearing in the ***Vocabulario*** and in the ***Vocabulario adicional*** lists. Passive vocabulary consists of those words and phrases that are given an English gloss in readings, exercises, activities, and authentic documents. These items are followed by a number indicating the lesson in which each word appears for the first time. ***Vocabulario adicional*** and *English glossed* items are indicated by the abbreviations *v.a.* and *g.,* respectively.

The following abbreviations are also used in the vocabularies:

adj.	adjective	*L.A.*	Latin America
adv.	adverb	*m.*	masculine noun
col.	colloquial	*Méx.*	Mexico
f.	feminine noun	*pl.*	plural noun
f.n.	foot note	*s.*	supplement
form.	formal	*sing.*	singular noun
inf.	infinitive	*Ven.*	Venezuela
l.	lectura	*t.*	trivia

A

a to, 1; at, 1
- **¿— cómo está el cambio?** What's the rate of exchange?, 2
- **— corto plazo** in a short term, g. 17
- **— favor de** on behalf of, v.a. 19
- **— fin de que** so that, 19
- **— jornada completa** full-time, v.a. 10
- **— la derecha (izquierda)** to the right (left), 2
- **— la hora del almuerzo** at lunch time, 4
- **— la llegada** upon arrival, v.a. 1
- **— la semana** weekly, 10
- **— la una** at one o'clock, g. 1
- **— la vista** as soon as presented (*bill of exchange*), s. 4
- **— las (+ *time*)** at (+ *time*), 1
- **— las (los) demás** to other people, g. 10
- **— media jornada** part-time, v.a. 10
- **— medio día** part-time, v.a. 10
- **— medio tiempo** part-time, v.a. 10
- **— nombre mío** in my name, v.a. 15
- **— partir de** starting, 3
- **— partir del día** as of (+ *date*), v.a 3
- **— pesar de (que)** in spite of (the fact that), 14
- **— plazo fijo** fixed term (deposit), 13
- **¿— qué distancia?** how far?, 3
- **¿— qué hora?** at what time?, 1
- **¿— quién(es)?** whom, v.a. 2
- **— su cargo** at your expense, s. 2
- **— sus órdenes** at your service, 10
- **— tiempo completo** full-time, v.a. 10
- **— toda plana** full-page, v.a. 14
- **— todo el mundo** the world over, 9
- **— tres cuadras de** three blocks from, 7
- **— veces** sometimes, 6
- **— ver** let's see, 6

abonar to pay, s. 4
abrasivo(a) abrasive, g. p
abrecartas (*m.*) letter opener, v.a. 10
abrigo (*m.*) coat, sweater, 14
abrir to open, 2
- **— un negocio** to set up a business, 16

abrocharse el cinturón de seguridad to fasten one's seat belt, v.a. 1
abuelo(a) grandfather, grandmother, 13
abusar de to abuse, 20
acceso (*m.*) access, 7
accesorio (*m.*) accessory, 5
accidente (*m.*) accident, 19
acción (*f.*) stock, 13; share, 13
aceite (*m.*) oil, v.a. 8
acelerador (*m.*) accelerator, v.a. 6
aceptar to accept, 2
acera (*f.*) sidewalk, 8
acerca de about, 7
aconsejar to advise, 16
acordarse (o:ue) to remember, 18
acreditado(a) well-established, 6
acreditar to credit, v.a. 11; to accredit, to give official authorization, 13
acreedor(a) (*m., f.*) creditor, v.a. 11
activo (*m.*) assets, v.a. 11
actual current, 6; present, 6
actualmente presently, 10
acuerdo (*m.*) agreement, 20
acumulador (*m.*) battery, v.a. 6
acuse de recibo (*m.*) return receipt, v.a. 7
adaptar to adapt, 18
adaptarse to become adapted to, g. 15
adecuado(a) adequate, s. 3
además besides, 6
adicional additional, g. 1
adiestramiento (*m.*) training, g. 5
adiós good-bye, p
adjetivo (*m.*) adjective, g. p
adjunto (*m.*) enclosure, s. 2
adjunto(a) attached, v.a. 11
administración (*f.*) administration, g. p
- **— de empresas (negocios)** business administration, 16
- **— de Pequeños Negocios** Small Business Administration, 16
- **— Federal de Hipotecas** Federal Housing Authority (FHA), v.a. 17

administrador(a) (*m., f.*) administrator, manager, g. p
adquirir to acquire, g. 20
aduana (*f.*) customs, 1
aéreo(a) air, 9
aerolínea (*f.*) airline, v.a. 1
aeropuerto (*m.*) airport, 1
afectar to affect, 18
agarrar to take, 8
agencia (*f.*) agency, g. p
- **— de publicidad** advertising agency, p

agente (*m., f.*) agent, g. p
- **— viajero(a)** (*m., f.*) traveling salesperson, 6

agrado (*m.*) pleasure, s. 3
agregar to add, 14
agrícola agricultural, g. 11
agua caliente (fría) (*f.,* but **el agua**) hot (cold) water, v.a. 3
aguacate (*m.*) avocado, v.a. 4
ahora now, 1
- **— mismo** right now, 17

ahorita now (*Méx.*), 1; in a while, 1
ahorrar to save, 7
ahorro (*m.*) savings, 6
aire(*m.*) air, 3
— **acondicionado** air conditioning, 3
ají (*m.*) chili (pepper), 4
ajustar to adjust, 1, 12
ajuste (*m.*) adjustment; reconciliation, v.a. 11
al to the, 4
— **alcance** within reach, g. 6
— **año** yearly, 10
— **contado** cash, g. 15
— **detall** retail, 5
— **detalle** retail, 5
— **día** daily, 8
— **día siguiente** the next day, 4
— **fondo** in the back, 5
— **gusto** any style, to order; to taste, v.a. 4
— **horno** baked, v.a. 4
— **igual** in the same way, g. 13
— **llegar** upon arrival, v.a. 1
— **mayoreo** wholesale, 5
— **menudeo** retail, 5
— **mes** monthly, 17
— **poco rato** a while later, 3
— **por mayor** wholesale, 5
— **por menor** retail, 5
— **respecto** about that, 10; about the matter, 10
— **ritmo de** according to, s. 3
— **toda plana** full-page, v.a. 14
— **vapor** steamed, v.a. 20
alberca (*f.*) (*Méx.*) swimming pool, v.a. 17
alboroto (*m.*) riot, s. 4
alcanzar to be enough, 19; to reach, 19
alcohólico(a) alcoholic, 2
alegrarse to be happy, 17; to be glad, 17
alfarería (*f.*) pottery (*i.e.*, the craft), 9; pottery shop, 9
alfombra (*f.*) carpet, 17
algo something, v.a. 5
¿— que declarar? anything to declare?, 2
¿— más? anything else?, 3
algodón (*m.*) cotton, 9
algún (alguno/a) any, 7
alguna vez ever, v.a. 5
algunas veces sometimes, 19
alimentar to feed, 12
alimentos frescos (*m., f.*) fresh foods, s. 1
allá there, over there, 3
allí there, 16
almacén (*m.*) warehouse, v.a. 5
grandes almacenes (*m. pl.*) department store, g. 1
almeja (*f.*) clam, v.a. 4
almohada (*f.*) pillow, 1
almorzar (o:ue) to have lunch, 10
almuerzo (*m.*) lunch, 4
alquilado(a) rented, 18
alquilar to rent, 8; to lease, v.a. 13
alquiler (*m.*) rent, 12
altavoz (*m.*) loudspeaker, 1
alto(a) high, 9
alto (*m.*) height, 7; depth (*of a container*), 7
altoparlante (*m.*) loudspeaker, 1
ambiguo(a) ambiguous
ambos(as) both, 3
americano(a) American, g. p
amistades (*f. pl.*) friends, g. 12
amortiguador (*m.*) shock absorber, 6
amparar to support, s. 4
ampliación (*f.*) enlargement, l. 12; expansion, v.a. 20
amplio(a) ample; extensive, 20
analizar to analyze, 20
analógico analog, v.a. 12
anaquel (*m.*) shelf, 18
ancho (*m.*) width, 7
anexo (*m.*) enclosure, s. 2
animales vivos (*m., pl.*) live animals, s. 1
anotar to write down, to note, to jot down, 5
antefirma (*f.*) sender's company name, s. 2
anterior previous, 11; former, 11
antes (de) before, 1
— **de decidir** before deciding, g. 6
anticipadamente ahead of time, s. 4
anticipo (*m.*) advance payment, v.a. 5
antiguo(a) former, l. 6
anual yearly, 10
anunciado(a) advertised, g. 1
anunciar to announce, 1; advertise, v.a. 14
anuncio (*m.*) ad, 14
— **panorámico** billboard, v.a. 14
año (*m.*) year, 10
apagar la luz to turn off the light, v.a. 3
aparecer to appear, 13
apariencia (*f.*) appearance, 14
apartado postal (*m.*) post office box, v.a. 7
apartamento (*m.*) apartment, 3
aparte separately, 7; in addition to, 7
apellido (*m.*) last name, p; surname, p
— **materno** mother's last name, s. 1
— **paterno** father's last name, s. 1
apenas scarcely, 9; hardly, 9
apio (*m.*) celery, v.a. 4
apostar (o:ue) to bet, 20
apoyar to favor, v.a. 20
apreciable noticeable, g. 4
aprobación (*f.*) approval, v.a. 16
aprobar (o:ue) to approve, 16
aprovechar to take advantage, g. 5
aquél (*m.*) that (over there), 18
aquí here, 2
— **tiene...** here's . . . , 4
aranceles (*m. pl.*) (customs) duty, 2
araña (*f.*) spider, g. 14
árboles frutales (*m. pl.*) fruit trees, 17
archivador (*m.*) file, filing cabinet (*España*), v.a. 10
archivar to file, v.a. 10
archivo (*m.*) file, filing cabinet, v.a. 10
área (*f.*, but **el área**) area, 7
arrancar to start, 8
arreglar to repair, to fix, v.a. 8
arreglo (*m.*) arrangement, 11
arrendador(a) lessor, landlord, s. 4
arrendamiento (*m.*) lease, v.a. 18
arrendar to rent, to lease, v.a. 13
arrendatario(a) (*m., f.*) lessee, v.a. 18; tenant, s. 4
arriendo (*m.*) lease, v.a. 18
arriesgarse to take risks, g. 11
arroz (*m.*) rice, 4
artesanía (*f.*) artcraft, 8; handicraft, 8
artículo (*m.*) article, 5; item, 5
asado(a) grilled, 4; broiled, 4; roasted, 4
asalto (*m.*) assault, v.a. 20
ascensor (*m.*) elevator, 3
aseado(a) clean, s. 4
asegurado(a) (*adj.*) insured, 15; (*m., f.*) policyholder, v.a. 19
asegurador(a) insurer (*m., f.*); insurance company, v.a. 19
aseguranza (*f.*) (*Méx.*) insurance, 19
asegurar to ensure, 3; to insure, 19
— **se** to make sure, g. 9
asesor(a) de inversiones (*m., f.*) investment officer, s. 3
asesoramiento (*m.*) advice, 16; consulting, 16
así thus, this way, g. 5
— **que** so, 10
asiduidad (*f.*) frequency (of business orders), s. *3*
asiento (*m.*) seat, 1; entry, 11
— **de diario** journal entry, 11
— **de pasillo** aisle seat, 1
— **de ventanilla** window seat, 1
asistencia (*f.*) attendance, 12
asistente (*m., f.*) assistant, 11
asociación (*f.*) association, g. p
aspirante (*m., f.*) applicant, v.a. 10
aspirar to aspire, l. 12
asumible assumable, 17
asumir to assume, 16
asunto (*m.*) reference line; subject, 2
atacar to attack, g. 11
atención (*f.*) attention, 1
— **médica y hospitalaria** medical and hospital care, 19
atender (e:ie) to assist, 5; to attend, 5; to wait on, 5
aterrizaje (*m.*) (plane) landing, v.a. 1
atraer to atract, g. 18
atún (*m.*) tuna, v.a. 4
audífonos (*m., pl.*) headset, v.a. 7
aumentar to increase, 9
aumento (*m.*) increase, 9; raise, 9
aún as yet, still, g. 11
aunque although, g. 4
ausencia (*f.*) absence, 12
auto (*m.*) car, 6
autobús (*m.*) bus, 8
automáticamente automatically, 12
automático(a) automatic, 8
automatizar to automate, 12
automóvil (*m.*) car, 6
autopista (*f.*) expressway, v.a. 14; freeway, v.a. 14
— **de cuota** (*f.*) toll road, g. 8
autorizar to authorize, 18
auxiliar de vuelo (*m., f.*) flight attendant, 1
aval (*m.*) collateral, 16
avenida (*f.*) avenue, 8
avería (*f.*) damage (merchandise during transport), 9

averiguar to find out, 9
aves (*f. pl.*) poultry, fowl, v.a. 4
avión (*m.*) plane
avisar to inform, 8; to give notice, 8
aviso (*m.*) notification, s. 4
ayer yesterday, 11
ayuda (*f.*) help, 12; assistance, 12
ayudante (*m., f.*) assistant, 11
ayudar to help, 9
azúcar (*m., f.*) sugar, 20

B

bacalao (*m.*) cod, v.a. 4
bagre (*m.*) bagre (*freshwater fish*), 4
bajar to go down, 2
bajarse to get off, 8
bajo(a) low, g. 14
balance (*m.*) balance, 11
— **de comprobación** trial balance, 11
— **general** balance sheet, 11
balboa (*m.*) currency of Panama, g. 2
baldosa (*f.*) tile, 17
bancario(a) (*adj.*) bank, banking, 6
bancarrota (*f.*) bankrupcy, insolvency, 15
banco (*m.*) bank, g. p
— **electrónico** electronic bank, 15
banda elástica (*f.*) rubber band, v.a. 10
banquero(a) (*m., f.*) banker, v.a. 15
banqueta (*f.*) sidewalk (*Méx.*), 8
bañadera (*f.*) bathtub, v.a. 3
baño (*m.*) bathroom, v.a. 1; toilet, v.a. 1
barato(a) inexpensive, v.a. 5; cheap, v.a. 5
barbería (*f.*) barber shop, v.a. 18
barco (*m.*) ship; boat, v.a. 9
barrera (*f.*) barrier, g. 11, v.a. 20
barrio (*m.*) neighborhood, 15
base (*f.*) base, g. 3
bastante quite, 19
batería (*f.*) battery, v.a. 6
baúl (*m.*) trunk, v.a. 6
bazar (*m.*) bazaar, store, 14
beber to drink, 4
bebida (*f.*) drink, 2
beca (*f.*) scholarship, 16
beneficiar to benefit; to do good, 20
beneficiario(a) (*m., f.*) beneficiary, g. p; person or business authorized to receive payment (bill of exchange), s. 4
beneficio (*m.*) benefit, 20
— **adicional (marginal)** (*m.*) fringe benefit, 10
beneficioso(a) advantageous, g. 5
berro (*m.*) watercress, v.a. 4
bien fine, p; well, p
— **cocido(a)** well done, v.a. 4
— **cocinado(a)** well done, v.a. 4
— **terminado(a)** well made, 5
bienes (*m. pl.*) assets
— **inmuebles** real estate, 13
— **muebles** personal property, 13
— **raíces** real estate, 13
bienvenido(a) welcome, 2
bife (*m.*) steak (*Arg.*), g. 4
biftec (*m.*) steak, g. 4
bilingüe bilingual, 10
billete (*m.*) ticket, 1
— **de banco** bill, v.a. 15; bank note, v.a. 15
— **de ida** one-way ticket, 1
— **de ida y vuelta** round-trip ticket, 1
— **falso** counterfeit bill, v.a. 15
billón trillion, g. 11
bistec (*m.*) steak, v.a. 4
blanquillo (*m.*) egg (*Méx.*), 4
blusa (*f.*) blouse, 14
bocina (*f.*) horn, klaxon, v.a. 6
bolígrafo (*m.*) ballpoint pen, v.a. 3
bolívar fuerte (*m.*) currency of Venezuela, g. 2
boliviano (*m.*) currency of Bolivia, g. 2
bolsa (*f.*) bag, 14; stock exchange, g. 18
— **de aire** (*f.*) air bag, v.a. 6
bolso(a) (*m.,f.*) handbag, 2; carry-on bag, 2
bomba de agua (*f.*) water pump, v.a. 8
bonito(a) beautiful, 17
bonito (*m.*) tuna, v.a. 4
bono (*m.*) bond, 13
botones (*m.*) bellhop, 3
boulevard, bulevar (*m.*) boulevard, 8
brécol (*m.*) broccoli, v.a. 4
breve brief, p
bróculi (*m.*) broccoli, v.a. 4
brutal brutal, v.a. 20
bruto(a) gross, v.a. 9
buen well, 9
buen(o)(a) good, 4
buenas noches good evening, p; good night, p
buenas tardes good afternoon, p
buenos días good morning, p; good day, p
bujía (*f.*) spark plug, v.a. 6
bulto (*m.*) package, 2; bundle, 2
buque (*m.*) ship; boat, v.a. 9
buró (*m.*) desk, v.a. 10
buscar to look for, 5
buzón (*m.*) mailbox, 7

C

caballero (*m.*) gentleman, v.a. 1
caber to fit, 9
cabeza (*f.*) head
— **de familia** (*m., f.*) head of household (of the family), 13
cable (*m.*) cable, v.a. 12
cada each, 5
cadena (*f.*) chain, 5
café (*m.*) coffee, 4
— **con leche** café au lait, 4
— **expreso** espresso, 4; strong black coffee, 4
— **solo** espresso, 4; strong black coffee, 4
cafetería (*f.*) cafeteria, 4
caja (*f.*) box; petty cash, s. 4
— **de bolas** ball bearings, v.a. 6
— **registradora** cash register, 12
cajero(a) (*m., f.*) teller, v.a. 15
cajero automático (*m.*) automatic teller machine, v.a. 15
cajuela (*f.*) trunk (*Méx.*), v.a. 6
cajetilla (*f.*) pack, package, g. 2
calamar (*m.*) squid, v.a. 4
calculador(a) (*m., f.*) calculator, g. p
— **de bolsillo** pocket calculator, v.a. 2
calcular to calculate, g. 13
calderilla (*f.*) small change, v.a. 15
calefacción (*f.*) heating, v.a. 3
calendario (*m.*) calendar, g. p
calidad (*f.*) quality, 5
calificación (*f.*) qualification, v.a. 10
calificado(a) qualified, g. 15
calificar (*col.*) to qualify, 16
calle (*f.*) street, p
cámara (*f.*) camera, 2
— **de video** video camera, 2
— **fotográfica** (photographic) camera, 2
camarero(a) (*m., f.*) waiter, 4; waitress, 4
camarón (*m.*) shrimp, v.a. 4
cambiar to change, 2; to exchange, 2
— **un cheque** to cash a check, v.a. 15
cambio (*m.*) change, v.a. 6; shift, 8
— **de aceite** oil change, v.a. 6
— **manual** standard shift, 8
— **mecánico** standard shift, 8
caminar to walk, 2
camión (*m.*) bus (*Méx.*), 8; truck, 9
camioneta (*f.*) van, v.a. 9
camisa (*f.*) shirt, 14
campaña de promoción (*f.*) promotion campaign, 14
campesino(a) farmer, g. 19
canasta (*f.*) basket, g. 7
cancelado(a) canceled, 13
candente burning, g. 11
candidato(a) (*m., f.*) candidate, 10; applicant, 10
cangrejo (*m.*) crab, v.a. 4
cantidad (*f.*) quantity, 5
caña de azúcar (*f.*) sugar cane, 20
capacidad (*f.*) means, capacity, 14
— **instalada** productive capacity, 14
capacitado(a) qualified, g. 12
capital (*f.*) capital (i.e., city), 6
capital (*m.*) capital (i.e., assets), v.a. 11
capitalista (*m., f.*) capitalist, v.a. 20
característica (*f.*) feature, 14
cárcel (*f.*) jail, g. 2
carga (*f.*) shipment, 9; load, 9
cargamento (*m.*) shipment, 9; load, 9
cargar to charge, 7; to load, 9
cargo (*m.*) title, v.a. 5; employment, v.a. 5
Caribe (*m.*) Caribbean, 20
caridad (*f.*) charity, 13
carne (*f.*) meat, v.a. 4
— **asada** steak (*Méx.*), v.a. 4
— **de res** beef, v.a. 4
carnicería (*f.*) meat market, v.a. 18
caro(a) expensive, 5
carrera (*f.*) studies, 13; schooling, 13; career, 13
carretera (*f.*) highway, v.a. 9
carro (*m.*) car, 6
carrocería (*f.*) body (*of an automobile*), v.a. 6
carta (*f.*) letter, 7
— **certificada** registered (certified) letter, v.a. 7

— **circular** circular, s. 2
— **de negocios** business letter, s. 2
— **de recomendación** letter of recommendation, v.a. 10
cartel (*m.*) poster, v.a. 14
cartera (*f.*) handbag, 14; purse, 14
cartero(a) (*m., f.*) mail carrier, v.a. 7
casa (*f.*) firm, 1; business, 1; company, g. 1; house, 4
— **de cambio** currency exchange office, 2
— **de empeño(s)** pawnshop, v.a. 18
— **de huéspedes** boarding house, g. 3
— **matriz** main office, v.a. 15
— **propia** one's own home
casado(a) married, p
casarse to get married, 16
casetera (*f.*) VCR, v.a. 2
casi almost, 2
casilla de correo (*f.*) post office box, v.a. 7
caso (*m.*) case, 11
causado(a) caused, 19
celular (*m.*) cellular telephone, v.a. 2
cena (*f.*) dinner; supper, g. 4
centavo (*m.*) cent, v.a. 2
centímetro (*m.*) centimeter, 7
centro (*m.*) center, 3
— **comercial** shopping center, 18; mall, 4
— **de la ciudad** downtown, 3; center of the city, 3
cerca (de) near, 17
cercano(a) near, 7; close by, 7
cerdo (*m.*) pork, v.a. 4
cerrar (e:ie) to close, 5
certificado de depósito certificate of deposit (C.D.), 13
cesantear to fire (*i.e.,* an employee), v.a. 10
césped (*m.*) lawn, 17; grass, 17
chamaco(a) (*m., f.*) (*Méx.*) child, 5
chamarra (*Méx.*) jacket, 14
champú shampoo, v.a. 3
chaqueta (*f.*) jacket, 14
chasis (*m.*) chassis, v.a. 6
checar (*col. Méx.*) to check, v.a. 8
cheque (*m.*) check, g. p
— **al portador** check to the bearer, v.a. 15
— **de caja** cashier's check, 15
— **de viajero** traveler's check, 2
— **sin fondos** bounced check, v.a. 15; overdrawn check, v.a. 15
chequear to check, v.a. 8
chequera (*f.*) checkbook, v.a. 15
chícharos (*m. pl.*) peas, v.a. 4
chile (*m.*) chili (pepper), 4
chimenea (*f.*) fireplace, 17
chinche (*f.*) thumbtack, v.a. 10
chocar to collide, 19; to have a collision, 19
chofer (*m., f.*) chauffeur, 8; driver, 8
cifra (*f.*) figure; number, 20
cigarrillo (*m.*) cigarette, 2
cinturón de seguridad (*m.*) seat belt, v.a. 1
circulación (*f.*) circulation, 14
circular (*f.*) circular, 12
circunstancias atenuantes (agravantes) (*f., pl.*) special circumstances, v.a. 20
cita (*f.*) appointment, 5
ciudad (*f.*) city, 4
ciudadano(a) (*m., f.*) citizen, 2
civilizado(a) civilized, g. p
claramente clearly, g. 15
claro of course, 15; clear, l. 12
clase (*f.*) class, g. 3
— **acomodada** upper class, g. 6
— **media** middle class, g. 3
— **turística** tourist class, v.a. 1
cláusula (*f.*) clause g. p
clave (*f.*) code, 7
claxon (*m.*) horn, klaxon, v.a. 6
cliente (*m., f.*) client, 5; customer, 5
cobertura (*f.*) coverage, 19
cobija (*f.*) (*Méx.*) blanket, 1
cobrar to charge, g. 1
— **o devolver (C.O.D.)** collect on delivery (C.O.D.), v.a. 9
— **un cheque** to cash a check, v.a. 15
cobre (*m.*) copper, 20
cobro (*m.*) collection (*of debts*), 12
cocina (*f.*) kitchen, 17; stove, 17
coche (*m.*) car, 6
código (*m.*) code, 7
coger to take, 8
cojinetes (*m. pl.*) roller bearings, v.a. 6
colocar to place, 18
colón (*m.*) currency of Costa Rica and El Salvador, g. 2
colonia (*Méx.*) (*f.*) neighborhood, 15
coma (*f.*) comma, g. 2
comedor (*m.*) dining room, 17
comején (*m.*) termite, 17
comenzar (e:ie) to begin, 5
comer to eat, 4
comercial commercial, g. p
comercio (*m.*) commerce, 20
comida (*f.*) lunch, 4; meal, 13; food, 13
— **chatarra** (*f.*) junk food, t. 4
comisión (*f.*) commission, 13
como as, 4
cómo no certainly, 1; of course, 1
¿cómo? how?, 4
¿— **está Ud.?** how are you?, p
¿— **son?** what are (they) like?, 4
compacto(a) compact, 8
compañía (*f.*) company, g. p
comparar to compare, 6
compatible compatible, 9
compensar to compensate, 6
competencia (*f.*) competition, 14
competir (e:i) to compete, 6
competitivo(a) competitive, 6
completar to fill out (a form), 1
completo(a) complete, full, 13
componente (*m.*) component, v.a. 12
composición de textos (*f.*) word processing, 10
compra (*f.*) buying, 6; purchase, v.a. 5
comprador(a) (*m., f.*) buyer, 1
comprar to buy, 5
compraventa (*f.*) purchase and sale agreement, v.a. 5
comprender to understand, 5
comprensivo(a) comprehensive, 19
comprobante (*m.*) claim check, 2; (written) proof or verification, 2; (written) proof or receipt, 13
— **del sueldo y de los descuentos** wage and tax statement (W-2), 13
computación (*f.*) computation, 12
computador(a) (*m., f.*) computer, g. p
— **portátil** laptop computer, 2
común usual, g. 18
comunicación (*f.*) communication, 7
con with, p
— **cargo** drawn on, s. 4
— **pocas millas** (*i.e.,* a car) with not too many miles on it. g. 8
— **propiedad** (*i.e.,* **hablar**) correctly, g. 10
— **que cuenta** available, 7
¿— **quién?** With whom?, 11
¿— **quién desea Ud. hablar?** With whom would you like to speak?, p
— **referencia a** with regard to, s. 2
conceder un crédito to extend credit, v.a. 5
concentrar(se) to concentrate, l. 12
concepto (*m.*) concept, 12
conciliar reconcile, v.a. 11
condado (*m.*) county, 16
condición (*f.*) condition, g. p
condiciones de costumbre en la plaza (el mercado) usual terms in the market, 6
condiciones de pago terms of payment, 6
condominio (*m.*) condominium, 16
conducir to drive, 8
condueño(a) (*m., f.*) co-owner, 14
conección para el cable cable outlet, v.a. 17
conectar to connect, 12
confeccionar to make, 14; to prepare, 14; to put together, 14
confecciones (*f., pl.*) ready-made clothes, 5
conferencia (*f.*) **telefónica** telephone conference, v.a. 7
confiar trust, g. 20
confidencial confidential, s. 2
confirmar to confirm, v.a. 1
conforme a according to, s. 4
congelado(a) frozen, 4
conjunto(a) joint, v.a. 13
conjunto (*m.*) set, 5
conmigo with me, 6
conocer to know, 7; to meet for the first time, 13
conocido(a) known, g. 5
conseguir (e:i) to obtain, 13; to get, 13
consejo (*m.*) advice, 14
conservar to maintain, g. 12
considerarse to see yourself, g. 20
consignatario(a) (*m., f.*) consignee, v.a. 9
consistir (en) to consist (of), 10
constancia (*f.*) proof, v.a. 18
construido(a) built, 17
— **a la orden** custom built, 17
consultar to consult, 11
consumidor(a) (*m., f.*) consumer, 6
contabilidad (*f.*) accounting, 11
contable accounting, 11
contador(a) (*m., f.*) accountant, 11
— **público(a) titulado(a)** Certified Public Accountant (C.P.A.), v.a. 11

contar (o:ue) to count, 13
contenedor (*m.*) container, 9
contener to contain, 7
contingencia (*f.*) contingency, 17
continuar to continue, 10
contra against, 19
contratar to hire, 10; to employ, 10
contrato (*m.*) contract, g. p
contribución (*f.*) contribution, 13; (real estate) tax, 13
contribuir to contribute, 10
contribuyente (*m., f.*) taxpayer, v.a. 13
conveniente convenient, 13
convenir to suit, 18; to be good for, 18
 — en to agree on, v.a. 18
 — le a uno to be to one's advantage, 15
conversación (*f.*) conversation, p
conversar to talk, 1
convertirse to become, l. 9
copa (*f.*) glass, 4
copia (*f.*) copy, g. p
copropietario (*m.*) co-owner, 14
corbina (*f.*) sea bass, 4
corchetera (*f.*) stapler, v.a. 10
cordero (*m.*) lamb, v.a. 4
córdoba (*m.*) currency of Nicaragua, g. 2
corredor(a) de bienes raíces (*m., f.*) real estate agent, 17; realtor, 17
correlativo(a) related, s. 4
correo (*m.*) post office, 7
 — aéreo air mail, 7
 — electrónico electronic mail (e-mail), 7
correr con to be in charge of, 9
correspondencia (*f.*) mail, correspondence, v.a. 7
 — comercial business correspondence, s. 2
cortinas (*f., pl.*) curtains, v.a. 3
cosa (*f.*) thing, 7
cosecha (*f.*) crop, 20
cosechero(a) grower, g. 7
costar (o:ue) to cost, 6
 — trabajo to pay dearly, g. 15
coste (*m.*) cost, g. p
costo (*m.*) cost, g. p
 —, seguro y flete (C.S.F.) cost, insurance, and freight (C.I.F.), v.a. 9
costoso(a) costly, 11
creación (*f.*) creation, 5
crecer to grow, 11
crédito (*m.*) credit, g. p
creer to believe, 6; to think, 6
crudo(a) rare, v.a. 4
cruzar to cross, 8
cuadra (*f.*) block, 7
cuadrado(a) square, 18
cuadrar to reconcile, v.a. 11
cual (*m., f.*) which, what, 13
¿cuál? which?, 3; what?, 3
cualquier(a) any, g. 2
cuando when, 4
 — termina de comer when he/she finishes eating, 4
¿cuándo? when?, 1
¿cuánto(a)? how much?, 3
¿cuántos(as)? how many?, 3
cuarto (*m.*) room, 3
 — de lavar laundry room, 17
 — principal master bedroom, v.a. 17
cúbico(a) cubic, 9
cubierto(a) covered, 19
cubrir to cover, 8
CUC (Cuban convertible peso) (*m.*) Cuban currency, g. 2
cuello (*m.*) neck, 20
cuenta (*f.*) bill, 4; account, 13
 — a (por) cobrar account receivable, v.a. 11
 — a (por) pagar account payable, v.a. 11
 — acreedora credit account, v.a. 11
 — conjunta joint account, 15
 — corriente checking account, v.a. 11
 — de ahorros savings account, 13
 — de cheques checking account (*Méx.*), 15
 — del mercado de dinero money market account, 15
 — deudora debit account, v.a. 11
 — individual de retiro individual retirement account (I.R.A.), 13
cuentas claras clean accounts, g. 12
cuero (*m.*) leather, 9
cuerpo (de la carta) (*m.*) body (of a letter), s. 2
cuidado (a) cared for, 17; kept, 17
cuidadosamente carefully, s. 2
cultivo (*m.*) cultivation; farming, 20
cumplir to fulfill, g. 9
cuota inicial (*f.*) down payment, 16
curioso(a) inquisitive; curious, g. 20
curriculum vitae (*m.*) résumé, v.a. 10

D

dama (*f.*) lady, v.a. 1
dañar to harm; to damage, 20
daño (*m.*) damage, 9
dar to give, 3
 — a la calle to overlook the street, 3
datos (*m. pl.*) information, 3; data, 3
de of, 1; from, 1
 — acuerdo (con) in accordance (with), 5
 — costumbre usual, 6
 — enganche deposit (down payment) (*Méx.*), 18
 — la izquierda (derecha) to the left (right), 2
 — nada. You're welcome., p
 — nuevo again, 12
 — primera (calidad) top quality, 5
 — todos modos anyway, 7; in any case, 7
 — un lugar a otro from one place to another, 8
 — uso used, 13
debajo (de) underneath, v.a. 1
debate (*m.*) debate, 20
debatir to debate, 20
debe (*m.*) debit, v.a. 11
deber must, 2; should, 2; to have to, 2; to owe, 13
debido(a) due, v.a. 13
debitar to debit, v.a. 11
decidir to decide, 8
decímetro (*m.*) decimeter, 9
decimosegundo(a) twelfth, l. 9
decir to say, 7; to tell, 7
declaración (*f.*)
 — de aduana customs form, 1
 — de impuestos tax return, 13
declarar to declare, 2
 — culpable to declare at fault, 19
 — se to declare oneself, 15
 — se en quiebra to declare bankruptcy, 15
dedicado(a) dedicated, v.a. 20
dedicar to dedicate, 20
deducción (*f.*) deduction, 13
 — general standard deduction, v.a. 13
deducible deductible, v.a. 13
deducir to deduct, 13
defender to defend, g. 11
defensa (*f.*) (car) bumper, v.a. 6
definitivamente definitely, 20
dejar to leave (behind), 4
 — de ser to be no longer, s. 3
 Se lo puedo — en... I can give it to you for . . . , 8
delito (*m.*) crime, g. 2
demanda (*f.*) demand, v.a. 20
demasiado too much, 12; too, 17
demora (*f.*) delay, 1
demorar to take (*time*), 4; to last (*a length of time*), 4
demostración (*f.*) show, v.a. 14
departamento (*m.*) apartment, v.a. 17
depender (de) to depend (on), 6
dependiente (*m., f.*) dependent, 13
depositante (*m., f.*) depositor, v.a. 15
depositar to deposit, 13
depositario(a) depositary; receiver, v.a. 15
derecho ajeno (*m.*) another's rights, g. 20
derechos aduaneros (de aduana) (*m., pl.*) customs duty, 20
derechos de autor (*m., pl.*) copyright, 20
derrumbe (*m.*) collapse, s. 4
desarrollar develop, v.a. 20
desarrollo (*m.*) development, g. 5
desayuno (*m.*) breakfast, 4
descafeinado(a) decaffeinated, 4
descarga (*f.*) unloading, 9
descargar to unload, 9
descartar to rule out, 16
descender to descend, g. p
descontar (o:ue) to give a discount of, 6
descripción del contenido de trabajo (*f.*) job description, 10
descuento (*m.*) discount, 5; deduction, 12; reduction, 12
desde from, 1; since, g. 5
 — luego of course, 6
 — que since, 13
desear to wish, 1; to want, 1
desempleo (*m.*) unemployment, v.a. 13
deshonesto(a) dishonest, g. 2
desnudo(a) naked, g. 20
desocupado(a) vacant, 18; empty, 18
desocupar la habitación to check out; to vacate a room, v.a. 3

despedida (*f.*) farewell, g. p; closing, s. 2
despedir (e:i) to fire (*i.e.*, an employee), v.a. 10
despegue (*m.*) take-off, v.a. 1
desperdiciar to squander, l. 12
después later, 2
después (de) after, 2
destacador (*m.*) highlighter, v.a. 10
destinatario(a) (*m., f.*) addressee, 7; recipient, s. 2
destino (*m.*) destination, v.a. 9
destruir to destroy, l. 6
desvergonzado(a) shameless, g. 20
detallista (*m., f.*) retailer, 10
deuda (*f.*) debt, v.a. 11, 16
deudor(a) (*m., f.*) debtor, v.a. 11
devolver (o:ue) to return, v.a. 9
día (*m.*) day, 2
— **de semana (de trabajo)** weekday, v.a. 14; workday, v.a. 14
— **hábil (laborable)** weekday; workday, v.a. 14
dibujo (*m.*) drawing, v.a. 14; design, v.a. 14
dicho (*m.*) saying, g. p
diferencia (*f.*) difference, 2
dificultad (*f.*) difficulty, 6
Dígale que pase. Tell him/her to come in., 10
digital digital, v.a. 12
digo I mean, 7
dinero (*m.*) money, 7
— **en efectivo** cash, v.a. 2
dirección (*f.*) address, p
directamente directly, 6
directorio telefónico (*m.*) telephone book, 7
disco (*m.*) diskette, v.a. 12
— **(de programación)** (*m.*) computer disk(ette), v.a. 12
— **duro** hard drive, v.a. 12
discutir to discuss, 5
diseñado(a) designed, 12
diseñar to design, 14
diseño (*m.*) design, 5
disfrazado(a) disguised, v.a. 20
disponerse to set (in place), s. 3
disponible available, 5
disposición (*f.*) regulation, 7
disquete (*m.*) computer disk(ette), v.a. 12
distinto(a) different, 9
distribuir to distribute, 14
distrito industrial (*f.*) industrial zone, 4
dividendo (*m.*) dividend, v.a. 13
divisa (*f.*) hard currency, g. 5
divorciado(a) divorced, p
doble (*m.*) double, 9; twice, 9
documento (*m.*) document, g. p
dólar (*m.*) dollar, 2; currency of the United States, Puerto Rico, and El Salvador
doler (o:ue) to hurt, 8; to feel pain, 8
domicilio (*m.*) address, p
dominar master, g. 20
donación (*f.*) donation, 13
donativo (*m.*) donation, 13
¿dónde? where?, 1
dormitorio (*m.*) bedroom
— **principal** master bedroom, v.a. 17

ducha (*f.*) shower, v.a. 3
dudar to doubt, 18
dueño(a) (*m., f.*) owner, 16
dulce (*m.*) sweet, 18; confection, 18
dulcería (*f.*) candy store, v.a. 18
durante during, v.a. 1
durar to last, 17

E

e and, g. 8
echar to drop, 7
económico(a) economic(al), 16
economista (*m., f.*) economist, v.a. 20
ecosistema (*m.*) ecosystem, 20
edad (*f.*) age, 5
edición (*f.*) edition, v.a. 14; issue, v.a. 14
edificio (*m.*) building, 18
efectivo (*m.*) cash, v.a. 11
efectivo(a) effective, 14
efecto (*m.*) effect, 20
efectuarse to take place, s. 3
eficientemente efficiently, v.a. 20
egreso (*m.*) expenditure, v.a. 11
ejemplar (*m.*) copy, v.a. 14; sample, v.a. 14
el the, g. p
electricidad (*f.*) electricity, 12
eléctrico(a) electric, 17
electrodoméstico (*m.*) appliance, v.a. 17
elegante elegant, 17
elevador (*m.*) elevator, 3
eliminar to remove, g. 11
ella misma herself, 8
elote (*m.*) (*Méx.*) ear of fresh corn, v.a. 4
embalaje (*m.*) packing, packaging, 9
emergencia (*f.*) emergency, v.a. 1
emigrar to emigrate, g. 17
empezar (e:ie) to begin, 5
empleado(a) (*m., f.*) employee, 1; clerk, 1; employed, g. 12; used, g. 12
— **de cuello blanco** white-collar worker
empleador(a) (*m., f.*) employer, 13
emplear to hire, 10; to employ, 10
empleo (*m.*) employment, 10
quedarse sin — lose your job, 20
emprender to undertake, l. 12
empresa (*f.*) enterprise, 11; company, 11
en in, 1; on, 1; at, 1
— **blanco y negro** in black and white, v.a. 14
— **casa** at home, 10
— **caso de que** in case, 19
— **colores** in color, v.a. 14
— **cuanto** as soon as, 19
— **cuanto a** in regard to, 7
— **depósito** (*m.*) deposit (*down payment*), 18
— **exceso (de)** in excess (of), v.a. 13
— **existencia** in stock, 6
— **fondo** (in) deposit (*down payment*), 18
— **la misma forma** in the same way, g. 13
— **lo adelante** from now on, s. 4
— **mi nombre** in my name, v.a. 15

— **primer lugar** in the first place, g. 15
— **primera clase** (*f.*) in first class, 1
— **punto** sharp, v.a. 5
¿— qué puedo (podemos) servirle? How may I (we) help you?, p
— **realidad** indeed, g. 2
— **seguida** right away, 1
— **seguida va para allá** he's on his way there, 3
— **todo el mundo** the world over, g. 7
encargar to entrust, 11
encargarse (de) to take charge (of), 9; to see after, 9
enchufe (*m.*) electrical outlet; socket, v.a. 17
encontrar (o:ue) to meet, 8
encuadernación (*f.*) binding, s. 4
encuesta (*f.*) poll, v.a. 14; survey, v.a. 14
energías alternativas (*f.*) alternative energies, p
enfrentar to encounter, l. 12
enganche (*m.*) (*Méx.*) down payment, 16
engrase (*m.*) lubrication, v.a. 6
ensalada (*f.*) salad, 4
ensamblar assemble, g. 5
enseguida (*f.*) right away
enseñar to show, 8
enseres (*m., f.*) fixtures, 19
entablar una demanda to file a lawsuit, 20; to sue, 20
entender (e:ie) to understand, 5
entonces then, 4
Entonces llamo más tarde. I'll call later, then., p
entrada (*f.*) arrival, 12; entry, 12; down payment, 16
— **para vehículos** driveway, v.a. 17
entrar to enter, 9
entre between, g. 5
entrega al día siguiente overnight delivery, v.a. 7
entrega especial (*f.*) special delivery, v.a. 7
entregar to deliver, v.a. 7
entrepaño (*m.*) shelf, 18
entrevista (*f.*) interview, 10
enviar to send, 7
envío (*m.*) shipment, s. 2
envuelto(a) wrapped, 14
equipaje (*m.*) baggage, 2
equipo (*m.*) equipment, 12; hardware, v.a. 12
— **de computación** computer hardware, 12
— **electrónico** electronic device, v.a. 1
equivalente equivalent, 10
error (*m.*) error, 11
es decir that is to say, g. 3; in other words, 12
Es la una. It's one o'clock., g. 1
es (una) lástima it's a pity, 17
escala (*f.*) stopover, 1
— **de impuestos** (*f.*) tax rate table, v.a. 13
escalera (*f.*) stairs, 2
— **mecánica** escalator, v.a. 2
— **rodante** escalator, 18
escáner (*m.*) scanner, v.a. 12

escanógrafo (*m.*) scanner, v.a. 12
escaparate (*m.*) shop window, 18; display window, 18
escasez (*f.*) scarcity, g. 20
escoger to choose, 10
escribir to write, 2
escritorio (*m.*) desk, v.a. 10
escritura (*f.*) deed, 17
escuchar to listen, 5
escuela (*f.*) school, 17
escusado (*m.*) bathroom (toilet) (*Méx.*), v.a. 1
ese(a) that, g. 6
eso es todo that's all, 3
espacio comercial (*m.*) commercial space, 18
español (*m.*) Spanish, g. p
especialidad (*f.*) specialty, 4
especialista (*m., f.*) specialist, 20
esperar to wait (for) 10; to expect, 10; to hope, 16
esposo(a) (*m., f.*) husband, 13; wife, 13
esquina (*f.*) corner, 8
— **superior derecha (izquierda)** upper right (left) corner, v.a. 7
estable stable, 2
establecer to establish, g. 14
establecimiento (*m.*) establishment, 9; shop, 9
— **comercial** business, g. 18
estación (*f.*) station, 9; season, 14
— **de servicio** service station, v.a. 8
estacionamiento (*m.*) parking; parking lot, v.a. 8
estacionar to park, v.a. 8
estado (*m.*) state, v.a. 2
— **civil** marital status, v.a. 13
— **de cuenta** statement of account, v.a. 2
— **de pérdidas y ganancias** profit and loss statement, 11
— **financiero** financial statement, 11
Estados Unidos (*m. pl.*) United States, g. 2
estafa (*f.*) fraud, v.a. 20
estampilla (*f.*) (postage) stamp, v.a. 7
estancia stay, g. 17
estante (*m.*) open cabinet with shelves, 18
estar to be, 3
— **a (su) disposición** to be at (your) disposal, 5
— **acostumbrado(a)** (*i.e.,* to a service) to take for granted, g. 8
— **bien si...** (to be) all right if . . . , 5
— **de acuerdo** to agree, g. 7
— **dispuesto(a) a** to be willing to, 17
— **seguro(a)** to be certain, 6
este(a) this, 5
estenógrafo(a) (*m., f.*) stenographer, shorthand writer, v.a. 20
estimar to estimate; to think, 20
estofado(a) stewed, v.a. 4
estos(as) these, 5
estructura (*f.*) structure, 18
estuco (*m.*) stucco, v.a. 17
estudiante (*m., f.*) student, 16
estudiar to study, 13
etiqueta (*f.*) label, 12
euro (*m.*) currency of the European Union, g. 2
evaluar to evaluate, 11; to assess, 11
evasión fiscal (*f.*) tax evasion, v.a. 13
eventualidad (*f.*) eventuality, 19
evitar to avoid, 1
exactamente exactly, 18
exceder to exceed, 7
excelente excellent, 20
excepto except, 19
exceso de velocidad (*m.*) speeding, 19
exclusión (*f.*) exclusion, v.a. 13
exclusivamente exclusively, 14
exclusivo(a) exclusive, 5
exención (*f.*) exemption, v.a. 13
exigir to require, 14; to demand, 14
éxito (*m.*) success, v.a. 14
expectativa de vida (*f.*) life expectancy, v.a. 19
expedir (e:i) to issue, s. 1
experiencia (*f.*) experience, 10
explicación (*f.*) explanation, g. 15
explicar to explain, 11
explotación (*f.*) exploitation, v.a. 20
exportación (*f.*) export, v.a. 5
exportar to export, 6
expreso(a) express, 9
extender (e:ie) un cheque to write a check, v.a. 15
exterior (*m.*) exterior, g. 17
extracción de dinero withdrawal, v.a. 15
extraer dinero to withdraw money, v.a. 15
extranjero(a) (*m., f.*) foreigner, 2

F

fábrica (*f.*) factory, 6
fabricación (*f.*) manufacture, 5
fabricado(a) manufactured, 5
fabricar to manufacture, 5
fachada (*f.*) façade, 17
fácil easy, g. 10
fácilmente easily, 12
facsímil(e) (*m.*) facsimile, 7; fax, 7
factoría (*f.*) factory, g. p
factura (*f.*) invoice, s. 4
facturar el equipaje to check the luggage, v.a. 1
falda (*f.*) skirt, 14
fallecer to die, 13
falsedad (*f.*) falsehood; untruth, g. 20
faltar to be lacking, 19
familiares (*m. pl.*) relatives, s. 1
farmacia (*f.*) drugstore, v.a. 18
farol (*m.*) light, v.a. 8
favor de (+ *inf.*) please (do something), 1
fax (*m.*) facsimile, 7; fax, 7
fecha (*f.*) date, 2
— **de cierre** closing date, v.a. 11
— **de nacimiento** date of birth, v.a. 2
— **de vencimiento** expiration, date, 3; due date, v.a. 11
— **fija** by a certain date, s. 4
federal federal, 15
fenómeno natural (*m.*) natural phenomenon, 19; act of God, 19
ferretería (*f.*) hardware store, v.a. 18
ferrocarril (*m.*) railroad, 9; train, 9
fiador(a) guarantor, s. 4
fibra (*f.*) fiber, 9
ficha (*f.*) token, v.a. 7
fielmente faithfully, g. 6
figurarse to imagine, 13
fijar to fix, g. 6
fijo(a) fixed, 16
fila (*f.*) row, 1; line, 2
filmar to film, v.a. 14
filme (*m.*) film, v.a. 14
filtro de aire (aceite) (*m.*) air (oil) filter, 6
fin (*m.*) end, 13
— **de semana** weekend, v.a. 14
final final, 11
financiamiento (*m.*) financing, 16
financiar to finance, 16
financiero(a) financial, 11
firma (*f.*) firm, g. p; business, 1; company, 1; signing, g. 5; signature, 2
firmar to sign, 2
fitosanitario(a) phytosanitary, 20
flete (*m.*) freight, 9
florería (*f.*) flowershop, v.a. 18
floristería (*España*) (*f.*) flowershop, v.a. 18
folio (*m.*) folio (page) (*i.e.,* in accounting books), v.a. 11
folleto (*m.*) booklet, 7
fondo (*m.*) down payment, 18
— **mutuo** (*m.*) mutual fund, 13
fondos (*m. pl.*) funds; deposits, v.a. 11
forma (*col.*) (*f.*) form, 13
— **corta (larga)** short (long) form, 13
— **de pago** (*f.*) means of payment, 6
formulario (*m.*) form, s. 1
fotocopiadora (*f.*) photocopier, g. p
frágil fragile, 9
franco a bordo free on board (F.O.B.), v.a. 9
franqueo (*m.*) postage, v.a. 7
frazada (*f.*) blanket, 1
frecuente frequent, g. 2
frecuentemente frequently, 20
freno (*m.*) brake, 6
frente a (*f.*) in front of, 8
fresco(a) fresh, 4
frijol (*m.*) bean, 4
frívolo(a) frivolous, g. p
frito(a) fried, v.a. 4
frontera (*f.*) border, 9; frontier, 9
fuego (*m.*) fire, 19
fuerte strong, 4
fuerza mayor (*f.*) natural phenomenon, 19; act of God, 19
fumar to smoke, 1
funcionar to work, 3
futuro (*m.*) future, g. 16

G

gabinete (*m.*) cabinet, v.a. 17
galleta (*f.*) cookie, 18
galletica (*f.*) cookie, 18
galletita (*f.*) cookie, 18
gamba (*f.*) shrimp (*España*), v.a. 4
ganancia (*f.*) profit, 11; earnings, 11

H

I

insolvente insolvent, v.a. 16
inspección (*f.*) inspection, 17
inspeccionar to inspect, v.a. 17
inspector(a) (*m., f.*) inspector, 2
instalado(a) installed, 14; available, 14
instantáneo(a) instant, 4
institución (*f.*) institution, 13
instrumentos de crédito (*m. pl.*) credit documents, s. 4
íntegro(a) entire, complete, s. 4
intensivo(a) intensive, g. 11
intercambio (*m.*) interchange, g. 9
intercomunicador (*m.*) intercom, 5
interés (*m.*) interest, g. p
— **simple (compuesto)** simple (compound) interest, v.a. 16
interesado(a) interested, 5
interesar to interest, 18
interior interior, 3
internacional international, 7
Internet (*f.*) Internet, 7
interurbano(a) inner cities, g. 8
introducción de datos (*f.*) data entry, 10
introducir to introduce, 14
inundación (*f.*) flood, 19
invalidez (*f.*) disability; disablement, v.a. 19
inventario (*m.*) inventory, v.a. 11
inversión (*f.*) investment, 12
invertir (e:ie) to invest, 10
investigar to investigate, 18
invierno (*m.*) winter, 14
invitación (*f.*) invitation, 13
invitar to invite, g. 20
ir to go, 3
— **a (+ *inf.*)** to be going (to do something), 3
— **por su cuenta** to be paid by you, 6
irse to leave, l. 6
— **se fue** left, l. 6
itinerario (*m.*) itinerary, v.a. 9

J

jabón (*m.*) soap, v.a. 3
jamás never, g. 15
jardín (*m.*) garden, 17
jefe(a) (*m.,f.*) boss, 5
— **de compras** purchasing manager, p
— **de familia** head of household, s. 1
— **de ventas** sales manager, 5
jornada (*f.*) working hours, day's work, s. 4
jornal (*m.*) daily wage(s), v.a. 10
joven young, 19
joyería (*f.*) jewelry store, v.a. 18
jubilación (*f.*) retirement, 10
jueves (*m.*) Thursday, 1
juguetería (*f.*) toy shop, 18
junta (*f.*) meeting, 5

K

kilo (*m.*) kilogram, 7
kilogramo (*m.*) kilogram, 7
kilómetro (*m.*) kilometer, 3

L

La línea está ocupada. The line is busy., p
la mayor parte the majority, 17; most, 17
la que that which, what
lado (*m.*) side, 18
ladrillo (*m.*) brick, v.a. 17
lamentablemente regrettably, 20
lamentar to be sorry for, 3; to regret, 3
lámpara (*f.*) lamp, v.a. 17
lana (*f.*) wool, 9
langosta (*f.*) lobster, v.a. 4
lápiz (*m.*) pencil, v.a. 10
larga distancia (*f.*) long distance, 7
largo (*m.*) length, 7
largo(a) long, 20
las de those, 6
las demás the rest, the others, 9
las nuestras ours, 6
lavabo (*m.*) bathroom sink, v.a. 3
lavadora (*f.*) washing machine, v.a. 17
— **de platos** dishwasher, 17
lavandería (*f.*) laundry, v.a. 18
lavaplatos (*m.*) dishwasher, 17
leche (*f.*) milk, 4
lechuga (*f.*) lettuce, v.a. 4
lectura (*f.*) reading, g. 1
leer to read, 4
legado (*m.*) bequest, 13
legal legal, 16
lejos (de) far (from), 7
lema (*m.*) slogan, 14
lempira (*m.*) currency of Honduras, g. 2
lenguado (*m.*) sole, 4
lesión (*f.*) injury, 19
letra de cambio (*f.*) bill of exchange, s. 4
ley (*f.*) law, g. 12
libra (*f.*) pound, 7
libre free, 20
— **juego** (*m.*) fair play, g. 20
libre de derechos (impuestos) duty-free, v.a. 2
— **a bordo (L.A.B.)** free on board (F.O.B.), v.a. 9
libro (*m.*) book, g. 1
— **de actas** minute book, v.a. 11
— **de caja** cash book, v.a. 11
— **de ventas** sales book, v.a. 11
— **diario** journal, 11
— **mayor** general ledger, 11
— **talonario** (*Spain*) checkbook, v.a. 15
licencia (*f.*) license, 8
liga (*f.*) rubber band (*Méx., Cuba*), v.a. 10
limpiaparabrisas (*m.*) windshield wiper, v.a. 6
limpio(a) clean, v.a. 3
lindo(a) beautiful, 17
línea (*f.*) line, 6
— **está ocupada** line is busy, p
linóleo (*m.*) linoleum, 17
liquidar to liquidate; to pay off, v.a. 11
liquidez (*f.*) liquidity, v.a. 16
líquido (*m.*) liquid, v.a. 6
— **de frenos** brake fluid, v.a. 6
— **de la transmisión** transmission fluid, v.a. 8

lista (*f.*) list, 6
listo(a) ready, 3
literatura (*f.*) literature, 19
llamada (*f.*) call, 7
— **a cobrar** collect call, v.a. 7
— **de larga distancia** long-distance call, 7
llamar to call, 2
Me llamo... My name is . . . , 3
llanta (*f.*) tire, v.a. 6
llave (*f.*) key, 3
llegar (a) to arrive (in), 1
llenar to fill out (a form), 1
— **los requisitos** to qualify, v.a. 10
lleno(a) full, 8
llevar to take (someone or something someplace), 2; to carry, 9
— **a cabo** to take place, g. 8
— **la contabilidad** to keep the books, 11
lo (la) it, 7
— **contrario** just the opposite, 20
— **mejor** the best thing
— **que** that which, 5
— **siento** I'm sorry, p
— **único** the only thing, 17
local (*adj.*) local, 6; commercial space, 18
logo(grama) (*m.*) logo, 14
lograr to succeed, to attain, g. 17
— **ponerse de acuerdo** to reach an agreement, g. 9
los the, g. p
los (las) de allá those over there, 20
— **de aquí** those here, 20
— **hacen** make them, v.a. 20
— **otros(as)** the others, 20
— **que** those who, g. 20
los demás the rest, 9; the others, 9
los nuestros ours, 6
losa (*f.*) tile, 17
lubricación (*f.*) lubrication, v.a. 6
luego then, later 1
lugar (*m.*) place, 18
lujo (*m.*) luxury, g. 6
lunes (*m.*) Monday, 6
luz (*f.*) light, v.a. 6

M

madera (*f.*) wood, v.a. 17
madre (*f.*) mother, 16
¡magnífico! great!, 7; magnificent, 7
maíz (*m.*) corn, v.a. 4
maleta (*f.*) suitcase, 2
maletero(a) (*m., f.*) car trunk, v.a. 6; porter, 2; skycap, 2
maletín de mano (*m.*) handbag, 2; carry-on bag, 2
malgastar to waste, l. 12
malo(a) bad, 5
manchado(a) stained, 17
mandar to send, 7
manejar to drive, 8; to operate; to manage, g. 15
— **bajo los efectos del alcohol (de las drogas)** driving while intoxicated, v.a. 20

Manifiesto Comunista (*m.*) Communist Manifesto, v.a. 20
mano de obra (*f.*) labor, g. 5
manta (*f.*) blanket, 1
mantener to keep, 15
mantenimiento adecuado (*m.*) adequate maintenance, g. 8
manual del usuario (dueño) (*m.*) user's (owner's) manual
manufacturero(a) manufacturing, g. 11
mañana tomorrow, 1; morning (*f.*), 10
máquina (*f.*) car (*Cuba*), 6; machine, 12
— **contestadora** (*f.*) answering machine, 10
— **copiadora** (*f.*) copying machine, v.a. 10
— **de escribir** (*f.*) typewriter, v.a. 10
marca (*f.*) brand, 6
— **de fábrica** manufacturer's trademark, v.a. 5
— **registrada** trademark, trade name, 14
marcado(a) marked, 5
marcador (*m.*) marker, v.a. 10
marcar to dial, 7; to mark, 8; to indicate, 8
marisco (*m.*) seafood, 4; shellfish, 4
mármol (*m.*) marble, v.a. 17
más plus, 3; further, g. 1
— **de** more than, g. 16
— **fácil** easier, g. 5
— **o menos** more or less, 3
— **tarde** later, 9
masivo(a) massive, 14
matasellos (*m.*) postmark, v.a. 7
materia prima (*f.*) raw material, v.a. 5
material (*m.*) material, 10
matrícula (*f.*) registration, 16; registration fees, 16
matrimonio (*m.*) marriage
mayor larger, s. 2; grown up 5; older, 19
— **de edad** of age, 13
la — parte the majority, 8
mayoría (*f.*) majority, g. 3
mayorista (*m., f.*) wholesaler, 10
mazorca de maíz tierno (*f.*) ear of fresh corn, v.a. 4
Me llamo My name is, 3
Me parece It looks to me, 20
Me temo que... I'm afraid that . . . , 12
media jornada part-time, 13
mediano(a) medium, 8
mediante through, 12; by means of, 12
medicamento (*m.*) medicine, 2; drug, 2
medicina (*f.*) medicine, 2; drug, 2
médico(a) medical, 13
medida (*f.*) measure, 7; measurement, 7; dimension, 7
medio(a) half, 2
medio (*m.*) middle, g. 3
medio publicitario advertising media, v.a. 14
medio tiempo part-time, 13
medios (*m. pl.*) means, 7; system, 7
— **de comunicación** media, 7
— **de transporte** means of transportation, 8
— **publicitarios** advertising, v.a. 14
medir (e:i) to measure, 7
mejor better, 4
mejorar to improve, 14
membrete (*m.*) letterhead, v.a. 7
memorando (*m.*) memorandum, memo, s. 3
memoria (*f.*) memory, v.a. 7
mencionar to mention, 10
menor less, 7
— **de edad** minor, 13
menos de less than, 4
mensaje (*m.*) message, 10
mensual monthly, v.a. 10
mensualmente monthly, 17
menú (*m.*) menu, 4
menudeo (*m.*) retail, 5
menudo (*m.*) small change (*Cuba*), v.a. 15
mercadería (*f.*) merchandise, 6
mercado (*m.*) market, 5
mercancía (*f.*) merchandise, g. p
mercancías (*f. pl.*) goods, v.a. 2
mero (*m.*) halibut, 4
mes (*m.*) month, 10
al — monthly, 14
mesa (*f.*) table, 4
mesero(a) (*m., f.*) waiter (waitress), 4
mesonero(a) (*Ven.*) waiter (waitress), 4
metro (*m.*) meter, 9; subway, g. 8
mexicano(a) Mexican, 1
México Mexico, 1
mi (mis) my, 2
microonda (*f.*) microwave, 17
mil one thousand, 17
millardo (*m.*) billion, g. 11
mínimo (*m.*) minimum, 17
minoría (*f.*) minority, g. 6
minorista (*m., f.*) retailer, 10
minuto (*m.*) minute, 1
mirar to look at, 2
miscelánea (*f.*) miscellany, v.a. 13
mismo(a) same, 15
ella — herself, 8
mixto(a) mixed, 4
mochila (*f.*) backpack, s. 4
modelo (*m.*) model, 5
módem (*m.*) modem, v.a. 12
modernizar modernize, 11
modo (*m.*) way, g. 4
molestar(se) to bother, 18
momento (*m.*) moment, 5
moneda (*f.*) currency; coin, v.a. 2
— **falsa** counterfeit coin, v.a. 15
— **fraccionaria** small change, v.a. 15
monte de piedad (*m.*) pawnshop, v.a. 18
montepío (*m.*) pawnshop, v.a. 18
monitor (*m.*) monitor, 2
mordida (*f.*) bite, g. 2; bribe (*Méx.*), g. 2
morir(se) (o:ue) to die, 13
mostrador (*m.*) counter, 1
mostrar (o:ue) to show, 8; to exhibit, g. 7
motín (*m.*) riot, 19
motivo (*m.*) reason, 19
motor (*m.*) motor, engine, v.a. 6
— **de arranque** starter, v.a. 6
móvil (*m.*) cellular telephone, v.a. 2
movimiento (*m.*) movement, g. 8
mozo(a) (*m., f.*) waiter (waitress), 4
muchas gracias thank you very much, p
mucho(a) much, 3
Mucho gusto en conocerlo(a). Pleased to meet you., 10
muchos(as) many, 4
mudarse to move (relocate), 15
mueblería (*f.*) furniture factory or store, v.a. 18
muebles (*m. pl.*) furniture, 13
muerte (*f.*) death, 19
muestra (*f.*) sample, 7
mujer (*f.*) woman, 3
— **de negocios** businesswoman, 3
multa (*f.*) fine, v.a. 13; ticket, 19; penalty, v.a. 13
multinacionales (*f., pl.*) transnational (multinational) companies, 20
mundo (*m.*) world, 9
— **de las empresas** corporate world, r. 1
a todo el — the world over, 9
municipal municipal, 13
muy very, 3
— **bien** very well, p

N

nacimiento (*m.*) birth. v.a. 2
nacional national, 9
nada nothing, 3
— **más** nothing else, 3
nadie no one, 6
navegar la red to surf the Web, v.a. 12
necesario(a) necessary, 12; needed, 12
necesidad (*f.*) necessity, 11; need, 11
necesitar to need, 1
negar (e:ie) to deny, 16
negociante (*m., f.*) businessperson, g. 13
negociar to negociate, 17
negocio(s) (*m.*) business, 1
neumático (*m.*) tire, v.a. 6
nevada (*f.*) snowstorm, 19
nevera (*f.*) refrigerator, v.a. 17
ni neither, nor, 6
— **...ni** neither . . . nor, g. 11
ni ... tampoco not either, 13; neither, 13
ningún (ninguno/a) none, 6
niño (*m.*) child, 5
nivel (*m.*) level, 17
no no, g. 1
no ha lugar the petition is not granted, v.a. 20
no obstante nevertheless, s. 2
nombre (*m.*) name, p
nómina (*f.*) payroll, 11
norma (*f.*) rule, l. 12
nos to us, 7
notablemente notably, 14
novio(a) (*m., f.*) fiancé(e), 16; boyfriend, 16; girlfriend, 16
nuestro(a) our, 2
nuevo(a) new, g. 9
nuevo sol (*m.*) currency of Peru, g. 2
número (*m.*) number, 1
— **de teléfono** (*m.*) telephone number, p
nunca never, 14

O

o or, 1
obligar to compel, g. 12
obrero(a) worker, g. 14
— **no calificado(a)** unqualified worker, g. 19
obsoleto(a) obsolete, 12
obtener to obtain, 13; to get, 13
ocupado(a) busy, 5
ocupar to occupy, g. 4
ocuparse de to deal with, 20
ocurrir to happen, v.a. 2; to occur, 9
oferta (*f.*) offer, 6; bid, 6; deal, 6; supply, v.a. 20
oficial de banco (*m., f.*) bank officer, 16
oficina (*f.*) office, g. p
— **de correos** post office, 7
— **principal** main office (*Puerto Rico*), v.a. 15
oficinista (*m., f.*) office clerk, 10
ofrecer to have available, 7
¡Ojalá! I hope, 17; if only, 17
omiso(a) omitted, s. 4
ómnibus (*m.*) bus, 8
opción (*f.*) option, 10
operación (*f.*) operation, 12
operador(a) (*m., f.*) operator, 7
operar to operate, g. p
oponerse to oppose, 20
opositor(a) opponent, v.a. 20
orden (*f.*) order, 5
— **de compra** (*f.*) purchase order
ordenador (*m.*) computer (*España*), 2
— **portátil** (*m.*) laptop computer, 2
ordenar to order, 6
Organización de Mantenimiento de la Salud Health Maintenance Organization (HMO), g. 10
organizar to organize, 14
origen (*m.*) origin, 14
oro (*m.*) gold, g. p
otorgar to issue, s. 4
otra vez again, 12
otro(a) other, another, 1

P

padre (*m.*) father, 16
padres (*m. pl.*) parents, 16
pagar to pay, 2
— **a plazos** to pay in installments, v.a. 5
— **al contado** to pay in cash, v.a. 5
— **exceso de equipaje** to pay excess luggage
pagaré (*m.*) promissory note, I.O.U., 4
página de la Web (*f.*) Web page, v.a. 12
páginas amarillas (*f. pl.*) Yellow Pages, v.a. 14
pago (*m.*) payment, 16
— **inicial** down payment, 16
país (*m.*) country, v.a. 2
países en desarrollo developing countries, g. 11
palabra (*f.*) word, g. p
pan (*m.*) bread, 4
— **francés** french toast (*Méx.*), g. 4
— **tostado** toast, 4
panadería (*f.*) bakery, v.a. 18
pantalones (*m., pl.*) trousers, 14
— **de vaqueros (de mezclilla)** jeans, 14
pantalla (*f.*) screen, v.a. 12
papa (*f.*) potato, v.a. 4
papel (*m.*) paper, l. 12
— **de cartas** stationery, v.a. 3
— **higiénico** toilet paper, v.a. 3
paquete (*m.*) package, 7
para to, 1; for, 1; in order to, 1
— **conversar** to talk, g. 1
— **que** so that, 19
— **servirle** at your service, p
— **uso personal** for personal use, 2
parabrisas (*m.*) windshield, v.a. 6
parachoques (*m.*) bumper, v.a. 6
parada (*f.*) (bus) stop, 8
— **de autobuses** bus stop, v.a. 2
— **de camiones** (*Méx.*) bus stop, v.a. 2
— **de taxis** taxi stop, 2
parar to stop, v.a. 8
parecer to look like, 12; to seem, 12
pargo (*m.*) red snapper, 4
parquímetro (*m.*) parking meter, v.a. 8
participar to participate, to give notice, s. 3
pasado(a) last, 10; past, 10
pasaje (*m.*) ticket, 1
— **de ida** one-way ticket, 1
— **de ida y vuelta** round-trip ticket, 1
pasajero(a) (*m., f.*) passenger, 1
pasaporte (*m.*) passport, 2
pasar to come in, p; to pass, 2; to go through 2; to happen
— **a ser** to become, l. 6
— **al mayor** to enter in the ledger, v.a. 11
Pase. Come in., p
pase (*m.*) entry; pass, 16
— **al mayor** general ledger entry, 11
— **de abordar** boarding pass, v.a. 1
pasivo (*m.*) liabilities, v.a. 11
paso (*m.*) step, 15
un — más one step further, g. 1
pastilla (*f.*) microchip, v.a. 12
pasto (*m.*) lawn, 17; grass, 17
patata (*f.*) potato, v.a. 4
patente (*f.*) patent, 14
patio (*m.*) patio, yard, v.a. 17
pato (*m.*) duck, v.a. 4
patria (*f.*) country, fatherland, g. 4
patrón(ona) (*m., f.*) employer, 13
pavo (*m.*) turkey, v.a. 4
paz (*f.*) peace, g. 20
pedido (*m.*) order, 5; purchase order, s. 2
pedir (e:i) to ask for, 7
— **prestado** to borrow, g. 15
pegar to hit, 20
película (*f.*) film, v.a. 14
peligroso(a) risky, g. 8
peluquería (*f.*) beauty parlor, v.a. 18; salon, v.a. 18
penetrar to penetrate, to enter (*i.e., a market*), 6
pensar (en) (e:ie) to think (about), g. 17; to plan, 9
pensión (*f.*) boarding house; g. 3 pension, 13
— **alimenticia** alimony, v.a. 13
pequeño(a) small, 2
perder (e:ie) to lose, 15
pérdida (*f.*) loss, 11
perdón pardon me, excuse me, 2
perdonar to forgive, 11
perdone excuse me, 11
¡perfecto! perfect!, 1
perfumería (*f.*) perfume store, v.a. 18
periférico (*m.*) peripheral (device), v.a. 12
periódicamente periodically, 11
periódico (*m.*) newspaper, 1
perjuicio (*m.*) damage, 20
permitir to allow, g. 19
pero but, 2
persona (*f.*) person, 3
personal (*m.*) personnel, 10; (*adj.*) personal, 12
personalizado(a) personalized, 12
pertenecer to belong, s. 4
pesar to weigh, 7
pescadería (*f.*) fish market, v.a. 18
pescado (*m.*) fish, 4
peseta (*f.*) currency of Spain, g. p
peso (*m.*) currency of several Latin American countries, g. 2; weight, 7
— **bruto** gross weight, v.a. 9
— **muerto** dead weight, v.a. 9
— **neto** net weight, v.a. 9
petrolero(a) oil (*adj.*), g. 6
pie (*m.*) **(cuadrado)** (square) foot, 18
piedra (*f.*) stone, 17
pieza (*f.*) piece, 5; part, 6
pinchado(a) flat (tire), v.a. 8
pintado(a) painted, 17
piscina (*f.*) swimming pool, v.a. 17
piso (*m.*) floor, 3
pito (*m.*) horn, klaxon, v.a. 6
pizarra (*f.*) bulletin board, v.a. 10
plan (*m.*) plan, g. p
planilla (*f.*) form, 13
— **de contribución sobre ingresos** tax return (*Puerto Rico*), 13
planta (*f.*) plant,
— **alta** upstairs, v.a. 2
— **baja** ground floor, 2; downstairs, 2
plástico (*m.*) plastic, 14
platillo (*Méx.*) dish, g. 4
plazo (*m.*) term, installment, s. 3
población (*f.*) people, g. 3
pobre poor, g. 3
pocas veces not frequently, 6
poco a little, 6
— **tiempo** a short time, g. 4
un — a little, 9
pocos(as) a few, g. 3
poder (o:ue) can, 6; to be able, 6; may, g. 2
poderoso(a) powerful, v.a. 12
policía (*f.*) police department; (*m., f.*) police officer, v.a. 20
póliza (*f.*) policy, 19
pollo (*m.*) chicken, v.a. 4
ponchado(a) (*col.*) flat (*tire*), v.a. 8

poner to put, 10
  — a la venta to put up for sale, 17
  — en vigor to enact, 20
  — un negocio to set up a business, 16
popular popular, 4
por by, 1; on, 1; through, 1; for, 3
  — adelantado in advance, 18
  — aquí this way, 3
  — ciento percent, 5
  — cierto by the way, 12
  — concepto (de) referring to (a specific item), 12; regarding, 12
  — cualquier motivo for any reason, 19
  — detrás from behind
  — día per day, 3
  — ejemplo for example, 14
  — escrito in writing, s. 4
  — ese motivo that is why, g. 6
  — favor please, p
  — fuera (from) the outside, 17
  — la mañana in the morning, 1
  — otra parte in addition, s. 2
  ¿— qué? why? 6
  — supuesto of course, 15
  — último finally, lastly, 7
  — vía aérea (férrea, marítima) by air (rail, boat), v.a. 9
porque because, 6
portátil portable, 2
porte (*m.*) postage, v.a. 7
  — debido postage due, v.a. 7
  — pagado postage paid, v.a. 7
posdata (*f.*) postscript, s. 2
posible possible, 12
posición (*f.*) job, 10; post, 10; position, 10
positivo(a) positive
postre (*m.*) dessert 4
postulante (*m., f.*) applicant, 10
practicar to practice, g. p
precedido(a) preceded, 14
precio (*m.*) price, 5
  — de compra purchase price, v.a. 5
  — de venta selling price, v.a. 5
precisamente precisely, 19; exactly, 19
preferible preferable, 20
preferir (e:ie) to prefer, 5
pregunta (*f.*) question, 7
preguntar to ask, 10
preguntarse to wonder, 9; to ask oneself, 9
premio (*m.*) prize, 13
prenda de vestir (*f.*) garment, 5; clothing, 5
prender la luz to turn on the light, v.a. 3
preocuparse to worry, g. 16
preparación (*f.*) qualification, v.a. 10
preparado(a) qualified, g. 18
preparar to prepare, g. 4
presencia (*f.*) presence, g. 10
presentación (*f.*) presentation, 14; appearance, 14
presentar to present, 14
presilla (*f.*) staple (*Cuba*), v.a. 10; paper clip (*Cuba*), v.a. 10
presilladora (*f.*) stapler (*Cuba*), v.a. 10
prestaciones adicionales (*f.*) fringe benefit, 10
prestamista (*m.*) lender; pawnbroker, 16
préstamo (*m.*) loan, 13
prestar to lend, 18
presupuesto (*m.*) estimate, 12; budget, 12
prima (*f.*) premium, 19
primer(o)(a) first, 5
primero first, 2
principalmente principally, 14; mostly, 14
principio (*m.*) beginning, g. 9
privado(a) private, 7
probabilidad de vida (*f.*) life expectancy, v.a. 19
probador (*m.*) fitting room, 18
probar (o:ue) to taste, 20
problema (*m.*) problem, 11
procesamiento de textos (*m.*) word processing, 10
proceso (*m.*) process, 20
producción (*f.*) production, 20
producir to manufacture, 5
producto (*m.*) product, g. p
profesional (*m., f.*) professional, 17
profesionista (*m., f.*) professional, 17
programa (*m.*) program, g. p; software, v.a. 12
  — de manejo (administración) (de base) de datos (*m.*) database management program, 10
programador(a) (*m., f.*) programmer, v.a. 12
prohibido(a) forbidden, v.a. 1
prolongar to prolong, 20
promedio (*m.*) average, 15
promover (o:ue) to promote, g. 5
propaganda (*f.*) advertisement, 7; advertising, 14; publicity, 14
propiedad (*f.*) property, 17
propietario(a) (*m., f.*) owner, 16
propina (*f.*) tip, 4
propio(a) own, g, 5
protección del medio ambiente (*f.*) environmental protection, 20
proteccionismo (*m.*) protectionism, 20
proteger protect, 20
proveedor(a) (*m., f.*) supplier, 6; provider, 6
provenir to come from, g. 19
proximidad (*f.*) proximity, 18
próximo(a) next, 6
prueba (*f.*) proof, 13
publicar to publish, v.a. 14
publicidad (*f.*) advertising, 14; publicity, 14
pueblo (*m.*) town, 8
puerta (*f.*) door, 1; gate, 1
pues because, 7; since, 7
puerco (*m.*) pork, v.a. 4
puesto (*m.*) job, 10; post, 10; position, 10
  — desempeñado position held
punto (*m.*) point, v.a. 17
  — de vista (*m.*) point of view, v.a. 20

Q

que than, 4; that, g. 2; which, 5
  — pasa passing by, 2
¡qué...! how . . . !, 18
¿qué? what, 1; which, 1
  ¿— hora es? What time is it?, 1
  ¿— se le ofrece? What can I do for you?, 9
  ¿— será de...? What will become of . . . ?, 19
quebrar (e:ie) to go bankrupt, 15
quedar to be located, 2
  — se (con) to take, 18; to keep, 18
querer (e:ie) to want, 5; to wish, 5
quetzal (*m.*) currency of Guatemala, g. 2
quiebra (*f.*) bankruptcy, 15; insolvency, 15
¿quién(es)? who?, v.a. 1
quincenal biweekly; every two weeks, v.a. 10
quizás maybe, g. 19

R

radiador (*m.*) radiator, v.a. 8
radio (*f.*) radio, 14
  — de batería (de pilas) battery-operated radio, v.a. 2
rastra (*Cuba*) (*f.*) trailer
ratón (*m.*) mouse, v.a. 12
razón (*f.*) reason
razón social (*f.*) trade name, s. 3
realidad (*f.*) reality, g. 4
rebajar to reduce, 12; to diminish, 12
recado (*m.*) message, 10
recalentarse (e:ie) to overheat, v.a. 8
recámara (*f.*) room (*Méx.*), 3
  — principal master bedroom, v.a. 17
recargo adicional (*m.*) additional charge, v.a. 13
recaudar to collect, g. 13
recepción (*f.*) reception desk, 3; front desk, 3
recepcionista (*m., f.*) receptionist, g. p
recibido(a) received, 13
recibir to receive, 6
recibo (*m.*) receipt, 13
recién recently, 16; newly, 16
reciente recently, 20
recientemente recently, 17
reclamación (*f.*) claim, v.a. 19
reclinar to recline, v.a. 1
recomendar (e:ie) to recommend, 7
recordar (o:ue) to remember, g. 19
recursos (*m. pl.*) resources, g. 12
red (*f.*) Internet, 7; Web, v.a. 12
  redes ferroviarias railroad lines, g. 8
redactar to write, to compose, 20
reembolso (*m.*) refund, 13; reimbursement; v.a. 13
referencia (*f.*) reference, 10
reflejar to reflex, g. 6
refrigerador (*m.*) refrigerator, v.a. 17
  — empotrado built-in refrigerator, v.a. 17
regadera (*Méx.*) shower, 3
regalo (*m.*) gift, 13
regatear to bargain, g. 1
regido(a) to be in force, s. 4
registrar to record, 12; to key into (a computer), 12; to file, v.a. 13
regresar to return, 1; to come (go) back, 1

regulación (*f.*) regulation, 7
regular to regulate, g. 12
relación (*f.*) relation, 9
relacionado(a) related, 17
reloj (*m.*) clock, v.a. 10; watch, v.a. 10
rellenar to fill out (*a form*), 1
relleno(a) stuffed, v.a. 4
remarcador del último número (*m.*) last number redial, v.a. 7
remitente (*m., f.*) sender, v.a. 7
remodelar to remodel, 17
remolcador (*m.*) tow truck, v.a. 8
rendimiento (*m.*) yield, v.a. 16
rendir (e:i) informe to report, 12; to give an account, 12
renglón (*m.*) line (*on paper*), v.a. 13; line (*of merchandise*), 14; item, v.a. 13
renta (*f.*) revenue, 13; income, 13
— **vitalicia** life annuity, v.a. 19
rentar (*col.*) to rent, 8
renunciar (a) to resign (from), 10
reo (*m., f.*) defendant (*in a criminal case*), v.a. 20
reorganizar to reorganize, 11
reparación (*f.*) repair, 6
taller de — (*m.*) repair shop, 6
reparar to repair, v.a. 8; to fix, 20
reportar to report, v.a. 13
representar to represent, 11
República de Chile (*f.*) Republic of Chile, 20
República Dominicana (*f.*) Dominican Republic, 14
repuesto (*m.*) spare part, 6
requerir (e:ie) to require, g. 14
requisito (*m.*) requirement, g. 9
rescate (*m.*) surrender value, v.a. 19
reserva (*f.*) reservation, v.a. 1
reservación (*f.*) reservation, g. p
reservar to reserve, 1
resolver (o:ue) to solve, g. 14
responsabilidad (*f.*) responsibility, 19
— **civil** liability, 19
reponsabilizarse to take responsibility for, 9
responsable responsible, 19
respuesta (*f.*) answer, 10
restaurante (*m.*) restaurant, g. p
restitución (*f.*) restitution, 19
resto (*m.*) rest, g. 13
restorán (*m.*) restaurant, 4
resumé (*m.*) résumé, v.a. 10
resumen (*m.*) résumé, v.a. 10
retirar dinero to withdraw money, v.a. 15
retiro (*m.*) retirement, 10
— **(de dinero)** withdrawal, v.a. 15
reunión (*f.*) meeting, 5
reunir los requisitos to qualify, v.a. 10
revisar to check, v.a. 8
revista (*f.*) magazine, 1
rico(a) rich, g. 11
riego automático (*m.*) automatic sprinkler, v. 17
riesgo (*m.*) risk, 9
robo (*m.*) theft, 19; burglary, 19; robbery, 19
rojo(a) red, 19
ropa (*f.*) clothing, 5; clothes, 5
— **hecha** ready-made clothes, g. 14
rotura (*f.*) breakage, 9
rudimentario(a) rudimentary, 12
ruido (*m.*) noise, 3
ruta (*f.*) route, 8

S

sábana (*f.*) sheet, v.a. 3
saber to know, 7
sacar to take out, to withdraw, v.a. 15
— **el dinero** to withdraw money, v.a. 15
— **la cuenta** to add up, 18
sacrificar to sacrifice, 17
sala (*f.*) living room, 17
— **de estar** family room, 17
salario (*m.*) salary, 10
saldo (*m.*) balance, v.a. 11
salida (*f.*) departure, 1; exit, 1
salir to leave, 11; to go out, 11
salmón (*m.*) salmon, 4
salón (*m.*) salon, 5
— **de belleza** beauty parlor; salon, v.a. 18
— **de estar** family room, 17
— **de exhibición** showroom, 5; exhibition hall, 5
salsa (*f.*) sauce, 4
salud (*f.*) health, 10
saludar to greet, 8; to say hello, 8
saludo (*m.*) greeting; salutation, g. p
salvapantallas (*m., pl.*) screensaver, v.a. 12
salvavidas (*m.*) life preserver, v.a. 1
sanitario(a) sanitary, 20
satisfecho(a) satisfied, 6
saya (*f.*) skirt, 14
se alquila for rent, v.a. 17
se dice is said, g. 10
se ha hecho has become, t. 4
se invierte is invested, 10
Se lo puedo dejar en... I can give it to you for . . . , 8
se mueve is moved, g. 9
se otorga is stipulated, s. 4
Se trata de... It is a question of . . . , 9
se vende for sale, 17
secadora (*f.*) dryer, v.a. 17
sección (*f.*) section, 1
secretario(a) (*m., f.*) secretary, 11
seguir (e:i) to continue, 11
según as, 12; according to, 6; depending on, 6
— **se reciben** as they are received (come in), 12
seguro (*m.*) insurance, 19
— **colectivo** group insurance, v.a. 19
— **de accidentes de trabajo** workers' compensation insurance, v.a. 19
— **de grupo** group insurance, v.a. 19
— **de salud** health insurance, v.a. 19
— **de vida** life insurance, 19
— **dotal** endowment insurance, v.a. 19
— **social** Social Security, 12
seleccionar to select, 5
sello (*m.*) (postage) stamp, v.a. 7
semáforo (*m.*) traffic light, 20
semana (*f.*) week, 10
semanal weekly, 10
sencillo(a) simple l. 12
sentar(e:ie) to enter accounting, s. 4
sentarse (e:ie) to sit down, 15
sentencia (*f.*) sentence, v.a. 20; decision, v.a. 20
sentir (e:ie) to regret, to be sorry, 17; to feel, g. 18
señal de parada (*f.*) stop sign, 19
señor (Sr.) (*m.*) Mr., p; sir, p; gentleman, p
señora (Sra.) (*f.*) Mrs., p; lady, p; Ma'am, p; Madam, p
señorita (Srta.) (*f.*) Miss, p; young lady, p
separado(a) separate, v.a. 13
ser to be, p
— **peligroso,** to be dangerous, g. 8
— **puntual** to be on time, g. 10
— **(una) lástima** to be a pity, 17
serio(a) (*col.*) serious
servicio (*m.*) service, 7; bathroom (toilet), v.a. 1
— **de habitación** room service, v.a. 3
— **de correo y paquetería privado** private courier, v.a. 7
servir (e:i) to serve, 11
— **(de)** to be (a), g. 1; to serve (as), g. 20
para servirle at your service, p
sesión (*f.*) session, 20
si if, g. 1
si es posible if possible, 5
sí yes, 1
siempre always, 6
sigla (*f.*) abbreviation in initials, g. 5
silenciador (*m.*) muffler, 6
silla (*f.*) chair, v.a. 10
simple simple, 20
sin without, 7
— **embargo** nevertheless, g. 7
— **perjuicio de** not affecting, s. 4
— **remedio** without hope, 20
sindicato (*m.*) union (worker's), s. 4
sino but, g. 16
sirva de... be a(n) . . . , g. 1
sírvase please, s. 3
sistema (*m.*) system, g. p
— **de riego automático** automatic sprinkler system, v.a. 17
— **de suspensión** suspension system, 6
— **operativo** operating system, 10
— **tributario** tax system, g. 13
sistemático(a) systematic, g. p
situación (*f.*) situation, g. p
situado(a) situated, 3
soborno (*m.*) bribe, v.a. 20
sobre about, 7; on, 13; above, 18; over, 18; (*m.*) envelope, v.a. 7
sobregiro (*m.*) overdraft, v.a. 15
sobrepasar to surpass, 14
socialista (*m., f.*) socialist, v.a. 20
sociedad (*f.*) society, g. 4
— **Anónima (S.A.)** corporation, 5
— **Cooperativa** cooperative, g. 12
— **de Beneficios Mutuos** mutual benefit company, g. 12
— **en Comandita** joint stock company, g. 12

— **Limitada (de Responsabilidad Limitada) (S.R.L.)** Limited Liability Company, s. 4
— **Regular Colectiva (en Nombre Colectivo)** general partnership, g. 12
socio(a) (*m., f.*) partner, 13
— **comanditario** silent or nominal partner, g. 12
socios solidarios joint liable partners, g. 12
sofisticado(a) sophisticated, 12
solamente only, 1
solicitante (*m., f.*) applicant, v.a. 15
solicitar to ask for, 10; to apply for, 10
solicitud (*f.*) application, 10
solo(a) alone, 14
sólo only, 1
soltero(a) single, p
Son las (+ *time*) It's (+ *time*), 1
sondeo de la opinión pública (*m.*) poll, v.a. 14; survey, v.a. 14
soplado(a) blown, 9
soporte (*m.*) support, v.a. 12
— **físico** hardware, v.a. 12
— **lógico** software, v.a. 12
su(s) your, his, her, their, 2
subir to go up, 2
subscriptor(a) (insurance) policyholder, v.a. 19
subsidiar subsidize, 20
subtotal (*m.*) subtotal, v.a. 13
suceder to happen, 9
sucio(a) dirty, v.a. 3
sucre (*m.*) currency of Ecuador, g. p
sucursal (*f.*) branch, v.a. 15
sueldo (*m.*) salary, 10
suelto (*m.*) small change (*Puerto Rico*), v.a. 15
sueño (*m.*) dream, g. 18
suficiente sufficient, 13; enough, 13
sufrimiento (*m.*) suffering, 20
sufrir to suffer, 11
sugerente catchy; suggestive, v.a. 14
sugerir (e:ie) to suggest, 16
sugestivo(a) catchy; suggestive, v.a. 14
suicidio (*m.*) suicide, 19
sujetapapeles (*m.*) paper clip, v.a. 10
sumar to add up, g. 15
suministrador(a) (*m., f.*) provider, 6; supplier, 6
superar to exceed, to overcome, g. 17
supermercado (*m.*) supermarket, v.a. 18
suponer to suppose, 9
sustituir substitute, v.a. 20
sutilmente subtly, g. 19

T

tabla de cotizaciones (*f.*) currency exchange table, v.a. 2
tablilla de avisos (*f.*) bulletin board, v.a. 10
tachuela (*f.*) thumbtack (*Puerto Rico*), v.a. 10
tal such, 17
talón (*m.*) (*Spain*) check, 2
talonario de cheques checkbook, v.a. 15
talla (*m.*) size, s. 2
taller (*m.*) workshop, g. 14
— **de mantenimiento** mechanic's shop, s. 3
— **de mecánica (reparación)** (*m.*) auto shop, 6
tamaño (*m.*) size, 7
también also, g. 3
tampoco neither, not either, 6
tan so, 4
— **... como** as . . . as, 4
— **pronto como** as soon as, 11
tanque (*m.*) tank, v.a. 8
tanto(a) so much, 14
tantos(as) so many, 14
tapicería (*f.*) upholstery, v.a. 6
tara (*f.*) tare, v.a. 9
tardar to take, to last (a length of time), 4
tarde (*f.*) afternoon, 1
tarifa (*f.*) tariff, 7; toll, 7; fare, 7
tarjeta (*f.*) card, 3
— **de crédito** credit card, v.a. 2
— **de embarque** boarding pass, v.a. 1
— **de registro (huésped)** registration card, 3
— **de residente** resident card, v.a. 2
— **postal** postcard
— **telefónica** prepaid telephone card, v.a. 7
— **verde** green card, g. 2
tasa (*f.*) rate, 2
— **de cambios** exchange rate, 2
— **de interés** interest rate, v.a. 16
tasador(a) (*m., f.*) appraiser, 17
tasar to value; to appraise, v.a. 16
taxi (*m.*) taxi, 2
taxímetro (*m.*) taximeter, 8
taxista (*m., f.*) taxi driver, 8
taza (*f.*) cup, 11
techo (*m.*) roof, 17
tecla (*f.*) key, v.a. 12
teclado (*m.*) keyboard, v.a. 12
teja (*f.*) roof tile, 17
tejamaní, tejamanil (*Méx.*) (*m.*) shingle, v.a. 17
tejido (*m.*) fabric, 9
tela (*f.*) fabric, 5
— **de araña** web, g. 14
telecomunicaciones (*f. pl.*) telecommunications, g. p
telefonista (*m., f.*) telephone operator, 7
teléfono (*m.*) telephone, g. p
— **celular** cellular phone, v.a. 7
— **portátil** cordless phone, v.a. 7
— **público** public phone, v.a. 7
telegrama (*m.*) telegram, 7
televisión (*f.*) television, v.a. 3
televisor (*m.*) TV set v.a. 3
— **portátil** portable television set v.a. 2
temblor de tierra (*m.*) earthquake, 19
temer to fear, 17; to be afraid of, g. 15
Me temo que... I am afraid that . . . , 12
tenedor(a) de libros (*m., f.*) bookkeeper, v.a. 11
tener to have, 4
— **aceptación** to be well received, 5; to be a demand for, 5
— **casa propia** to own a house, 16
— **hambre** to be hungry, 4
— **prisa** to be in a hurry, 4
— **que (+ *inf.*)** to have to (do something), 4
— **razón** to be right, 18
— **suerte** to be lucky, 14
tercer mundo (*m.*) third world, g. 14
tercera persona (*f.*) third party, v.a. 19
tercero (*m.*) third party, v.a. 19
tercero(a) third, 3
terminar (de) to finish, 4
término (*m.*) term, s. 3
— **medio** medium, v.a. 4
termita (*f.*) termite, 17
ternera (*f.*) veal, v.a. 4
terremoto (*m.*) earthquake, 19
testigo (*m., f.*) witness, v.a. 16
texto (*m.*) text, v.a. 14
tiempo (*m.*) time, 9
— **extra** overtime, v.a. 10
tienda (*f.*) store, 5
— **de comestibles** grocery store, g. 18
— **por departamentos** department store, v.a. 18
tierra (*f.*) land, 9
timbre (*m.*) (postage) stamp (*Méx.*), v.a. 7
timón (*m.*) steering wheel, v.a. 6
tintorería (*f.*) dry cleaning shop, v.a. 18
típico(a) typical, p; model, s. 2
tipo (*m.*) type, 4
— **de cambio** exchange rate, 2
— **de interés** interest rate, v.a. 16
tirada (*f.*) circulation, 14
título (*m.*) title, g. p
toalla (*f.*) towel, v.a. 3
todavía yet, g. 12; still, g. 12
todo (*m.*) all, 6; everything, 6
— **el mundo** everybody, l. 6
— **tipo** all types, v.a. 5
todos(as) all, 1; all of them, 4
todos los días every day, 2
tomar to take, 2; to drink, 2
— **algo** to have something to drink
— **una decisión** to make a decision, 11
tomate (*m.*) tomato, 4
tonelada (*f.*) ton, v.a. 9
tópico (*m.*) topic, g. 11
tornado (*m.*) tornado, 19
torreja (*f.*) French toast, g. 4
tortilla (*f.*) tortilla (*Méx.*), 4; omelette (*España and other countries*), 4
tostada (*f.*) toast, 4
total total, 20
trabajador(a) (*m., f.*) worker, 19
trabajar to work, 6
— **por cuenta propia** to be self-employed, 13
trabajo (*m.*) work, 10; job, g. 6
tradicional traditional, 13
traductor(a) (*m., f.*) translator, v.a. 20
traer to bring, 11
tráiler (*m.*) trailer, 9
trámite (*m.*) procedure, 9
transacción (*f.*) transaction, 17
transbordar to transfer, 9
transbordo (*m.*) transfer, 9
transeúnte (*m., f.*) passerby, 8
transferencia (*f.*) transfer, 8

tránsito (*m.*) traffic, 19
transmisión (*f.*) transmission gear, v.a. 6
transnacionales (*f. ,pl.*) transnational (multinational) companies, 20
transparente transparent, 14
transportar to transport, 9
transporte (*m.*) transport g. p; shipping, 6
— **por tierra** land transportation, 9
trasbordar to transfer, 9
trasbordo (*m.*) transfer, 9
trasladar to move, 3; to relocate, 3
traspasar to transfer, v.a. 17
traspaso (*m.*) transfer, 17
tratado (*m.*) agreement, g. 5
Tratado de Libre Comercio de América del Norte (TLCAN) North American Free Trade Agreement (NAFTA), 9
tratar to deal, 9
—**de** to try (to), g. 2
—**se de** to be a question of, 9
tren (*m.*) railroad, 9; train, 9
tributario(a), tributary, l. 12
tropas (*f. pl.*) troops, g. 4
trucha (*f.*) trout, v.a. 4
tubo de escape (*m.*) exhaust pipe, 6
turista (*m., f.*) tourist, 8
tutor (*m.*) guardian, v.a. 20

U

u or, g. 4
último(a) last (in a series), 1
un(a) a, g. p
un momento one moment, p
un paso más one step further, g. 1
únicamente only, 14
único: lo — the only thing, 17
unidad (*f.*) unit, 6
— **óptica** scanner, 12; optic unit, 12
universidad (*f.*) university, 13
uno one, g. 1
unos, unas some, g. 11
— **(+*number*)** about (+ *number*), 3
urgencia (*f.*) urgency, 9
usado(a) used, g. 12
usar to use, v.a. 1
uso (*m.*) use, 12
usted you, g. p
usualmente usually, 17
utilidad (*f.*) profit, 13
— **bruta** gross profit, v.a. 5
— **neta** net profit, v.a. 5
utilizar to use, 6; to utilize, 6

V

vacaciones (*f. pl.*) vacation, 10
vacío(a) vacant, 18; empty, 18
vale (*m.*) voucher, s. 4
valer to be worth, 17
— **la pena** to be worth it, 19
válido(a) valid, g. p
valija (*f.*) suitcase, 2
valioso(a) valuable, 12
valor (*m.*) value, 7; worth, 7
valla (*f.*) billboard, v.a. 14
Vamos a... Let's . . . , g. p
variable variable, 16
variar to change, 14; to vary, 14
variedad (*f.*) variety, 5
varios(as) various, 5; several, 5
vecindario (*m.*) neighborhood, 15
vecino(a) (*m., f.*) neighbor, 17
vegetales (*m. pl.*) vegetables, 4
veliz (*m.*) (*Méx.*), handbag, 2; carry-on bag, 2
velocidad (*f.*) speed, v.a. 12
vencido(a) due, v.a. 13
vencimiento (*m.*) due (date), s. 4
vender to sell, 5
se vende for sale, 17
venderse bien to sell well, 14
venir to come, 4
venta (*f.*) sale, 5
ventaja (*f.*) advantage, 16
ventanilla (*f.*) (service) window, 7
ver to see, 2
verano (*m.*) summer, 14
verbo (*m.*) verb, g. p
verdad (*f.*) truth, g. 15
¿— ? right?, 2
versión (*f.*) version, v.a. 12
vestido (*m.*) dress, 14
vestidura (*f.*) upholstery, v.a. 6
vez (*f.*) time, 12
viajante (*m., f.*) traveling salesperson, 6
viajar to travel, 1
viaje de negocios (*m.*) business trip, 1
víctima (*f.*) victim, g. 1
vida (*f.*) life, 19
videograbadora (*f.*) VCR, v.a. 2
vidriera (*f.*) (store) window, 18
vidrio (*m.*) glass, 9
viejo(a) old, g. 8
viernes (*m.*) Friday, 6
vigilancia (*f.*) vigilance, g. p
vino (*m.*) wine, 4
violación (*f.*) violation, 19
visitar to visit, 6
viudo(a) (*m., f.*) widower, 13; widow, 13
vivienda (*f.*) housing, g. 17
vivir to live, g. 3
vocabulario (*m.*) vocabulary, g. p
volante (*m.*) steering wheel, v.a. 6
volumen (*m.*) volume, 6
volver (o:ue) to return, 6; to come (go) back, 6
vuelco (*m.*) overturning, s. 4
vuelo (*m.*) flight, 1

Y

y and, p
ya already, 4
— **lo sé** I know, 15
yerba (*f.*) lawn, grass, v.a. 17
yo solo(a) just me, 4

Z

zacate (*m.*) (*Méx.*) lawn, v.a. 17
zanahoria (*f.*) carrot, v.a. 4
zapatería (*f.*) shoe store or factory, v.a. 18
zona (*f.*) zone, g. p
— **industrial** industrial zone

English-Spanish Vocabulary

A

about acerca de, 7
— **(+ *number*)** unos... **(+ *number*)**, 3
— **that (the matter)** al respecto, 10
above sobre, 18
absence ausencia (*f.*), 12
abuse abusar de, 20
accelerator acelerador (*m.*)
accept aceptar, 2
access acceso (*m.*), 7
accessory accesorio (*m.*), 5
accident accidente (*m.*), 19
accompany acompañar, 17
according to según, 6; al ritmo de
account cuenta (*f.*), 15
— **payable** cuenta a pagar
— **receivable** cuenta a cobrar
accountant contador(a) (*m., f.*), 11
accounting contabilidad (*f.*), 11; (*adj.*) contable, 11
accredit acreditar, 13
acknowledgement of receipt acuse de recibo (*m.*)
acquire adquirir, g. 20
act of God fenómeno natural (*m.*), 19; fuerza mayor (*f.*), 19
ad anuncio (*m.*), 14
adapt adaptar, 18
add agregar, 14
— **up** sacar la cuenta, 18
addition: in — to aparte de, 7
additional adicional
— **charge** recargo adicional (*m.*)
address dirección (*f.*), p; domicilio (*m.*), p
addressee destinatario(a) (*m., f.*), 7
adequate maintenance mantenimiento adecuado (*m.*)
adjective adjetivo (*m.*)
adjust ajustar, l. 12
adjusted gross income ingreso bruto ajustado (*m.*), 13
adjustment ajuste (*m.*)
administrator administrador(a) (*m., f.*)
advance payment anticipo (*m.*)
advantage ventaja (*f.*), 16
advertise anunciar
advertisement propaganda (*f.*), 7
advertising publicidad (*f.*), 14; propaganda (*f.*), 14
— **agency** agencia de publicidad (*f.*), p
— **media** medio publicitario (*m.*)
advice consejo (*m.*), 14; asesoramiento (*m.*), 16
advise aconsejar, 16
affect afectar, 18
afternoon tarde (*f.*), 1
again de nuevo, 12; otra vez, 12
against contra, 19
age edad (*f.*)
agency agencia (*f.*), 7
agent agente (*m., f.*), 14
agree on convenir (en)
agreement acuerdo (*m.*), 20
air aéreo(a) (*adj.*), 9; aire (*m.*)
— **conditioning** aire acondicionado (*m.*), 3
— **mail** correo aéreo (*m.*), 7
airline línea aérea (*f.*), 2
airport aeropuerto (*m.*), 1
aisle seat asiento de pasillo (*m.*), 1
alcoholic alcohólico(a), 2
alimony pensión alimenticia (*f.*)
all todos(as), 1; todo (*m.*), 6
all of them todos(as), 4
almost casi, 2
alone solo(a), 14
already ya, 4
also también, 4
alternative energies energías alternativas (*f.*), p
although aunque, 17
always siempre, 6
ambiguous ambiguo(a)
American americano(a), 4
among entre, 9
amount importe (*m.*), 12
ample amplio(a), 20
analyze analizar, 20
and y, p
announce anunciar, 1
another otro(a), 3
another's right derecho ajeno (*m.*), g. 20
answer respuesta (*f.*), 10
answering machine máquina contestadora (*f.*)
any algún(alguno/a), 7; cualquier(a)
any style al gusto
anything algo
— **else?** ¿algo más?, 3
— **to declare?** ¿algo que declarar?, 2
anyway de todos modos, 7
apartment apartamento (*m.*), 3
appear aparecer, 13
appearance presentación (*f.*), 14; apariencia (*f.*), 14
appliance electrodoméstico (*m.*)
applicant candidato(a) (*m., f.*), 10; aspirante (*m., f.*); postulante (*m., f.*)
application solicitud (*f.*), 10
apply for solicitar, 10
appoint nombrar, 20
appointment cita (*f.*), 5
appraise tasar
appraiser tasador(a) (*m., f.*), 17
approval aprobación (*f.*)
approve aprobar (o:ue), 16
area área (*f. but* el área), 7
around más o menos, 3
arrangement arreglo (*m.*), 11; iguala (*f.*), (*Cuba*), 11
arrival entrada (*f.*), 12
arrive (in) llegar (a), 1
artcraft artesanía (*f.*), 8
article artículo (*m.*), 5
as según, 12
— **. . . as** tan... como, 4
— **of (+ *date*)** a partir del día, 3
— **soon as** tan pronto como, 11, 19, en cuanto, 19
— **they are received (come in)** según se reciben, 12
ask (for) pedir (e:i), 7; solicitar, 10
— **a question** preguntar, 10
— **oneself** preguntarse, 9
aspire aspirar, l. 12
assault asalto (*m.*)
assess evaluar, 11
assist atender (e:ie), 5
assistance ayuda (*f.*), 12
assistant asistente (*m., f.*), 11
association asociación (*f.*)
assume asumir, 16, 17
at a, 1; en, 1
— **(+ *time*)** a la(s) (+ *time*), 1
— **fault** culpable, 19
— **lunch time** a la hora del almuerzo, 4
— **your expense** a su cargo
— **your service** para servirle, p; a sus órdenes, 10
attached adjunto(a)
attend atender (e:ie), 5
attendance asistencia (*f.*), 12
attention atención (*f.*), 1
authorize autorizar, 18
auto shop taller de mecánica (*m.*)
automate automatizar, 12
automatic automático(a), 8
automatically automáticamente, 12
available disponible, 5; instalado(a), 14
to have — contar (o:ue) con, 7
avenue avenida (*f.*), 8
avocado aguacate (*m.*)
avoid evitar, 1
awarded adjudicado(a), 20

B

bazaar bazar (*m.*), 14
backpack mochila (*f.*)
bad malo(a)
baggage equipaje (*m.*), 2; velices (*m. pl.*) (*Méx.*), 2
baked al horno
bakery panadería (*f.*)
balance saldo (*m.*), 15; balance (*m.*)
— **sheet** balance general, 11
ball bearings caja de bolas (*f.*)
ballpoint pen bolígrafo (*m.*)
bank (*adj.*) bancario(a), 6; banco (*m.*)
— **note** billete (de banco) (*m.*)
— **officer** oficial de banco (*m., f.*), 16
banker banquero(a) (*m., f.*)
bankruptcy bancarrota (*f.*), 20; quiebra (*f.*), 20
barber shop barbería (*f.*)
barrier barerra (*f.*), v.a. 20
bathroom baño (*m.*), 17; servicio (*m.*); excusado (*m.*) (*Méx.*)
— **sink** lavabo (*m.*)

battery acumulador (*m.*), batería (*f.*)
— **operated radio** radio de batería (pilas) (*f.*)
be ser, p; estar, 3
— **a question of** tratarse de, 9
— **able** poder (o:ue), 6
— **afraid of** temer, 17
— **afraid that . . .** temer que..., 12
— **at (your) disposal** estar a su disposición, 5
— **certain of** estar seguro(a) de, 6
— **enough** alcanzar, 19
— **glad** alegrarse, 17
— **going (to do something)** ir a (+ *inf.*), 5
— **good for** convenir, 18
— **happy** alegrarse, 17
— **hungry** tener hambre, 4
— **in charge (of)** correr con, 9
— **lacking** faltar, 19
— **located** quedar, 2
— **lucky** tener suerte, 14
— **necessary (to do something)** hay que (+ *inf.*), 6
— **no longer** dejar de ser
— **paid by you** ir por su cuenta, 6
— **right** tener razón, 18
— **self-employed** trabajar por cuenta propia, 13
— **sorry for** lamentar, 3
— **to one's advantage** convenirle a uno, 15
— **well received** tener aceptación, 5
— **willing to** estar dispuesto(a), 17
— **worth** valer, 17
— **worth it** valer la pena, 19
bean frijol (*m.*), 4
beautiful bonito(a), 17; lindo(a), 17
beauty parlor peluquería (*f.*); salón de belleza (*m.*)
because pues, 7; porque, 6, 10
become pasar a ser, l. 6; convertirse, l. 9
beef carne de res (*f.*)
before antes (de), 1
— **deciding** antes de decidir
begin empezar (e:ie), 14; comenzar (e:ie), 14
believe creer, 6
bellhop botones (*m.*), 3
beneficiary beneficiario(a) (*m., f.*), 15
benefit beneficio (*m.*), 20
to benefit beneficiar, 20
bequest legado (*m.*), 13
bet apostar (o:ue), 20
better mejor, 4
between entre, 6
bid oferta (*f.*), 6
big grande, 2
bilingual bilingüe, 10
bill cuenta (*f.*), 4; billete (de banco) (*m.*)
— **of exchange** letra de cambio (*f.*)
billboard valla (*f.*)
birth nacimiento (*m.*)
biweekly quincenal
black negro(a)
— **coffee (strong)** café expreso (*m.*), 4; café solo (*m.*), 4
in — and white en blanco y negro

blanket manta (*f.*), 1; frazada (*f.*), 1; cobija (*f.*) (*Méx.*), 1
block cuadra (*f.*), 7
three blocks from a tres cuadras de, 7
blown soplado(a), 9
boarding pass pase de abordar (*m.*); tarjeta de embarque (*f.*)
boat barco (*m.*); buque (*m.*)
body cuerpo (*m.*)
— **of a car** carrocería (*f.*)
boiled hervido(a)
bond bono (*m.*), 13
book libro (*m.*), g.1
bookkeeper tenedor(a) de libros (*m., f.*)
booklet folleto (*m.*), 7
border frontera (*f.*), 9
boss jefe(a) (*m., f.*), 5
both ambos(as), 3
bother molestar(se), 18
boulevard boulevard (*m.*), 8
bounced check cheque sin fondos (*m.*)
boyfriend novio (*m.*), 16
brake freno (*m.*), 6
— **fluid** líquido de frenos (*m.*)
branch (office) sucursal (*f.*)
brand marca (*f.*), 6
bread pan (*m.*), 4
breakage rotura (*f.*), 9
breakfast desayuno (*m.*), 4
bribe soborno (*m.*); mordida (*f.*) (*Méx.*)
brick ladrillo (*m.*)
brief breve, p
bring traer, 11
broccoli brécol (*m.*); bróculi (*m.*)
broiled asado(a), 4
brother hermano (hno.) (*m.*), 10
brutal brutal, v.a. 20
budget presupuesto (*m.*), 12
building edificio (*m.*), 18; inmueble (*m.*)
built construido(a), 17
bulletin board pizarra (*f.*); tablilla de avisos (*f.*)
bumper defensa (*f.*); parachoques (*m.*)
bundle bulto (*m.*), 2
burglary robo (*m.*), 19
bus autobús (*m.*), 8; ómnibus (*m.*), 8; camión (*m.*) (*Méx.*), 8
— **stop** parada (*f.*), 8
business negocio(s) (*m.*), 1; firma (*f.*), 1; casa (*f.*), 1; establecimiento comercial (*m.*)
— **administration** administración de empresas (negocios) (*f.*), 16
— **correspondence** correspondencia comercial (*f.*)
— **documents** documentos mercantiles (*m. pl.*)
— **letter** carta de negocios (*f.*)
— **trip** viaje de negocios (*m.*), 1
busy ocupado(a), p
but pero, 3
buy comprar, 5
buyer comprador(a) (*m., f.*), 1
buying compra (*f.*), 6
by por, 1
— **a certain date** fecha fija
— **air** por vía aérea
— **boat** por vía marítma
— **rail** por vía férrea
— **the way** por cierto, 12

C

cabinet gabinete (*m.*)
café au lait café con leche (*m.*), 4
cafeteria cafetería (*f.*), 4
calculator calculador(a) (*m., f.*), 18
call llamar, 2; llamada (*f.*), 7
camera cámara fotográfica (*f.*), 2
campaign (for promotion) campaña de promoción (*f.*), 14
cancelled cancelado(a), 13
candidate candidato(a) (*m., f.*), 10
candy store dulcería (*f.*)
capital capital (*m.*)
capitalist capitalista (*m., f.*), v.a. 20
car auto (*m.*), 6; automóvil (*m.*), 6; carro (*m.*), 6; coche (*m.*), 6; máquina (*f.*) (*Cuba*), 8
— **related** automovilístico(a)
card tarjeta (*f.*), 3
cared (for) cuidado(a), 17
career carrera (*f.*), 13
carefully cuidadosamente
Caribbean Caribe (*m.*), 20
carpet alfombra (*f.*), 17
carrot zanahoria (*f.*)
carry llevar, 9
— **out** desempeñar
carry-on bag bolso(a) (*m., f.*), 2; maletín de mano (*m.*), 2
case caso (*m.*), 11
cash efectivo (*m.*), 15; dinero en efectivo (*m.*)
— **a check** cobrar un cheque
— **book** libro de caja (*m.*)
— **register** caja registradora (*f.*), 12
cashier's check cheque de caja (*m.*), 15
catchy sugestivo(a); sugerente
cause motivo (*m.*), 19
caused causado(a), 19
celery apio (*m.*)
cellular telephone celular (*m.*), v.a. 2; móvil (*m.*), v.a. 2
center of the city centro de la ciudad (*m.*), 3
centimeter centímetro (*m.*), 7
certainly cómo no, 1
certificate of deposit (C.D.) certificado de depósito (*m.*), 13
certified certificado(a)
— **letter** carta certificada (*f.*)
— **Public Accountant** Contador(a) Público(a) Titulado(a) (*m., f.*)
chain cadena (*f.*), 13
chair silla (*f.*)
change cambiar, 2; variar, 14; cambio (*m.*)
charge cargar, 7; cobrar, 7
charity caridad (*f.*), 13
chassis chasis (*m.*)
chauffeur chofer (*m., f.*), 8
cheap barato(a), 5

check cheque (*m.*), 2; chequear; revisar
— **out** desocupar la habitación
— **to the bearer** cheque al portador (*m.*)
checkbook chequera (*f.*); talonario de cheques (*m.*)
checking account cuenta corriente (*f.*), 15; cuenta de cheques (*f.*) (*Méx.*), 5
chicken pollo (*m.*)
child niño(a) (*m., f.*), 16
children hijos (*m. pl.*), 13
chile (bell pepper) chile (*m.*), 4
choose escoger, 10
church iglesia (*f.*), 13
cigarette cigarrillo (*m.*), 2
circular circular (*f.*), 12; carta circular (*f.*)
circulation circulación (*f.*), 14; tirada (*f.*), 14
citizen ciudadano(a) (*m., f.*), 2
claim reclamación (*f.*)
— **check** comprobante (*m.*), 2
clam almeja (*f.*)
class clase (*f.*)
clause cláusula (*f.*)
clean limpio(a)
clear claro(a), l. 12
clerk empleado(a) (*m., f.*), 7
client cliente(a) (*m., f.*), 5, 6
clock reloj (*m.*), 12
close cerrar (e:ie), 15
close by cercano(a), 7
closing despedida (*f.*)
— **costs** gastos de cierre (*m.*), 17
— **date** fecha de cierre (*f.*)
clothes ropa (*f.*), 14
clothing prenda de vestir (*f.*), 5; ropa (*f.*), 14
co-applicant for joint account solicitante de cuenta conjunta (*m., f.*)
co-owner condueño(a) (*m., f.*), 14
cod bacalao (*m.*)
code código (*m.*), 7; clave (*f.*), 7
coffee café (*m.*), 4
— **shop** cafetería (*f.*), 4
coin moneda (*f.*)
cold frío(a)
collateral aval (*m.*), 16
collect on delivery (C.O.D.) cobrar o devolver (C.O.D.)
collection (of debts) cobro (*m.*), 12
collide chocar, 19
color: in — en colores
come venir, 4
— **(go) back** regresar, 1; volver (o:ue), 6
— **in** pasar, p
comfortable cómodo(a)
commence iniciar, 20
commerce comercio (*m.*), 20
commercial comercial, 7
— **space** local (*m.*), 18; espacio (*m.*), 18
commission comisión (*f.*), 13
communication comunicación (*f.*), 7
Communist Manifesto Manifiesto Comunista (*m.*), v.a. 20
compact compacto(a), 8
company firma (*f.*), 5; compañía (*f.*), 9; empresa (*f.*), 11
compare comparar, 6
compatible compatible
compensate compensar, 6
compete competir (e:i), 6
competition competencia (*f.*), 14
complete completo(a), 13
compound interest interés compuesto (*m.*)
comprehensive comprensivo(a), 19
computation computación (*f.*), 12
computer computador(a), 2; ordenador (*m.*) (*España*), 2
— **disk(ette)** disco (de programación) (*m.*); disquete (*m.*)
— **hardware** equipo de computación (*m.*), 12
concentrate concentrar(se), l. 12
concept concepto (*m.*), 12
condition condición (*f.*), 5
condominium condominio (*m.*), 16
confections dulces (*m. pl.*), 18
confirm confirmar
connect conectar, 12
consignee consignatario(a) (*m., f.*)
consignment note (trucking) guía (*f.*)
consist (of) consistir (en), 10
consult consultar, 11
consultation consulta (*f.*)
consulting asesoramiento (*m.*), 16
consumer consumidor(a) (*m., f.*), 6
contain contener, 7
container contenedor (*m.*), 9
continue seguir (e:i), 11
contract contrato (*m.*), 10
contribute contribuir, 10
contribution contribución (*f.*), 13
convenient conveniente, 13
conversation conversación (*f.*), p
cookie galleta (*f.*), 18; galletica (*f.*), 18; galletita (*f.*), 18
copper cobre (*m.*), 20
copy copia (*f.*), 19; ejemplar (*f.*)
— **machine** máquina copiadora (*f.*)
copyright derechos de autor (*m., pl.*), 20
corn maíz (*m.*), v.a. 4
ear of fresh — elote (m.) (*Méx.*)
corner esquina (*f.*), 8
upper right (left) — esquina superior derecha (izquierda)
the — of la esquina de
corporation sociedad anónima (S.A.) (*f.*), 5
correspondence correspondencia (*f.*)
cost costo (*m.*), 5; coste (*m.*), 5
— **insurance, and freight (C.I.F.)** costo, seguro y flete (C.S.F.)
costly costoso(a), 11
cotton algodón (*m.*), 9
count contar (o:ue), 13
counter mostrador (*m.*), 1
counterfeit bill billete falso (*m.*)
country país (*m.*), 4
county condado (*m.*), 16
cover cubrir, 8
coverage cobertura (*f.*), 19
covered cubierto(a), 19
crab cangrejo (*m.*)
creation creación (*f.*), 5
credit crédito (*m.*), 3; haber (*m.*); acreditar
— **account** cuenta acreedora (*f.*)
— **card** tarjeta de crédito (*f.*), 3
— **documents** instrumentos de crédito (*m. pl.*)
creditor acreedor(a) (*m., f.*)
crop cosecha (*f.*), 20
cross cruzar, 8
Cuban currency CUC (Cuban convertible peso) (*m.*), g. 2
cubic cúbico(a), 9
cultivation cultivo (*m.*), 20
cup taza (*f.*), 11
currency moneda (*f.*)
— **exchange office** casa de cambio (*f.*), 2
— **table** tabla de cotizaciones (*f.*)
current actual, 6
curtain cortina (*f.*)
custom built hecho(a) a la orden, 17; construido(a) a la orden, 17
customer cliente (*m., f.*), 5
customs aduana (*f.*), 1
— **duty** derechos aduaneros (de aduana) (*m., pl.*), 20
— **form** declaración de aduana (*f.*), 1

D

daily al día, 8
— **wage(s)** jornal (*m.*)
damage daño (*m.*), 9; avería (*f.*), 9; perjuicio (*m.*), 20
to damage dañar, 20
data datos (*m. pl.*), 3
— **base** base de datos (*f.*)
— **base management program** programa de manejo (administración) de base de datos (*m.*), 10
— **entry** introducción de datos (*f.*), 10
date fecha (*f.*), 2
daughter hija (*f.*), 7
day día (*m.*)
dead weight peso muerto (*m.*)
deal oferta (*f.*), 6; tratar, 9
— **with** ocuparse de, 20
death muerte (*f.*), 19
debate debate (*m.*), 20, debatir; 20
debit debe (*m.*); debitar
— **account** cuenta deudora (*f.*)
debt deuda (*f.*), 16
debtor deudor(a) (*m., f.*)
decaffeinated descafeinado(a), 4
decide decidir, 8
decimeter decímetro (*m.*), 9
declare declarar
— **at fault** declarar culpable, 19
— **bankruptcy** declararse en quiebra, 15
— **oneself** declararse, 15
decrease disminución (*f.*)
dedicate dedica, 20
dedicated dedicado(a), v.a. 20
deduct deducir, 13

deductible deducible
deduction descuento (*m.*), 12; deducción (*f.*), 13
deed escritura (*f.*), 17
defendant (criminal) acusado(a) (*m., f.*); reo (*m., f.*); **(civil)** demandado(a) (*m., f.*)
definitely definitivamente, 20
degree grado (*m.*)
delay demora (*f.*), 1
deliver entregar, 9
demand exigir, 14; demanda (*f.*), v.a. 20
deny negar (e:ie), 16
department store grandes almacenes (*m. pl.*)
departure salida (*f.*), 1
depend (on) depender (de), 6
dependent dependiente (*m., f.*), 13
depending on según, 6
deposit depositar, 13
depositary depositario(a)
depositor depositante (*m., f.*)
depth (of a container) alto (*m.*), 7
design diseño (*m.*), 5; dibujo (*m.*); diseñar, 14
designed diseñado(a), 12
desk escritorio (*m.*); buró (*m.*)
dessert postre (*m.*), 4
destination destino (*m.*)
destroy destruir, l. 6
develop desarrollar, v.a. 20
dial marcar, 7
die morir (o:ue), 13; fallecer, 13
difference diferencia (*f.*), 13
different distinto(a), 9
difficulty dificultad (*f.*), 6
dimension medida (*f.*), 7
diminish rebajar, 12
dining room comedor (*m.*), 17
dinner cena (*f.*), 4
directly directamente, 6
director director(a) (*m., f.*), 5
dirty sucio(a)
disability (disablement) invalidez (*f.*)
discount descuento (*m.*), 5; rebaja (*f.*)
disaster desastre (*m.*)
discuss discutir, 5
disguised disfrazado(a), v.a. 20
dishwasher lavadora de platos (*f.*), 17; lavaplatos (*m.*), 17
display window escaparate (*m.*), 18; vidriera (*f.*), 18
distribute distribuir, 14
district attorney fiscal (*m., f.*)
divide repartir, 20
dividend dividendo (*m.*)
divorced divorciado(a), p
do hacer, 5
— **good** beneficiar, 20
— **the right thing** hacer bien
you did the right thing hizo bien, 11
document documento (*m.*), 9
dollar dólar (*m.*), 2
Dominican Republic República Dominicana (*f.*), 14
donate donar, 20
donation donación (*f.*), 13; donativo (*m.*)
door puerta (*f.*), 1
double doble (*m.*), 9
doubt dudar, 18
down payment entrada (*f.*), 17; cuota inicial (*f.*), 17; enganche (*m.*) (*Méx.*), 17
downstairs planta baja (*f.*), 2
downtown centro de la ciudad (*m.*), 3
drawing dibujo (*m.*)
drawn girado(a), 15
dress vestido (*m.*), 14
drink bebida (*f.*), 2; tomar, 4; beber, 4
drive manejar, 8; conducir, 8
driver chofer (*m., f.*), 8
driving while intoxicated manejar bajo los efectos del alcohol
drop echar, 7
drug medicina (*f.*), 2; medicamento (*m.*), 2
drugstore farmacia (*f.*)
dryer secadora (*f.*)
duck pato (*m.*)
due debido(a); vencido(a)
— **date** fecha de vencimiento (*f.*)
during durante, 14
duty (customs) derechos (*m. pl.*), 2; aranceles (*m. pl.*), 2; impuesto (*m. pl.*), 2
— **free** libre de derechos (impuestos)

E

each cada, 5
earn ganar, 13
earnings ganancia (*f.*), 11
earthquake terremoto (*m.*), 19; temblor (*m.*), 19
easily fácilmente, 12
eat (breakfast) tomar, 3; comer, 4
economic(al) económico(a), 16
economist economista (*m., f.*), v.a. 20
ecosystem ecosistema (*m.*), 20
edition edición (*f.*)
effect efecto (*m.*), 20
effective efectivo(a), 14
efficiently eficientemente, v.a. 20
electric eléctrico(a), 17
electrical outlet enchufe (*m.*)
electricity electricidad (*f.*), 12
electronic electrónico(a)
— **device** equipo electrónico (*m.*)
— **mail (e-mail)** correo electrónico (*m.*), 7
elegant elegante, 17
elevator ascensor (*m.*), 3; elevador (*m.*), 3
emergency emergencia (*f.*)
emphasize hacer resaltar, 14
employ contratar, 10; emplear, 10
employee empleado(a) (*m., f.*), 7
employer empleador(a) (*m., f.*), 13; patrón(ona) (*m., f.*), 13
employment empleo (*m.*), 10
empty desocupado(a), 18; vacío(a), 18
enact poner en vigor, 20
enclosure anexo (*m.*); adjunto (*m.*)
encounter enfrentar, l. 12
end fin (*m.*), 13
endowment insurance seguro dotal (*m.*)
engine motor (*m.*)
engineer ingeniero(a) (*m., f.*)
enlargement ampliación (*f.*), l. 12
enough suficiente, 13
ensure asegurar, 3
enter (i.e., a market) penetrar, 6
enter in the ledger pasar al mayor
enterprise empresa (*f.*), 11
entertainment expenses gastos de representación (*m. pl.*)
entrust encargar, 11
entry entrada (*f.*), 12
envelope sobre (*m.*)
environmental protection protección del medio ambiente (*f.*), 20
equal to igual (que), 10
equipment equipo (*m.*), 12
equivalent equivalente, 10
error error (*m.*), 11
escalator escalera rodante (*f.*), escalera mecánica (*f.*), 18
espresso café expreso (*m.*), 4; café solo (*m.*), 4
establish establecer, 20
establishment establecimiento (*m.*), 9
estimate presupuesto (*m.*), 12; estimar, 20
evaluate evaluar, 11
eventuality eventualidad (*f.*), 19
ever alguna vez
every todo(a), todos(as)
— **body** todo el mundo, l. 6
— **day** todos los días, 2
— **two weeks** quincenal
everything todo (*m.*), 6
exactly exactamente, 18; precisamente, 19
exceed exceder, 7; superar
excellent excelente, 20
except excepto, 19
exchange cambiar, 2
— **rate** tasa de cambios (*f.*), 2
exclusion exclusión (*f.*)
exclusive exclusivo(a), 5
exclusively exclusivamente, 14
excuse me perdón, 2; con (su) permiso, 6
exemption exención (*f.*)
exhaust pipe tubo de escape (*m.*), 6
exhibition hall salón de exhibición (*m.*), 5
exit salida (*f.*), 1
expansion ampliación (*f.*), v.a. 20
expect esperar, 10
expenditure egreso (*m.*)
expense gasto (*m.*), 12
expensive caro(a), 5
experience experiencia (*f.*), 10
expert witness experto(a) (*m., f.*); perito(a) (*m., f.*)
expiration date fecha de vencimiento (*f.*), 3
explain explicar, 11
explanation explicación (*f.*)
exploitation explotación (*f.*), v.a. 20
export exportación (*f.*), 6; exportar, 6
express expreso(a), 9
expressway autopista (*f.*)
extend credit conceder un crédito
extensive amplio(a), 20
extortion extorsión (*f.*)

F

fabric tejido (*m.*), 9; tela (*f.*), 14
facade fachada (*f.*), 17
face (the street) dar a (la calle), 3
facsimile facsímil(e) (*m.*), 7; fax (*m.*), 7
fair equitativo(a), 20
— **play** libre juego (*m.*), g. 20
falsehood falsedad (*f.*), g. 20
family room sala de estar (*f.*), 17; salón de estar (*m.*), 17
far (from) lejos (de), 7
fare tarifa (*f.*), 7
farming cultivo (*m.*), 20
fasten abrocharse
father padre (*m.*), 16
favor apoyar, v.a. 20
fax facsímil(e) (*m.*), 7; fax (*m.*), 7
fear temer, 17
feature característica (*f.*), 14
federal federal, 15
fee honorario (*m.*), 20
feed alimentar, 12
feel pain doler (o:ue), 8
felony delito mayor (grave) (*m.*)
fender guardabarros (*m.*); guardafangos (*m.*)
fiancé(e) novio(a) (*m., f.*), 16
fiber fibra (*f.*), 9
figure (number) cifra (*f.*), 20
file registrar; archivador (*m.*)
filing cabinet archivador (*m.*) (*España*), archivo
fill out (a form) llenar, 1; rellenar, 1
film película (*f.*); filme (*m.*); filmar
final final (*m.*), 11
finally por último, 7
financial financiero(a), 11
— **statement** estado financiero (*m.*), 11
find out averiguar, 9
fine bien, p; multa (*f.*), 19
finish terminar (de), 4
fire fuego (*m.*), 19; incendio (*m.*), 19
fireplace chimenea (*f.*), 17
firm firma (*f.*), 1
first (*adv.*) primero, 2; (*adj.*) primero(a), 2
— **(second) degree murder** asesinato de primer (segundo) grado (*m.*)
fish pescado (*m.*), 4
— **market** pescadería (*f.*)
fit caber, 9
fitting room probador (*m.*), 18
fix reparar
fixed fijo(a), 16
— **rate** a plazo fijo, 13
— **term (deposit)** a plazo fijo, 13
fixtures enseres (*m. pl.*), 19
flight vuelo (*m.*), 1
— **attendant** auxiliar de vuelo (*m., f.*), 1
flood inundación (*f.*), 19
floor piso (*m.*), 3
flower flor (*f.*)
— **shop** florería (*f.*)
folio folio (*m.*)
food comida (*f.*), 13
foot pie (*m.*), 18
for para, 1; por, 3
— **any reason** por cualquier motivo, 19
— **personal use** para uso personal, 2
— **rent** se alquila
— **sale** se vende, 17
forbidden prohibido(a), 7
foreigner extranjero(a) (*m., f.*), 2
forgive perdonar, 11
form planilla (*f.*), 13; forma (*f.*), 13
former anterior, 11; antiguo(a), l. 6
fourth cuarto(a), 3
fowl aves (*f. pl.*)
fragile frágil, 9
fraud fraude (*m.*)
free libre, 20
free (of charge) gratis, 7; libre, 20
— **on board (F.O.B.)** libre a bordo (F.A.B.)
freeway autopista (*f.*)
freight flete (*m.*), 9
French toast pan francés (*m.*) (*Méx.*), torrejas
frequency (of business orders) asiduidad (*f.*)
frequently frecuentemente, 20
fresh fresco(a), 4
— **foods** alimentos frescos (*m. pl.*)
Friday viernes (*m.*), 6
fried frito(a)
fringe benefit beneficio adicional (*m.*), 10
from de, 1; desde, 6
— **behind** por detrás
— **one place to another** de un lugar a otro, 8
front: in — (of) frente (a), 8
— **desk** recepción (*f.*), 3
frontier frontera (*f.*), 9
fruit tree árbol frutal (*m.*)
full lleno(a), 8; completo(a), 13
full-page a toda plana
full-time a tiempo completo
funds fondos (*m.*)
furniture muebles (*m. pl.*), 13
— **factory or store** mueblería (*f.*)
further más
future futuro (*m.*)

G

garage garaje (*m.*), 17
garden jardín (*m.*), 17
garment prenda de vestir (*f.*), 5
gasoline gasolina (*f.*)
gate puerta (*f.*), 1
general general
— **ledger** (libro) mayor (*m.*), 11
— **ledger entry** pase al mayor (*m.*), 11
— **manager** gerente general (*m., f.*), p
— **partnership** sociedad regular colectiva (*f.*)
generate generar, g. 20
generation generación (*f.*)
generic genérico(a)
gentleman señor (*m.*), p; caballero (*m.*)
get obtener, 13; conseguir (e:i), 13
— **married** casarse, 16
— **off** bajarse, 8
gift regalo (*m.*), 13
girlfriend novia (*f.*), 16
give dar, 3
— **a discount** descontar (o:ue), 6
— **an account** rendir (e:i) informe, 12
— **notice** avisar, 8; participarse
— **official authorization** acreditar, 13
I can — it to you for . . . Se lo puedo dejar en..., 8
glass copa (*f.*), 4; vidrio (*m.*), 9
globalization globalización (*f.*), 20
glove compartment guantero(a) (*m., f.*)
go ir, 3
— **back** regresar, 1
— **bankrupt** quebrar (e:ie), 15
— **down** bajar, 2
— **out** salir, 11
— **straight ahead** siga derecho
— **up** subir, 2
good buen(o)(a)
— **afternoon** buenas tardes, p
— **evening** buenas noches, p
— **morning (day)** buenos días, p
— **night** buenas noches, p
good-bye adiós, p
goods géneros (*m. pl.*); mercancías (*f. pl.*)
government gobierno (*m.*), 15
grade point average (G.P.A.) promedio de notas (*m.*)
graduate graduarse, 13
grandmother abuela (*f.*), 13
graphic gráfico (*m.*)
grass césped (*m.*); zacate (*m.*) (*Méx.*)
great! ¡magnífico!, 7
green verde
— **card** tarjeta verde (*f.*)
— **salad** ensalada de lechuga (*f.*)
greet saludar, 8
grilled asado(a), v.a. 4
gross bruto(a)
— **income** ingreso bruto (*m.*)
— **profit** utilidad bruta (*f.*)
— **weight** peso bruto (*m.*)
ground floor planta baja (*f.*), 2
group insurance seguro de grupo (*m.*); seguro colectivo (*m.*)
grow crecer, 11
guarantee garantía (*f.*), 16
guardian tutor(a) (*m., f.*)
guest huésped (*m., f.*), 3
guilty culpable (*m., f.*), 19
not — inocente

H

half medio(a), 8
handbag maletín de mano (*m.*), 2; bolso(a) (*m., f.*), 2; cartera (*f.*), 14
handicraft artesanía (*f.*), 8
happen ocurrir, 9; suceder, 9
hard drive disco duro (*m.*)
hardly apenas, 9
hardware soporte físico (*m.*)
— **store** ferretería (*f.*)

harm dañar, 20
has become se ha hecho, t. 4
have tener, 4
— **a collision** chocar, 19
— **available** ofrecer, 7
— **lunch** almorzar (o:ue), 10
— **to** deber, 2; tener que (+ *inf.*), 4
head cabeza (*f.*), 20
— **of household (of the family)** cabeza de familia (*m., f.*), 13; jefe(a) de familia (*m., f.*)
health salud (*f.*), 10
— **insurance** seguro de salud (*m.*)
heating calefacción, (*f.*), 17
height alto (*m.*), 7
hello: to say — saludar, 8
help ayudar, 9; ayuda (*f.*), 12
her su(s), 2
here's . . . Aquí tiene..., 4
herself ella misma, 8
high alto(a), 9
highway carretera (*f.*)
hire contratar, 10; emplear, 10
his su(s), 2
hold (a position) desempeñar
home hogar (*m.*), p
hope esperar, 16
I — . . . Ojalá..., 17
horn bocina (*f.*), claxon (*m.*); pito (*m.*)
hot caliente
hotel hotel (*m.*), 3
house casa (*f.*), g. 1
housing vivienda (*f.*)
how? ¿cómo?, 4
— **are you?** ¿Cómo está Ud.?, p
— **are you doing?** ¿Qué tal?, 6
— **far?** ¿A qué distancia?, 3
— **many?** ¿Cuántos(as)?, 3
— **may I (we) help you?** ¿En qué puedo (podemos) servirle?, p
— **much?** ¿Cuánto(a)?, 3
How . . . ! ¡Qué...!, 18
hurricane huracán (*m.*), 19
hurt doler (o:ue), 8
husband esposo (*m.*), 13

I

idea idea (*f.*), 14
identification (I.D.) identificación (*f.*)
If only . . . Ojalá..., 17
if possible si es posible, 5
imagine figurarse, 13
import importar, 5
imported importado(a)
importer importador(a) (*m., f.*), 14
improve mejorar, 14
in en, 1
— **accordance (with)** de acuerdo (con), 5
— **addition** por otra parte
— **advance** por adelantado, 18
— **any case** de todos modos, 7
— **case** en caso de que, 19
— **deposit** en fondo, 18; en depósito, 18
— **excess (of)** en exceso (de)
— **order to** para, 1
— **other words** es decir, 12
— **stock** en existencia, 6
— **the back** al fondo, 5
— **the morning** por la mañana, 4
include incluir, 19
included incluido(a), 10
including incluido(a), 10
income ingreso (*m.*), 13; renta (*f.*), 13
inconvenience inconveniente (*m.*), 3
increase aumento (*m.*), 9; aumentar, 9
indeed en realidad, 6
indemnification indemnización (*f.*)
indicate indicar, 6; marcar, 8
individual individual, 15
— **retirement account (I.R.A.)** cuenta individual de retiro (*f.*), 13
industry industria (*f.*), 14
inexpensive barato(a), 5
inflation inflación (*f.*), 20
inform avisar, 8
information datos (*m.*), 3; información (*f.*), 8; informes (*m.*), 8
infrasturcture infraestructura (*f.*), v.a. 20
inheritance herencia (*f.*), 13
initate iniciar, 20
initial inicial (*f.*)
injury lesión (*f.*), 19
inquisitive curioso(a), g. 20
insolvency insolvencia (*f.*), 15
insolvent insolvente
inspect inspeccionar
inspection inspección (*f.*), 17
inspector inspector(a) (*m., f.*), 2
installed instalado(a), 14
instant instantáneo(a), 4
institution institución (*f.*), 13
insurance seguro (*m.*)
— **company** asegurador(a) (*m., f.*)
insure asegurar, 19
insured asegurado(a) (*m., f.*), 15
intercom intercomunicador (*m.*), 5
interest interés (*m.*), 13; interesar, 18
— **rate** tipo de interés (*m.*); tasa de interés (*f.*)
interested interesado(a), 5
interior interior, 3
international internacional, 7
Internet Internet (*f.*), 7; red (*f.*)
interpreter intérprete (*m., f.*)
intersection of la esquina de
interview entrevista (*f.*), 10
introduce introducir, 14
inventory inventario (*m.*), 12
invest invertir (e:ie)
investigate investigar, 18
investment inversión (*f.*), 12
— **officer** asesor de inversiones (*m.*)
invitation invitación (*f.*), 13
invite invitar, g. 20
invoice factura (*f.*)
issue edición (*f.*)
issuer país que lo expide (*m.*)
it looks to me me parece, 20
It's (+ *time*) Es (son) la(s) (+ *time*), 1
item artículo (*m.*), 5; renglón (*m.*), 14
itinerary itinerario (*m.*)

J

jacket chaqueta (*f.*), 14; chamarra (*f.*) (*Méx.*), 14
jewelry store joyería (*f.*)
job puesto (*m.*), 10; posición (*f.*), 10; empleo (*m.*)
— **description** descripción del contenido de trabajo (*f.*), 10
joint account cuenta conjunta (*f.*), 15
jot down anotar, 5
journal (libro) diario (*m.*), 11
— **entry** asiento de diario (*m.*), 11
judge juez (*m., f.*)
junk food comida chatarra (*f.*), t. 4
jury jurado (*m.*)
just: — me yo solo(a), 4
— **the opposite** lo contrario, 20

K

keep quedarse (con), 18
— **the books** llevar la contabilidad, 11
kept cuidado(a), 17
key llave (*f.*), 3; **(into a computer)** registrar, 12; tecla (*f.*)
keyboard teclado (*m.*)
kilo kilo (*m.*), 7; kilogramo (*m.*), 7
kilogram kilo (*m.*), 7; kilogramo (*m.*), 7
kilometer kilómetro (*m.*), 3
kitchen cocina (*f.*), 17
klaxon bocina (*f.*), claxon (*m.*)
know saber, 7; conocer, 7
I — ya lo sé, 15
known conocido(a), 6

L

label etiqueta (*f.*), 12
labor mano de obra (*f.*), 14
lady señora (*f.*), p; dama (*f.*)
lamb cordero (*m.*)
lamp lámpara (*f.*)
land tierra (*f.*), 9
— **transportation** transporte por tierra (*m.*), 9
language idioma (*m.*)
laptop computer computador(a) portátil (*m., f.*), 2; ordenador portátil, (*m.*), (*España*), 2
large grande, 2
last (a length of time) demorar, 4; pasado(a), 10; durar, 17
— **(in a series)** último(a), 1
— **name** apellido (*m.*), p
— **name (mother's)** apellido materno (*m.*)
— **name (father's)** apellido paterno (*m.*)
lastly por último, 7
later después, 2; más tarde, 9
laundry room cuarto de lavar (*m.*), 17
law ley (*f.*), 14
lawn césped (*m.*); zacate (*m.*) (*Méx.*)

lease alquilar, 13; arrendar; arrendamiento (*m.*)
leather cuero (*m.*), 5
leave salir, 11; irse, l. 6
— **(behind)** dejar, 4
left se fue, l. 6
legal legal, 16
lend prestar, 18
lender prestamista (*m., f.*)
length largo (*m.*), 7
less than menos de, 4; menor, 7
lessee arrendatario(a) (*m., f.*)
let's see a ver, 6
letter carta (*f.*), 7
— **of recommendation** carta de recomendación (*f.*)
— **opener** abrecartas (*m.*)
letterhead membrete (*m.*)
lettuce lechuga (*f.*)
level nivel (*m.*), 17
liabilities pasivo (*m.*)
liability responsabilidad civil (*f.*), 19
license licencia (*f.*), 8
life vida (*f.*), 19
— **annuity** renta vitalicia (*f.*)
— **expectancy** probabilidad de vida (*f.*)
— **insurance** seguro de vida (*m.*)
— **preserver** salvavidas (*m.*)
light luz (*f.*), 19; lámpara (*f.*)
like gustar, 8
Limited Liability Company sociedad de responsabilidad limitada (S.R.L.) (*f.*)
line línea (*f.*), p; fila (*f.*), 2
— **of business** giro (*m.*), p
— **of merchandise** renglón (*m.*), 14
linoleum linóleo (*m.*), 17
liquidate liquidar
liquidity liquidez (*f.*)
list lista (*f.*), 6
listen escuchar, 5
literature literatura (*f.*), 19
little: a — un poco, 6
live vivir, 13
live animals animales vivos (*m. pl.*)
living room sala (*f.*), 17
load cargamento (*m.*), 9; carga (*f.*), 9; cargar, 9
loan préstamo (*f.*), 13
lobster langosta (*f.*)
local local, 6
locked inmovilizado(a), 15
logo logo(grama) (*m.*), 14
long largo(a), 20
— **distance** larga distancia (*f.*), 7
look (at) mirar, 2
— **for** buscar, 5
— **like** parecer, 12
lose perder (e:ie), 15
— **your job** quedarse sin empleo (trabajo), 20
loss pérdida (*f.*), 11
loudspeaker altavoz (*m.*), 1; altoparlante (*m.*), 1
low bajo(a), 16
lube and oil change engrase (*m.*)
lubrication engrase (*m.*); lubricación (*f.*)
lunch almuerzo (*m.*), 4; comida (*f.*), 4

M

Ma'am señora (*f.*), p
machine máquina (*f.*), 12
Madam señora (*f.*), p
magazine revista (*f.*), 1
magnificent! ¡magnífico!, 7
mail correspondencia (*f.*), correo (*m.*)
— **carrier** cartero(a) (*m., f.*)
mailbox buzón (*m.*), 7
main office casa matriz (*f.*)
majority mayor parte (*f.*), 17; mayoría (*f.*), 18
make hacer, 5; confeccionar, 14
— **a decision** tomar una decisión, 11
— **them** los (las) hacen, v.a. 20
mall centro comercial (*m.*), 4
man hombre (*m.*), 5
manager gerente (*m., f.*), p
manslaughter homicidio (*m.*)
manufacture fabricación (*f.*), 5
manufactured fabricado(a), 5
manufacturer's trade mark marca de fábrica (*f.*)
manufacturing manufacturero(a), 14
many muchos(as), 4
marital status estado civil (*m.*)
mark marcar, 8
marked marcado(a), 5
market mercado (*m.*), 5
married casado(a), p
massive masivo(a), 14
master dominar, g. 20
master bedroom cuarto principal (*m.*)
material material (*m.*), 10
matter importar, 11
meal comida (*f.*), 13
I mean digo, 7
means medios (*m. pl.*), 7; capacidad (*f.*), 14
— **of payment** forma de pago (*f.*), 6
— **of transportation** medios de transporte (*m. pl.*), 8
measure medida (*f.*), 7; medir (e:i), 7
measurement medida (*f.*), 7
meat carne (*f.*)
— **market** carnicería (*f.*)
mechanic's shop taller de reparaciones (*m.*)
medical médico(a), 13
— **and hospital care** atención médica y hospitalaria, 19
medicine medicina (*f.*), 2; medicamento (*m.*), 2
medium mediano(a), 8
meet encontrar (o:ue), 8; conocer, 13
meeting reunión (*f.*), 5; junta (*f.*) (*Méx.*), 5
memorandum memorando (*m.*)
memory memoria (*f.*)
mention mencionar, 10
menu menú (*m.*), 4
merchandise mercancía, (*f.*), 6; mercadería (*f.*), 6
message mensaje (*m.*)
meter metro (*m.*), 9
Mexican mexicano(a), 2
Mexico México, 1
microchip pastilla (*f.*)
microwave microonda (*f.*), 17
milk leche (*f.*), 4
minimum mínimo (*m.*), 17
minor menor de edad, 13
minute minuto (*m.*), 1
— **book** libro de actas (*m.*)
miscellaneous expenses gastos varios (*m. pl.*)
miscellany miscelánea (*f.*)
misdemeanor delito menor (menos grave) (*m.*)
Miss señorita (Srta.) (*f.*), p
mixed mixto(a), 4
model modelo (*m.*), 5
modem módem (*m.*)
modernize modernizar, 11
moment momento (*m.*), 5
Monday lunes (*m.*)
money dinero (*m.*), 7
— **market account** cuenta del mercado de dinero (*f.*), 15
— **order** giro postal (*m.*), 7
monitor monitor (*m.*)
month mes (*m.*), 10
monthly mensual, 13; al mes, 13
— **payment** mensualidad (*f.*), 13
— **salary** sueldo mensual (*m.*)
more or less más o menos, 3
morning mañana (*f.*), 10
mortgage hipoteca (*f.*), 13
most la mayor parte, 17
mostly principalmente, 14
mother madre (*f.*), 16
motor motor (*m.*)
mouse ratón (*m.*)
move trasladar, 3; (*relocate*) mudarse, 15
Mr. señor (Sr.) (*m.*), p
Mrs. señora (Sra.) (*f.*), p
much mucho(a), 3
muffler silenciador (*m.*), 6
multinational companies transnacionales (*f., pl.*), 20
municipal municipal, 13
must deber, 2
my mi(s), 2

N

naked desnudo(a), g. 20
name nombre (*m.*), p; nombrar
in my — a nombre mío; en mi nombre
My — is . . . Me llamo..., 3
sender's company — antefirma (*f.*)
national nacional, 9
natural phenomenon fenómeno natural (*m.*), 19; fuerza mayor (*f.*), 19
near cercano(a), 7; cerca (de), 17
necessary necesario(a), 12
necessity necesidad (*f.*), 11
neck cuello (*m.*), 20
need necesitar, 1; necesidad (*f.*), 11; hacer falta, 14
needed necesario (a), 12
negociate negociar, 17
neighbor vecino(a) (*m., f.*), 17
neighborhood barrio (*m.*), 15; vecindario (*m.*), 15

neither ni, 6; tampoco, 6; ni... tampoco, 13
net neto(a)
— **profit** utilidad neta (*f.*)
— **weight** peso neto (*m.*)
never nunca, 14
nevertheless sin embargo
new nuevo(a), 12
newly recién, 17
newspaper periódico (*m.*), 1
next próximo(a), 6
next day al día siguiente, 4
no one nadie, 6
noise ruido (*m.*), 3
none ningún (ninguno/a), 6, 8
noodle fideo (*m.*)
nor ni, 6
North American Free Trade Agreement (NAFTA) Tratado de Libre Comercio de América del Norte (TLCAN) (*m.*)
not no
— **either** tampoco, 6; ni... tampoco, 13
— **guilty** inocente (*m., f.*)
notably notablemente, 14
note anotar, 5
nothing nada, 3
— **else** nada más, 3
noun nombre (*m.*), p
now ahora, 1; ahorita, 1
number cifra (*f.*), 20

O

obsolete obsoleto(a), 12
obtain obtener, 13; conseguir (e:i), 13
occupied (a house) habitado(a), 16
occur ocurrir
of de, 1
— **age** mayor de edad, 13
— **course** cómo no, 1; desde luego, 6
offer oferta, 6
office oficina (*f.*), 5
— **clerk** oficinista (*m., f.*), 10
oil aceite (*m.*)
— **change** cambio de aceite (*m.*)
old viejo(a), 19
older mayor, 19
omelette tortilla (*f.*)
on en, 1; por, 1; sobre, 13
— **behalf of** a favor de
— **the way there (he is)** en seguida va para allá, 3
one moment un momento, p
one-way ticket pasaje (billete) de ida (*m.*), 1
only solamente, 1; sólo, 13; únicamente, 14
the — thing lo único, 17
open abrir, 2
operate manejar
operating system sistema operativo (*m.*), 10
operation operación (*f.*), 12
opponent opositor(a), v.a. 20
oppose oponerse, 20
optic unit unidad óptica (*f.*), 12
option opción (*f.*), 10
or o, 1
order pedido (*m.*), 5; orden (*f.*); ordenar, 6
organize organizar, 14
origin origen (*m.*), 14; procedencia (*f.*)
other otro(a)
others: the — los (las) demás, 9
our nuestro(a), 6
ours los (las) nuestros(as), 6
outside por fuera, 17
oven horno (*m.*), 17
over sobre, 18
— **there** allá, 3; por allá, 6
overdraft sobregiro (*m.*)
overdrawn check cheque sin fondos (*m.*)
overhead expenses gastos generales (*m.*)
overheat recalentarse (e:ie)
overlooks the street da a la calle, 3
overtime tiempo extra (*m.*)
owe deber, 13
own a house tener casa propia, 16
owner dueño(a) (*m., f.*), 16; propietario(a) (*m., f.*), 1

P

pack cajetilla (*f.*)
package bulto (*m.*), 2; paquete (*m.*), 7; cajetilla
packing embalaje (*m.*), 9
page (accounting books) folio (*m.*)
paid by you va a su cuenta
painted pintado(a), 17
paper papel (*m.*), l. 12
paper clip sujetapapeles (*m.*)
parents padres (*m.*), 16
pardon me perdón, 2
park estacionar
parking estacionamiento (*m.*)
— **lot** estacionamiento (*m.*)
— **meter** parquímetro (*m.*)
part pieza (*f.*), 6; parte (*f.*), 8
part-time medio tiempo, 13; medio día
participate participar
participation participación (*f.*)
partner socio(a) (*m., f.*), 13
pass pasar, 11
passenger pasajero(a) (*m., f.*), 1
passerby transeúnte (*m., f.*), 8
passing by que pasa, 2
passport pasaporte (*m.*), 2
past pasado(a), 10
patent patente (*f.*), 14
patio patio (*m.*)
pawnbroker prestamista (*m., f.*)
pay pagar, 2
— **attention** hacer caso, 19
— **in cash** pagar al contado
— **in installments** pagar a plazos
— **off** liquidar
payroll nómina (*f.*), 11
peace paz (*f.*), g. 20
peas chícharos (*m. pl.*); guisantes (*m. pl.*)
penalty multa (*f.*)
pencil lápiz (*m.*)
penetrate penetrar
pension pensión (*f.*), 13
per por
— **day** por día, 3
— **unit** por unidad, 6
percent por ciento (*m.*), 6
perfume store perfumería (*f.*)
periodically periódicamente, 11
peripheral (device) periférico (*m.*)
person persona (*f.*), 3
personal personal, 12
— **property** bienes muebles (*m. pl.*), 13
personalized personalizado(a), 12
personnel personal (*m.*), 10
petty cash caja (*f.*)
phone teléfono (*m.*)
— **book** guía de teléfonos (*f.*), 7; directorio telefónico (*m.*), 7
— **number** número de teléfono (*m.*), p
photocopier fotocopiadora (*f.*)
phytosanitary fitosanitario(a), 20
pie pastel (*m.*)
pillow almohada (*f.*), 1
pity: It's a — Es una lástima, 17
place lugar (*m.*), 18
— **an order** hacer un pedido, 6
plan pensar (en) (e:ie), 9; plan (*m.*), 10
plane avión (*m.*)
please por favor, p; favor de (+ *inf.*), 1; gustar, 8; Sírvase...
pleasure agrado (*m.*)
pleased to meet you mucho gusto (en conocerla a), 10
plus más, 3
pocket calculator calculadora de bolsillo (*f.*)
police (department) policía (*f.*)
— **officer** policía (*m., f.*)
policy póliza (*f.*), 19
— **holder** asegurado(a) (*m., f.*); subscriptor(a) (*m., f.*)
point of view punto de vista (*m.*), v.a. 20
poll sondeo de la opinión pública (*m.*)
popular popular, 4
pork puerco (*m.*); cerdo (*m.*)
portable portátil, 2
porter maletero(a) (*m., f.*), 2
position puesto (*m.*), 10; posición (*f.*), 10
— **held** puesto desempeñado (*m.*)
possession posesión (*f.*)
possible posible, 12
post puesto (*m.*), 10; posición (*f.*), 10
— **office** oficina de correos (*f.*), 7; correo (*m.*), 7
— **office box** apartado postal (*m.*); casilla de correo (*f.*)
postage franqueo (*m.*); porte (*m.*)
— **due (paid)** porte debido (pagado)
poster cartel (*m.*)
postmark matasellos (*m.*)
postscript posdata (*f.*)
potato papa (*f.*); patata (*f.*)
pottery (the craft) alfarería (*f.*), 9
pottery shop (factory) alfarería (*f.*), 9
poultry aves (*f. pl.*)
pound libra (*f.*), 7
powerful poderoso(a)

practice practicar
preceded precedido(a), 14
precisely precisamente, 19
prefer preferir (e:ie), 5
premium prima (*f.*), 19
prepaid response contestación pagada (*f.*)
prepare preparar, 6; confeccionar, 14
present actual, 6; presentar, 14
presentation presentación (*f.*), 14
presently actualmente, 10
previous anterior, 11
price precio (*m.*), 5; importe (*m.*), 12
principally principalmente, 14
print imprimir; letra de molde (*f.*)
printed matter impreso (*m.*), 7
printer impresor(a) (*m., f.*)
printing impresión (*f.*), 15; letra de molde (*f.*)
private privado(a), 7
prize premio (*m.*), 13
problem problema (*m.*), 11
procedure trámite (*m.*), 9
process proceso (*m.*), 20
product producto (*m.*), 5
production producción (*f.*), 20
professional profesional (*m., f.*), 17; profesionalista (*m., f.*), 17
profit ganancia (*f.*), 11; utilidad (*f.*), 13
  — and loss statement estado de pérdidas y ganancias (*m.*), 11
program programa (*m.*), 10
programmer programador(a) (*m., f.*)
prolong prolongar, 20
promissory note (I.O.U.) pagaré (*m.*)
proof (written) comprobante (*m.*), 2; prueba (*f.*), 13; constancia (*f.*)
property propiedad (*f.*), 17
  — tax impuesto a la propiedad (*m.*)
prosecutor abogado(a) acusador(a) (*m., f.*)
protect proteger, 20
protectionism proteccionismo (*m.*), 20
provided that con tal que, 18
provider suministrador(a) (*m., f.*), 6; proveedor(a) (*m., f.*), 12
proximity proximidad (*f.*), 18
publicity publicidad (*f.*), 14; propaganda (*f.*), 14
publish publicar
purchase compra (*f.*), 13; comprar
  — and sale agreement compraventa (*f.*)
  — order orden de compra (*f.*); pedido (*m.*)
  — price precio de compra (*m.*)
purchasing manager jefe(a) de compras (*m., f.*), p
purse cartera (*f.*), 14
put poner, 10
  — together confeccionar, 14
  — up for sale poner a la venta, 17

Q

qualification calificación (*f.*)
qualify calificar, 16
quality calidad (*f.*), 5
quantity cantidad (*f.*), 5
question pregunta (*f.*), 7
quite bastante, 19

R

radiator radiador (*m.*)
radio radio (*f.*), 14
railroad ferrocarril (*m.*), 9; tren (*m.*), 9
raise aumento (*m.*), 9
rare crudo(a)
raw material materia prima (*f.*)
reach alcanzar, 19
read leer, 4
ready listo(a), 3
real estate bienes inmuebles (*m. pl.*), 13; inmuebles (*m. pl.*), 13; bienes raíces (*m. pl.*), 13
  — agent corredor(a) de bienes raíces (*m., f.*), 17
  — tax contribución (*f.*), 17
reason motivo (*m.*), 19
reasonable equitativo(a), 20
receipt recibo (*m.*), 13; comprobante (*m.*), 13
receive recibir, 6
received recibido(a), 13
receiver depositario(a) (*m., f.*)
recent reciente, 20
recently recientemente, 16; recién, 16
reception desk recepción (*f.*), 3
receptionist recepcionista (*m., f.*), 5
recipient destinatario(a) (*m., f.*)
recline reclinar
recommend recomendar (e:ie), 7, 12
reconcile conciliar; cuadrar
reconciliation ajuste (*m.*)
record registrar, 12
red rojo(a), 19
  — snapper huachinango (*m.*) (*Méx.*), pargo (*m.*), 4
reduce rebajar, 12
reduction descuento (*m.*), 12
reference referencia (*f.*), 10
referring to (a specific item) por concepto (de), 12
refrigerator refrigerador (*m.*)
refund reembolso (*m.*), 13
regard: in — to en cuanto a, 7; con referencia a
regarding por concepto (de), 12
registered brand marca registrada (*f.*), 14
registered letter carta certificada (*f.*); certificado (*m.*)
registration matrícula (*f.*), 16
  — card tarjeta de registro (*f.*), 3; tarjeta de huésped (*f.*), 3
  — fees matrícula (*f.*), 16
regret lamentar, 3; sentir (e:ie), 17
regrettably lamentablemente, 20
regulation regulación (*f.*), 7; disposición (*f.*), 16
reimbursement reembolso (*m.*)
related relacionado(a)
relation relación (*f.*), 9
relationship (family) parentesco (*m.*)
relatives familiares (*m. pl.*)
relocate trasladar, 3
remember recordar (o:ue); acordarse (de) (o:ue), 18
remodel remodelar, 17
rent alquilar, 8; rentar, 8; alquiler (*m.*), 12
rented alquilado(a), 18
renter inquilino(a) (*m., f.*)
reorganize reorganizar, 11
repair reparación (*f.*), 6; reparar
  — shop taller de reparación (*m.*), 6
report informe (*m.*), 11; rendir (e:i) informe, 12; reportar
represent representar, 11
reproduction réplica (*f.*), 5
Republic of Chile República de Chile (*f.*), 20
require exigir, 14; requerir (e:ie), 17
reservation reservación (*f.*), 3; reserva (*f.*), 3
reserve reservar, 1
resident card tarjeta de residente (*f.*)
resign (from) renunciar (a), 10
respective correspondiente, 6
responsible responsable, 19
rest: the — los (las) demás, 9
restaurant restaurante (*m.*), 4; restorán (*m.*), 4
restitution restitución (*f.*), 19
résumé resumen, curriculum vitae (*m.*)
retail al por menor, 5; menudeo, 5; al detall, 5; al detalle, 5
retailer detallista (*m., f.*), 10; minorista (*m.*), 10
retirement retiro (*m.*), 10; jubilación (*f.*), 10
return regresar, 1; volver (o:ue), 6; devolver (o:ue)
  — receipt acuse de recibo (*m.*)
revenue renta (*f.*), 13
rice arroz (*m.*), 4
right derecho(a)
  — ? ¿verdad?, 2
  — away en seguida, 1
  — now ahora mismo, 17
riot motín (*m.*), 19
risk riesgo (*m.*), 9
roasted asado(a), 4
robbery robo (*m.*), 19
roller bearings cojinetes (*m. pl.*)
roof techo (*m.*), 17
  — tile teja (*f.*), 17
room habitación (*f.*), 3; cuarto (*m.*), 3; recámara (*f.*) (*Méx.*), 3
  — service servicio de habitación (*m.*)
round-trip ticket pasaje (billete) de ida y vuelta (*m.*), 1
route ruta (*f.*), 8
row fila (*f.*), 1
rubber band banda elástica (*f.*); goma (*f.*) (*Puerto Rico*); liga (*f.*) (*Méx., Cuba*)
rudimentary rudimentario(a), 12
rule norma (*f.*), l. 12
  — out descartar, 16

S

sacrifice sacrificar, 17
safe seguro(a), 15
salad ensalada (*f.*), 4
salary sueldo (*m.*), 10; salario (*m.*), 10
sale venta (*f.*), 5
sales ventas
— manager jefe(a) de ventas (*m., f.*), 5
— tax impuesto sobre la venta (*m.*)
salmon salmón (*m.*)
salon peluquería (*f.*); salón de belleza (*m.*)
salutation saludo (*m.*)
same mismo(a), 20
— as igual (que), 10
sample muestra (*f.*), 7; ejemplar (*m.*)
sanitary sanitario(a), 20
satisfied satisfecho(a), 6
sauce salsa (*f.*), 4
save ahorrar, 7
saving ahorro (*m.*), 12
savings ahorros (*m.*), 6
— account cuenta de ahorros (*f.*)
say decir, 7
scanner escáner (*m.*), 12; escanógrafo (*m.*), 12
scarcely apenas, 9
scarcity escasez (*f.*), g. 20
schedule horario (*m.*), 10
scholarship beca (*f.*), 16
schooling carrera (*f.*)
screen pantalla (*f.*)
sea bass corbina (*f.*), 4
seafood marisco (*m.*), 4
season estación (*f.*), 14
seat asiento (*m.*), 1
secretary secretario(a) (*m., f.*), 11
section sección (*f.*), 1
see ver, 2
— after encargarse (de), 9
— you tomorrow hasta mañana, p
— yourself considerarse, g. 20
seem parecer, 12
select seleccionar, 5
sell vender, 5
— well venderse bien, 14
selling price precio de venta (*m.*)
send enviar, 7; mandar, 7
sender remitente (*m., f.*)
separate separado(a)
separately aparte, 7
serious grave, 20; serio(a)
seriously gravemente, 20
serve servir (e:i), 11
service servicio (*m.*), 7
— station gasolinera (*f.*); estación de servicio (*f.*)
session sesión (*f.*), 20
set (in place) disponer
set up a business poner (abrir) un negocio, 16
several varios(as), 5
shameless desvergonzado(a), g. 20
share acción (*f.*), 13
sheet sábana (*f.*)
shelf estante (*m.*), 18
shellfish marisco (*m.*), 4
shift turno (*m.*)
ship barco (*m.*); buque (*m.*)
shipment cargamento (*m.*), 9; carga (*f.*), 9
shock absorber amortiguador (*m.*)
shoe store zapatería (*f.*)
shop establecimiento (*m.*), 9
— window escaparate (*m.*), 18; vidriera (*f.*), 18
shopping center centro comercial (*m.*), 4
should deber, 2
show enseñar, 8; mostrar (o:ue), 8, 15; demostración (*f.*)
shower ducha (*f.*); regadera (*f.*) (*Méx.*), 3
showroom salón de exhibición (*m.*), 5
shrimp camarón (*m.*); gamba (*f.*) (*España*)
side lado (*m.*), 18
sidewalk acera (*f.*), 8; banqueta (*f.*) (*Méx.*), 8
sign firmar, 2
signature firma (*f.*), 19
signing firma (*f.*), 19
simple sencillo(a), l. 12
since pues, 7; desde que, 13
single soltero(a)
sir señor (*m.*), p
sit down sentarse (e:ie), 15
situated situado(a), 3
size tamaño (*m.*), 7; talla (*f.*)
skycap maletero(a) (*m., f.*), 2
slogan lema (*m.*), 14
small pequeño(a), 2
— Business Administration Administración de Pequeños Negocios (*f.*), 16
— change calderilla (*f.*); moneda fraccionaria (*f.*); menudo (*m.*) (*Cuba*); suelto (*m.*) (*Puerto Rico*)
smoke fumar, 1
snowstorm nevada (*f.*), 19
so así que, 10
— many tantos(as), 14
— much tanto(a)
— that para que, 19
soap jabón (*m.*)
Social Security seguro social (*m.*), 12
socialist socialista (*m., f.*), v.a. 20
socket enchufe (*m.*)
software soporte lógico (*m.*)
sole lenguado (*m.*), 4
solve resolver (o:ue), 16
something algo, 5
sometimes algunas veces, 19; a veces, 6
son hijo (*m.*), 7
sophisticated sofisticado(a), 1
sorry: I'm — Lo siento, p
soup sopa (*f.*)
spare part repuesto (*m.*), 6; pieza de repuesto (*f.*)
spark plug bujía (*f.*)
speak hablar, 5
special especial
— delivery entrega especial (*f.*)
specialty especialidad (*f.*), 4
specification indicación (*f.*), 14
speeding exceso de velocidad (*m.*), 19
spend gastar, 12
spite: in — of (the fact that) a pesar de (que), 14
spreadsheet hoja de análisis (*f.*), 12; hoja de cálculo (*f.*), 12
sprinkler system sistema de regadío (*m.*)
squander desperdiciar, l. 12
square cuadrado(a), 18
squid calamar (*m.*)
stable estable
stained manchado(a), 17
stairs escalera (*f.*), 2
stamp (postage) estampilla (*f.*); sello (*m.*); timbre (*m.*) (*Méx.*)
standard shift cambio mecánico (*m.*), 8
standard deduction deducción general (*f.*)
staple grapa (*f.*); presilla (*f.*) (*Cuba*)
stapler grapadora (*f.*); presilladora (*f.*) (*Cuba*)
start (car) arrancar
starter motor de arranque (*m.*)
starting a partir de, 3
state estado (*m.*), 17
— tax impuesto estatal (del estado) (*m.*)
statement of account estado de cuenta (*m.*)
station estación (*f.*), 9
steak bistec (*m.*); bife (*m.*); biftec (*m.*); carne asada (*f.*)
steamed al vapor
step paso (*m.*)
one — further un paso más
steering wheel volante (*m.*); timón (*m.*)
stewed estofado(a); guisado(a)
stock acción (*f.*), 13
stone piedra (*f.*), 17
stop parar
— sign señal de parada (*f.*), 19
store tienda (*f.*), 5; bazar (*m.*), 14
stove cocina (*f.*), 17
street calle (*f.*), p
strong fuerte, 4
structure estructura (*f.*), 18
stucco estuco (*m.*)
student estudiante (*m., f.*), 16
studies carrera (*f.*)
study estudiar, 13
stuffed relleno(a)
subject asunto (*m.*)
subsidize subsidiar, 20
substitute sustituir, v.a. 20
subtotal subtotal (*m.*)
success éxito (*m.*)
suffer sufrir, 11
sufficient suficiente, 13
sugar azúcar (*m., f.*), 20
— cane caña de azúcar (*f.*), 20
suggest sugerir (e:ie), 16
suggestive sugestivo(a); sugerente
suicide suicidio (*m.*), 19
suit convenir, 18
suitcase maleta (*f.*), 2; valija (*f.*), 2
summer verano (*m.*), 14
sunken hundido(a), 17

supermarket supermercado (*m.*); hipermercado (*m.*)
supper cena (*f.*), 4
supplier suministrador(a) (*m., f.*), 6; proveedor (a) (*m., f.*), 12
supply oferta (*f.*), v.a. 20
suppose suponer, 9
surname apellido (*m.*), p
surpass sobrepasar, 14
surrender value rescate (*m.*)
survey sondeo de opinión pública (*m.*); encuesta (*f.*)
suspension sistema de suspensión (*m.*), 6
sweets dulces (*m. pl.*), 18
swimming pool piscina (*f.*); alberca (*f.*) (*Méx.*)
system medios (*m. pl.*), 7; sistema (*m.*), 11

T

table mesa (*f.*), 4
take tomar, 2; **(time)** demorar, 4; coger, 8; quedarse (con), 18
— **advantage** aprovechar, 16
— **charge (of)** encargarse (de), 9
— **responsibility for** responsabilizarse, 9
— **(someone or something someplace)** llevar, 2
talk hablar, 5; conversar
tank tanque (*m.*)
tare tara (*f.*)
tariff tarifa (*f.*), 7
taste gusto; probar (o:ue), 20
tax impuesto (*m.*), 3
— **evasion** evasión fiscal (*f.*)
— **payer** contribuyente (*m., f.*)
— **rate table** escala de impuestos (*f.*)
— **return** declaración de impuestos (*f.*), 13; planilla de contribución sobre ingresos (*f.*) (*Puerto Rico*), 13
taxable income ingresos sujetos a impuestos (*m.*)
taxi taxi (*m.*), 2
— **driver** taxista (*m., f.*), 8
— **stop** parada de taxi (*f.*), 2
taximeter taxímetro (*m.*), 8
telecommunications telecomunicaciones (*f. pl.*)
telegram telegrama (*m.*), 7
telegraphy telegrafía (*f.*)
telephone teléfono (*m.*), 3
— **operator** telefonista (*m., f.*), 7; operador(a) (*m., f.*), 7
television televisión (*f.*), 14
— **(TV) set** televisor (*m.*)
tell decir, 7
term plazo (*m.*); término (*m.*)
— **of payment** condición de pago (*f.*)
termite comején (*m.*), 17; termita (*f.*), 17
test prueba (*f.*), 20
than que, 4
thank you (very much) (muchas) gracias, p
that que, 5
— **is to say** es decir, 12, 18
— **(over there)** aquél (*m.*), 18
— **'s all** eso es todo, 3
— **which** lo que, 9
the others los (las) otras, 20
theft robo (*m.*), 19
their su(s), 2
then entonces, 4; luego, 12
there allá, 3; allí, 16
— **are all kinds of things** hay de todo, 4
— **is (are)** hay, 3
these estos(as), 5
— **here** los (las) de aquí, 20
thing cosa (*f.*), 7
think creer, 6; estimar, 20
— **about** pensar (en) **(e:ie),** 9
third tercero(a), 7
— **party** tercera persona (*f.*); tercero(a) (*m.*)
this este(a), 5
— **very day** hoy mismo, 5
— **way** por aquí, 3
those los de, 6
— **over there** los (las) de allá, 20
— **who** los (las) que, g. 20
thousand mil, 17
three tres
through por, 1; mediante, 12
thumbtack chinche (*f.*); tachuela (*f.*) (*Puerto Rico*)
Thursday jueves (*m.*)
ticket pasaje (*m.*), 1; billete (*m.*), 1; multa (*f.*), 19
tied up inmovilizado(a), 15
tile losa (*f.*), 17; baldosa (*f.*), 17
time tiempo (*m.*), 9; vez (*f.*), 12; hora (*f.*)
— **of arrival** hora de llegada (*f.*)
tip propina (*f.*), 4
tire llanta (*f.*); goma (*f.*); neumático (*m.*)
title cargo (*m.*)
to a, 1; para, 1; hacia, 3
— **order** al gusto
— **taste** al gusto
— **the left** a (de) la izquierda, 2
— **the right** a (de) la derecha, 2
— **us** nos, 7
toast tostada (*f.*), 4; pan tostado (*m.*), 4
today hoy, 3
together with junto con
toilet inodoro (*m.*)
token ficha (*f.*)
toll tarifa (*f.*), 7
— **road** autopista de cuota (*f.*), g. 8
tomato tomate (*m.*), 4
tomorrow mañana, 1
ton tonelada (*f.*)
too demasiado, 17
— **much** demasiado, 12
tool herramienta (*f.*), g. 20
top quality de primera calidad, 5; de primera, 17
tornado tornado (*m.*), 19
tortilla tortilla (*f.*) (*Méx.*), 4
tourist turista (*m., f.*), 8
tow truck remolcador (*m.*)
toward hacia, 3
towel toalla (*f.*)
town pueblo (*m.*), 8
toy shop juguetería (*f.*), 18
trademark marca registrada (*f.*), 14
trade name razón social (*f.*)
traditional tradicional
traffic tráfico (*m.*), 19
train ferrocarril (*m.*), 9; tren (*m.*), 9
transaction transacción (*f.*)
transfer transferencia (*f.*), 8; transbordo (*m.*), 9; trasbordo (*m.*), 9; transbordar, 9; trasbordar, 9; traspaso (*m.*), 17
translator traductor(a) (*m., f.*)
transmission fluid líquido de transmisión (*m.*)
transmission gear transmisión (*f.*)
transnational (multinational) companies multinacionales (*f., pl.*), 20; transnacionales (*f. pl.*), 20
transparent transparente, 14
transport transportar, 9
travel viajar, 1
traveler's check cheque de viajero (*m.*), 2
traveling salesperson viajante (*m., f.*), 6; agente viajero (*m., f.*), 6
trespassing entrada ilegal (*f.*)
trial juicio (*m.*)
— **balance** balance de comprobación (*m.*), 11
tributary tributario(a), l. 12
trillion billón (*m.*), g. 11
trout trucha (*f.*)
truck camión (*m.*), 9
true verdadero(a)
trunk baúl (*m.*); cajuela (*f.*) (*Méx.*); maletero (*m.*)
trust confiar, g. 20
truth verdad (*f.*)
try (to) tratar (de), 6, 20
tuna atún (*m.*); bonito (*m.*)
turkey pavo (*m.*); guajalote (*m.*) (*México*); guanajo (*m.*) (*Cuba*)
turn doblar; voltear
turn on (off) the light encender **(e:ie)** (apagar) la luz
twelfth decimosegundo(a), l. 9
twice doble (*m.*), 9
type tipo (*m.*), 4
typewriter máquina de escribir (*f.*)
typical típico(a), 4

U

underneath debajo (de)
understand comprender, 5; entender **(e:ie),** 5
undertake emprender, l. 12
unemployment desempleo (*m.*)
unit unidad (*f.*), 6
United States Estados Unidos (*m. pl.*), 4
university universidad (*f.*), 13
unleaded gasoline gasolina sin plomo (*f.*)
unload descargar, 9
unloading descarga (*f.*), 9
unnecessary innecesario, 6
until hasta, 3
— **one hits** hasta llegar a

Hispanos en Estados Unidos

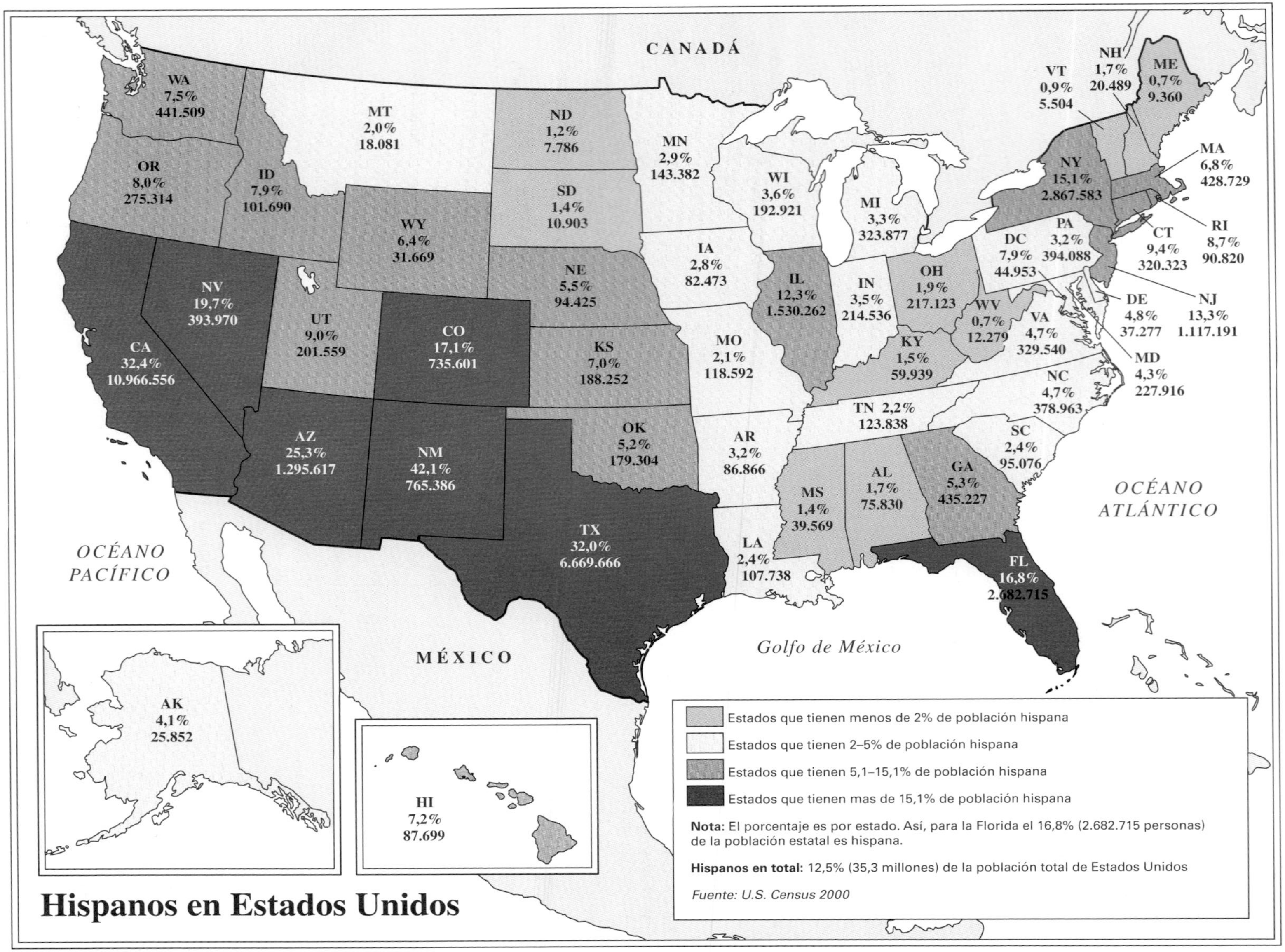

América del Sur
Mar Caribe
OCÉANO ATLÁNTICO
OCÉANO PACÍFICO
TRINIDAD Y TOBAGO
Puerto España
Barranquilla
Cartagena
Maracaibo
Caracas
La Guaira
San Carlos
Ciudad Bolívar
VENEZUELA
Río Orinoco
Georgetown
Paramaribo
Cayena
Salto Ángel
GUYANA
SURINAM
GUAYANA FRANCESA
Medellín
Río Magdalena
Zipaquirá
Bogotá
Cali
COLOMBIA
Popayán
San Agustín
Otavalo
Pichincha
Santo Domingo de los Colorados
Quito
ECUADOR
Chimborazo
Guayaquil
Ecuador
CORDILLERA DE LOS ANDES
Río Negro
Río Amazonas
Manaos
Belén
Iquitos
Río Madeira
Sipán
Trujillo
BRASIL
Recife
PERÚ
Machu Picchu
Callao
Lima
Cuzco
Lago Titicaca
La Paz
Puno
Arequipa
Tiahuanaco
Cochabamba
Río Paraguay
Salvador
Brasilia
BOLIVIA
Sucre
Potosí
Arica
Iquique
Bello Horizonte
Filadelfia
PARAGUAY
Asunción
Río Paraná
Río de Janeiro
San Pablo
Santos
Trópico de Capricornio
Antofagasta
Salta
San Miguel de Tucumán
Puerto Iguazú
Resistencia
CHILE
Río Uruguay
Puerto Alegre
Córdoba
Aconcagua
Mendoza
Viña del Mar
Valparaíso
Santiago
Rosario
URUGUAY
Montevideo
Buenos Aires
La Plata
Punta del Este
ARGENTINA
Río de la Plata
Concepción
Río Colorado
Mar del Plata
Bahía Blanca
Bariloche
Puerto Montt
PATAGONIA
Estrecho de Magallanes
Islas Malvinas
Punta Arenas
TIERRA DEL FUEGO
Cabo de Hornos
ISLAS GALÁPAGOS
San Salvador
Santa Cruz
San Cristóbal
Isabela
0 250 500 Km.
0 250 500 Mi.

España
Mar Cantábrico
Golfo de Vizcaya
FRANCIA
MONTES PIRINEOS
ANDORRA
OCÉANO ATLÁNTICO
Mar Mediterráneo
La Coruña
Avilés
Gijón
Oviedo
Santander
Bilbao
San Sebastián
GALICIA
Santiago de Compostela
ASTURIAS
MONTES CANTÁBRICOS
CANTABRIA
PAÍS VASCO
Pamplona
Pontevedra
Vigo
León
Burgos
Río Ebro
NAVARRA
CATALUÑA
Costa Brava
Palencia
Valladolid
Soria
LA RIOJA
Zaragoza
Lérida
Barcelona
Tarragona
Braga
Oporto
Zamora
Río Duero
CASTILLA-LEÓN
Salamanca
ARAGÓN
Segovia
Ávila
Madrid
SIERRA DE GUADARRAMA
MADRID
Toledo
Coimbra
SIERRA DE ESTRELLA
PORTUGAL
Río Tajo
ESPAÑA
CASTILLA-LA MANCHA
COMUNIDAD VALENCIANA
Valencia
Río Júcar
Cáceres
EXTREMADURA
Lisboa
Setúbal
Badajoz
Mérida
Río Guadiana
Ciudad Real
Albacete
Almadén
MURCIA
Alicante
Menorca
Mallorca
Palma
ISLAS BALEARES
Ibiza
Formentera
SIERRA MORENA
Linares
Córdoba
Río Guadalquivir
Jaén
Murcia
Costa Blanca
Cartagena
Sevilla
Huelva
ANDALUCÍA
Granada
Mulhacén
SIERRA NEVADA
Almería
Costa de la Luz
Jerez de la Frontera
Cádiz
Málaga
Costa del Sol
Mar Mediterráneo
Algeciras
Gibraltar (G.B.)
Tánger
Ceuta (Esp.)
Melilla (Esp.)
MARRUECOS
0 50 100 150 200 Km.
0 50 100 150 200 Mi.
OCÉANO ATLÁNTICO
ESPAÑA
ISLAS CANARIAS
ÁFRICA
ISLAS CANARIAS
La Palma
Santa Cruz de la Palma
Tenerife
Santa Cruz de Tenerife
Gomera
Hierro
Gran Canaria
Las Palmas
Lanzarote
Arrecife
Puerto del Rosario
Fuerteventura
0 100 Km.
0 100 Mi.
OCÉANO ATLÁNTICO
MARRUECOS